AF521639

Preventive Detention of Terror Suspects

Preventive detention as a counter-terrorism tool is fraught with conceptual and procedural problems and risks of misuse, excess, and abuse. Many have debated the inadequacies of the current legal frameworks for detention, and the need for finding the most appropriate legal model to govern detention of terror suspects that might serve as a global paradigm.

This book offers a comprehensive and critical analysis of the detention of terror suspects under domestic criminal law, the law of armed conflict and international human rights law. The book looks comparatively at the law in a number of key jurisdictions including the U.S.A., the U.K., Israel, France, India, Australia, and Canada and in turn compares this to preventive detention under the law of armed conflict and various human rights treaties. The book demonstrates that the procedures governing the use of preventive detention are deficient in each framework and that these deficiencies often have an adverse and serious impact on the human rights of detainees, thereby delegitimizing the use of preventive detention.

Based on her investigation, Diane Webber puts forward a new approach to preventive detention, setting out ten key minimum criteria drawn from international human rights principles and best practices from domestic laws. The minimum criteria are designed to cure the current flaws and deficiencies and provide a base line of guidance for the many countries that choose to use preventive detention, in a way that both respects human rights and maintains security.

Diane Webber is a British solicitor who earned her doctorate at Georgetown University Law Center in Washington DC. She has worked in London in private practice, focusing on criminal law (particularly white-collar fraud), employment and discrimination law, and sports and entertainment law.

Routledge Research in Terrorism and the Law

Available titles in this series include:

The United States, International Law and the Struggle against Terrorism
Thomas McDonnell

Counter-Terrorism and Beyond
The Culture of Law and Justice After 9/11
Nicola McGarrity, Andrew Lynch and George Williams

Counter-terrorism and the Detention of Suspected Terrorists
Preventative Confinement and International Human Rights Law
Claire Macken

Gender, National Security and Counter-terrorism
Human rights perspectives
Margaret L. Satterthwaite and Jayne Huckerby

Surveillance, Counter-Terrorism and Comparative Constitutionalism
Fergal Davis, Nicola McGarrity and George Williams

Homeland Security, its Law and its State
A Design of Power for the 21st Century
Christos Boukalas

Anti-Terrorism Law and Normalising Northern Ireland
Jessie Blackbourn

The Impact, Legitimacy and Effectiveness of EU Counter-Terrorism
Fiona de Londras and Josephine Doody

Preventive Detention of Terror Suspects
A New Legal Framework

Diane Webber

LONDON AND NEW YORK

First published 2016
by Routledge
2 Park Square, Milton Park, Abingdon, Oxon OX14 4RN

and by Routledge
711 Third Avenue, New York, NY 10017

Routledge is an imprint of the Taylor & Francis Group, an informa business

British Library Cataloguing in Publication Data
A catalogue record for this book is available from the British Library

Library of Congress Cataloging in Publication Data
A catalog record has been requested for this book

ISBN: 978-1-138-93689-8 (hbk)
ISBN: 978-1-315-67654-8 (ebk)

Typeset in Galliard
by Fish Books Ltd.

Printed and bound by CPI Group (UK) Ltd, Croydon, CR0 4YY

Contents

Acknowledgments

This book, and the doctoral thesis on which the book is based, could not have been written without the advice, encouragement, and support of many people. In particular, I could not have done any of this without my wonderful supportive family, John, Daniel, Katie, and Jonathan, all of whom were with me every step of the way.

Special thanks are due to my doctoral supervisor David Stewart and doctoral committee members David Cole and David Koplow, for their patience, encouragement, questions, and suggestions both during the doctoral process and whilst the thesis was being transformed into this book.

I also want to thank the SJD Director Alexa Freeman, and Dean Nan Hunter at Georgetown University Law Center for their encouragement and support, as well as all the many people who reviewed different sections and provided helpful comments along the way.

Table of cases

Australia

Canada

European Court of Human Rights

France

India

Inter-American Court of Human Rights

International Court of Justice

International Criminal Tribunal for the former Yugoslavia

Israel

United Kingdom

United Nations Human Rights Committee

United States

Table of legislation

Algeria

Australia

Canada

France

India

Israel

Malaysia

Security Offences (Special Measures Act) 2012, Act 747.......................238

United Kingdom

Anti-Terrorism, Crime and Security Act, 2001 c.24....70, 78, 109, 110, 237
Counter-Terrorism Act, 2008, c.28..98, 110, 111
Counter-Terrorism and Security Act 2015, c.8......................................115
Criminal Justice Act 1993, c.44. 115
Criminal Justice and Public Order Act 1994, c.33. 111
Draft Detention of Terrorist Suspects (Temporary Extension) Bills, CM 8018, February 2011. 111
Enhanced Terrorism Prevention and Investigation Measures Bill, CM 8166 September, 2011. ....108, 116
Human Rights Act 1998, c.42. ....25, 40, 92
Magna Carta (1215). 3, 19
Police & Criminal Evidence Act 1984, c.60, Code F, Code of Practice on Visual Recording with Sound of Interviews with Suspects, 2013. 243
Police & Criminal Evidence Act 1984, Code H, Revised Code of Practice, 2013. ....111, 239, 240
Prevention of Terrorism Act, 2005, c.2..103, 109, 110, 113, 115, 135, 242
Protection of Freedoms Act 2012, c.9..111
Terrorism Act 2000 c.11. 239
Terrorism Act 2006, c.11. 22
Terrorist Prevention and Investigation Measures Act, 2011, c.23. ....104, 105, 242

United States

8 United States Code §1226. 195
18 United States Code §2332. 194
18 United States Code §2339. ....172, 173, 193, 194
18 United States Code §3144. ....194, 195
28 C.F.R. §501.3(a). 192
Alien Tort Statute, 28 U.S.C. §1350. 244
Authorization for Use of Military Force (AUMF), Pub. L. No. 107-40, 115 Stat. 224 (2001). 177, 196
Classified Information Procedures Act, P. L. 96–456, 94 Stat. 2025 (1980). 225, 242, 243, 276
Detainee Treatment Act of 2005, Pub. L. No. 109-148, 119 Stat. 2739 (2005). 182, 200
Executive Order No. 13,567, Periodic Review of Individuals Detained at Guantánamo. 201

Table of treaties and other sources

Treaties

Other sources

Africa

Europe

Organization of American States

United Nations

Introduction

The problem

The catastrophic terror attacks in the United States on September 11, 2001 (9/11) were the trigger for many countries to re-evaluate their counter-terrorism strategies and laws, and adopt stringent counter-terrorism legislation. Notwithstanding this, the number of terrorist attacks around the world appears to have escalated exponentially between 2001 and 2015.[1] In 2014 alone, 13,463 terrorist attacks occurred in 95 countries,[2] killing more than 32,700 and wounding more than 34,700.[3]

Much of the counter-terrorism legislation was crafted to tackle terrorist attacks from al-Qaeda and its offshoots. However, terror from another equal, if not more violent, source began to emerge from a group established in 2006, originally called the Islamic State of Iraq.[4] The group merged with an al-Qaeda affiliate in 2013, and took the name Islamic State of Iraq and the Levant, or Da'esh, ISIL, or ISIS (hereinafter Da'esh). In February 2014, al-Qaeda cut its ties with Da'esh. After capturing territory in Iraq and Syria, Da'esh announced the establishment of a caliphate in June 2014.[5] Not content with the wholesale slaughter, bloodshed, rape, and enslavement of women that resulted from their territorial rampage in Iraq and Syria, Da'esh honed another terrible trade-mark: the brutal killings of non-believers (in common with groups such as Boko Haram)[6] and barbaric beheadings of Western hostages.[7]

The emergence of Da'esh generated something else quite unprecedented. Thousands of foreigners – estimated in May 2015 to be over 25,000 – have been attracted to join Da'esh in Iraq and Syria to fight or give other support.[8] However, many have returned home.[9] Law enforcement officials in many countries are worried that new challenges will be posed both by returning fighters, and homegrown Da'esh supporters incited to commit terror attacks on home soil.[10] Concerns have also been expressed that Da'esh now poses a greater threat than al-Qaeda.[11]

As terrorists do not appear to be fully deterred by the prospect of arrest, trial, and punishment after an attack, or even of death in the course of an attack,[12] many states have resorted to more preemptive counter-terrorism methods to prevent terrorist acts, such as targeted killing, surveillance, and preventive detention. These methods could be termed "necessary evils," and each of them may be effective in forestalling terrorist activity to a lesser or greater extent, but often at a high price involving the sacrifice of individual human rights.

The purpose of this book is to evaluate preventive detention as a tool to forestall terrorist attacks. Preventive detention is used in at least forty countries, which between them are home to approximately 70 percent of the world's population.[13] With new challenges posed by Da'esh, the spotlight is back on evaluating when and how preventive detention might be used.

Preventive detention as a counter-terrorism tool is fraught with conceptual and procedural problems and risks of misuse, excess, and abuse. It is sometimes necessary to use it to save lives, but it has numerous drawbacks. Many scholars have debated the inadequacies of the current legal frameworks for detention, and the need for finding the most appropriate legal model to govern detention of terror suspects that might serve as a global paradigm.[14] However, to date no one has examined together and comprehensively detention under the law enforcement model,[15] the law of armed conflict (LOAC) model,[16] and the international human rights model,[17] and compared each one against the others.

This study undertakes to fill that analytical gap by analyzing and comparing in depth the laws relating to detention of terror suspects in a sample of seven countries, and detention under the LOAC, against the background of detention in five general human rights treaties. The analysis reveals conceptual problems and demonstrates that the procedures governing the use of preventive detention are deficient in each framework. These deficiencies often have an adverse and serious impact on the human rights of detainees, thereby delegitimizing the use of preventive detention. In order to halt these abuses in the many countries that use preventive detention, the legal framework governing detention must be properly tailored to guarantee the human rights of detainees in a meaningful way, without adversely compromising counter-terrorism tools.

Each of the seven countries examined has independently developed its counter-terrorism laws, and specifically its detention laws, in response to particular threats in ways that reflect local domestic history, custom, and culture. Unsurprisingly, those domestic laws may not be tailored to deal with the current and continuing global terrorist threat. Neither is the law of armed conflict designed to detain terror suspects.

To many people the potential reach of preventive detention signals the importance and necessity of ensuring that this tool is used in the most rights-compliant way, without compromising the essential counter-terrorism work of law enforcement authorities. And the more it is used within a human rights-compliant framework and in accordance with the rule of law, the less likely it is to attract complaints that it is unfair, immoral, and contrary to principles of justice. Thus detention can be a valuable tool in appropriate circumstances to forestall terror attacks, provided certain safeguards are in place.

This book: (1) contends that with all the counter-terrorism legislation enacted since 9/11, the three main legal frameworks by which preventive detention can be evaluated are still not tailored to the current global terrorist threat, and nor do they provide adequate protections for the human rights of individuals; (2) shows that very few common core principles can be extracted from the analysis of domestic detention laws, the LOAC, and the detention provisions in five general human rights treaties; (3) explains why there is a need for a new set of common core principles; (4) advocates the placing of human rights concerns at the heart of a framework for detention of terror suspects;[18] and (5) recommends a new approach, by suggesting key minimum criteria based mainly on international human rights law principles and some best practices drawn from the domestic laws. These minimum criteria are aimed at curing the current flaws and deficiencies in the law and could form the basis for crafting fundamental core principles. They are designed to give a base line of guidance to the many countries that choose to use the tool of preventive detention.

Preventive detention

Conceptual issues

Preventive detention is not a novel concept: it long predates 9/11 in many countries of the world. For example, it was first known in an elemental way in Magna Carta[19] and its modern form in the United Kingdom may date from its use in India in the interests of national security in the mid-nineteenth century.[20] In the United States, preventive detention appears to date from 1786 when the Massachusetts legislature passed a law permitting preventive detention in order to deal with a rebellion.[21]

The concept of preventive detention is extremely problematic because people are treated in the same way as persons on remand post-charge and pre-trial, or as convicted criminals, merely because some level of suspicion exists that they might commit a terrorist act at some time in the future. Yet there are times when detention may be the only means to remove a potential terror suspect from the streets.

Rationales for detention include incapacitation of terror suspects and disrupting terror plots,[22] and to facilitate interrogation of a suspect in isolation before he is charged and entitled to rights to silence and to consult counsel.[23] The scope of those rights and the timing of when the rights apply differ from country to country. One reason why the Bush administration embraced the LOAC approach of treating suspects as enemy combatants may have been because it thought that suspects held under LOAC without charge would not have these due process rights.[24]

Preventive detention is a counter-terrorism tool that carries a grave risk of abuse, because of conceptual and procedural flaws relating to its use. While many think it is a necessary and useful counter-terrorism tool, others have expressed legitimate concerns. For example, the counter-terrorism context of preventive detention relates to future conduct, which is impossible to predict with complete accuracy, and poses a risk of detaining innocent people.[25] The prediction problem is not unique to the terrorism context – it applies equally to detention of persons after they have served a prison sentence, such as sex offenders, when such post-sentence incarceration is said to be therapeutic and not punitive.[26] Some critics approach the problem of preventive detention[27] by discussing the balance (or lack of balance) between liberty of the individual and security of the people as a whole.[28]

Preventive detention is a term that has been used by different countries and commentators in several contexts, such as administrative detention,[29] investigative detention,[30] pre-charge detention,[31] or security detention.[32] These terms will be discussed throughout this book.

As the review of current practice reveals, preventive detention is a "fact of life."[33] It has its uses, and it has its drawbacks. It is not a perfect counter-terrorism tool by any means, as will be seen throughout this work, and it "is not susceptible to absolute answers."[34] This book does not make any recommendations about whether any state should, or should not opt for preventive detention as a counter-terrorism tool, but flaws and deficiencies in the three main frameworks are identified and addressed.

Terminology issues

This study is concerned with the phenomenon of preventive detention, irrespective of how it is labeled. For the purposes of the analysis that follows, "preventive detention" refers to *detention before or without charge for the purpose of preventing a future terrorist act.* This means detention in three types of situation: (1) when a person is arrested on suspicion of being about to commit a terrorist offense. For example, he is suspected of having carried out some early steps of terrorist activity but has not done any sufficiently overt act to enable police to make an immediate charge. The person may be detained for incapacitation and/or interrogation purposes; (2) when a person is detained under immigration law for security reasons; and (3) when a person who cannot be criminally prosecuted because of issues such as the danger of compromising sources, is detained for security reasons.

Some national laws also currently permit detention of persons perceived as dangerous to others in a variety of situations. These include persons accused of criminal offenses awaiting trial, persons accused of immigration violations awaiting deportation, persons who have served a sentence but pose a continuing risk, and persons with mental disorders who pose a risk to themselves or others.[35] The common denominator is that this type of detention is security based.

Sometimes, confusingly, countries give one label to detention, when in fact detention is imposed for some additional or different purpose. For example, the United Kingdom permits detention without charge of terror suspects for fourteen days.[36] The rationale is ostensibly to amass sufficient evidence to charge the suspect. Whilst this is true, another implicit purpose of this detention is to incapacitate a suspect or disrupt potential plots.[37]

United States law permits the detention of persons who have done nothing other than witness an alleged crime, if there is probable cause to believe that they have relevant testimony and would not appear if served with a subpoena.[38] In the aftermath of 9/11 the "material witness" laws were frequently used as a pretext to preventively detain suspected terrorists. In a number of countries, including Australia, Canada, the United Kingdom and the United States, immigration law is frequently used for counter-terrorism purposes to preventively detain non-national suspected terrorists.

Preventive detention is also permitted under the LOAC, but a number of extremely complicated issues have emerged from the United States' detention of suspected terrorists at Guantánamo and in Afghanistan. In the case of wars between two or more states, or certain types of protracted internal conflicts involving the state and organized armed groups,[39] detention is governed to a limited extent by the Geneva Conventions.[40]

As is demonstrated in this book, the LOAC, as set out in the Geneva Conventions, other instruments, and customary international law, is not tailored to address contemporary transnational terrorism, which now can involve random and intermittent attacks anywhere in the world by non-state actors. These sporadic attacks may continue intermittently and indefinitely. LOAC detention does not fit neatly into the category of preventive detention that is the main subject of scrutiny in this book. However, Israel's references to LOAC in its detention cases, and the United States' use of LOAC to detain terror suspects captured overseas, are relevant and important within the overall discussion of preventive detention of terror suspects.

Terrorism

It is important to understand what the tool of preventive detention is aimed at preventing, as well as its context and limits. In the absence of an internationally agreed definition of "terrorism,"[41] the following working definition is adopted for the purposes of this discussion: *the unlawful use, or threat, of violence by non-state actors,*[42] *against persons, property, critical infrastructures, or key resources, intended to intimidate or coerce a government, or all or part of the general public, in furtherance of political, religious, or ideological objectives.*

To date at least 109 variations of the term can be found,[43] together with a proliferation of scholarly literature on the subject.[44] Not only is there no *international* consensus on the meaning of terrorism,[45] in some countries such as the United States, no single *national* agreement of a terrorism definition exists, with some twenty-two variations of the term.[46]

The need for a definition of terrorism "is of real practical importance. It triggers powers, as well as contributing to the description of offences,"[47] and has legal consequences.[48]

One result of the lack of agreement internationally is that some countries have expanded their definitions of terrorism in domestic law,[49] in some cases with "vague, unclear or overbroad definitions of terrorism,"[50] which have adversely affected the exercise of some fundamental freedoms.[51]

For example, the United Kingdom has one of the broadest definitions of terrorism, including the use or threat of action,[52] instigation of, or preparation for action, and even glorification of terrorism.[53] In October 2013, in *R. v. Gul*, whilst holding that the statutory definition of terrorism includes any or all military attacks by a non-state armed group against any or all state or inter-governmental organization armed forces in the context of a non-international armed conflict, the United Kingdom Supreme Court expressed concerns about the breadth of the definition of terrorism and its impact on counter-terrorism measures, including detention.[54]

The broader the definition of terrorism, the more opportunity there is for governments to preventively detain terror suspects for offenses that lie far from core terrorist activity as described in the working definition above. For example, in Saudi Arabia, terrorist acts include "disturbing public order," "endangering national unity," and "defaming the state or its status."[55] In India, terrorist activity includes the causing of "damage to the monetary stability of India by way of production or smuggling or circulation of high quality counterfeit Indian paper currency, coin or of any other material."[56]

The effect of many different laws

United Nations and regional activity after 9/11[57] that urged states to prevent terrorism generated a cornucopia of different laws and regulations: some criminalizing various activities; and others providing tools to combat terrorist activity, with greater cooperation between law enforcement authorities across national borders. Although preventive detention had been in use to forestall terror attacks in some countries prior to 9/11, such as the United Kingdom, India, and Israel; other countries, such as Australia, and the United States (via the law of armed conflict) also turned to preventive detention in one form or another.

The laws and tools vary from country to country, as one would expect. The laws may differ as to what constitutes an act of terrorism, what grounds authorities must have to arrest and detain suspects, and what tools are available to prevent terror attacks. Furthermore, from the civil liberties perspective, due process, speech, and association rights vary considerably from place to place.

Australia's counter-terrorism strategy is similar to that of the United Kingdom, with four strands: intelligence analysis; taking "all necessary and practical action" to protect the country and its citizens; providing an "immediate and targeted response" to attacks; and building a strong community to resist the development of violent extremism and terrorism on the home front.[100] One key difference derives from the federal nature of Australia, where the Commonwealth (federal) Parliament has worked in tandem with the states and territories in formulating counter-terrorist laws.

Canada's detention laws are of interest because of the way they choose to balance liberty and security. Canada's first counter-terrorism strategy[101] highlights the importance of human rights, as enshrined in the Canadian Charter of Rights and Freedoms,[102] and in international human rights and international humanitarian law,[103] whilst at the same time declaring that "[s]ecurity is also a human right."[104] The strategy also echoes the United Kingdom strategy with four strands: prevent; detect; deny; and respond.[105] Canada is a party to the ICCPR.

India, out of all the countries surveyed, faces the second highest terror threat, and the effectiveness of its laws together with the liberty/security balance are evaluated. India still has not implemented an official counter-terrorism strategy because of "turf wars and the increasingly fractured nature of Indian politics."[106] India is a party to the ICCPR but its detention laws are largely incompatible with it.

Detention in Israel is the subject of Chapter 7. Unlike most of the other countries surveyed in this book, where the main terrorist threat emanates from al-Qaeda and affiliates, and Da'esh, the principal threat to Israel derives from Palestinian armed groups operating from Palestinian territories, as well as from Hezbollah, which has a strong base in southern Lebanon.[107] No formal national security or counter-terrorism strategy exists.[108] Israel's approach involves "an incessant struggle for both physical and cultural survival."[109]

In many cases the applicable normative system is the law relating to international armed conflicts.[110] "Alongside the international law dealing with armed conflicts, fundamental principles of Israeli public law … may apply."[111] Although Israel is party to the four Geneva Conventions (GCs), GC IV has not been enacted through domestic Israeli legislation. However, its customary provisions are part of Israeli law.[112] Israel's position is that the laws of belligerent occupation in GC IV do not apply to activities in Judea, Samaria, and the Gaza Strip, but Israel does honor the humanitarian provisions of GC IV.[113] Because the terrorists do not distinguish between military and civilian targets, and do not fulfill the criteria to be classified as combatants,[114] which would afford them the protections of GC III,[115] they are regarded as civilians who are unlawful combatants.[116]

Different issues are presented. First, Israel has been in a perpetual state of emergency since the state was established in 1948. Administrative detention applicable in Israel for suspects who cannot be prosecuted is found in emergency legislation.[117] Consequently, Israel has derogated from some of its human rights guarantees under the ICCPR.[118] Second, the Israeli Supreme Court brings a distinctive twist on LOAC to its interpretation of the constitutionality of various detention measures.[119]

The LOAC is "based upon a delicate balance"[120] of the rights of the individual, weighed against the military need to maintain and protect the security of the country and its citizens. Thus "human rights are protected by the law of armed conflict, but not to their full scope."[121] Third, Israel adopts a unique approach to providing sensitive evidence to detainees.[122]

Chapter 8 concerns law enforcement detention in France, a civil law country. France is included in this study because of its long history in combating terrorism, and because a real tension in France exists between the right to freedom from arbitrary arrest and detention, enshrined in the French Bill of Rights of 1789, the ICCPR, and the European Convention, and the statutory fundamental right to security.[123] France is party to both the ICCPR and European Convention. Once a treaty is ratified in France it prevails over domestic legislation,[124] and the provisions are directly applicable in French law. The French counter-terrorism strategy emphasizes prevention, disruption, and repression,[125] "preventive judicial neutralization,"[126] and deportation of foreign nationals.[127] Terrorism crimes are defined broadly in the Penal Code,[128] allowing investigation and prosecution "before any concrete act has taken place," as well as the arrest, detention and questioning of individuals suspected of associating with others involved in terrorist networks.[129] France has a "judge-centered model with inquisitorial roots, in which the defense in particular plays a subsidiary role."[130]

Chapter 9 discusses the approach of the United States to detaining persons suspected of involvement in terror activity, related to both international and domestic terrorism.[131] The chapter highlights the "devices" that have been employed to achieve detention of terror suspects without charge, such as the material witness statute, immigration law, and the LOAC model within the context of the United States' never-ending war with al-Qaeda and affiliates.

President Obama has asserted that as a matter of policy, "the preference of the United States is to capture terrorist suspects."[132] The 2015 National Security Strategy envisages a place for detention:

> Outside of areas of active hostilities, we endeavor to detain, interrogate, and prosecute terrorists through law enforcement. However, when there is a continuing, imminent threat, and when capture or other actions to disrupt the threat are not feasible, we will not hesitate to take decisive action.[133]

As to captures, seven persons have been captured and detained off-the-battlefield during the Obama Administration.[134] On the issue of overseas detentions and human rights, although the United States is a party to the ICCPR, it does not accept that the Covenant has any jurisdiction overseas.

Chapter 10 reflects on the lessons learned from evaluating the flaws in international human rights law and the problems encountered in both the law enforcement and LOAC models of preventive detention, many of which relate to inadequate process. In order to craft useful reference guidelines for countries, this book advocates drawing on elements of international human rights law, and some examples of good practice from domestic laws.

A set of ten minimum criteria is recommended to guide all states that choose to use preventive detention. Each principle is subjected to three tests: (1) whether it is compatible with international human rights standards; (2) if the principle is adopted, how would it affect the ability of law enforcement authorities to prevent terrorist acts; and (3) if the principle is adopted, what changes are needed in the LOAC and domestic laws of the surveyed countries. Finally, the hypothetical example described above is revisited to show the effect of applying the principles to that scenario.

Notes

1 Statistics differ enormously. *See e.g.* Global Terrorism Database (GTD), www.start.umd.edu/gtd/search/Results.aspx?region, showing under 3,000 incidents in 2001, rising to nearly 17,000 in 2013. *Also see* US Department Of State, Country Reports On Terrorism 2014 www.state.gov/documents/organization/10287.pdf, showing 531 international attacks in 2001, rising to over 13,000 in 2014. The escalation in the number of terrorist attacks can of course be attributed to different reasons, including global conditions, and it cannot be known how many more attacks might have taken place without all the lawmaking and preventive activity. The "lack of emphasis on measuring effectiveness" of counter-terrorism methods since 9/11 has been described as "astounding." *See* Susan Donkin and Simon Bronitt, *Critical Perspectives on the Evaluation of Counter-terrorism Strategies. Counting the Costs of the "War on Terror" in Australia, in* Counter-Terrorism, Human Rights And The Rule Of Law, 171. (Ancieto Masferrer and Clive Walker, eds. Edward Elgar Publishing Limited, 2013).

2 GTD. Over half of all attacks occurred in Iraq, Pakistan, Afghanistan, India, and Nigeria.

3 US Department Of State, Country Reports On Terrorism 2014, National Counterterrorism Center: Annex Of Statistical Information, www.state.gov/j/ct/rls/crt/2014/239416.htm.

4 Erin McClam, *Tracing the rise of ISIS into a menace of terror*, NBC News (September 29, 2014), www.nbcnews.com/storyline/isis-terror/tracing-rise-isis-menace-terror-n214266.

5 *Id.*

6 Farouk Chotia, *Who are Nigeria's Boko Haram Islamists?* BBC News (January 21, 2015), www.bbc.com/news/world-africa-13809501.

7 Erin McClam, *Tracing the rise of ISIS into a menace of terror.*

8 Press Release, Security Council, Action against Threat of Foreign Terrorist Fighters Must Be Ramped Up, Security Council Urges in High-Level Meeting, U.N. Doc. SC/11912 (May 19, 2015).

9 Ian Traynor, *Major terrorist attack is 'inevitable' as Isis fighters return, say EU officials*, THE GUARDIAN (September 25, 2014), www.theguardian.com/world/2014/sep/25/major-terrorist-attack-inevitable-isis-eu; DANIEL L. BYMAN AND JEREMY SHAPIRO, BE AFRAID. BE A LITTLE AFRAID: THE THREAT OF TERRORISM FROM WESTERN FOREIGN FIGHTERS IN SYRIA AND IRAQ (Brookings, January 2015).

10 MICHAEL MCCAUL, CHAIRMAN OF THE COMMITTEE ON HOMELAND SECURITY, OPENING STATEMENT AT HEARING ON PREVENTING TERROR TRAVEL AND HOMEGROWN TERRORISM (February 11, 2015), http://homeland.house.gov/press-release/chairman-mccaul-opening-statement-hearing-preventing-terror-travel-and-homegrown; Graham Keeley and Fiona Hamilton, *800 extremists 'are ready to strike,'* THE TIMES (August 25, 2015), www.thetimes.co.uk/tto/news/world/europe/article4537140.ece.

11 Eric Schmitt, *ISIS or Al Qaeda? American Officials Split Over Biggest Threat*, N.Y. TIMES (August 4, 2015), www.nytimes.com/2015/08/05/world/middleeast/isis-or-al-qaeda-american-officials-split-over-biggest-threat.html?action=click&pgtype=Homepage&module=first-column-region®ion=top-news&WT.nav=top-news&hp.

12 Donkin and Bronitt, *Critical Perspectives on the Evaluation of Counter-terrorism Strategies*, 176–7 (referring to numerous studies, e.g. L. Dugan, G. LaFree and A.R. Piquero, *Testing a rational choice model of airline hijackings*, 43 CRIMINOLOGY 1031 (2005) and C. LUM, L.W KENNEDY AND A.J. SHERLEY, THE EFFECTIVENESS OF COUNTER-TERRORISM STRATEGIES (Campbell Systematic Reviews, 2006)).

13 *See* Appendix 1 for list of countries.

14 Some examples of scholarly literature from an international and comparative perspective include Stella Burch Elias, *Rethinking "Preventive Detention" from a Comparative Perspective: Three Frameworks for Detaining Terrorist Suspects*, 41 COLUM. HUM. RTS. L. REV. 99 (2009); Monica Hakimi, *International Standards for Detaining Terror Suspects: Moving Beyond the Armed Conflict-Criminal Divide*, 40 CASE W. RES. J. INT'L L. 593 (2009); David Cole, *Out of the Shadows: Preventive Detention, Suspected Terrorist, and War*, 97 CALIF. L. REV. 693 (2009); CLAIRE MACKEN, COUNTER-TERRORISM AND DETENTION OF SUSPECTED TERRORISTS (Routledge, 2011); KENT ROACH, THE 9/11 EFFECT: COMPARATIVE COUNTER-TERRORISM (Cambridge University Press, 2011); Monica Hakimi, *A Functional Approach to Targeting and Detention*, 110 MICH. L. REV. 1365 (2012); Christopher Slobogin, *Preventive Detention in Europe, the United States and Australia*, *in* PREVENTIVE DETENTION: ASKING THE FUNDAMENTAL QUESTIONS (Patrick Keyzer, ed., Intersentia, 2013).

15 The law enforcement model treats terrorism as a crime in accordance with the domestic law of states. Persons are arrested and detained in circumstances permitted by the criminal law.

16 The LOAC model applies in time of war. Detentions are designed to prevent combatants returning to the battlefield and are tied to the duration of hostilities.

17 The international human rights law model is drawn from five general international human rights treaties that purport to underpin the domestic detention laws and arguably how detentions are conducted under LOAC. The treaties are the International Covenant on Civil and Political Rights, G.A. res. 2200A

(XXI), 21 U.N. GAOR Supp. (No. 16) at 52, U.N. Doc. A/6316 (1966), 999 U.N.T.S. 171, (entered into force March 23, 1976) [ICCPR]; the European Convention for the Protection of Human Rights and Fundamental Freedoms, opened for signature November 4, 1950, 213 UNTS 222 (entered into force September 3, 1953) [European Convention]; American Convention on Human Rights, O.A.S. Treaty Series No. 36, 1144 U.N.T.S. 123, (entered into force July 18, 1978) [American Convention]; African (Banjul) Charter of Human and Peoples' Rights, adopted June 27, 1981, OAU Doc. CAB/LEG/67/3 rev. 5, 21 I.L.M. 58 (1982), (entered into force October 21, 1986) [African Charter]; and the Arab Charter on Human Rights, adopted May 22, 2004, reprinted in 12 Int'l Hum. Rts. Rep. 893 (2005), (entered into force March 15, 2008) [Arab Charter]. Detention is mentioned also in some specific universal instruments, *see e.g.* the International Convention for the Protection of All Persons from Enforced Disappearances, G.A. Res.61/177, U.N. Doc. A/RES/61/177 (2006), (adopted December 20, 2006); the Convention on the Rights of the Child, G.A. Res. 44/25, annex, 44 U.N. GAOR Supp. (No. 49) at 167, U.N. Doc. A/44/49 (1989), (entered into force September 2, 1990).

18 This approach is discussed to a limited extent by Hakimi, *International Standards for Detaining Terror Suspects*, 640, noting that although administrative detention exists within a human rights law framework, the law in that area requires further development.

19 Magna Carta, §39 "No freemen shall be taken or imprisoned or disseised or exiled or in any way destroyed, nor will we go upon him nor send upon him, except by the lawful judgment of his peers or by the law of the land." (U.K.). (1215). *See also* PREVENTIVE DETENTION AND SECURITY LAW, A COMPARATIVE SURVEY, 5 (Andrew Harding & John Hatchard, eds) (Kluwer Academic Publishers, 1993): noting that some provisions of Magna Carta imply that there were irregular detentions at that time.

20 Derek P. Jinks, *The Anatomy of an Institutionalized Emergency: Preventive Detention and Personal Liberty in India*, 22 MICH. J. INT'L L. 311, 324 (2001).

21 Adam Klein and Benjamin Wittes, *Preventive Detention in American Theory and Practice*, 2 HARV. NAT'L SECURITY J. 85, 116–7 (2011).

22 Matthew Waxman, *Administrative Detention*, 51 *in* LEGISLATING THE WAR ON TERROR: AN AGENDA FOR REFORM (Benjamin Wittes, ed.) (Brookings Institution Press, 2010).

23 STEPHANIE COOPER BLUM, THE NECESSARY EVIL OF PREVENTIVE DETENTION ON THE WAR ON TERROR, 54 (Cambria Press, 2008).

24 *Id.*, 53 (citing an exchange between Deputy Solicitor General Paul Clements and Justice Ginsburg in Oral Argument at 27, Hamdi v Rumsfeld, 542 U.S. 507 (2004) (No. 03-6696) *available at* www.supremecourt.gov/oral_arguments/argument_transcripts/03-6696.pdf. *Also* 58 (citing George W. Bush, President of the United States, President Discusses Creation of Military Commissions to Try Suspected Terrorists (September 2006) www.whitehouse.gov/news/releases/2006/09/20060906-3.html (noting the intelligence value from captured terrorists, "this is intelligence that cannot be found in any other place. And our security depends on getting this kind of information.").

25 Cole, *Out of the Shadows*, 696.

26 Slobogin, *Preventive Detention in Europe, the United States and Australia*, 31–54. *See* Kansas v. Hendricks, 521 U.S. 346, 358 (1997), where a person who is "dangerous beyond [his] control" can be detained if there is also a prediction of dangerousness. In Kansas v. Crane, 534 U.S. 407 (2002), the Court held that lack of control merely required proof of serious difficulty in controlling behavior. The bar can be as low as personality disorders (Slobogin, 39). *See also* M v. Germany [2010] ECHR No. 19359/04 and Fardon v. Australia, HRC UN Doc CCPR/C/98/D1629/2007 (May 10, 2010).

27 Preventive detention is also known as "preventative detention" in Australia, or "administrative detention" in Israel.

28 *See e.g.* Hakimi, *A Functional Approach to Targeting and Detention*, 1409: "As the liberty costs increase, the benefits of containing the threat must be more substantial to remain proportional;" Brendan Gogarty, Benedict Bartl, and Patrick Keyzer, *The Rehabilitation of Preventive Detention*, *in* PREVENTIVE DETENTION: ASKING THE FUNDAMENTAL QUESTIONS, 111 (Patrick Keyzer, ed., Intersentia, 2013): "the right to personal liberty is not absolute, with the state having a legitimate right to ensure public safety."

29 Waxman, *Administrative Detention*; Andrew McCarthy, *We Need an Administrative Detention Law*, National Review Online (September 21, 2009), *www.nationalreview.com/articles/228277/we-need-administrative-detention-law/andrew-c-mccarthy.*

30 *See e.g.* DAN STIGALL, COUNTERTERRORISM AND THE COMPARATIVE LAW OF INVESTIGATIVE DETENTION, 160 (Cambria Press, 2009).

31 PREVENTIVE DETENTION, 1 (Stanislaw Frankowski and Dinah Shelton, eds) (Kluwer Academic Publishers, 1992); MACKEN, COUNTER-TERRORISM AND DETENTION OF SUSPECTED TERRORISTS.

32 PREVENTIVE DETENTION AND SECURITY LAW, A COMPARATIVE SURVEY, 4–5; Doug Cassel, *Security Detention: The International Legal Framework: International Human Rights Law and Security Detention*, 40 CASE W. RES. J. INT'L L. 383 (2009); Hakimi, *A Functional Approach to Targeting and Detention.*

33 PREVENTIVE DETENTION AND SECURITY LAW – A COMPARATIVE SURVEY, 2.

34 Cole, *Out of the Shadows: Preventive Detention, Suspected Terrorist, and War*, 695.

35 *See e.g.* Cole, *Out of the Shadows*, 700.

36 *See Chapter 5, infra.*

37 Preventive detention may have been used in London to prevent terror attacks during the Olympics in 2012, *see* DAVID ANDERSON Q.C., REPORT OF THE INDEPENDENT REVIEWER ON THE OPERATION OF THE TERRORISM ACT 2000 AND PART 1 OF THE TERRORISM ACT 2006, THE TERRORISM ACTS IN 2012, ¶3.14(b) (Jul. 2013), https://terrorismlegislationreviewer.independent.gov.uk/wp-content/uploads/2013/07/Report-on-the-Terrorism-Acts-in-2012-FINAL_WEB1.pdf, referring to preventive arrests made before the London Olympic Games: "this may have served as a deterrent to other extremists, as well as removing potential threats to the Games."

38 *See Chapter 9, infra.*

39 Rome Statute of the International Criminal Court, U.N. Doc. A/CONF. 183/9* (July 17, 1998).

40 *See* Geneva Convention for the Amelioration of the Condition of the Wounded and Sick in Armed Forces in the Field, (August 12, 1949), 6 U.S.T. 3114, 75

U.N.T.S. 31 [GC I]; Geneva Convention for the Amelioration of the Condition of the Wounded, Sick and Shipwrecked Members of Armed Forces at Sea, (August 12, 1949), 6 U.S.T. 3217, 75 U.N.T.S. 85 [GC II]; Geneva Convention Relative to the Treatment of Prisoners of War, (August 12, 1949), 6 U.S.T. 3316, 75 U.N.T.S. 135 [GC III]; Geneva Convention Relative to the Protection of Civilian Persons in Time of War, (August 12, 1949), 6 U.S.T. 3516, 75 U.N.T.S. 287 [GC IV]; Protocol Additional to the Geneva Conventions of August 12, 1949, and Relating to the Protection of Victims of International Armed Conflicts, (June 8, 1977), 1125 U.N.T.S. 3 [AP I]; Protocol Additional to the Geneva Conventions of August 12, 1949, and Relating to the Protection of Victims of Non-International Armed Conflicts, (June 8, 1977), 1125 U.N.T.S. 609 [AP II].

41 *See* Al-Sirri v. Secretary of State for the Home Department (United Nations High Commissioner for Refugees intervening) [2013] 1 AC 745 (U.K.), ¶37, "there is as yet no internationally agreed definition of terrorism [and] no comprehensive international Convention binding Member States to take action against it..."

42 This working definition is specifically limited to activities by individuals or groups that are not endorsed by a state.

43 *See e.g.* ALEX P. SCHMID, POLITICAL TERRORISM: A RESEARCH GUIDE TO CONCEPTS, THEORIES, DATA BASES AND LITERATURE, 119–52 (Transaction Books, 1984); WALTHER LAQUEUR, THE AGE OF TERRORISM, 143 (Brown, Little, 1987); Alex Schmid, *"Terrorism on Trial": Terrorism – the Definitional Problem*, 36 CASE W. RES. J. INT'L L. 375 (2004); BRUCE HOFFMAN, INSIDE TERRORISM, 1–41 (Columbia University Press, 2006).

44 *See e.g.* HOFFMAN, INSIDE TERRORISM, 40, terrorism, is "the deliberate creation and exploitation of fear through violence in the pursuit of political change;" BEN SAUL, DEFINING TERRORISM IN INTERNATIONAL LAW, 66 (Oxford University Press, 2006): MARTHA CRENSHAW, EXPLAINING TERRORISM: CAUSES, PROCESSES AND CONSEQUENCES, 1–32 (Routledge, 2010).

45 In 1996 the U.N. General Assembly decided to establish an Ad Hoc Committee *inter alia* to develop a comprehensive legal framework of conventions dealing with international terrorism. U.N.G.A. Res. 51/210 (Dec. 17, 1996). To date there has been no consensus. *See* Mahmoud Hmoud, *Negotiating the Draft Comprehensive Convention on International Terrorism*, ICJ 4 5 (1031) (2006).

46 Nicholas J. Perry, *The Numerous Federal Legal Definitions of Terrorism: The Problem of Too Many Grails*, 30 J. LEGIS. 249 (2004).

47 LORD CARLILE OF BERRIEW Q.C., INDEPENDENT REVIEWER OF TERRORISM LEGISLATION, THE DEFINITION OF TERRORISM, 6 ¶12, Cm. 7052 (March 2007).

48 SAUL, DEFINING TERRORISM IN INTERNATIONAL LAW, 5 (commenting that without an agreed definition, states can unilaterally decide on what amounts to terrorism, and this can lead to arbitrary and excessive responses).

49 *See e.g.* Sudha Setty, *What's in a Name? How Nations Define Terrorism Ten Years After 9/11*, 33 U. PA. J. INT'L L, 61–62 (2011).

50 U.N. Human Rights Council, Report of the High Commissioner for Human Rights on the Protection of Human Rights and Fundamental Freedoms while Countering Terrorism, UN Doc. A/HRC/8/13, ¶20 (2008).

51 *Id. Also see* Ben Saul, *Legislating from a Radical Hague: the United Nations Special Tribunal for Lebanon Invents an International Crime of Transnational Terrorism*, LEIDEN J. INT'L L. 2011 24(3) 677, 685 (noting that many states defined terrorism "to suit their own political purposes and to camouflage assaults on fundamental rights," as well as to depart from procedural protections found in the criminal law).

52 Terrorism Act 2000 c.11, §1 (U.K.).

53 Terrorism Act 2006, c.11, §2 (U.K.).

54 R. v. Gul [2013] UKSC 64, ¶¶29–40, 63–64 (U.K.).

55 Lori Plotkin Boghardt, *Saudi Arabia: Outlawing Terrorism and the Arab Spring*, Policy Watch 2187, WASH. INSTITUTE FOR NEAR EAST POLICY (December 27, 2013), www.washingtoninstitute.org/policy-analysis/view/25640.

56 Unlawful Activities (Prevention) Act, 2012 No. 3 (2013), §4 (India).

57 U.N. Doc. S/RES/1373 (September 28, 2001), e.g., ¶2b decides that member states shall "take the necessary steps to prevent the commission of terrorist acts;" UN Doc. S/RES/1456, ¶6 (adopted January 20, 2003), repeating call for prevention but also refers to respecting human rights; this was repeated again by UN Doc. A/RES/60/158 (February 28, 2006), and in the UN Global Counter-Terrorism Strategy, UN Doc. A/RES/60/288 (September 20, 2006). A number of regional counter-terrorism frameworks were created both pre and post 9/11: Inter-American Committee Against Terrorism in 1999, OEA/Ser. P AG/RES. 1650 (XXIX-O/99) (June 7, 1999); TWENTY-THIRD MEETING OF CONSULTATION OEA OF MINISTERS OF FOREIGN AFFAIRS, /Ser.F/II.23 RC.23/RES.1/01, STRENGTHENING HEMISPHERIC COOPERATION TO PREVENT, COMBAT, AND ELIMINATE TERRORISM (September 21, 2001); TWENTY-FOURTH MEETING OF CONSULTATION OF MINISTERS OF FOREIGN AFFAIRS, OEA/Ser.F/II.24, RC.24/.RES.1/01, TERRORIST THREAT TO THE AMERICAS (September 21, 2001); Inter-American Convention Against Terrorism, AG/RES. 1840 (XXXII-O/02) (adopted March 6, 2002, (entered into force October 7, 2003); COUNCIL OF EUROPE FRAMEWORK DECISION (2002/475/JHA) (June 13, 2002); THE EUROPEAN UNION COUNTER-TERRORISM STRATEGY, 14469/4/05 REV 4 (November 30, 2005).

58 Duncan Gardham, *Airline bomb plot: investigation 'one of the biggest since WW2,'* THE TELEGRAPH (September 8, 2009), www.telegraph.co.uk/news/uknews/terrorism-in-the-uk/6152185/Airline-bomb-plot-investigation-one-of-biggest-since-WW2.html; Duncan Gardham, *Suicide bombers convicted at end of Britain's biggest terrorism investigation*, THE TELEGRAPH (July 8, 2010), www.telegraph.co.uk/news/uknews/terrorism-in-the-uk/7879970/Suicide-bombers-convicted-at-end-of-Britains-biggest-terrorism-investigation.html.

59 ICCPR, Art. 4 permits derogation in a state of emergency from a number of guarantees, including from art. 9, which governs the right to liberty. It is not possible to derogate from the right to permit detainees to challenge detention, see CCPR General Comment No. 29. States of Emergency (Article 4), U.N. Doc. CCPR/C/21/Rev.1/Add.11, ¶16 (2001).

60 ICCPR, art. 9(4); European Convention, Art. 5(4); American Convention, Art. 7(6); African Charter, Art. 7(1); and Arab Charter Art. 14(7).

61 India Const. Art. 22(5) merely provides that if an order of preventive detention has been made, "the authority making the order shall, as soon as may be,

communicate to such person the grounds on which the order has been made and shall afford him the earliest opportunity of making a representation against the order." No further details appear in either the Constitution or the Code of Criminal Procedure. In Australia, under the Criminal Code Act (Cth.) 1995, §105.51, federal detention orders can only be challenged if there is an error of law, and that challenge may only take place after the detention order has expired. For detention under LOAC in Afghanistan, *see* al-Maqaleh v. Gates, 605 F.3d 84 (D.C. Cir. 2010).

62 Secretary of State for the Home Department v. AF (FC) [2004] UKHL 56, ¶¶65, 66 (U.K.)

63 18 U.S.C. app 3. §6(c)(1).

64 Emergency Powers (Detention) Law, 5739-1979, S.H. 76, 33 L.S.I. 89-92 (Isr. 1979), §6(c); Incarceration of Unlawful Combatants Law, 5762-2002 (Isr. 2002), §5(5).

65 ICCPR, Art. 9(2); European Convention, Art. 5(2); American Convention, Art. 7(4); Arab Charter, Art. 14(3).

66 ICCPR, Art. 14; European Convention, Art. 6; American Convention, Art. 8; African Charter, Art. 7(1); Arab Charter, Art. 13.

67 European Convention, Art. 6.(1) This provision includes proceedings for the "determination of civil rights."

68 A. v. United Kingdom, Appl. No. 34455/05, ECHR (Feb. 19, 2009) ¶¶21–220.

69 *See e.g.* A. v. State of Israel, CrimA 6659/06 (June 11, 2008).

70 Terrorism Act 2000, Sch. 8, §§6, 8 (U.K.).

71 Criminal Procedure Law (Powers of Enforcement – Arrest), 1996, §35D. (Isr.).

72 Order Regarding Security Provisions [consolidated version] (Judea and Samaria) (No. 1651) 5770-2009, Article B, Temporary Order §287.

73 Criminal Code Act (Cth.) 1995, 105.38 (Austrl.).

74 Criminal Code Act (Cth.) 1995, 105.35. (Austrl.).

75 India Const. Art 22(3)(b).

76 Hakimi, *International Standards for Detaining Terrorism Suspects*, 626: the United States has "almost singularly asserted the authority to detain non-battlefield terrorism suspects in accordance with the LOAC."

77 Spencer Ackerman, *US transfers Umm Sayyaf, wife of suspected ISIS member to Iraqi Kurds*, THE GUARDIAN (August 7, 2015), www.theguardian.com/world/2015/aug/07/us-transfers-umm-sayyaf-wife-of-suspected-isis-member-to-iraqi-kurds.

78 *See e.g.* Nancy A. Youssef and Shane Harris, *The Women Who Keep ISIS Secretly Running*, DAILY BEAST (July 5, 2015), *www.thedailybeast.com/articles/2015/07/05/the-women-who-secretly-keep-isis-running*.html; Jonathan Horowitz, *The U.S. Must Ensure Umm Sayyaf Is Not Subjected to Human Rights Abuses*, JUST SECURITY (July 9, 2015), http://justsecurity.org/24513/umm-sayyaf-non refoulement/.

79 *See e.g.*. John B. Bellinger III and Vijay M. Padmanabhan, *Detention Operations in Contemporary Conflict: Four Challenges for the Geneva Conventions and Other Existing Law*, 105 AM. J INT'L L. 201, 202 (2011); Philip B. Heymann, *Detention*, 2 HARV. NAT'L SECURITY J. (2011), available at http://harvard nsj.com/wp-content/uploads/2011/03/Vol.-2; GABRIELLA BLUM AND PHILLIP B. HEYMANN, LAWS, OUTLAWS AND TERRORISTS, xii (MIT Press, 2010).

80 For criminal law issues, *see* ROACH, THE 9/11 EFFECT, 19; Eric Posner, *The War on Terror Will be Ever With Us*, SLATE (December 11, 2012), www.slate.com/articles/news_and_politics/view_from_chicago/2012/12/jeh_johnson_is_wrong_the_fight_with_al_qaida_continues.html; ROBERT CHESNEY, JACK GOLDSMITH, MATTHEW C. WAXMAN AND BENJAMIN WITTES, A STATUTORY FRAMEWORK FOR NEXT-GENERATION TERRORIST THREATS, 5 (Hoover Institution, Stanford University, 2013). For LOAC issues, *see* ROACH, THE 9/11 EFFECT, 439; Charles G. Kels, *The Perilous Position of the Laws of War*, HARV. NAT'L SECURITY J. (December 6, 2012), http://harvardnsj.org/2012/12/the-perilous-position-of-the-laws-of-war/; Emanuel Gross, *Fighting Terrorism with One Hand Tied Behind the Back: Delineating the Normative Framework for Conducting the Struggle Against Terrorism within a Democratic Paradigm*, 29 WIS. INT'L L. J. 1,13 (2011); Michael H. Hoffman, *State Practice, The Customary Law of War and Terrorism: Adapting Old Rules to Meet New Threats*, *in* 34 ISRAEL YEARBOOK ON HUMAN RIGHTS, 231, 232 (Martinus Nijhoff Publisher, 2004).

81 PREVENTIVE DETENTION, 1.

82 Universal Declaration of Human Rights. Adopted by the General Assembly of the United Nations in Res. 217 A (III), U.N. Doc. A/RES/217(111) Dec.10, 1948. UDHR has not been formally adopted as a legally binding document but the international community has recognized its importance as the basis for fundamental human rights.

83 ICCPR; European Convention; American Convention; African Charter Human Rights; Arab Charter.

84 *E.g.*, Hakimi, *International Standards for Detaining Terrorism Suspects*, 614–7. Administrative detention is security detention that is not connected to the criminal law model, and does not depend on criminal arrest or charge.

85 ALEX CONTE AND BOAZ GANOR, LEGAL AND POLICY ISSUES IN ESTABLISHING AN INTERNATIONAL FRAMEWORK FOR HUMAN RIGHTS COMPLIANCE WHEN COUNTERING TERRORISM, 17–18, INTERNATIONAL POLICY INSTITUTE FOR COUNTER-TERRORISM (2005), www.ict.org.il/Portals/0/Articles/20471-Ganor_Conte_Human_Rights.pdf (commenting that one of the main motivations for regular criminal activity is personal gain, whereas terrorists are motivated by altruism).

86 *Id.* So if the ideology mandates killing non-believers, that killing would be seen as lawful and appropriate.

87 *Id.* 21–23.

88 *Id.* 18.

89 *E.g.* in both countries terror suspects can be detained in police custody for longer periods than suspects arrested in connection with other criminal offenses, and access to lawyers can be delayed in terror cases.

90 ROACH, THE 9/11 EFFECT, 309, 361.

91 This book discusses Australia, Canada and India in detail, but the laws of many other countries are based on British law. *See e.g.* Abu Bakar Munir, *Malaysia*, 131–149 *in* PREVENTIVE DETENTION AND SECURITY LAW, A COMPARATIVE SURVEY.

92 Kent Roach, *The Post-9/11 Migration of Britain's Terrorism Act 2000*, *in* THE MIGRATION OF CONSTITUTIONAL IDEAS (ed., Sujit Choudry, Cambridge University Press, 2006).

93 CONTEST: THE UNITED KINGDOM'S STRATEGY FOR COUNTERING TERRORISM: ANNUAL REPORT FOR 2014, CM 9048, ¶1.3 (March 2015, UK).
94 PURSUE, PREVENT, PROTECT, PREPARE: THE UNITED KINGDOM'S STRATEGY FOR COUNTERING IINTERNATIONAL TERRORISM, HOME OFFICE, CM 7547, ¶019 (March 2009, UK).
95 U.N. Human Rights Committee, Replies to the List of Issues to be Taken up in Connection with the Consideration of the Sixth Periodic Report of the Government of the United Kingdom of Great Britain and Northern Ireland, CCPR/C/GBR/Q/6/Add.1, ¶¶ 1,2, 3, 4, 18 June 2008.
96 Human Rights Act 1998, c.42, §§2, 3 (U.K.). The British government is currently considering repealing the Human Rights Act and replacing it with a Bill of Rights that will not compel the automatic deference to ECHR decisions, *see e.g.* Jon Stone, *Government delays Human Rights Act repeal amid opposition from senior Tories*, THE INDEPENDENT (May 27, 2015), www.independent.co.uk/news/uk/politics/government-delays-human-rights-act-repeal-amid-opposition-from-senior-tories-10277687.html.
97 Nicola McGarrity, *'Let the Punishment Fit the Offence': Determining Sentences for Australian Terrorists*, 2 INT'L J. CRIM. JUST. 1 (2013).
98 BRET WALKER, INDEPENDENT NATIONAL SECURITY LEGISLATION MONITOR, DECLASSIFIED ANNUAL REPORT 20 DECEMBER 2012, 28 Commonwealth of Australia (2013).
99 George Williams, *Anti-terror legislation in Australia and New Zealand*, *in* GLOBAL ANTI-TERRORISM LAW AND POLICY, *in* GLOBAL ANTI-TERRORISM LAW AND POLICY, 545–6 (Victor V. Ramraj, Michael Hor, Kent Roach and George Williams, eds) (Cambridge University Press, 2012).
100 AUSTRALIAN GOVERNMENT, COUNTER-TERRORISM WHITE PAPER, 19 (2010), www.asio.gov.au/img/files/counter-terrorism_white-paper.pdf.
101 GOVERNMENT OF CANADA, BUILDING RESILIENCE AGAINST TERRORISM: CANADA'S COUNTER-TERRORISM STRATEGY, 7 (2011).
102 Constitution Act 1982 *being* Schedule B to the Canada Act, 1982, c.11 (U.K.), *available at* http://laws.justice.gc.ca/eng/charter/CHART_E.PDF.
103 GOVERNMENT OF CANADA, BUILDING RESILIENCE AGAINST TERRORISM, 11.
104 *Id.*
105 *Id.*, 4–5.
106 Rama Lakshmi, *India's counterterror measures in disarray*, WASH. POST, A7 (May 2, 2012).
107 Gabriella Blum, *Judicial review of counterterrorism operations*, 47 JUSTICE 17, 18 (2010).
108 AMICHAI COHEN AND STUART A. COHEN, ISRAEL'S NATIONAL SECURITY LAW, 11 (Routledge, 2012).
109 *Id.*
110 Public Committee Against Torture in Israel v. Government of Israel, HCJ 769/02, ¶18 (citing ANTONIO CASSESE, INTERNATIONAL LAW, 420 (2nd ed. 2005)).
111 Public Committee Against Torture in Israel v. Government of Israel, ¶18.
112 *Id.*, ¶20.
113 *Id.*
114 GC III Art. 4A. (The conditions to be fulfilled are: (a) that of being commanded by a person responsible for his subordinates; (b) that of having a fixed

distinctive sign recognizable at a distance; (c) that of carrying arms openly; (d) that of conducting their operations in accordance with the laws and customs of war.)

115 GC III gives combatants a number of rights, including the right to be treated formally as a prisoner of war if detained on the battlefield.

116 Public Committee Against Torture in Israel v. Government of Israel, HCJ 769/02, ¶28.

117 Emergency Powers (Detention) Law. Similar provisions promulgated by military order apply in the Occupied Territories, *see e.g.* Order Regarding Security Provisions [consolidated version] (Judea and Samaria) (No. 1651) at Article B, Temporary Order.

118 ICCPR, Art. 4 permits derogation from some guarantees in times of emergency. As Israel has derogated from the ICCPR, it is not obliged to ensure that detention is not arbitrary. Israel is not, however, released from the right to afford detainees the right to challenge detention, because that right is non-derogable.

119 In evaluating the proportionality of administrative detention pursuant to the Incarceration of Unlawful Combatants Law, 5762-2002, the Supreme Court reasoned that civilians participating in hostilities against the State of Israel are unlawful combatants. They are subject to the Fourth Geneva Convention relative to civilians (GC IV) and can be detained when they represent a threat to the security of the state. An unlawful combatant would not, however, be entitled to the same degree of protection to which innocent civilians are entitled under GC IV. The Court held indefinite detention to be proportionate, relying once more on the applicability of international humanitarian law, in particular to GC III, which allows prisoners of war to be interned until hostilities have ended. *See* A. v. Israel, A. v. State of Israel, ¶¶13 and 49 (citing the Third Geneva Convention, relative to prisoners of war, art. 118, providing that detention is possible until the cessation of hostilities).

120 *Id.*, ¶22.

121 *Id.*

122 The judge will see all the evidence, without the detainee or his representative being present, and may decide to accept evidence without disclosing it to the detainee or his lawyer if he is "satisfied that disclosure of the evidence to either of them may impair state security or public security." *See* Emergency Powers (Detention) Law, 5739-1979, §6(c).

123 Loi No. 2003-239, Art.1 (Fr. March 18, 2003).

124 Const. of October 4, 1958, Art. 55 (Fr.).

125 Jacqueline Hodgson, The Investigation and Prosecution of Terrorist Suspects in France, 4 (Report commissioned by Home Office, 2006).

126 Human Rights Watch, Preempting Justice. Counterterrorism Laws And Procedures In France, 11 (Jul. 2008) (quoting Christophe Chaboud, a former head of the special anti-terrorism unit of the Ministry of Interior).

127 Frank Foley, Countering Terrorism In Britain And France, 303–7 (Cambridge University Press, 2013).

128 Code Pénale (Fr.).

129 Hodgson, The Investigation and Prosecution of Terrorist Suspects in France, 4.

130 Jacqueline Hodgson, *The French Prosecutor in Question*, 67 WASH. AND LEE L. REV. 1361, 1363 (2010).

131 Some reports suggest that more terrorist fatalities since 9/11 can be attributed to non-Islamist homegrown extremists than those with international ties. *See e.g.* Scott Shane, *Homegrown Extremists Tied to Deadlier Toll Than Jihadists in U.S. Since 9/11*, N.Y. TIMES (June 24, 2015), www.nytimes.com/2015/06/25/us/tally-of-attacks-in-us-challenges-perceptions-of-top-terror-threat.html?_r=0.

132 THE WHITE HOUSE, OFFICE OF THE PRESS SECRETARY, REMARKS BY THE PRESIDENT AT THE NATIONAL DEFENSE UNIVERSITY (May 23, 2013), www.whitehouse.gov/the-press-office/2013/05/23/remarks-president-national-defense-university.

133 THE WHITE HOUSE, OFFICE OF THE PRESS SECRETARY, NATIONAL SECURITY STRATEGY, 9 (February 2015), www.whitehouse.gov/sites/default/files/docs/2015_national_security_strategy.pdf.

134 *See Chapter 9*, *infra*.

Part I

Detention provisions in Human Rights Treaties and Geneva Conventions

1 Introducing the Treaties

Human rights law underpins all the domestic detention laws surveyed in this work, and also has a part to play in the law of armed conflict (LOAC). Part I analyzes the detention of terror suspects in international law in five general human rights treaties, and in LOAC.[1] The detention provisions are set out in Appendix 3, Table 1. This chapter introduces the human rights treaties and their jurisdiction, focusing on the thorny problem of the extraterritorial reach of the treaties. This issue is particularly relevant to detention, in cases where a state captures and detains individuals outside of its home territory.

The Treaties

The detention provisions in the International Covenant on Civil and Political Rights[2] (ICCPR) provide the foundation for the treatment of detention in the regional human rights treaties. However, the treaty wording is very broad and has generated an enormous amount of comment and interpretive, but non-binding, jurisprudence from the United Nations Human Rights Committee (HRC), from which can be gleaned many important criteria to form the basis of core global principles.

The European Convention for the Protection of Human Rights and Fundamental Freedoms (European Convention),[3] through the judgments of the European Court of Human Rights (ECHR), has become a dynamic and powerful instrument in the response to new challenges and the ongoing promotion of the rule of law and democracy in Europe.[4] The ECHR has developed an extensive body of case law, much of it concerned with detention. The Council of Europe describes the ECHR as the "conscience of Europe"[5] and its landmark judgments in detention and other cases have prompted changes in national laws.[6] Its interpretive jurisprudence yields much useful and important material to assist in the search for global core principles.

The American Convention on Human Rights (American Convention)[7] was modeled on both the ICCPR and the European Convention.[8] The rights and freedoms it guarantees are those set forth in the American Declaration on the Rights and Duties of Man.[9] Although the American

Declaration was adopted as a non-binding declaration, it is generally recognized that it provides an authoritative definition and interpretation of the human rights obligations by which Organization of American States (OAS) member states are bound under their Charter.[10] The Inter-American Court of Human Rights (IACHR) has confirmed that the American Declaration defines the human rights set out in the OAS Charter and is "a source of international obligations related to the Charter of the Organization for those states."[11]

The African Charter of Human and Peoples' Rights[12] (African Charter) does not have a robust enforcement mechanism, and little can be done to police or sanction violations effectively. In 1998 the Organization of African States adopted a Protocol to the African Charter to establish an African Court on Human and Peoples' Rights.[13] The African Commission and states may submit cases to the Court,[14] but NGOs and individuals may only do so if their state has made a declaration "accepting the competence of the Court" to receive such cases.[15] It appears that the Court has not dealt with any cases alleging a violation of Article 6 of the African Charter.[16]

The most recent regional human rights instrument is the Arab Charter on Human Rights (Arab Charter).[17] Although it is an improvement on an earlier 1994 version,[18] critics of the Charter point out that it is still inconsistent with international human rights law.[19]

Jurisdiction

ICCPR

The issue of territorial reach is particularly relevant to whether the ICCPR applies to the practice of detention by the United States in Guantánamo Bay, Afghanistan and Iraq, and by Israel in the Occupied Territories. Contrary to most other countries, the United States has consistently maintained that its human rights obligations do not apply extraterritorially.[20] The United States eschews international human rights laws as far as LOAC detention in Guantánamo and Afghanistan is concerned, and presumably will do so in respect of any future detention in any place outside of the United States.

Israel's position is that the ICCPR and similar instruments "did not apply directly to the current situation in the occupied territories."[21] Israel maintains that it has been in a state of emergency since 1948 and has derogated from its ICCPR obligations.[22]

The interpretation of Article 2 has been, and still is, the subject of extensive debate and discussion, by the HRC,[23] the International Court of Justice (ICJ),[24] human rights organizations,[25] and scholars.[26] The debate centers round whether certain words are to be interpreted conjunctively or disjunctively.[27] The controversy derives from the interpretation of highlighted words of Article 2(1): "Each State Party to the present Covenant undertakes to respect and to ensure to **all individuals within its territory and**

subject to its jurisdiction the rights recognized in the present Covenant ..." (emphasis added).

No presumptions can be found either against or in favor of extra-territoriality in international law, and the only guidance that can be discovered is in the "text, object and purpose of each particular treaty."[28] The basic rule governing interpretation of treaties is in Article 31 of the Vienna Convention,[29] which prescribes looking at the ordinary meaning of the words. However, if the meaning is "ambiguous or obscure" or "leads to a result which is manifestly absurd or unreasonable" then recourse may be had to "supplementary means of interpretation, including the preparatory work of the treaty and the circumstances of its conclusion."[30] It has often been necessary to turn to the *travaux préparatoires* that documented treaty negotiations, but the debates have not always reached clear conclusions.

It might seem obvious to read the words conjunctively, as do the United States[31] and Israel,[32] but the literature suggests that the position is far from clear. One suggestion is that the conjunctive interpretation could lead to a result that is inconsistent with the object and purpose of the ICCPR or one that is manifestly absurd.[33] It is therefore pertinent to see what light, if any, is shed on the interpretation of the relevant words in the *travaux préparatoires*. The United States had introduced the notion of territory into the drafting, and had suggested the wording that found its way into the final form of Article 2(1).[34]

Many commentators have analyzed the explanation given by the United States delegate, Eleanor Roosevelt, that the purpose of the wording in Article 2(1) was to make it clear that the draft Covenant would apply only to persons within the territory and subject to the jurisdiction of contracting states.[35] The context of her comments is important as she was concerned that the ICCPR might oblige state parties to enact legislation that affected persons who, although outside their state's territory, were technically within its jurisdiction for certain purposes, such as those in the then occupied territories of Germany, Austria, and Japan.[36]

However, according to Michal Gondek, Eleanor Roosevelt did not clearly explain how the phrase "within the territory and subject to its jurisdiction" was to be interpreted. He opines that the United States intended to avoid acquiring positive obligations by legislating with regard to persons in occupied territories in situations that were outside United States jurisdiction as an occupying power.[37] In short, it may be that the rationale in this particular context was to avoid assuming obligations that a state could not meet.[38] Dominic McGoldrick supports this interpretation, noting that the record in the *travaux préparatoires* affirms that the words would have to be read disjunctively in order to protect the Covenant rights.[39]

Quite soon after the coming into force of the ICCPR in 1976, the HRC began to depart from the literal reading of the text.[40] It then "abandoned the literal meaning altogether" in its General Comment No. 31 of 2004,[41] instead prescribing a disjunctive interpretation – that the rights be available to all individuals who may find themselves in the territory **or** subject to the jurisdiction of the state party.[42] This formula is repeated in General Comment 35 of 2014.[43]

The ICJ has commented that the *travaux préparatoires* confirm the HRC's interpretation of Article 2(1),[44] although Dennis and Surena consider it significant that the ICJ did not cite General Comment 31 in its opinion,[45] but relied on the HRC rulings in *Lopez Burgos*[46] *v. Uruguay* and *Celiberti v. Uruguay.*[47] The commentators are firmly of the view that the *travaux préparatoires* confirm the conjunctive interpretation.[48] In support of their argument they point to the words of HRC member Christian Tomuschat in *Lopez Burgos* concerning the correct interpretation of Article 2(1) that "[t]he formula was intended to take care of objective difficulties which might impede the implementation of the Covenant in specific situations."[49] However, they fail to cite the sentence that precedes the words just cited, as well as the last three sentences of the same paragraph, which seem to support the ruling in the case and do not advance the commentators' contention that the conjunctive interpretation applies.[50]

Marko Milanovic comments that the United States' interpretation not only excludes the application of the ICCPR to occupied territories but also to activities in leased territories, such as Guantánamo Bay.[51] He does not believe that the *travaux préparatoires* are clear about how the elusive phrase is to be interpreted, rather that they provide "an ample dose of confusion and doubt."[52] He highlights a United States' concern that extending human rights obligations in occupied or leased territories might result in questions of conflicting authority.[53] Furthermore, in 2010 the ICJ made it clear that Article 9 applied "in principle to any form of arrest or detention decided upon and carried out by a public authority, whatever its legal basis and the objective being pursued."[54]

The United States has consistently maintained that the treatment of its detainees in Guantánamo, Afghanistan, and Iraq is governed by the *lex specialis*, the law of armed conflict, and not international human rights law.[55] The HRC has disagreed,[56] and has commented that the obligations of the United States under international human rights law extend to persons detained at Guantánamo Bay.[57] The impasse continues, but some indications can be discerned of a "more relaxed" approach to the international human rights law (IHRL) and international humanitarian law (IHL) relationship, and where they do not directly conflict, a willingness to harmonize legal obligations.[58] The United States has confirmed its stance in recent discussions with the HRC.[59]

European Convention

In this Convention too, the interpretation of extraterritorial jurisdiction, which is relevant to detention, has been controversial. Initially the jurisdiction clause was drafted to guarantee rights to all persons residing within the territories of the contracting parties,[60] but this was thought to be too restrictive.[61] Although the words in the final version (the "High Contracting Parties shall secure to everyone within their jurisdiction the rights and freedoms defined in Section I of this Convention")[62] appear clear, the phrase "within their jurisdiction" has generated a lot of discussion and debate.[63] Although Article 1 does not mention territory, it should be read in tandem with Article 56, which provides that any state can notify the Secretary General of the Council of Europe that the European Convention extends to "all or any of the territories for whose international relations it is responsible,"[64] but there is a proviso that "the Convention shall be applied in such territories, with due regard, however, to local requirements,"[65] whatever that means.

The issue of the applicability of extraterritorial jurisdiction has been frequently disputed in places where states have been in some sort of military occupation. In *Loizidou v. Turkey*, the Court opined:

> [b]earing in mind the object and purpose of the Convention, the responsibility of a Contracting Party may also arise when as a consequence of military action – whether lawful or unlawful – it exercises effective control of an area outside its national territory. The obligation to secure, in such an area, the rights and freedoms set out in the Convention, derives from the fact of such control whether it be exercised directly, through its armed forces, or through a subordinate local administration.[66]

However, effective control of an area has been hard to define.[67] Until 2011 the leading case was *Bankovic v. Belgium*,[68] which generated much academic comment.[69] It involved a complaint by relatives of Yugoslav citizens killed in a NATO (North Atlantic Treaty Organization) operated strike in Belgrade that various Convention rights had been violated. The Court did not find a jurisdictional link between the applicants and the respondent state for an extraterritorial act. It commented that the case law:

> demonstrates that its recognition of the exercise of extra-territorial jurisdiction by a Contracting State is exceptional: it has done so when the respondent State, through the effective control of the relevant territory and its inhabitants abroad as a consequence of military occupation or through the consent, invitation or acquiescence of the Government of that territory, exercises all or some of the public powers normally to be exercised by that Government.[70]

In this case the exceptional exercise of extraterritorial jurisdiction was limited to action on the territory of another contracting party except in some special circumstances.[71]

The scope of extraterritorial jurisdiction was broadened further in 2004 in *Ilascu v. Moldova and Russia*.[72] The case concerned the pre- and post-trial detention of Moldovan nationals in Moldova. The applicants claimed first that Moldova had violated the Convention. Moldova asserted that at the relevant time it did not have effective control. The extraterritorial aspect related to the allegation that Moldova was under *de facto* Russian control on account of the presence of Russian troops and equipment as well as support that Russia allegedly gave to the separatist regime.[73] The Court gave a very wide interpretation of jurisdiction in respect of Moldova,[74] and also concluded that there was a "continuous and uninterrupted link of responsibility on the part of the Russian Federation for the applicants' fate."[75] One view is that the Court's principles of extraterritorial application of the ECHR are valid both in cases of actual military occupation, and where a state party provides political, military, and economic support to a separatist regime in another state, which enables the separatist regime to survive.[76]

In 2011 *Al-Skeini v. United Kingdom*[77] concerned a complaint of a violation of Article 2, relating to an investigation into the death of Iraqi civilians involving British soldiers in an area of southern Iraq under British control. The United Kingdom government argued that it did not have effective control over any part of Iraq and that in any event, Iraq fell outside the Convention space, and that none of the exceptions in *Bankovic* applied. The Court commented that "the question whether exceptional circumstances exist which require and justify a finding by the Court that the State was exercising jurisdiction extra-territorially must be determined with reference to the particular facts."[78]

The Court gave the example of *Al-Saadoon and Mufdhi v. the United Kingdom*, where it was held that "two Iraqi nationals detained in British-controlled military prisons in Iraq fell within the jurisdiction of the United Kingdom, since the United Kingdom exercised total and exclusive control over the prisons and the individuals detained in them."[79]

In considering whether extraterritorial jurisdiction could apply in a place that was non-Convention territory, the *Al-Skeini* Court commented that the importance of establishing jurisdiction of an occupying state does not imply that "jurisdiction under Article 1 of the Convention can never exist outside the territory covered by the Council of Europe Member States. The Court has not in its case-law applied any such restriction."[80] Thus in the exceptional circumstances of this case, the Court considered:

> that the United Kingdom, through its soldiers engaged in security operations in Basrah during the period in question, exercised authority and control over individuals killed in the course of such security operations, so as to establish a jurisdictional link between the deceased and the United Kingdom for the purposes of Article 1 of the Convention.[81]

The ECHR thus extended the concept of extraterritorial jurisdiction, albeit limited to what it called exceptional circumstances, to acts committed anywhere. In *Al-Jedda v. United Kingdom*, decided on the same day as *Al-Skeini*, the Court held that an Iraqi detained in British custody in Iraq was within the authority and control of the United Kingdom throughout his detention, and therefore within the jurisdiction of the United Kingdom and thus the European Convention was applicable to his case.[82] Similar rulings have been made in *Hassan v. United Kingdom*,[83] and *Jaloud v. The Netherlands*.[84]

American Convention

The scope of jurisdiction in the American Convention is expressed as requiring state parties to respect the rights and freedoms in the document and to ensure "to all persons subject to their jurisdiction the free and full exercise of those rights and freedoms…"[85] The extraterritorial scope of the American Convention is a relevant issue in the context of preventive detention measures used by many state parties, not least the United States at Guantánamo Bay. The United States, which has not ratified the Convention,[86] is considered subject to the American Declaration,[87] which has no jurisdictional scope.[88]

The first case on extraterritoriality under the American Convention was *Saldano v. Argentina*[89] where an Argentinian national applicant incarcerated on death row in the United States claimed that Argentina had failed to protect him. The Commission noted that a state party "may be responsible under certain circumstances for the acts and omissions of its agents which produces effects or are undertaken outside that State's own territory."[90] No evidence could be found to establish that Argentina had in any way exercised its authority or control over Saldano either prior or subsequent to his arrest in the United States, or over the local officials in the United States involved in the criminal proceedings against him.[91] Thus he was not within Argentinian jurisdiction.

One early case under the American Declaration concerning detention is *Coard v. United States*.[92] Seventeen Grenadians complained about their detention for a period of between nine and twelve days, during the United States' occupation of Grenada in 1983. The United States maintained that they were civilian detainees, held briefly for reasons of military necessity in accordance with the Geneva Conventions,[93] and that the matter was governed exclusively by the LOAC, which the Commission had no mandate to apply.[94] The Commission declared that it was competent to hear the complaint,[95] and although it was not in issue, went on to consider the subject of extraterritoriality.[96] On the facts, the Commission held that the claimants had been subjected to the extraterritorial authority and control of the United States authorities and had not been afforded access to a review of the legality of their detention with the least possible delay.[97] Thus the United States had violated the American Declaration.

Pursuant to Article 25 of the Rules of Procedure of the IACHR, in serious and urgent cases, on its own initiative or at the request of a party, the Commission can request that states adopt precautionary measures to prevent irreparable harm to persons.[98] In March 2002, after the arrival of the first detainees at Guantánamo, several human rights organizations applied for precautionary measures to protect the human rights of the detainees.[99] Rather like the approach of the ECHR, the Commission decided that the detainees were within the authority and control of the United States, noting in March 2002 that:

> where persons find themselves within the authority and control of a state and where a circumstance of armed conflict may be involved, their fundamental rights may be determined in part by reference to international humanitarian law as well as international human rights law. Where it may be considered that the protections of international humanitarian law do not apply, however, such persons remain the beneficiaries at least of the non-derogable protections under international human rights law. In short, no person under the authority and control of a state, regardless of his or her circumstances, is devoid of legal protection for his or her fundamental and non-derogable human rights.[100]

During February and March 2003, the petitioner submitted further information to the Commission about the Guantánamo detainees, and again requested that the Commission adopt precautionary measures.[101] The Commission made a formal request in this connection to the United States government, which responded that the Commission lacked competence, both to apply international humanitarian law, and to request precautionary measures.[102] The measures were reiterated and amplified in 2004, 2005, and 2006 in respect of Omar Khadr,[103] but had no impact on the detention policy and practice at Guantánamo.

The first Guantánamo case to come before the IACHR was *Ameziane v. United States*,[104] in March 2012, where an Algerian national who was captured in Pakistan in 2002 was held briefly at a United States airbase in Kandahar, Afghanistan, and then transferred to Guantánamo, where he was cleared for release in 2009. He alleged arbitrary detention,[105] and complained about his treatment whilst detained, both in Kandahar and at Guantánamo.[106] The IACHR's decision on admissibility concluded that at every stage of the arrest and detention, the United States brought the petitioner under United States jurisdiction.[107] Although the IACHR paved the way to continue with an analysis of the merits of the case, further consideration of the issues was pre-empted by Ameziane being transferred to Algeria in December 2013.[108]

African Charter

Article 2 states that every individual shall be entitled to the rights and freedoms recognized and guaranteed under the Charter. There does not appear to be any case law relating to jurisdiction in the context of detention.

Arab Charter

Under Article 3 each state party undertakes to ensure to all individuals subject to its jurisdiction the right to enjoy the rights and freedoms set out in the Charter.

Detention and human rights in LOAC sources

Introduction

LOAC, also known as international humanitarian law (IHL), derives from two sources: international treaties,[109] and customary international law.[110] Conflicts arising between two or more of the parties to the Geneva Conventions (GCs) are known as international armed conflicts[111] (IACs) and the rules of the GCs and Additional Protocol (AP) I apply as they did during the brief period when the United States participated in the war in Afghanistan between October and December 2001.

In non-international armed conflicts (NIACs), such as between a government and armed groups, only Common Article 3 of the GCs (so named because the same article appears in all four GCs in the same place) and perhaps AP II apply.[112] Common Article 3 is a relatively short statement prescribing humane treatment and listing a number of prohibited acts.[113] Otherwise IHRL applies, such as reflected in GC IV.[114] When there are gaps in treaty law, customary international law applies.[115] In 2012 a number of states concluded the Copenhagen Process, which resulted in the formulation of a set of non-binding principles and guidelines governing detention in NIACs.[116] Some of those principles are seen in the relevant sections of the United States Department of Defense Law of War Manual.[117]

Some of the later stages of the United States' presence in Afghanistan and Iraq can fit into the traditional understanding of a non-international armed conflict,[118] with the United States supporting the respective current governments in their fight against insurgents, but waging a "war on terror" or "countering violent extremism" around the world wherever al-Qaeda may be, does not.[119] As terror attacks led or inspired by al-Qaeda or Da'esh are not carried out by states (and parties to the GCs), the attacks cannot be classified as international armed conflicts either.

Applying human rights in LOAC

Opinions differ as to the extent of the application of IHRL. Europeans, the International Committee of the Red Cross (ICRC), ICJ, and human rights activists maintain that IHRL "*always* applies, hand in hand with the LOAC on the battlefield."[120] The HRC, in General Comment 35, also states that Article 9 ICCPR relating to detention applies in "situations of armed conflict to which the rules of international humanitarian law are applicable."[121] As mentioned above, several ECHR decisions dealing with IACs confirm that Article 5 regarding detention applies extraterritorially in armed conflicts.

A British court has commented that LOAC would only apply to detention in a NIAC context if the law governing NIACs provided an authority to detain,[122] and the Court did not believe any such authority currently existed in LOAC or customary international law.[123] Thus, in that case, in the absence of applicable LOAC, IHRL, i.e. Article 5 ECHR applied.

Conversely, Israel and the United States posit that "during situations of armed conflict international humanitarian law is the *lex specialis*, to the exclusion of human rights law applicable to the treatment of captured 'enemy combatants.'"[124] The Copenhagen Process did not change this approach: Israel was not a participant; and the wording of the relevant section permits the United States to maintain its stance.[125]

Notes

1 This book analyzes many decisions and commentaries relating to preventive detention in the context of human rights, but limitations on the size of this work preclude delving into all the decisions, recommendations, and interpretations of every country and treaty body.

2 International Covenant on Civil and Political Rights, G.A. res. 2200A (XXI), 21 U.N. GAOR Supp. (No. 16) at 52, U.N. Doc. A/6316 (1966), 999 U.N.T.S. 171 (entered into force March 23, 1976) [ICCPR].

3 European Convention for the Protection of Human Rights and Fundamental Freedoms, opened for signature November 4, 1950, 213 UNTS 222 (entered into force September 3, 1953) [European Convention].

4 Council Of Europe, *European Court of Human Rights, Landmark Judgments*, http://human-rights-convention.org/the-main-judgments.

5 *Id.*

6 The burden caused by this may be one reason why the United Kingdom is considering whether to repeal its Human Rights Act and replace it with a Bill of Rights. *See e.g.* Jon Stone, *Government delays Human Rights Act repeal amid opposition from senior Tories*, The Independent (May 27, 2015), www.independent.co.uk/news/uk/politics/government-delays-human-rights-act-repeal-amid-opposition-from-senior-tories-10277687.html.

7 American Convention on Human Rights, O.A.S. Treaty Series No. 36, 1144 U.N.T.S. 123 (entered into force July 18, 1978) [American Convention].

8 MICHAL GONDEK, THE REACH OF HUMAN RIGHTS IN A GLOBALISING WORLD: EXTRATERRITORIAL APPLICATION OF HUMAN RIGHTS TREATIES, 109 (Intersentia, 2009).

9 American Declaration on the Rights and Duties of Man (adopted by the Ninth International Conference of American States, Bogotá, Colombia, 1948) [American Declaration].

10 Brian Farrell, *The Right to Habeas Corpus in the Inter-American Human Rights System*, 33 SUFFOLK TRANSNAT'L L. REV. 197, 202 (2010).

11 *Id.* fn. 28 (quoting Interpretation of the American Declaration of the Rights and Duties of Man Within the Framework of Article 64 of the American Convention of Human Rights, No. 10 (ser. A) 1989 IACHR P.45 (July 14, 1989)).

12 African (Banjul) Charter of Human and Peoples' Rights (adopted June 27, 1981, OAU Doc. CAB/LEG/67/3 rev. 5, 21 I.L.M. 58 (1982), entered into force October 21, 1986) [African Charter].

13 Protocol to the African Charter on Human and Peoples' Rights on the Establishment of the African Court on Human and Peoples' Rights, 1998 (entered into force in 2004), *available at* www.achpr.org/instruments/court-establishment/#1.

14 *Id.*, Art. 5.

15 *Id.*, Arts. 5(3), 34(6).

16 A search on the African Court of Human Rights' website has not revealed any cases dealing with arbitrary detention.

17 Arab Charter on Human Rights, adopted May 22, 2004, reprinted in 12 Int'l Hum. Rts. Rep. 893 (2005) (entered into force March 15, 2008), *available at* www1.umn.edu/humanrts/instree/loas2005.html [Arab Charter].

18 Arab Charter on Human Rights (adopted Sep. 15 1994, by the League of Arab State), reprinted in 18 Hum. Rts. L.J. 151 (1997).

19 *See e.g.* Mervat Rishmawi, The Arab Charter on Human Rights and the League of Arab States: An Update, 10 HUM. RTS. L. REV. 169, 170 (2010).

20 *See e.g.*, MARKO MILANOVIC, EXTRATERRITORIAL APPLICATION OF HUMAN RIGHTS TREATIES, 58 (Oxford University Press, 2011); Beth Van Schaack, *The United States' Position on the Extraterritorial Application of Human Rights Obligations: Now is the Time for Change*, 90 INT'L L. STUDIES 20, 22 (2014).

21 Legal Consequences of the Construction of a Wall in the Occupied Palestinian Territory, Advisory Opinion, I.C.J. Reports 2004 136, 179, ¶110.

22 *See Chapter 7 infra.*

23 *See e.g.*, Lopez Burgos v. Uruguay, HRC Communication No. R.12/52, U.N. (July 29, 1981), Doc. Supp. No. 40 (A/36/40) 176; Human Rights Committee, General Comment No. 31 [80], Nature of the General Legal Obligation Imposed on States Parties to the Covenant, CCPR/C/21/Rev.1/Add.13. (General Comments) (May 26, 2004), ¶10.

24 Legal Consequences of the Construction of a Wall in the Occupied Palestinian Territory, 179, ¶109; Armed Activities on the Territory of the Congo (Democratic Republic of the Congo v. Uganda), Judgment, I.C.J. Reports 2005, 168, 242–3, ¶216.

25 *See e.g.* HUMAN RIGHTS WATCH, IN THE NAME OF SECURITY. COUNTERTERRORISM LAWS WORLDWIDE SINCE SEPTEMBER 11, 6 (2012); INTERNATIONAL COMMISSION OF JURISTS, ASSESSING DAMAGE, URGING ACTION, REPORT OF

The Eminent Jurists Panel On Terrorism, Counter-Terrorism And Human Rights, 24 (2009), 55–6.

26 *See e.g.* Dominic McGoldrick, *Extraterritorial Application of the International Covenant on Civil and Political Rights*, 41–81, *in* Extraterritorial Application Of Human Rights Treaties (Fons Coomans and Menno T. Kamminga (eds)) (Intersentia, 2004); Gondek, The Reach Of Human Rights In A Globalising World, 119, 132–7; Milanovic, Extraterritorial Application Of Human Rights Treaties, 10–11, 58–60, 222–7; Van Schaack, *The United States' Position on the Extraterritorial Application of Human Rights Obligations.*

27 Gondek, The Reach Of Human Rights In A Globalising World, 132.

28 Milanovic, Extraterritorial Application Of Human Rights Treaties, 10–11.

29 Vienna Convention on the Law of Treaties, U.N.T.S. vol. 1155, p. 331, dated May 23, 1969 (entered into force January 27, 1980), Art. 31.

30 *Id.*, Art. 32.

31 Gondek, The Reach Of Human Rights In A Globalising World, 239–43 (commenting that the US supported the "cumulative" or "conjunctive" approach, "ignoring the jurisprudence of the Committee and focusing largely on its own interpretation of the *travaux préparatoires*"); Milanovic, Extraterritorial Application Of Human Rights Treaties, 58 (saying that the United States maintain that the language is clear and supported by the negotiating history).

32 Gondek, The Reach Of Human Rights In A Globalising World, 234–9 (commenting that Israel believes that LOAC alone applies to the situation in the Occupied Territories, "which excludes the applicability of human rights").

33 McGoldrick, *Extraterritorial Application of the International Covenant on Civil and Political Rights*, 48.

34 Marc J. Bossuyt, Guide To The *"Travaux Préparatoires"* Of The International Covenant On Civil And Political Rights, 53, 54 (Martinus Nijhoff Publishers, 1987) (citing Commission on Human Rights, 5th Session (1949) [Proposal E/CN.4/224 (USA); and the US introduced a further amendment which set the wording into its final form: Commission on Human Rights, 6th Session (1950), amendment E/CN.4/365 (USA)).

35 Gondek, The Reach Of Human Rights In A Globalising World, 93–4 (citing Compilation of the comments of Governments on the Draft International Covenant on Human Rights and on the Proposed Additional Articles (memorandum by the Secretary General) dated March 22, 1950, UN Doc. E/CN.4/365, §34, and Summary of the Record of the 193rd Meeting of the Commission on Human Rights (Sixth Session), May 15, 1950 UN Doc. E/CN.4/SR.193 §53).

36 *Id.*

37 *Id.*, 99.

38 *Id.* 103. *See also* Van Schaack, *The United States' Position on the Extraterritorial Application of Human Rights Obligations*, 24 (commenting that the 'legal position' of the US "actually reflects a strategic policy choice to endeavor to evade scrutiny of its extraterritorial exploits on the merits").

39 McGoldrick, *Extraterritorial Application of the International Covenant on Civil and Political Rights*, 66.

40 Michael J. Dennis, *Application of Human Rights Treaties Extraterritorially in Times of Armed Conflict and Military Occupation*, 99 AM. J. INT'L L. 119, 122–3 (January 2005) (citing Lopez Burgos, Celiberti de Casariego v. Uruguay, Comm. No. 56/1979, UN Doc. CCPR/C/13/D/56/1979 (1979), and Montero v. Uruguay, Comm. No. 106/1981, UN Doc. CCPR/C/OP/2 136 (1983/1990)).

41 *Id.*, 123 (citing Human Rights Committee General Comment No. 31, ¶10).

42 *Id.*

43 Human Rights Committee, General Comment No. 35, ¶63, CCPR/C/GC35 (Dec. 16, 2014).

44 Legal Consequences of the Construction of a Wall in the Occupied Palestinian Territory, ¶109: "The *travaux préparatoires* ... show that, in adopting the wording chosen, the drafters of the Covenant did not intend to allow States to escape from their obligations when they exercise jurisdiction outside their national territory. They only intended to prevent persons residing abroad from asserting, vis-à-vis their State of origin, rights that do not fall within the competence of that State, but of that of the State of residence (see the discussion of the preliminary draft in the Commission on Human Rights, ElCN.4lSR.194, ¶46; and United Nations, *Officia1 record*, *of the General Assembly*, *Tenth Session*, *Annexes*, Al2929, Part II, Chap. V, ¶4 (1955))."

45 Michael J. Dennis and Andre Surena, *Application of the International Covenant on Political Rights in times of armed conflict and military occupation: the gap between legal theory and state practice*, E.H.R.L.R. 2008, 6, 714, 721. But Sir Nigel Rodley, a member of the HRC, suggests that the failure of the ICJ to mention General Comment No. 31 may have been because there was no evidence to suggest that the document was before the Court as it had not been finalized at the time the Court was considering the submissions before it, see Nigel Rodley, *The extraterritorial reach and applicability in armed conflict of the International Covenant on Civil and Political Rights: a rejoinder to Dennis and Surena*, E.H.LR.L.R. 2009, 5, 628, 631–2.

46 Lopez Burgos.

47 Celiberti de Casariego.

48 Dennis and Surena, *Application of the International Covenant on Political Rights in times of armed conflict and military occupation*, 727.

49 *Id.*, 721 (quoting Christian Tomuschat in Lopez Burgos v. Uruguay).

50 GONDEK, THE REACH OF HUMAN RIGHTS IN A GLOBALISING WORLD, 107 (quoting Individual Opinion of Christian Tomuschat in Lopez Burgos v. Uruguay, in Appendix: "To construe the words 'within its territory' pursuant to their strict literal meaning as excluding any responsibility for conduct occurring beyond the national boundaries would, however, lead to utterly absurd results ... It may be concluded, therefore, that it was the intention of the drafters, whose sovereign decision cannot be challenged, to restrict the territorial scope of the Covenant in view of such situations where enforcing the Covenant would be likely to encounter exceptional obstacles. Never was it envisaged, however, to grant States parties unfettered discretionary power to carry out willful and deliberate attacks against the freedom and personal integrity against their citizens living abroad").

51 MILANOVIC, EXTRATERRITORIAL APPLICATION OF HUMAN RIGHTS TREATIES, 224.

52 *Id.*

53 *Id.*, 224–5.

54 Ahmadou Sadio Diallo (Republic of Guinea v. Democratic Republic of the Congo), Merits, Judgment I.C.J. Reports 2010 639, ¶77.

55 H.R.C., Consideration of Reports Submitted by States Parties under Article 40 of the Covenant, Third Periodic Reports of States Parties Due in 2003: United States of America, Annex I, U.N. Doc. CCPR/C/USA/3 ¶130 (Nov. 28, 2005). *See also* Van Schaack, *The United States' Position on the Extraterritorial Application of Human Rights Obligations*, 53–61 (for a discussion of the United States' Periodic Reports to the Human Rights Committee).

56 H.R.C., Consideration of Reports Submitted by States Parties Under Article 40 of the Covenant, Concluding Observations of the Human Rights Committee: United States of America, ¶¶ 3, 10, U.N. Doc. CCPR/C/USA/CO/3/Rev.1 (December 18, 2006) (calling on the United States to "acknowledge the applicability of the Covenant with respect to individuals under its jurisdiction but outside its territory, as well as its applicability in time of war").

57 *Id.*

58 Van Schaack, *The United States' Position on the Extraterritorial Application of Human Rights Obligations*, 59–61 (citing U.N. H.R.C., Consideration of Reports Submitted by States Parties Under Article 40 of the Covenant, Fourth Period Report: United States of America, U.N. Doc. CCPR /C/USA/4, ¶¶505-7 (May 22, 2012)).

59 Charlie Savage, *U.S., Rebuffing U.N., Maintains Stance That Rights Treaty Does Not Apply Abroad.* N.Y. TIMES (March 13, 2014) A. 12.

60 COMMITTEE OF EXPERTS, COLLECTED EDITION OF THE 'TRAVAUX PRÉPARATOIRES', Vol III, 260 (Martinus Nijhoff, The Hague, 1976).

61 *Id.*

62 European Convention, Art. 1.

63 *See e.g.* Fons Coomans and Menno T. Kamminga, *Comparative Introductory Comments*, 1–5 *in* EXTRATERRITORIAL APPLICATION OF HUMAN RIGHTS TREATIES (Fons Coomans and Menno T. Kamminga, eds) (Intersentia, 2004); McGoldrick, *Extraterritorial Application of the International Covenant on Civil and Political Rights*, 67–72; Rick Lawson, *Life After Bankovic: On the Extraterritorial Application of the European Convention on Human Rights*, 88–90 *in* EXTRATERRITORIAL APPLICATION OF HUMAN RIGHTS TREATIES (Fons Coomans and Menno T. Kamminga, eds) (Intersentia, 2004); MILANOVIC, EXTRATERRITORIAL APPLICATION OF HUMAN RIGHTS TREATIES, 15; GONDEK, THE REACH OF HUMAN RIGHTS IN A GLOBALISING WORLD, 263–79.

64 European Convention, Art. 56(1).

65 *Id.*, Art. 56(3).

66 Loizidou v. Turkey, App. No. 15318/89 ECHR (1995) Series A no. 310, ¶62.

67 Symeon Karagiannis, *The Territorial Application of Treaties*, 322, *in* THE OXFORD GUIDE TO TREATIES (Duncan B. Hollis, ed.) (Oxford University Press, 2012) (citing Loizidou; Ilascu v. Moldova and Russia, App. No. 48787/99 ECHR 2004-VII (Jul. 2004) and Issa v. Turkey, App. No. 31821/96 ECHR November 16, 2004, ¶71).

68 Bankovic v. Belgium, App. No. 52207/99 ECHR [2001] ECHR 890 (December 12, 2001).

69 *See e.g.* Coomans and Kamminga, *Comparative Introductory Comments*, 5; McGoldrick, *Extraterritorial Application of the International Covenant on Civil and Political Rights*, 68; Lawson, *Life After Bankovic*, 107–16; Milanovic, Extraterritorial Application Of Human Rights Treaties, 84–6; Gondek, The Reach Of Human Rights In A Globalising World, 265–6.

70 Bankovic, ¶71.

71 *Id.*, ¶80.

72 Ilascu (Merits) (Jul. 8, 2004).

73 *Id.*, ¶3.

74 *Id.*, ¶333.

75 *Id.*, ¶393.

76 Gondek, The Reach Of Human Rights In A Globalising World, 189.

77 Al-Skeini v. United Kingdom, Appl. No. 55721/07 ECHR (July 7, 2011).

78 *Id.*, ¶132.

79 *Id*, ¶136 (citing Al-Saadoon and Mufhdi v. United Kingdom, Appl. No. 61498/08, ECHR at §§ 86–89 (June 30, 2009)).

80 Al-Skeini, ¶142.

81 *Id.*, ¶149.

82 Al-Jedda v. United Kingdom, Appl. No. 27021/08, ECHR (2011) 53 EHRR 23 (July 7, 2011), ¶¶85, 86. At ¶107 the European Court of Human Rights did "not find it established that international humanitarian law places an obligation on an Occupying Power to use indefinite internment without trial … [U]nder international humanitarian law internment is to be viewed not as an obligation on the Occupying Power but as a measure of last resort." Jelena Pejic, in *The European Court of Human Rights' Al Jedda judgment: the oversight of international humanitarian law*, 883, 851 Int'l Rev. Red Cross 837 (September 2011), criticizes the judgment and suggests that it implies that parties to the European Convention may not intern civilians unless there is a binding and explicit UN Security Council mandate, or a derogation to Article 5 of the European Convention has been entered. Pejic comments that the ECHR has "failed to grasp the logic of IHL" and that the case "casts a chilling shadow on the current and future lawfulness of detention operations" overseas. The UK Supreme Court applied the extraterritorial principles of Al-Skeini in Smith and Ors. v. Ministry of Defence [2013] UKSC 41, ¶55, as did the UK Court of Appeal in Serdar Mohamed and Ors. v. Secretary of State for Defence [2015] EWCA Civ. 843, ¶8, 105.

83 Hassan v. United Kingdom, Appl. No. 29750/09, Judgment of Grand Chamber, ECHR (September 16, 2014) which related to detention in an international armed conflict and noted at ¶104 that "even in situations of international armed conflict, the safeguards under the Convention continue to apply, albeit interpreted against the background of the provisions of international humanitarian law."

84 Jaloud v. The Netherlands, Appl. No. 47708/08, Judgment of Grand Chamber, ECHR (November 20, 2014), which related to a wrongful death in Iraq.

85 American Convention, Art. 1(1). Notably, the drafters' first approach to crafting this clause was to model it on the ICCPR, using the words "within their territory and subject to their jurisdiction," but after objections from Panama,

the reference to territory was deleted. Panama's objected was rooted in their desire to protect the human rights of persons residing in the Panama Canal Zone, which was subject to US jurisdiction, but not US territory. Gondek notes that fact that the US did not object to this was inconsistent with the US position on jurisdiction in the ICCPR. *See* GONDEK, THE REACH OF HUMAN RIGHTS IN A GLOBALISING WORLD, 111.

86 Nor have Canada and Cuba. *See* GONDEK, THE REACH OF HUMAN RIGHTS IN A GLOBALISING WORLD, 79.

87 Christina M. Cerna, *Extraterritorial Application of the Human Rights Instruments of the Inter-American System*, 142 *in* EXTRATERRITORIAL APPLICATION OF HUMAN RIGHTS TREATIES (Fons Coomans and Menno T. Kamminga, eds) (Intersentia, 2004).

88 *Id.*, 141.

89 Saldano v. Argentina, Report No. 38/99, Inter-Am. Comm'n H.R. March 11, 1999 (Annual Report 1998).

90 *Id.*, ¶17.

91 *Id.*, ¶21. *See* Cerna, *Extraterritorial Application of the Human Rights Instruments of the Inter-American System*, 144–7.

92 Coard v. United States, Inter-Am. Comm'n. H.R. Case No. 10.951, Report No. 109/99 (September 29, 1999) (discussed by CERNA, Extraterritorial Application of the Human Rights Instruments of the Inter-American System, 153–6).

93 *Id.*, ¶32.

94 *Id.*, ¶35.

95 *Id.*, ¶36.

96 *Id.*, ¶37: "under certain circumstances, the exercise of its jurisdiction over acts with an extraterritorial locus will not only be consistent with but required by the norms which pertain. The fundamental rights of the individual are proclaimed in the Americas on the basis of the principles of equality and non-discrimination – 'without distinction as to race, nationality, creed or sex.' Given that individual rights inhere simply by virtue of a person's humanity, each American State is obliged to uphold the protected rights of any person subject to its jurisdiction. While this most commonly refers to persons within a state's territory, it may, under given circumstances, refer to conduct with an extraterritorial locus where the person concerned is present in the territory of one state, but subject to the control of another state – usually through the acts of the latter's agents abroad. In principle, the inquiry turns not on the presumed victim's nationality or presence within a particular geographic area, but on whether, under the specific circumstances, the State observed the rights of a person subject to its authority and control."

97 *Id.*, ¶60; Cerna, *Extraterritorial Application of the Human Rights Instruments of the Inter-American System*, 155; GONDEK, THE REACH OF HUMAN RIGHTS IN A GLOBALISING WORLD, 145.

98 Rules of Procedure of the Inter-Am. Ct. H.R., approved December 4–8, 2000, during its 109th extraordinary period of sessions.

99 GONDEK, THE REACH OF HUMAN RIGHTS IN A GLOBALISING WORLD, 217.

100 Guantánamo Bay Precautionary Measures Communication of March 16, 2002 from Inter-Am. Comm'n H. R. President Juan E. Mendez to US Secretary of State Colin Powell.

101 Cerna, *Extraterritorial Application of the Human Rights Instruments of the Inter-American System*, 163–4.

102 *Id.* 164. *See also* GONDEK, THE REACH OF HUMAN RIGHTS IN A GLOBALISING WORLD, 218 (citing Inter-Am. Comm'n H.R., Extension of the Guantánamo Bay Precautionary Measures (No. 259) (March 18, 2003)).

103 GONDEK, THE REACH OF HUMAN RIGHTS IN A GLOBALISING WORLD, 218–9 (*citing* Inter-Am. Comm'n H.R. Extension of the Guantánamo Bay Precautionary Measures (July 29, 2004), Inter-Am. Comm'n H.R. Extension of the Guantánamo Bay Precautionary Measures (No. 259) (October 28, 2005) and Inter-Am. Comm'n H.R., Resolution No. 1/06 on Guantánamo Bay Precautionary Measures (July 28, 2006) Press release No. 27/06).

104 Ameziane v United States, Inter-Am. Ct. H.R. Report No. 17/12. Petition P-900-08, Admissibility (March 20, 2012).

105 *Id.*, ¶¶19, 21.

106 *Id.*, ¶¶10–18.

107 *Id.*, ¶¶31–5.

108 OAS Press Release, IACHR Condemns Forced Transfer of Djamel Ameziane from Guantanamo to Algeria (December 19. 2013), www.oas.org/en/iachr/media_center/PReleases/2013/103.asp.

109 Second Hague Peace Conference Convention Regarding the Laws of and Customs of Land Warfare, (October 18, 1907), pmbl., 36 Stat. 2277, 3 Martens (3d) 461, *reprinted in* 2 AM. J. INT'L L. 90, 91–92 (Supp. 1908) [Hague Regulations]; Geneva Convention for the Amelioration of the Condition of the Wounded and Sick in Armed Forces in the Field, (August 12, 1949), 6 U.S.T. 3114, 75 U.N.T.S. 31 [GC I]; Geneva Convention for the Amelioration of the Condition of the Wounded, Sick and Shipwrecked Members of Armed Forces at Sea, (August 12, 1949), 6 U.S.T. 3217, 75 U.N.T.S. 85 [GC II]; Geneva Convention Relative to the Treatment of Prisoners of War, (August 12, 1949), 6 U.S.T. 3316, 75 U.N.T.S. 135 [GC III]; Geneva Convention Relative to the Protection of Civilian Persons in Time of War, (August 12, 1949), 6 U.S.T. 3516, 75 U.N.T.S. 287 [GC IV]; Protocol Additional to the Geneva Conventions of August 12, 1949, and Relating to the Protection of Victims of International Armed Conflicts, (June 8, 1977), 1125 U.N.T.S. 3 [AP I]; Protocol Additional to the Geneva Conventions of August 12, 1949, and Relating to the Protection of Victims of Non-International Armed Conflicts, (June 8, 1977), 1125 U.N.T.S. 609 [AP II]. The purpose of the GCs is to protect the sick and wounded, prisoners of war and civilians.

110 GARY D. SOLIS, THE LAW OF ARMED CONFLICT 24 (Cambridge University Press, 2010).

111 GCs, Art 2. For further definition of Prosecutor v. Tadic, IT-94-1, Appeals Chamber Decision on Jurisdiction (Int'l Crim. Trib. for the Former Yugoslavia, October 2, 1995) ¶70: "an armed conflict exists whenever there is a resort to armed force between States or protracted armed violence between governmental authorities and organized armed groups within a State."

112 *Id.*,153.

113 GCs, Art 3.

114 *Id.*, e.*g.*, Art. 5, dealing with derogations has echoes of Art. 15 ICCPR, and AP I, Arts. 72 and 75 reflect human rights law principles.

115 David Glazier, *Playing by the Rules: Combating Al Qaeda Within the Law of War*, 51 WM. AND MARY L. REV. 957, 963 (2009).

116 THE COPENHAGEN PROCESS ON THE HANDLING OF DETAINEES IN INTERNATIONAL MILITARY OPERATIONS [COPENHAGEN PROCESS] (October 19. 2012).

117 UNITED STATES DEPARTMENT OF DEFENSE, LAW OF WAR MANUAL, §1.3.2 [LAW OF WAR MANUAL] (June 2015).

118 Non-international armed conflicts are sometimes hard to define. *See e.g.* Prosecutor v. Tadic, IT-94-1-T, Judgment (Int'l Crim. Trib. for the Former Yugoslavia, (May 7, 1997) ¶562: "the test for the existence of a non-international armed conflict "focuses on two aspects of a conflict; the intensity of the conflict and the organization of the parties to the conflict. In an armed conflict of an internal or mixed character, these closely related criteria are used solely for the purpose, at a minimum, of distinguishing an armed conflict from banditry, unorganized and short-lived insurrections, or terrorist activities, which are not subject to international humanitarian law." *Also see* Rome Statute of the International Criminal Court, UN Doc. A/CONF.183/9* (July 17, 1998): stating that non-international armed conflicts "are not situations of internal disturbances and tensions, such as riots, isolated and sporadic acts of violence or other acts of a similar nature." Rather, they are "armed conflicts that take place in the territory of a State when there is protracted armed conflict between governmental authorities and organized armed groups or between such groups." *Also see* UN Human Rights Council, Fourteenth Session, Report of the Special Rapporteur on extrajudicial, summary or arbitrary executions, UNGA, A/HRC/14/24/Add.6, ¶52 (May 28, 2010), setting out further tests for identifying non-international armed conflicts.

119 SOLIS, THE LAW OF ARMED CONFLICT, 106.

120 *Id.* 24. *See also* HRC Opinions adopted by the Working Group on Arbitrary Detention at its sixty-sixth session, 29 April–3 May 2013, No. 10/2013 (United States of America), Communication addressed to the Government, Concerning Mr. Obaidullah, ¶¶24, 31, 32 (A/HRC/WGAD/2013/10 (June 12, 2013) (citing Ahmadou Sadio Diallo ¶ 77: Article 9(1) and (2) ICCPR applies in principle to any form of detention, "whatever its legal basis and the objective being pursued").

121 Human Rights Committee, General Comment No. 35, ¶64, CCPR/C/GC35 (December 16, 2014).

122 Serdar Mohamed and Ors. v. Secretary of State for Defence, ¶123.

123 *Id.*, ¶¶246, 256.

124 INTERNATIONAL COMMISSION OF JURISTS, ASSESSING DAMAGE, URGING ACTION, 51; ON THE US POSITION ONLY, SEE LAW OF WAR MANUAL, §1.3.2.

125 COPENHAGEN PROCESS, Guidelines, ¶4.5: the *lex specialis* in armed conflicts is IHL, which can be supplemented or informed by IHRL depending on the detaining authority's legal obligations.

2 Detention provisions

This chapter compares the meaning and effect of detention as set out in the five human rights treaties[1] and the Geneva Conventions (GCs),[2] in the context of detaining persons preventively in the face of an actual or imminent terrorist attack. The detention provisions are laid out in Appendix 3, Table 1.

ICCPR

Arbitrary detention

The drafting of the International Covenant on Civil and Political Rights (ICCPR) began in June 1947[3] and work commenced at the outset on Article 9, which deals with detention. A key phrase in Article 9(1) is that no one shall be subjected to "arbitrary arrest and detention," and this phrase has been echoed in three of the four regional human rights instruments discussed below. Thus it is important to understand what it means. Again it is pertinent to look at the *travaux préparatoires.*

The phrase "arbitrary arrest and detention" was used from the very outset of drafting, submitted by the Secretariat at the first session of the drafting committee in 1947.[4] It echoes Article 9 of the Universal Declaration of Human Rights.[5] Many of the drafters of the Declaration had considered that "arbitrary" was the "most vital word" in Article 9.[6] In that first drafting session of the Covenant, Great Britain proposed a different set of wording that permitted detention only in specified circumstances,[7] instead of using the broader phrase "arbitrary detention." The British wording was a forerunner of Article 5(1)(c) of the European Convention, although the drafting of that Convention did not begin until February1950.[8]

By 1948 it seemed that the wording "no one shall be subjected to arbitrary arrest or detention" was acceptable to the drafting committee,[9] but discussion continued as to whether possible grounds justifying the deprivation of liberty should be set out in the Covenant.[10] By 1952 it was decided that it seemed unlikely that any list proposed, even with as many as forty grounds could cover all possible cases of legitimate arrest or detention.[11] It was also argued that "by using the word 'arbitrary' all legislation would have to conform to the principle of justice."[12] Ultimately, in 1958 the current wording of Article 9(1) was adopted unanimously.[13]

But what does "arbitrary detention" mean? The United Nations Department of Economic and Social Affairs' Study of the Right of Everyone to be Free from Arbitrary Arrest, Detention and Exile concluded in 1964 that "an arrest or detention is arbitrary if it is (a) on grounds or in accordance with procedures other than those established by law, or (b) under the provisions of a law the purpose of which is incompatible with respect for the right to liberty and security of person."[14] In 2012 the United Nations Working Group on Arbitrary Detention regarded deprivation of liberty in five classes of cases as arbitrary detention under customary international law.[15]

Guidance

No guidance can be found in the ICCPR itself as to when detention would be contrary to Article 9. In General Comment No. 8, the Human Rights Committee (HRC) made specific mention of preventive detention, but did not take definitional matters much further.[16]

General Comment No. 8 was replaced by General Comment No. 35 in December 2014. The HRC commented that preventive or security detention, made without contemplation of criminal prosecution "presents severe risks of arbitrary deprivation of liberty."[17] The HRC seems to suggest that preventive detention can only be used in exceptional circumstances, by invoking a "present, direct and imperative threat."[18] In these situations the state parties have the burden of proving that no alternative measures can be used, and this burden "increases with the length of detention."[19] The detention must not last longer than "absolutely necessary, … the overall length of possible detention is limited," and state parties must fully respect all of the Article 9 guarantees in every case.[20] This language is still very general, with no authorities cited or explanatory examples, and does not bring greater clarity to the definitional problems.[21] The HRC also comments on security detention in armed conflict situations, noting that "security detention authorized and regulated by and complying with international humanitarian law in principle is not arbitrary."[22] The meaning of this paragraph is not entirely clear.[23]

A number of key HRC cases aid interpretation of "arbitrary detention."[24] In *Hugo van Alphen v. The Netherlands* the HRC said:

> The drafting history of article 9, paragraph 1 confirms that 'arbitrariness' is not to be equated with 'against the law,' but must be interpreted more broadly to include elements of inappropriateness, injustice, and lack of predictability. That means that remand in custody pursuant to lawful arrest must not only be lawful but reasonable in all the circumstances. Further, remand in custody must be necessary in all the circumstances, for example, to prevent flight, interference with evidence or the recurrence of crime.[25]

Thus detention could not be inappropriate, unjust, unpredictable, unreasonable, or unnecessary. The HRC further refined the interpretation of arbitrary detention by adding the criterion of proportionality in *A v. Australia*.[26] In that case too, the HRC proscribed indefinite detention, commenting that "detention should not continue beyond the period for which the State can provide appropriate justification."[27] In *C v. Australia* the test was repeated, with the further refinement of a proviso that the state should demonstrate that "there were not less invasive means of achieving the same ends."[28]

Arbitrary detention remains problematic

Arbitrary detention remains a live issue. For example, in 2012 the Working Group on Arbitrary Detention adopted 69 opinions concerning the detention of 198 persons in 37 countries[29] and also transmitted a total of 104 urgent appeals to 44 states concerning 606 individuals.[30] In 2013 the HRC Working Group on Arbitrary Detention issued an opinion in the case of *Obaidullah* and concluded that his detention by the United States, first in Bagram, Afghanistan from July through October 2002, and since October 2002 in Guantánamo was arbitrary.[31] Three reasons were given: first, that the domestic law used by the United States to detain Obaidullah did not conform to either human rights law or international humanitarian law because the detention was prolonged and indefinite;[32] second, that the prolonged detention was due to Obaidullah's foreign status – this was a discriminatory reason that made the detention arbitrary;[33] and third, the failure to afford Obaidullah due process and fair trial protections gave the detention an arbitrary character.[34]

Duration

Although the HRC has opined on the duration of detention without judicial authority, i.e. the length of time a person could be detained without an opportunity to challenge the lawfulness of detention,[35] and pre-trial detention,[36] it has not issued any opinions as to the duration of detention *per se*, other than a nebulous comment that it should not continue beyond a justifiable period.[37] The HRC notes that in cases of detention other than sentences of imprisonment, failure to conduct periodic re-evaluation of the justification of continued confinement will render that detention arbitrary.[38]

Preventive detention

Preventive detention *per se* does not feature explicitly in Article 9, but has been contemplated in General Comment No. 35,[39] and in the case of *Campora Schweizer v. Uruguay*.[40] In May 2013, a statement was issued by the Human Rights Council Working Group on Arbitrary Detention, the Inter-American Commission of Human Rights and United Nations Rapporteurs on Human Rights and Counter-Terrorism, Torture and Health. It called for the closure of the Guantánamo Bay detention facility, for an end to indefinite detention of persons and stressed:

> that even in extraordinary circumstances, when the indefinite detention of individuals, most of whom have not been charged, goes beyond a minimally reasonable period of time, this constitutes a flagrant violation of international human rights law and in itself constitutes a form of cruel, inhuman, and degrading treatment.[41]

Core principles

In order that detention does not violate the Covenant by being arbitrary, the core principles are that detention has to be: (1) appropriate; (2) just; (3) predictable; (4) reasonable; (5) necessary; (6) proportionate; (7) it should not continue longer than can be justified; (8) detention should not be imposed if a less invasive method can be used to achieve the same ends; and (9) it must be on grounds and in accordance with procedures established by law. Macken suggests that the above list may be "summarized as a statement of the 'principle of proportionality.'"[42] Yet her definition does not seem to cover all the elements listed above.[43]

European Convention

Arbitrary detention

The European Convention is based on an earlier draft of the ICCPR,[44] but there are some significant differences in the final version, particularly relating to detention, which is dealt with in Article 5. The words "freedom from arbitrary arrest or detention" do not appear in the European Convention, but the European Court of Human Rights (ECHR) has implied such a term into the interpretation of Article 5.[45] In *Fox, Hartley and Campbell v. United Kingdom* the applicants challenged their detention on the basis that they had not been arrested or detained on "reasonable" suspicion of having committed an offense, as prescribed in Article 5(i)(c). Although the Court noted that the interpretation of reasonableness depended on all the circumstances, it made it clear that "[t]he reasonableness of the suspicion on which an arrest must be based forms an essential part of the safeguard against arbitrary arrest and detention."[46] The ECHR applied the margin of appreciation[47] in this case, by noting that there would be some deference to the state as it accepted that terrorist crime fell into a special category.[48] The Court went on to show that police expertise alone in dealing with terrorism would not be determinative, and police would need to provide evidence to the ECHR that there was reasonable suspicion for holding applicants.[49]

Six grounds for detention

Article 5(1) makes it clear that detention will only be permitted in accordance with a procedure prescribed by law,[50] and only on the six grounds specified in the Article. Compliance with the law by itself is not sufficient; any deprivation of liberty should "be in keeping with the purpose of protecting the individual from arbitrariness."[51]

In *Saadi v. United Kingdom*, which concerned an immigration detention for a period of seven days, the Court noted that it had not previously formulated a global definition of arbitrariness, but that key principles had been developed on a case-by-case basis. Further, the notion of arbitrariness varied "to a certain extent on the type of detention involved."[52]

A number of general principles apply to Article 5 as a whole: bad faith or deception on the part of the authorities is not permitted;[53] the detention must genuinely conform with the purpose of the restrictions in Article 5(1);[54] and some relationship must exist between the ground of permitted detention and the place and conditions of detention.[55] This means that, for example, someone detained on a mental health ground should be placed in a hospital, and someone detained for immigration purposes should be detained in an immigration center.

The Court went on to discuss Article 5(1)(c), which is the relevant clause for preventive detention. It stated that arbitrariness includes "an assessment of whether detention was necessary to achieve the stated aim."[56] Furthermore, detention is justified "only as a last resort where other, less severe measures have been considered and found to be insufficient to safeguard the individual or public interest which might require that the person concerned be detained."[57] The Court also noted that detention must be proportionate.[58]

Proportionality

Interestingly, the word "proportionality" is nowhere to be found in the European Convention, but the idea it expresses appears as a central principle in the jurisprudence of the ECHR.[59] Proportionality analysis may consist of suitability, necessity, and proportionality that reasonably balances the goal sought and the limiting measure.[60]

However, a fair or reasonable balance must be struck between the rights of individuals and the general public interests of society.[61] In the context of preventive detention of terror suspects, a proportionate balance is required between preventive detention and prevention of terrorism.[62]

Article 5(1)(c) appears to contain three separate grounds for detention on reasonable suspicion: (1) after an offense has been committed; (2) when it is reasonably considered necessary to prevent the commission of an offense; or (3) if someone flees after committing an offense.[63] This looks clear enough, but in fact is riddled with ambiguity.

The ordinary reading of the words seems to suggest that it is permissible to detain a person when it is reasonably considered necessary to prevent him committing an offense. One view is that because the three grounds are set out in one paragraph rather than listed separately, there must be proof that the detainee is linked with the commission of a criminal offense, and the Article does not allow preventive detention just because criminal activity may be expected to occur.[64]

If there is ambiguity when interpreting the meaning of treaty provisions, reference may be made to the *travaux préparatoires*,[65] and it appears that detention to prevent the commission of a crime was contemplated by the drafters.[66] However, despite that, the jurisprudence of the ECHR indicates a restrictive approach.

In *Guzzardi v. Italy*, which concerned the imposition of certain restrictions of liberty, the Court held that Article 5(1)(c):

> is not adapted to a policy of general prevention directed against an individual or a category of individuals who, like mafiosi, present a danger on account of their continuing propensity to crime; it does no more than afford the Contracting States a means of preventing a concrete and specific offence.[67]

The paragraph continues with a purported justification for this interpretation deriving from the use of the singular words "an offense" and "celle-ci" in the French text of the European Covenant, as well as reliance on the object of Article 5 to ensure that no one is dispossessed of liberty in an arbitrary fashion.[68]

This is baffling and seems to be something of a *non sequitur*. The French text,[69] if translated literally, reads as follows:

> [detention is permitted] if he is arrested and detained in order to be brought before the competent judicial authority, when there are plausible reasons to suspect that he has committed an offense or that there are reasonable reasons to believe that it is necessary to prevent the commission of an offense or flight after having done this.

Thus the French words do not appear to make the position any clearer.

Preventive detention

In *M. v. Germany*, which involved the detention of a convicted person after the conclusion of his sentence to prevent the commission of future crimes, the Court repeated the *Guzzardi* formula,[70] and added that the "potential further offenses are not however, sufficiently concrete and specific, as required by the Court's case law as regards, in particular, the place and time of their commission and their victims, and do not, therefore, fall within the ambit of art. 5(1)(c)."[71]

In *Schwabe and MG v. Germany*[72] a G8 Summit of Heads of State and Government was held in Rostock in June 2007. The police thought that Islamist terrorists posed a threat of terror attacks during the summit. The applicants drove to Rostock in order to participate in demonstrations. They parked their car in a car park in front of a prison. The police did a routine identity check, and when one of the applicants physically resisted the identity check, the police searched the car and found banners with the words "Freedom for all prisoners" and "Free all now." The applicants were arrested and detained under a local statute. The local district court ruled that their detention had been lawful to prevent the imminent commission or continuation of a criminal offense. Because they had banners calling for the liberation of prisoners, and they were in a car park in front of a prison, the Court ruled that it had to be assumed that they had been about to commit or aid and abet a criminal offense.

Appeals to both the Court of Appeal and the Federal Constitutional Court were dismissed, but the ECHR ruled that the applicants' right to liberty pursuant to Article 5 (1)(c) had been violated. The Court held that although the detention of a person may be justified when it is considered reasonably necessary to prevent his committing an offense, that ground of detention does no more than afford the contracting states a means of preventing "a concrete and specific offense ... as regards, in particular, the place and time of its commission and its victim(s)."[73] The Court also reiterated that "detention to prevent a person from committing an offense, must in addition, be 'effected for the purpose of bringing him before the competent legal authority,' a requirement which qualifies every category of detention referred to in Article 5(1)(c)."[74]

Article 5(1) (c) thus envisages that detention is only permissible if it is connected with bringing the detainee before a competent legal authority. The words could simply imply that a detainee cannot be detained without some court process. In *Lawless* the government argued that Article 5(1)(c) referred to two different types of case: the first where a person is detained on reasonable suspicion that an offense has been committed; and the second where a person is detained to prevent the commission of an offense. They argued that the obligation to bring a detainee before a court did not apply in the second narrower situation.[75] The Court rejected the narrow approach and held that Article 5(1)(c) had to be read together with Article 5(3) with the effect that if a person has been arrested to prevent an offense from taking place, he has to be brought promptly before a judge so that the judge can decide if the detention is justified.[76]

However, as regards preventive detention, the position is not clear. *Jecius v. Lithuania*[77] and *Ciulla v. Italy*[78] suggest that detention to prevent an offense from taking place is only permitted in the context of criminal proceedings. One view is that the words in *Ciulla* mean that "detention is only permitted if it is related to proceedings that could lead to conviction for a specific criminal charge."[79] This reading appears to neuter the effect of the second limb of Article 5(1)(c), which ostensibly has been interpreted to permit detention to prevent a specific and concrete offense.

A broader approach is seen in the comments of the Court in *Al-Jedda v. United Kingdom*, where British forces in Iraq detained an Iraqi national on the grounds of alleged imperative reasons of security. The Court noted that it has "long been established that the list of grounds of permissible detention in art. 5(1) does not include internment or preventive detention where there is no intention to bring criminal charges within a reasonable time."[80] This could be interpreted to give the authorities a window of time to detain for a short time within the parameters of Articles 5(1) (c) and 5(3) before it is clear that there is no intention to bring criminal charges, provided the detainee is brought promptly before the legal authority.

Furthermore, the Grand Chamber in *Hassan* rejected the notion that Article 5(1)(c) extended to situations of security internment in an international armed conflict.[81] However, security detention in armed conflict must comply with Article 5. In particular, it "should be in keeping with the fundamental purpose of Article 5(1), which is to protect the individual from arbitrariness."[82]

American Convention

Grounds for detention

Detention is dealt with in Article 7, the terms of which have many similarities to Article 9 ICCPR and Article 5 European Convention. Article 7 has been a central focus of Inter-American case law.[83] In 1994, in *Gangaram Panday* the Court stated that:

> no person may be deprived of his or her personal freedom except for reasons, cases or circumstances expressly defined by law (material aspect) and, furthermore, subject to strict adherence to the procedures objectively set forth in that law (formal aspect) … [N]o one may be subjected to arrest or imprisonment for reasons and by methods which, although classified as legal, could be deemed to be incompatible with the respect for the fundamental rights of the individual because, among other things, they are unreasonable, unforeseeable or lacking in proportionality.[84]

The Court has repeated this formula in a number of cases involving alleged violations of Article 7 in several states.[85] The Commission has also restated this in it its 2009 report entitled Citizen Security and Human Rights.[86]

Preventive detention

The Court specifically mentioned preventive detention in *Lopez Alvarez*, which involved preventive detention in Honduras (although unconnected with terrorism):

> The preventive detention is limited by the principles of legality, the presumption of innocence, need, and proportionality, all of which are strictly necessary in a democratic society ... The legitimacy of the preventive detention does not arise only from the fact that the law allows its application under certain general hypotheses. The adoption of this precautionary measure requires a judgment of proportionality between said measure, the evidence to issue it, and the facts under investigation. If the proportionality does not exist, the measure will be arbitrary.[87]

The Court has also specifically mentioned preventive detention, again not in a terrorism situation, but in a pre-trial context in *Barreto Leiva v. Venezuela*.[88] The applicant had been requested to give evidence in criminal proceedings, and did so. He was arrested on a warrant, but not told of the charges against him, and was placed in preventive detention for over a year. He was denied representation by a lawyer of his choice, and was denied access to the evidence in the case. He was eventually sentenced to a period of one year and two months, but denied a right of appeal. The Court declared that the imposition of preventive detention violated Article 7(3), and noted that "the deprivation of liberty of the accused cannot be based on general preventive or special preventive purposes, which could be attributed to the punishment, but ... based on a legitimate purpose..."[89] The Court also stated that preventive detention is "limited by the principle of proportionality."[90]

Valencia and Llanos concerned detentions in Colombia.[91] For the purpose of determining whether detention is compatible with the provisions of Article 7 (2) and (3), the Court considered that there are three steps to follow:

> 1) in the first place, the legality of the detention must be determined, in the material and formal sense of the term, for which purpose it must be found to be consistent with the domestic legislation of the state in question; 2) in the second place, said domestic laws must be examined in light of the guarantees established in the American Convention, to determine if they are arbitrary; and 3) finally, if the detention meets the requirements established in domestic laws that are compatible with the American Convention, it must be determined whether application of that provision to the specific case was arbitrary.[92]

Article 5 guarantees the right of persons deprived of liberty to be treated with due respect for human dignity. Yet there have been frequent concerns about the appalling conditions of detention.[93] The Court has frequently stated that detainees have the right to enjoy conditions of detention that are compatible with their personal dignity.[94]

African Charter

Article 6 proscribes arbitrary detention, and states that freedom may only be deprived for reasons and conditions previously laid down by law. No case law pertaining to preventive detention has been found.

Arab Charter

The totality of any guidance can be found in Article 14, which proscribes detention without a legal warrant, and states that detention may only be on grounds and in accordance with procedures established by law.

Geneva Conventions

International armed conflicts

The Geneva Conventions (GCs) contain very few provisions relating to detention, and the few that do exist are found within the context of international armed conflicts (IACs), and link to the duration of hostilities. The basis for, and standards of, detention are governed by Additional Protocol (AP) I, Common Article 3 (i.e. identical in all GCs), AP II and customary international law, but these provisions do not set out the rights sufficiently.[95] In reviewing the standards for preventive detention under the name of "internment" or "administrative detention" of members of armed groups, the International Committee of the Red Cross (ICRC) discusses the rights of unlawful combatants, as well as participants in non-international armed conflicts. Although the United States has not ratified AP I, it accepts that much of AP I has become part of customary international law.[96] AP I merely provides for humane treatment "as a minimum,"[97] and gives detainees the right to be informed promptly of the reasons for detention, and the right, except where the detention is for "penal offences," to be released as soon as possible, or at least "as soon as the circumstances justifying the … detention … have ceased to exist."[98] For example, AP I Article 72 states that the provisions of AP I are additional to GC IV and international human rights law.[99]

Detention of prisoners of war

GC III provides for detention of prisoners of war (POWs) during IACs. Article 21 states that POWs "may not be held in close confinement except where necessary to safeguard their health and then only during the continuation of the circumstances which make such confinement necessary."[100] Additionally, Article 118 permits the detention of POWs "for the duration of hostilities."[101]

Civilians

GC IV deals with the rights of detained civilians, also in the context of IACs. Article 42 allows for internment "if the security of the Detaining Power makes it absolutely necessary." Article 78 authorizes internment if an "Occupying Power" considers it necessary for "imperative reasons of security." There is a right of appeal and periodic further reviews.

ICRC experts comment that imperative reasons of security do not include information gathering, nor must detention be used as an alternative to criminal prosecution.[102] They found that there is a power to capture persons deemed to pose a serious security threat, and such persons may be detained as long as they continue to pose a threat.[103]

Non-international armed conflicts

According to the ICRC, neither the law of armed conflict (LOAC) nor international human rights law provide an explicit legal basis for internment in non-international armed conflicts (NIACs) – states should look to their own domestic law, provided it complies with the LOAC and international human rights law.[104] Common Article 3 contains no language to assist regulation of detention, other than the guiding principle of humane treatment. Nor does AP II (which the United States has also not ratified, but which President Obama hopes soon will be).[105] AP II provides for humane treatment, as a minimum,[106] and the preamble reminds readers that human rights laws and treaties offer a basic protection for individuals.[107]

To meet the challenges posed by the handling of detainees in NIACs, a number of states[108] concluded the Copenhagen Process in 2012. This resulted in the formulation of a set of principles and guidelines governing detention in NIACs only.[109] These are non-binding and not intended to justify any departure from international law.[110] In essence, the principles build upon Common Article 3, and provide greater procedural protections for detainees, as discussed in Chapter 4. Many echoes of human rights law can be discerned, such as the requirement that detentions must be lawful, i.e. not arbitrary, which is interpreted as reasonable and necessary in all the circumstances, with a lawful and continuing legitimate objective.[111]

Notes

1 International Covenant on Civil and Political Rights, G.A. res. 2200A (XXI), 21 U.N. GAOR Supp. (No. 16) at 52, U.N. Doc. A/6316 (1966), 999 U.N.T.S. 171 (entered into force March 23, 1976) [ICCPR]; European Convention for the Protection of Human Rights and Fundamental Freedoms, opened for signature November 4, 1950, 213 UNTS 222 (entered into force September 3, 1953) [European Convention]; American Convention on Human Rights, O.A.S. Treaty Series No. 36, 1144 U.N.T.S. 123 (entered into force July 18, 1978) [American Convention]; African (Banjul) Charter of

Human and Peoples' Rights, adopted June 27, 1981, OAU Doc. CAB/LEG/67/3 rev. 5, 21 I.L.M. 58 (1982) (entered into force October, 21 1986) [African Charter]; Arab Charter on Human Rights, adopted May 22, 2004, reprinted in 12 Int'l Hum. Rts. Rep. 893 (2005) (entered into force March 15, 2008) [Arab Charter].

2 Geneva Convention for the Amelioration of the Condition of the Wounded and Sick in Armed Forces in the Field, (August 12, 1949), 6 U.S.T. 3114, 75 U.N.T.S. 31 [GC I]; Geneva Convention for the Amelioration of the Condition of the Wounded, Sick and Shipwrecked Members of Armed Forces at Sea (Aug. 12, 1949), 6 U.S.T. 3217, 75 U.N.T.S. 85 [GC II]; Geneva Convention Relative to the Treatment of Prisoners of War (August 12 1949), 6 U.S.T. 3316, 75 U.N.T.S. 135 [GC III]; Geneva Convention Relative to the Protection of Civilian Persons in Time of War (August 12, 1949), 6 U.S.T. 3516, 75 U.N.T.S. 287 [GC IV]; Protocol Additional to the Geneva Conventions of 12 August 1949, and Relating to the Protection of Victims of International Armed Conflicts (June 8, 1977), 1125 U.N.T.S. 3 [AP I]; Protocol Additional to the Geneva Conventions of August 12, 1949, and Relating to the Protection of Victims of Non-International Armed Conflicts (June 8, 1977), 1125 U.N.T.S. 609 [AP II].

3 MARC J. BOSSUYT, GUIDE TO THE *"TRAVAUX PRÉPARATOIRES"* OF THE INTERNATIONAL COVENANT ON CIVIL AND POLITICAL RIGHTS, XIX, 187 (Martinus Nijhoff Publishers, 1987).

4 *Id.*, 187, Proposal E/CN.4/21, annex A (Secretariat) Art. 6 and 7(9). ("Every one shall be protected against arbitrary and unauthorized arrest.").

5 Universal Declaration of Human Rights, UNGA RES 217 A(III) (December 10, 1948), Art. 9: "No one shall be subjected to arbitrary arrest, detention or exile."

6 Laurent Marcoux Jr., *Protection from Arbitrary Arrest and Detention under International Law*, 5 B.C. INT'L & COMP. L. REV. 345, 354 (1982) (noting at fn. 56–57, the words of Eleanor Roosevelt that the word arbitrary "summed up the meaning of the whole article," General Assembly. Third Session, Summary Record of the 113th Meeting. 3 U.N. GAOR C.3, pI. I. 247. U.N. Doc. AlC.3/SR.113 (1948)).

7 MARC J. BOSSUYT, GUIDE TO THE *"TRAVAUX PRÉPARATOIRES"* OF THE INTERNATIONAL COVENANT ON CIVIL AND POLITICAL RIGHTS, 187, Proposal E/CN.4.21, annex B (GB), art. 10 (9).

8 COLLECTED EDITION OF THE "TRAVAUX PRÉPARATOIRES," VOL. I, PREPARATORY COMMISSION OF THE COUNCIL OF EUROPE, COMMITTEE OF MEMBERS, CONSULTATIVE ASSEMBLY, 11 MAY–8 SEPTEMBER 1949, XXVI (Martinus Nijhoff, 1975).

9 MARC J. BOSSUYT, GUIDE TO THE *"TRAVAUX PRÉPARATOIRES"* OF THE INTERNATIONAL COVENANT ON CIVIL AND POLITICAL RIGHTS, 189.

10 *Id.*, 190–1.

11 *Id*,. 193 (citing Commission on Human Rights, 5th Session (1949), 6th Session (1950), 8th Session (1952), A/2929, Chapt. VI, §28).

12 *Id.*, 198 (citing A/2929, Chapt. VI, §31).

13 *Id.*, 202 (citing Third Committee, 13th Session (1958), A/4045, §66(c)).

14 U.N. DEPT. OF ECONOMIC AND SOCIAL AFFAIRS, STUDY OF THE RIGHT OF EVERYONE TO BE FREE FROM ARBITRARY ARREST, DETENTION AND EXILE, E/CN.4/826 Rev. 1, 7 ¶27 (1964).

15 U.N.G.A. Human Rights Council, Report of the Working Group on Arbitrary Detention, A/HRC/22/44, 16 IIIA (2012) ¶38.

16 Claire Macken, Counter-Terrorism And The Detention Of Suspected Terrorists, 42 (Routledge, 2011) (citing Human Rights Committee, General Comment No. 8 (General Comments) (Right to liberty and security of persons) (Article 9) (Sixteenth session, 1982) U.N. Doc. HRI/GEN/1/Rev. 1 {8}, ¶4).

17 U.N. HRC General Comment No. 35, CCPR/C/GC/35 (Dec. 16, 2014), ¶15.

18 *Id.*

19 *Id.*

20 *Id.*

21 Shaheed Fatima, *UN HRC'S General Comment 35 on the Right to Liberty and Security: A Missed Opportunity?* Just Security (November 19, 2014), http://justsecurity.org/17587/uns-comment-liberty-security/.

22 U.N. HRC General Comment No. 35, ¶64.

23 Shaheed Fatima, *UN HRC'S General Comment 35 on the Right to Liberty and Security: A Missed Opportunity? (Part Two)*, Just Security (November 20, 2014), http://justsecurity.org/17596/human-rights-committees-general-comment-no-35-security-detention/.

24 After March 23, 1976, when the First Optional Protocol (opened for signature December 16, 1966, entered into force March 23, 1976), 999 UNTS 302 (list of signatories: http://www2.ohchr.org/english/law/ccpr-one.htm) came into effect, individuals of signatory states were able to take complaints of ICCPR violations to the Human Rights Committee.

25 Hugo van Alphen v. The Netherlands, HRC Communication No. 305/1988, (August 15, 1990) CCPR/C/39/D/305/1988, ¶5.8.

26 A v. Australia, HRC Communication No.560/1993 (April 30, 1997) CCPR/C/59/D/560/1993, ¶9.2.

27 *Id.*, ¶9.4.

28 C v. Australia, HRC Communication No. 900/1999 (November 13, 2002) CCPR/C/76/D/900/1999, ¶8.2.

29 U.N.G.A. Human Rights Council, Report of the Working Group on Arbitrary Detention, 5, §A1 ¶9.

30 *Id.*, 13, §A6 ¶23.

31 HRC Communication No. 10/2013 (United States of America), ¶44 (June 12, 2013).

32 *Id.* ¶37.

33 *Id.*, ¶42.

34 *Id.*

35 CCPR General Comment No. 35, ¶¶32, 33: "Persons arrested or detained on a criminal charge must be brought "promptly" before a judge or other officer," (citing Komaravski v Turkmenistan, 1450/2006 (August 5, 2008), CCPR/C/93/D/1450/2006, ¶7.4: "the length of custody without judicial authorization should not exceed a few days"). "48 hours should ordinarily suffice," (citing Kovsh v. Belarus, 1787/2008 (June 17, 2013). ¶¶7.3–7.5).

36 CCPR General Comment No. 35, ¶38: "Pre-trial detention should be the exception rather than the rule."

37 A v. Australia, ¶9.2. *See also* U. N. Dept. Of Economic And Social Affairs, Study Of The Right Of Everyone To Be Free From Arbitrary Arrest, Detention And Exile, ¶¶141–144.

38 H.R.C. General Comment No. 35, ¶12.

39 *Id.*, ¶15 (noting that security detention "presents severe risks of deprivation of liberty").

40 David Alberto Campora Schweizer v. Uruguay, Communication 66/1980 (March 15, 1980) U.N. Doc Supp. No. 40 (A/38/40), 117: "According to Article 9(1) of the Covenant, no one shall be subjected to arbitrary arrest or detention. Although administrative detention may not be objectionable in circumstances where the person concerned constitutes a clear and serious threat to society which cannot be contained in any other manner, the Committee emphasizes that that the guarantees enshrined in the following paragraphs of Article 9 fully apply in such instances."

41 United Nations Office of the High Commissioner for Human Rights, IACHR, U.N. Working Group on Arbitrary Detention, U.N. Rapporteur on Torture, U.N. Rapporteur on Human Rights and Counter-Terrorism, and U.N. Rapporteur on Health reiterate need to end the indefinite detention of individuals at Guantánamo Naval Base in light of current human rights crisis, (May 1, 2013), www.ohchr.org/EN/NewsEvents/Pages/DisplayNews.aspx?NewsID=13278&LangID=E.

42 Macken, Counter-Terrorism And Detention Of Suspected Terrorists, 50.

43 *Id.* "The principle of proportionality requires consideration as to whether a particular measure is for a legitimate aim, and if so, whether that measure is reasonably necessary to achieve that purpose, having regard to whether a less restrictive measure is available as an alternative to the measure in question."

44 U.N. Dept. Of Economic And Social Affairs, Study Of The Right Of Everyone To Be Free From Arbitrary Arrest, Detention And Exile, E/CN.4/826 Rev. 1, 7, ¶75 (1964).

45 Macken, Counter-Terrorism And The Detention Of Suspected Terrorists, 52 (citing Lawless v. Ireland (No.3) ECHR Series A no. 3 (July 1, 1961) ¶ 14). *Also see* Ammur v France, 17/1995/523/609, ECHR (June 25, 1996), ¶50; Trifkovic v. Croatia, Appl. No. 36653/09, Judgment (Merits and Just Satisfaction) ECHR (First Section) (November 6, 2012), ¶93; Saadi v. the United Kingdom [GC], no. 13229/03, ECHR (January 29, 2008), ¶67.

46 Fox, Campbell and Hartley v. United Kingdom, Appl. No. 12244/86; 12245/86; 12383/86, ECHR (August 30, 1990), ¶32.

47 This is a mechanism created by the ECHR to decide the degree of deference it will give to national governments in fulfilling their obligations under the European Convention. *See* Jeffrey Brauch, *The Dangerous Search for an Elusive Consensus: What the Supreme Court Should Learn from the European Court of Human Rights*, 52 How. L. J. 277, 279 (2009); Howard Charles Yourow, *the Margin of Appreciation and the Dynamics of European Human Rights Jurisprudence*, 3 Conn. J. Int'l L. 111,118 (1987); Andrew Legg, The Margin Of Appreciation In International Human Rights Law, 3 (Oxford University Press, 2012).

48 Fox, Campbell and Hartley, ¶32.

49 *Id.*, ¶34. "*Also see* LEGG, THE MARGIN OF APPRECIATION IN INTERNATIONAL HUMAN RIGHTS LAW, 155–6.

50 The domestic law needs to be scrutinized to ensure it is not arbitrary. Amuur, ¶50.

51 Grubic, Appl. No. 5384/11, ECHR (Oct. 30, 2012), ¶38; Trifkovic, ¶93.

52 Saadi, ¶68.

53 *Id.*, ¶69 (citing Bozano v. France, ECHR (1987) 9 EHRR 297, Conka v. Belgium, ECHR (2000) 11 EHRR 54).

54 *Id.*, ¶69 (citing Winterwerp v. The Netherlands, ¶37, Bouamar v. Belgium ECHR (1989) 11 EHRR 1, ¶50, and O'Hara v. United Kingdom, ECHR (2002) 34 EHRR 32, ¶34).

55 *Id.*, ¶69 (citing Bouamar v. Belgium, ¶50, Aerts v. Belgium, ECHR (2000) 11 EHRR 50, ¶46, and Enforn v. Sweden, ECHR (2005) 41 EHRR 30, ¶42.)

56 *Id*, ¶70.

57 *Id.* (citing Litwa v. Poland, ECHR (2001) 33 EHRR 53, ¶78, Hafsteinsdottir v. Iceland, App. No. 40905/98, ECHR (Jun. 8, 2004), ¶51, Enhorn v. Sweden, ¶44).

58 *Id.*, ¶70. (citing Vasileva v. Denmark, ECHR (2005) 40 EHRR 27, 37).

59 *See e.g.* Marc-Andre Eissen, *The Principle of Proportionality in the Case Law of the European Court of Human Rights*, 125, 131 *in* THE EUROPEAN SYSTEM FOR THE PROTECTION OF HUMAN RIGHTS (R. St. Macdonald, F. Matscher and H. Petzold, eds) (Martiinus Nijhoff, 1993); Jeremy McBride, *Proportionality and the European Convention on Human Rights*, 23 *in* THE PRINCIPLE OF PROPORTIONALITY IN THE LAWS OF EUROPE (Evelyn Ellis, ed.) (Hart Publishing, 1999); YUTAKA ARAI-TAKAHASHI, THE MARGIN OF APPRECIATION DOCTRINE AND THE PRINCIPLE OF PROPORTIONALITY IN THE JURISPRUDENCE OF THE ECHR, 14, 193 (Intersentia, 2002); STEFAN SOTTIAUX, TERRORISM AND THE LIMITATION OF RIGHTS, 44–5 (Hart Publishing, 2008); MACKEN, COUNTER-TERRORISM AND THE DETENTION OF SUSPECTED TERRORISTS, 56.

60 SOTTIAUX, TERRORISM AND THE LIMITATION OF RIGHTS, 45.

61 ARAI-TAKAHASHI, THE MARGIN OF APPRECIATION DOCTRINE AND THE PRINCIPLE OF PROPORTIONALITY IN THE JURISPRUDENCE OF THE ECHR, 14.

62 MACKEN, COUNTER-TERRORISM AND THE DETENTION OF SUSPECTED TERRORISTS, 56.

63 *Id.*

64 *Id.*, 53 (citing P. VAN DIJK AND G.J.H. VAN HOOF, THEORY AND PRACTICE OF THE EUROPEAN CONVENTION ON HUMAN RIGHTS, 260–1 3rd ed. (1994)).

65 Vienna Convention on the Law of Treaties, U.N.T.S. vol. 1155, 331, dated May 23, 1969 (entered into force January 27, 1980) Art. 32.

66 COMMITTEE OF EXPERTS, COLLECTED EDITION OF THE 'TRAVAUX PRÉPARATOIRES', Vol. IV, 260 (June 8–17, 1950).

67 Guzzardi v Italy, App. No. 7367/76, ECHR, ¶102, (November 6, 1980).

68 *Id.*

69 Article 5 (1)(c): "s'il a été arrêté et détenu en vue d'être conduit devant l'autorité judiciaire compétente, lorsqu'il y a des raisons plausibles de soupçonner qu'il a commis une infraction ou qu'il y a des motifs raisonnables de croire à la nécessité de l'empêcher de commettre une infraction ou de s'enfuir après l'accomplissement de celle-ci."

70 M. v. Germany, App. No. 19359/04, ECHR,¶89 (December 17, 2009).

71 *Id.*, ¶102.

72 Schwabe v. Germany, Appl. Nos. 8080/08 and 8577/08, ECHR (March 1, 2012).

73 *Id.*, ¶70.

74 *Id.*, ¶71.

75 MACKEN, COUNTER-TERRORISM AND THE DETENTION OF SUSPECTED TERRORISTS, 62–3 (citing Lawless v. Ireland (No. 3), ¶10).

76 *Id.* (citing Lawless v. Ireland (No. 3), ¶14).

77 MACKEN, COUNTER-TERRORISM AND THE DETENTION OF SUSPECTED TERRORISTS, 55 (citing Jecius v. Lithuania, App. No. 34578/97, ECHR ¶50 (Jul. 31, 2000)).

78 *Id.* (citing Ciulla v Italy, App. No. 11152/84, ECHR, ¶40 (Feb. 22, 1989)).

79 *Id.* 55. Macken suggests that this reasoning is supported by the holding in Jecius, ¶47, where there were no grounds for preventive detention "as no criminal proceedings had been pending against him at that time. Moreover, there were no crimes which he should have been prevented from committing."

80 Al-Jedda ¶100.

81 Hassan v. United Kingdom, Appl. No. 29750/09, Judgment of Grand Chamber, ECHR (September 16, 2014), ¶97.

82 *Id.*, ¶105.

83 Sergio Garcia Ramirez, *The Inter-American Court of Human Rights' Perspective on Terrorism*, 805, *in* COUNTER-TERRORISM, INTERNATIONAL LAW AND PRACTICE (Ana Maria Salinade Frias, Katja LH Samuel, Nigel D White, eds), (Oxford University Press, 2012).

84 Case of Gangaram Panday, Inter-Am. Ct. H.R. (Ser. C) No.16, Judgment of January 21, 1994 ¶47 (involving alleged violations in Suriname).

85 *See e.g.* Garcia Ramirez, *The Inter-American Court of Human Rights' Perspective on Terrorism*, 805, (citing Case of Cesti Hurtado, Inter-Am. Ct. H.R. (Series C) No. 56, Judgment of September 29, 1999, ¶140 (Peru), Case of Durand and Uguarte, Inter-Am. Ct. H.R. (Series C) No. 68, Judgment of August 16, 2000 (Peru), Case of Bamca Velasquez, Inter-Am. Ct. H.R. (Series C) No. No. 70, Judgment of November 25, 2000, ¶139 (Guatemala), Case of Juan Humberto Sanchez, Inter-Am. Ct. H.R. (Series C) No. 99, Judgment of June 7, 2003, ¶78 (Honduras), Case of Maritza Urrutia, Inter-Am. Ct. H.R. (Series C) No. 103, Judgment of November 27, 2003, ¶65 (Guatemala), Case of Gomez Paquiyauri Brothers, Inter-Am. Ct. H.R. (Series C) No. 110, Judgment of July 8, 2004 (Peru), Case of Tibi, Inter-Am. Ct. H.R. (Series C) No. 114, Judgment of September 7, 2004 (Ecuador), Case of Acosta Calderon, Inter-Am. Ct. H.R. (Series C) No. 129, Judgment of June 24, 2005, ¶57 (Ecuador)).

86 INTER-AMERICAN COMMISSION ON HUMAN RIGHTS, REPORT ON CITIZEN SECURITY AND HUMAN RIGHTS, OEA/Ser.L/V/II, Doc. 57 (December 31, 2009), ¶¶144–5.

87 Case of Lopez-Alvarez, Inter-Am. Ct. H.R., Judgment of February 1, 2006, ¶¶67,68 (Honduras).

88 Barreto Leiva v. Venezuela (Merits, Reparations and Costs), 19 IHRR 810 (November 17, 2009).

89 *Id.*, ¶111.

90 *Id.*, ¶122.
91 Case of James Zapata Valencia and Jose Heriberto Ramírez Llanos, Inter-Am. Ct. H.R., Report No. 79/11, Case No. 10.916 (July 21, 2011).
92 *Id.*, ¶128.
93 Garcia Ramirez, *The Inter-American Court of Human Rights' Perspective on Terrorism*, 806–7, (citing *e.g.* Case of Castillo Petruzzi, Inter-Am. Ct. H.R., Series C No.20, May 30, 1999 (Peru)).
94 *Id.* (citing *e.g.* the Case of Tibi, and the Case of Durand and Ugarte).
95 Jelena Pejic, *Procedural Principles and Safeguards for Internment/Administrative Detention in Armed Conflict and Other Situations of Violence*, 87 INT'L REV. RED CROSS 375, 377 (2005).
96 GARY D. SOLIS, THE LAW OF ARMED CONFLICT 134–135 (Cambridge University Press, 2010).
97 AP I, Art. 75.
98 *Id.*, Art. 75(3).
99 Pejic, *Procedural Principles and Safeguards for Internment/Administrative Detention in Armed Conflict and Other Situations of Violence* 378.
100 GC III, Art. 21.
101 *Id.*, Art. 118.
102 Chatham House and Int'l Comm. of the Red Cross, *Expert Meeting On Procedural Safeguards for Security Detention in Non-International Armed Conflict*, 91 INT'L REV. RED CROSS 859, 866 (2009).
103 *Id.*, 863.
104 *Id.*, 870. Many scholars have commented that international armed conflict procedures should apply to non-international armed conflicts. *See* e.g. Ashley S. Deeks, *Administrative Detention in Armed Conflict*, 40 CASE W. RES. J. INT'L L. 403, 434 (2009) (arguing that the core procedures in GC IV provide an excellent basis for detention); Ryan Goodman, *The Detention of Civilians in Armed Conflict*, 103 AM. J. INT'L L. 48, 50 (2009) (arguing that GC IV contains the most closely analogous rules concerning the detention of civilians, and that it constitutes the best approximation of IHL rules when interpretive gaps arise). *Contra see* John B. Bellinger III and Vijay M. Padmanabhan, *Detention Operations in Contemporary Conflict: Four Challenges for the Geneva Conventions and Other Existing Law*, 105 AM. J INT'L L. 201, 209 (2011) (arguing that the rules relating to international armed conflicts do not address the full range of detention issues in conflicts with non-state actors). *Also see* Serdar Mohamed and Ors. v. Secretary of State for Defence [2015] EWCA Civ. 843, ¶¶123, 246, 256 and Chapter 1 *infra*.
105 THE WHITE HOUSE, OFFICE OF THE PRESS SECRETARY, FACT SHEET: NEW ACTIONS ON GUANTÁNAMO AND DETAINEE POLICY (March 7, 2011), *available at* www.whitehouse.gov/the-press-office/2011/03/07/fact-sheet-new-actions-guant-namo-and-detainee-policy.
106 AP II, Arts. 2, 4, 5, 6.
107 Pejic, *Procedural Principles and Safeguards for Internment /Administrative Detention in Armed Conflict and Other Situations of Violence* 378–9.
108 Argentina, Australia, Belgium, Canada, China, Denmark, Finland, France, Germany, India, Malaysia, New Zealand, Nigeria, Norway, Pakistan, Russia, South Africa, Sweden, Tanzania, Netherlands, Turkey, Uganda, United Kingdom, and United States.

109 The Copenhagen Process On The Handling Of Detainees In International Military Operations [Copenhagen Process] (October 19, 2012).
110 *Id.*, Guidelines, ¶16.2–3.
111 *Id.*, ¶4.4.

3 Derogation

In some situations states may be released (or permitted to derogate) from the obligation to guarantee certain treaty rights.[1] This chapter compares derogation in the context of detention in the five human rights treaties,[2] and examines whether states are relieved from providing certain guarantees if they wish to preventively detain persons in the face of an actual or imminent terrorist attack. However, in derogating, states must be mindful of, and respect their obligations under international law.[3] This has been interpreted as including consistency with other international human rights treaty obligations.[4]

Relevant treaty provisions are set out in Appendix 3, Table 1.

ICCPR

Grounds for derogation

The derogation formula of "in time of public emergency when the life of the nation is threatened, and when its existence has been officially proclaimed"[5] evolved in discussions by the drafters of the International Covenant on Civil and Political Rights (ICCPR) after many other proposals had been considered and rejected.[6] The *travaux préparatoires* reflect the view that each government would have to decide for itself when such a situation existed, and each government should be allowed a certain latitude in judgment.[7] This discussion made reference to the "margin of appreciation" standard of deference in the European Convention,[8] which is discussed below, but that wording was not adopted. In fact, very little has been written about the use of a margin of appreciation by the Human Rights Committee (HRC), and it is unclear whether it exists at all in practice in respect of the ICCPR.[9] One view is that cases that can be found supporting the proposition that the HRC has been "speaking silently the language of the margin."[10]

In 1964, whilst drafting of the ICCPR was still ongoing, the United Nations Department of Economic and Social Affairs', Study of the Right of Everyone to be Free from Arbitrary Arrest, Detention and Exile reviewed derogation, and the use of preventive detention in times of emergency by nearly fifty countries.[11] They concluded that the right to derogate could apply "to the extent strictly required by the exigencies of the situation,"[12] echoing the phraseology in the then current draft of the ICCPR.

Guidance

In September 1984 the United Nations Economic and Social Council issued the non-binding Siracusa Principles,[13] in 1985 the International Law Association adopted the non-binding Paris Minimum Standards of Human Rights Norms in a State of Emergency,[14] and on August 31, 2001 the HRC issued General Comment No. 29,[15] as guidance on how to interpret Article 4. Additionally, the HRC has issued comments in its review of state party reports as well as in individual communications, although case law on the subject is scarce.[16]

Five core principles relating to derogation are discerned from the guidance:

1 There has to be a state of emergency that threatens the life of the nation.[17] The Siracusa Principles,[18] and the Paris Minimum Standards[19] provide some guidance. Both of these interpretation aids prescribe that the situation must be exceptional, affect the whole of the nation and relate to actual or imminent danger. Before 9/11, states such as Chile, Colombia, Peru, and Uruguay have cited terrorism as causing a state of emergency.[20] However, after 9/11 not many states derogated from the ICCPR, and none of the Latin American states that did derogate did so for reasons directly connected to the threat of international terrorism.[21] However, as to threats, it is not possible to derogate to face "possible exceptional situations which have not yet arisen."[22]
2 A state wishing to derogate must have officially proclaimed a state of emergency,[23] as a last resort.[24] The reason for this is to "prevent states from derogating arbitrarily from their obligations where such an action was not warranted by events."[25]
3 Derogating measures must be necessary and proportionate.[26] The HRC has from time to time expressed concern that insufficient attention has been paid to the principle of proportionality.[27]
4 Judicial review is not derogable in a state of emergency, in particular the right to apply to a court for a decision on the lawfulness of detention.[28]
5 Measures derogating from the ICCPR must be of an "exceptional and temporary" nature.[29] The "restoration of a state of normalcy" should be the predominant objective of a derogating state.[30] Thus derogating measures cannot be used to implement preventive detention as a counter-terrorism strategy,[31] because a strategy by definition is unlikely to be temporary.

Permanent emergencies

The principle relating to the use of emergency measures on a temporary basis only is one that has generated much controversy over what have been described as "permanent or entrenched emergencies." Examples involving terrorist activity include Northern Ireland (over eighty years), Israel (over fifty years), and Turkey (fifteen years),[32] Egypt, Uruguay, and Argentina, [33]as well as the United States' "war" on terror against al-Qaeda.[34] One main area of concern is that emergency legislation becomes normalized.[35] For example, the emergency regulations dating from the British Mandate in Palestine remained in place when the state of Israel was established in 1948, and are still in effect in current legislation. The continued use of the emergency regulations "became acceptable; it came to be considered as an evil perhaps, but an evil that one had to live with because of external circumstances imposed on the nation."[36]

European Convention

Grounds for derogation

If preventive detention does not fall into any of the categories in Article 5(1)(c) as analyzed in Chapter 2, states can only lawfully use this tool if the detention takes place in an emergency. The jurisprudence of the European Court of Human Rights (ECHR) illustrates that terrorism is such an emergency.[37] States may derogate from Article 5 in emergency situations that meet the criteria set out in Article 15. The wording of Article 15 is broadly similar to that in Article 4 ICCPR, with the addition of the words "in time of war," and the absence of the reference to non-discrimination in Article 15.

There are two tests. The first is that there must be a "public emergency." In *Lawless v. Ireland* the European Commission defined this as "a situation of exceptional and imminent danger or crisis affecting the general public, as distinct from particular groups, and constituting a threat to the organized life of the community which composes the State in question."[38]

In the *Greek* case,[39] where it was not accepted that a public emergency existed, the European Commission identified four characteristics of a public emergency:

1 It must be actual or imminent;[40]
2 Its effects must involve the whole nation;[41]
3 The continuance of the organized life of the community must be threatened;
4 The crisis or danger must be exceptional, in that the normal measures or restrictions, permitted by the Convention for the maintenance of public safety, health and order, are plainly inadequate.[42]

The second test is that derogating measures are only permitted to the extent strictly required by the exigencies of the situation. Any suspension measure must be "proportionate to strict necessity."[43]

Margin of appreciation

The ECHR has consistently recognized a margin of appreciation in assessing the necessity for derogating measures and the scope of the actual derogating measures.[44] A difference in approach can be discerned between various members of the European Commission and the ECHR in their exercise of the margin of appreciation in construing proportionality.[45] These range from the strict approach that a government had no other measure available to deal with the emergency,[46] to a less rigorous approach that affords each government a wide margin of appreciation, where "notions like good faith and reasonableness play an important role in assessing the proportionality of the measures."[47] Discussion of both approaches can be seen in *Lawless* and *Ireland*, but in each case the less rigorous approach prevailed.[48]

The jurisprudence thus indicates that the ECHR is unwilling to interfere with governmental discretion when states seek to derogate from human rights for reasons of public emergency that may detrimentally affect the life of that state.[49] This is particularly true in respect of detention in some cases involving terrorism.[50]

After 9/11, the United Kingdom enacted the Anti-Terrorism, Crime and Security Act 2001. Section 23 permitted indefinite detention of suspected international terrorists.[51] The British home secretary issued a derogation order on November 11, 2001. The ECHR recalled that it fell to states to determine whether the life of the nation was threatened by a public emergency, and that in that connection:

> a wide margin of appreciation should be left to the national authorities. Nonetheless, Contracting Parties do not enjoy an unlimited discretion. It is for the Court to rule whether, inter alia, the States have gone beyond the "extent strictly required by the exigencies" of the crisis. The domestic margin of appreciation is thus accompanied by a European supervision. In exercising this supervision, the Court must give appropriate weight to such relevant factors as the nature of the rights affected by the derogation and the circumstances leading to, and the duration of, the emergency situation.[52]

The Court agreed that there was a public emergency threatening the life of the nation,[53] but that was not the end of the story, as it was for the Court to assess the proportionality of the measures used:

> When the Court comes to consider a derogation under Article 15, it allows the national authorities a wide margin of appreciation to decide

> on the nature and scope of the derogating measures necessary to avert the emergency. Nonetheless, it is ultimately for the Court to rule whether the measures were "strictly required". In particular, where a derogating measure encroaches upon a fundamental Convention right, such as the right to liberty, the Court must be satisfied that it was a genuine response to the emergency situation, that it was fully justified by the special circumstances of the emergency and that adequate safeguards were provided against abuse ... the question of proportionality is ultimately a judicial decision.[54]

The Court concluded that the derogating measures were disproportionate in that they discriminated unjustifiably between nationals and non-nationals. The detention measures were therefore found to be in violation of Article 5.[55] The case triggered a change in United Kingdom law.

Permanent emergencies – comparison with ICCPR

In the guidance to the ICCPR, there is reference to the fact that a state of emergency should be a temporary situation.[56] However, in respect of the European Convention, the jurisprudence in *Lawless* and the *Greek case* does not allude to any temporal limitation. Instead each application has been assessed on a case-by-case basis. [57]

The jurisprudence reflects several examples of implicit acceptance of long and entrenched states of emergency, in Northern Ireland[58] and Turkey.[59] However, although the margin of appreciation may be wide, as regards the Court's analysis of whether a state of emergency exists, it may be narrower and less deferential when it comes to the evaluation of the proportionality of the derogating measures.[60] The length of detention measures will be a factor to be considered in the Court's proportionality.

American Convention

Grounds for derogation

No derogation clause is found in the American Declaration, merely a general limitation clause.[61] States may derogate from Article 7 of the American Convention in emergency situations provided that the criteria in Article 27 are satisfied.

Comparison with ICCPR and European Convention

Two differences from the wording in Article 4 ICCPR and Article 15 European Convention are immediately apparent. The first difference is in the definition of "emergency." In the American Convention, derogation is permitted "in time of war, public danger, or other emergency that threatens the independence or security of a State Party," whereas derogation pursuant to the other two instruments is permitted in a "public emergency threatening the life of the nation." Some scholars have commented that the distinctive terminology in the American Convention may have been chosen as a reflection of the emergency terms used in the various constitutions of the American states.[62]

The second difference in the wording is the addition of the words "for the period of time" in the limitation section of sub-paragraph 1. The time limitation has been mentioned in the Human Rights Committee (HRC) guidance to the ICCPR,[63] but not in the European Convention.[64] On the issue of interpretation, some commentators note the lack of a thorough analysis by the Inter-American Court of Human Rights (IACHR), mainly because many cases have required factual determination.[65] In its Doctrine on States of Emergency, some guidance on the interpretation of Article 27 can be extracted from the comments of the Inter-American Commission. It notes that state of emergency is "an institution which is essentially transitory in nature," and which "may only be justified in the face of real threats to the public order or the security of the state."[66]

In the 1987 Advisory Opinion in Emergency Situations, the Court stated that derogation is:

> a provision for exceptional situations only. It applies solely "in time of war, public danger, or other emergency that threatens the independence or security of a State Party."
>
> And even then, it permits the suspension of certain rights and freedoms only "to the extent and for the period of time strictly required by the exigencies of the situation." Such measures must also not violate the State Party's other international legal obligations, nor may they involve "discrimination on the ground of race, color, sex, language, religion or social origin."[67]

In the Commission's 1983 report concerning Nicaragua, it noted that the emergency had to be "of a serious nature, created by an exceptional situation that truly represents a threat to the organized life of the state."[68] In the 1987 Advisory Opinion on Judicial Guarantees in States of Emergency, the Court noted that:

> [f]rom Article 27(1), moreover, comes the general requirement that in any state of emergency, there be appropriate means to control the measures taken, so that they are proportionate to the needs and do not exceed the strict limits imposed by the Convention or derived from it.[69]

The Commission referred to the European Convention and the ICCPR in its analysis, and noted that those instruments, as well as the American Convention, "require the existence of a serious national emergency, that the measures adopted be 'strictly required by the exigencies of the situation' (these terms are the same in all three instruments) and that those measures be compatible with the state's other international obligations."[70] This means that "the measures adopted should be proportionate to the danger, both with respect to degree and duration; thus, once the danger that threatens the security of the State has been overcome, the special provisions should also be terminated."[71]

Permanent emergencies

A number of states have not observed the temporal limitation in Article 27. The Commission has frequently found violations of Article 27 because of lengthy entrenched emergencies.[72] For example, the government of Nicaragua invoked a state of emergency in early 1982, because of attacks by armed insurgents. Several hundred Miskitos were detained on grounds of alleged involvement in counter-revolutionary activities for various periods of up to ten months, and many cases of disappearances were reported. Similarly the Commission has criticized Colombia in respect of an emergency involving a state of siege for more than thirty years.[73]

Permanent states of emergency have been described as those that are "perpetuated, with or without proclamation, either as a result of *de facto* systematic extension or because the Constitution has not provided any time limit a priori."[74] Often, permanent states of emergency have been declared unlawful.[75] More recently the Commission complained that in Honduras, "the *de facto* government has continued to use curfews and to extend the state of emergency arbitrarily, without any basis in law or legitimate grounds."[76]

Proportionality

The IACHR has applied the principles governing assessment of the existence of a public emergency to state non-parties to the American Convention, that were members of the Organization of American States (OAS).[77] On the issue of assessment of whether the measures taken are lawful, the Court has said:

> Since Article 27(1) envisages different situations and since, moreover, the measures that may be taken in any of these emergencies must be tailored to "the exigencies of the situation," it is clear that what might be permissible in one type of emergency would not be lawful in another. The lawfulness of the measures taken to deal with each of the special situations referred to in Article 27(1) will depend, moreover, upon the character, intensity, pervasiveness, and particular context of the emergency and upon the corresponding proportionality and reasonableness of the measures.[78]

The Court has not produced a clear analysis of proportionality. A mixture of examples can be found where the principle has been applied, and where it has not been mentioned.[79] However, it is never lawful to suspend *habeas corpus* in a situation of emergency.[80] Scant mention of the margin of appreciation is found in IACHR cases; the doctrine does not seem to have been accepted to any great extent by the Court.[81] One example where the margin of appreciation seems to have been exercised, but not labeled as such, is in *Zambrano Velez*, a case dealing with the use of lethal force during an alleged situation of emergency in Ecuador.[82]

African Charter

The Charter contains no provision for derogation in times of emergency, thus all articles apply at all times.

Arab Charter

In time of (exceptional) public emergency it is permitted to derogate from the provisions relating to detention, but not the right to challenge detention at that time.[83]

Notes

1 One explanation of the rationale of derogation can be seen in Emilie M. Hafner-Burton, Lawrence R. Helfer and Christopher J. Fariss, *Emergency and Escape: Explaining Derogations form Human Rights Treaties*, 65 INTERNATIONAL ORGANIZATION 673, 681 (2011) (commenting that in emergencies governments need time and policy breathing space to adopt emergency measures, even those that restrict civil and political liberties. Their actions must also reduce the risk of censure from voters, interest groups, and domestic judges. "A derogation from a human rights treaty helps to achieve both of these ends").

2 International Covenant on Civil and Political Rights, G.A. res. 2200A (XXI), 21 U.N. GAOR Supp. (No. 16) at 52, U.N. Doc. A/6316 (1966), 999 U.N.T.S. 171 (entered into force March 23, 1976) [ICCPR]; European Convention for the Protection of Human Rights and Fundamental Freedoms, opened for signature Nov. 4, 1950, 213 UNTS 222 (entered into force September 3, 1953) [European Convention]; American Convention on Human Rights, O.A.S. Treaty Series No. 36, 1144 U.N.T.S. 123 (entered into force July 18, 1978) [American Convention]; African (Banjul) Charter of Human and Peoples' Rights, adopted June 27, 1981, OAU Doc. CAB/LEG/67/3 rev. 5, 21 I.L.M. 58 (1982) (entered into force October 21, 1986) [African Charter]; Arab Charter on Human Rights, adopted May 22, 2004, reprinted in 12 Int'l Hum. Rts. Rep. 893 (2005) (entered into force March 15, 2008) [Arab Charter].

3 ICCPR, Art. 4(1); European Convention, Art. 15(1); American Convention, Art. 27(1); Arab Charter, Art. 4(1).

4 DIANE A. DESIERTO, NECESSITY AND NATIONAL EMERGENCY CLAUSES, 279 (Martinus Nijhoff, 2012).

5 ICCPR, Art. 4(1).

6 MARC J. BOSSUYT, GUIDE TO THE *"TRAVAUX PRÉPARATOIRES"* OF THE INTERNATIONAL COVENANT ON CIVIL AND POLITICAL RIGHTS, 85 (citing Commission on Human Rights, 5th Session (1949), 6th Session (1950), 8th Session (11952), A/2929 Chapt. V, §§38,39).

7 *Id.*, 87 (citing Third Committee 18th Session (1963), A/5655, §49).

8 *Id.*

9 ANDREW LEGG, THE MARGIN OF APPRECIATION IN INTERNATIONAL HUMAN RIGHTS LAW, 5–6, (Oxford University Press, 2012); Christopher Michaelson, *Permanent Legal Emergencies and the Derogation Clause in International Human Rights Treaties: A Contradiction? in* POST 9/11 AND THE STATE OF PERMANENT LEGAL EMERGENCY, 297 (Aniceto Masferrer, ed., Springer 2012).

10 LEGG, THE MARGIN OF APPRECIATION IN INTERNATIONAL HUMAN RIGHTS LAW, 6 (citing James Crawford, *Preface*, ix, *in* YUTAKA ARAI-TAKAHASHI, THE MARGIN OF APPRECIATION DOCTRINE AND THE PRINCIPLE OF PROPORTIONALITY IN THE JURISPRUDENCE OF THE ECHR (Intersentia, 2002)). At 158 Legg describes two cases where there is a margin of appreciation to the national security expertise of states (citing Celepi v. Sweden, CCPR/C/51/D/456/1991 (1994)) but notes that such deference does not lead to the judicial abdication of responsibility, nor the nature of a state's response to perceived threats (Jeong-Eun Lee v. Republic of Korea, CCPR/C/84/D/11119/2002 (2005)).

11 U.N. DEPT. OF ECONOMIC AND SOCIAL AFFAIRS, STUDY OF THE RIGHT OF EVERYONE TO BE FREE FROM ARBITRARY ARREST, DETENTION AND EXILE, ¶¶753–82.

12 *Id.*, ¶783.

13 U.N. ECONOMIC AND SOCIAL COUNCIL, COMMISSION ON HUMAN RIGHTS, THE SIRACUSA PRINCIPLES ON THE LIMITATION AND DEROGATION PROVISIONS IN THE INTERNATIONAL COVENANT ON CIVIL AND POLITICAL RIGHTS (September 28, 1984), E/CN.4/1985/4, [Siracusa Principles].

14 Richard B. Lillich, *The Paris Minimum Standards of Human Rights Norms in a State of Emergency*, 79 AM. J. INT'L L. 1072 (1985) [Paris Minimum Standards].

15 CCPR General Comment No. 29. States of Emergency (Article 4), U.N. Doc. CCPR/C/21/Rev.1/Add.11 (2001).

16 Michaelson, *Permanent Legal Emergencies and the Derogation Clause in International Human Rights Treaties: A Contradiction?* 293.

17 CCPR General Comment No. 29, ¶2.

18 Siracusa Principles, ¶39, 40.

19 Paris Minimum Standards (A)1.

20 JAIME ORAA, HUMAN RIGHTS IN STATES OF EMERGENCY IN INTERNATIONAL LAW, 22 (Clarendon Press Oxford, 1992).

21 Michaelson, *Permanent Legal Emergencies and the Derogation Clause in International Human Rights Treaties: A Contradiction?* 309.

22 ORAA, HUMAN RIGHTS IN STATES OF EMERGENCY IN INTERNATIONAL LAW, 27.

23 CCPR General Comment No. 29, ¶2.

24 ORAA, HUMAN RIGHTS IN STATES OF EMERGENCY IN INTERNATIONAL LAW, 29.

25 Marc J. Bossuyt, Guide To The *"Travaux Préparatoires"* Of The International Covenant On Civil And Political Rights, 87 (citing Commission on Human Rights, 6th Session (1950), 8th Session (1952), A/2929 Chapt. V, §41).

26 CCPR General Comment No. 29, ¶4: the measures have to be "limited to the extent strictly required by the exigencies of the situation. This requirement relates to the duration, geographical coverage, and material scope of the state of emergency and any measures of derogation resorted to because of the emergency...[T]he obligation to limit any derogations to those strictly required by the exigencies of the situation reflects the principle of proportionality which is common to derogation and limitation powers."

27 *Id.*, fn 3 (citing concluding observations on Israel (1998), CCPR/C/79/Add.93. ¶11).

28 CCPR General Comment No. 29, ¶16; Claire Macken, Counter-Terrorism And The Detention Of Suspected Terrorists, 91–3 (Routledge, 2011) (citing Concluding Observations of the Human Rights Committee: Israel 18/08/98, U.N. Doc CCPR/C/79/Add.93 (Concluding Observations/Comments) ¶2.1, and Concluding Observations of the Human Rights Committee: Peru UN Doc A/51/40 (1996) ¶362).

29 CCPR General Comment No. 29, ¶2.

30 *Id.*, ¶1. *See also* Desierto, Necessity And National Emergency Clauses, 258.

31 Macken, Counter-Terrorism And The Detention Of Suspected Terrorists, 94.

32 Edel Hughes, *Entrenched Emergencies and the "War on Terror": Time to Reform the Derogation Procedure in International Law?* 20 N.Y. Int'l L. Rev. 1, 3 (2007).

33 Michaelson, *Permanent Legal Emergencies and the Derogation Clause in International Human Rights Treaties: A Contradiction?* 309.

34 Greg Miller, *Plan for hunting terrorists signals U.S. intends to keep adding names to kill lists*, Wash. Post (October 24, 2012), A1.

35 *See e.g.* Oraa, Human Rights In States Of Emergency In International Law, 22; Oren Gross, *"Once More Unto the Breach": The Systemic Failure of Applying the European Convention on Human Rights to Entrenched Emergencies*, 23 Yale J. Int'l L. 437, 455–6 (1998); Oren Gross, *"Chaos and Rules" Should Responses to Violent Crises Always be Constitutional?*, 112 Yale L. J. 1011, 1090 (2003); Hughes, *Entrenched Emergencies and the "War on Terror"*, 3; Macken, Counter-Terrorism And The Detention Of Suspected Terrorists, 94.

36 Gross, *"Chaos and Rules"*, 1092 (quoting the official commentary to the Emergency Powers (Detention) Bill, 1 Amnon Rubinstein, Ha-Mishpat Ha-Konstitutsyoni Shel Medinat Israel 263 (5th rev. ed. 1996): "In the state of siege to which the State is subject since its establishment, one cannot relinquish special measures designed to ensure adequate defense of the Sate and the public against those who conspire to eliminate the State. Still, one should not be content with the existence of those radical regulations ... Perceived necessity made thinkable what had previously been considered unthinkable").

37 Al-Jeddah v. United Kingdom, 81 (citing Lawless v Ireland, Ireland v. United Kingdom, 5310/71, ECHR (December 13, 1977), Brannigan and McBride v.

United Kingdom, Appl. No. 5/1992/350/423–4, ECHR (April 22 1993), Aksoy v. Turkey, Appl. No. 21987/93, ECHR (December 18, 1996)). *See also* A. v. United Kingdom, Appl. No. 3455/05 ECHR (February 19, 2009).

38 Lawless v. Ireland, Report of the European Commission (Adopted on December 19, 1959), Appl. N. 332/57 (Commission) 1 ECHR (Ser. B), §90.

39 The Greek Case, European Commission's Report of Nov. 5, 1969, 12 Ybk (the Greek Case).

40 MACKEN, COUNTER-TERRORISM AND THE DETENTION OF SUSPECTED TERRORISTS, 82–3 (noting that the Court gave very wide reading of actual and imminent threat in Lawless because although the facts did not appear to satisfy the criteria, the Court concluded that the Irish government was justified in declaring a state of emergency).

41 In cases where terrorist activity has taken place in a section of a territory, this has been open to both narrow and wide interpretation. See MACKEN, COUNTER-TERRORISM AND THE DETENTION OF SUSPECTED TERRORISTS, 85–8. *E.g.*, the narrow approach is reflected in Aksoy, ¶70, where the Court accepted there was a public emergency in the region of South East Turkey, and considered a deprivation of liberty that took place in that region. In Sakik v. Turkey, 87/1996/67/897-902, ECHR (Nov. 26, 1997), ¶39, in relation to an public emergency in South East Turkey, the Court would be not extend the effect of derogation to a part of Turkish territory not explicitly named in the notice of derogation. *Contra*, the wide approach is seen where the influence of terrorist activity is deemed to have an effect on the entire nation. *E.g.* although terrorist activity in Northern Ireland had comparatively little impact on daily life of the general public in the entire region of Northern Ireland and/or the UK, a wide interpretation was given by the Court, which accepted that there was a public emergency. *See* Lawless v. Ireland, ¶30, and Ireland v. United Kingdom, ¶205.

42 The Greek Case, ¶153.

43 ARAI-TAKAHASHI, THE MARGIN OF APPRECIATION DOCTRINE AND THE PRINCIPLE OF PROPORTIONALITY IN THE JURISPRUDENCE OF THE ECHR, 177 (citing Brannigan and McBride ¶43). *See also* Michaelson, *Permanent Legal Emergencies and the Derogation Clause in International Human Rights Treaties: A Contradiction?* 295 (quoting Handyside v. United Kingdom ECHR (1976) I EHRR 737, ¶48 where the Court "differentiated the 'strictly required' standard in Article 15 from the ordinary standard of necessity which the Court translates into the principle of proportionality").

44 ARAI-TAKAHASHI, THE MARGIN OF APPRECIATION DOCTRINE AND THE PRINCIPLE OF PROPORTIONALITY IN THE JURISPRUDENCE OF THE ECHR, 178. *See also* Lawless v. Ireland, Report of the European Commission, §90.

45 ORAA, HUMAN RIGHTS IN STATES OF EMERGENCY IN INTERNATIONAL LAW, 144–52.

46 *Id.*, 145.

47 *Id.*

48 *Id.*, (citing Lawless v. Ireland, and Ireland v. United Kingdom).

49 Gross, *"Once More Unto the Breach"*, 463.

50 *E.g.* The Court has accepted the State's assessments of a state of emergency in Lawless v. Ireland, ¶37; in Brannigan and McBride, ¶¶59, 60; and Ireland v. United Kingdom, 25, ¶214. In Aksoy, the Court accepted that there was a state

of emergency, but the measures taken were not sufficiently required by the exigencies of the situation. In this case no judicial intervention took place for forteen days, see ¶84.

51 Anti-Terrorism, Crime and Security Act 2001, c.24 §23 (2001) (Eng.).

52 A. v. United Kingdom, Appl. No. 3455/05 ECHR. (Feb. 19, 2009), ¶173.

53 *Id.*, ¶181.

54 *Id.*, ¶184.

55 *Id.*, ¶190.

56 CCPR General Comment No. 29, ¶2. The text of the ICCPR in Article 4(1) merely permits the use of derogating measures "to the extent strictly required by the exigencies of the situation."

57 Hughes, *Entrenched Emergencies and the "War on Terror"*, 10–11.

58 *See e.g.* Gross, *"Once More Unto the Breach"*, 472–3.

59 *See e.g.* Hughes, *Entrenched Emergencies and the "War on Terror"*, 20–3.

60 Stefan Sottiaux, Terrorism And The Limitation Of Rights, 259. Examples of the Court refusing to accept that measures were proportionate can be found in Brannigan and McBride, Aksoy, and A. v. United Kingdom.

61 American Declaration, Art. XXVIII: "The rights of man are limited by the rights of others, by the security of all, and by the just demands of the general welfare and the advancement of democracy."

62 Michaelson, *Permanent Legal Emergencies and the Derogation Clause in International Human Rights Treaties: A Contradiction?* 291 (citing Anna-Lena Svensson-McCarthy, The International Law Of Human Rights And States Of Exception: With Special Reference To Travaux Preparatiores And Case Law Of The International Monitoring Organs, 281 (Martinus Nijhoff, 1998)).

63 CCPR General Comment No. 29, ¶2.

64 Hughes, *Entrenched Emergencies and the "War on Terror"*, 10–11.

65 *See e.g.*, Oraa, Human Rights In States Of Emergency In International Law, 24; Legg, The Margin Of Appreciation In International Human Rights Law, 4–5.

66 Inter-American Commission On Human Rights, Ten Years Of Activities 1971–1981, 337, 338 (OAS, 1982).

67 Habeas Corpus in Emergency Situations (Arts. 27(2) and 7(6) of the American Convention on Human Rights), Advisory Opinion OC-8/87, January 30, 1987, Inter-Am.Ct. H.R. (Ser. A) No. 8 (1987), ¶19.

68 Hughes, *Entrenched Emergencies and the "War on Terror"*, 43 (citing Inter-Am. Comm'n H.R. Report On The Situation Of Human Rights Of A Segment Of Miskito Origin, at Pt. II, subdiv. E, ¶8, OEA/Ser.L/V.II.62 doc. 10, rev. 3 (November 29, 1983)).

69 Judicial Guarantees in States of Emergency (Arts. 27(2), 25 and 8 of the American Convention on Human Rights), Advisory Opinion OC-9/87, October 6, 1987, Inter-Am. Ct. H.R. (Ser. A) No. 9 (1987), ¶21.

70 Inter-Am. Comm'n H.R. Report On The Situation Of Human Rights Of A Segment Of Miskito Origin Pt. II, subdiv. E ¶¶6–8.

71 *Id.*, ¶14.

72 Hughes, *Entrenched Emergencies and the "War on Terror"*, 43.

73 *Id.*, (citing Inter-Am. Comm'n H.R., Report On The Situation Of Human Rights In The Republic Of Colombia, Conclusions And

RECOMMENDATIONS, subdiv. A, ¶2, OEA/Ser.L/V/II.53 doc.22 (June 30, 1981)). *Also see* ORAA, HUMAN RIGHTS IN STATES OF EMERGENCY IN INTERNATIONAL LAW, 25 (noting that the Commission failed to give a clear opinion as to the actual existence of a state of emergency).

74 ORAA, HUMAN RIGHTS IN STATES OF EMERGENCY IN INTERNATIONAL LAW, 30 (citing *e.g.* IACHR REPORT ON THE SITUATION OF HUMAN RIGHTS IN PARAGUAY (1978) OAS Ser.L/V/11.43, doc. 13, pp. 14–15, 88 ¶1).

75 *Id.*

76 INTER-AM. COMM'N H.R REPORT ON HONDURAS AND THE COUP D'ETAT. §5 HUMAN RIGHTS VIOLATIONS, A ¶213, II. Doc. 55, Dec. 30, 2009.

77 ORAA, HUMAN RIGHTS IN STATES OF EMERGENCY IN INTERNATIONAL LAW, 26, 32–3, 159. *E.g.* the Commission applied the doctrine to situations in Chile and Paraguay before the American Convention entered into force.

78 Habeas Corpus in Emergency Situations (Arts. 27(2) and 7(6) of the American Convention on Human Rights), Advisory Opinion, ¶22.

79 ORAA, HUMAN RIGHTS IN STATES OF EMERGENCY IN INTERNATIONAL LAW, 161–8.

80 *Id.*, 160 (citing Habeas Corpus in Emergency Situations (Arts. 27(2) and 7(6) of the American Convention on Human Rights), Advisory Opinion, ¶¶37–38). *See also* Case of Neira Alegria, Inter-Am. Ct. H.R. Series C No. 21 (January 19, 1995) ¶84.

81 *See e.g.* Benedict Kingsbury, *Foreword: Is the Proliferation of International Courts and Tribunals a Systemic Problem?* 31 N.Y.U. J. INT'L L. & POL. 679, 695 (1999); Douglas Lee Donoho, *Autonomy, Self-Governance, and the Margin of Appreciation: Developing a Jurisprudence of Diversity within Universal Human Rights*, 15 EMORY INT'L L. REV. 391, fn.140 (2001).

82 Case of Zambrano Velez, Inter-Am. Ct. H.R. Series C. No. 166 (July 4, 2007), ¶47.

83 Arab Charter, Art. 4(1) (2).

4 Due process and conclusions to Part I

This chapter compares the due process of detention as set out in the five human rights treaties[1] and the Geneva Conventions,[2] in the context of preventively detaining persons to forestall a terrorist attack. The detention provisions are laid out in Appendix 3, Table 1. The second part of the chapter draws conclusions from the analysis in Part I.

Due process

ICCPR

Knowing the reason for detention

Article 9(2) states that anyone who is arrested shall be informed at the time of his arrest of the reasons for the arrest. The detainee should be given enough factual specifics to indicate the substance of the complaint, to enable him to challenge the detention if the reasons are invalid or unfounded.[3]

Challenging detention

Article 9(3) requires anyone arrested or detained on a criminal charge to be brought "promptly" before a judge with entitlement to trial within a reasonable time. In *Berry v. Jamaica* the Human Rights Committee (HRC) held that there was a violation of Article 9(3) because he should have been brought "promptly" before a judge.[4] The notion of promptness is considered key,[5] and the HRC has found violations in cases of delays of "more than a few days."[6] However, Article 9(3), which regulates pre-trial detention, technically does not apply to those preventively detained without charge, as it envisages that a charge has been preferred.[7]

Persons detained without charge are entitled to apply to a court pursuant to Article 9(4) so that the court may decide without delay if the detention is lawful, in what are effectively *habeas corpus* proceedings. Article 9(4) does not say that the detainee must be brought before a court without delay, and the word "promptly," which applies in the bringing of a person who has been charged before a court pursuant to Article 9(3), is absent. The right to challenge detention must involve the ability of the court to order the release of a detainee if the detention is unlawful. An example where the domestic law does not permit release is Australia, which has been criticized by human rights groups and the HRC for this serious procedural flaw.[8]

Evidence

Other aspects of process are not explicitly found in the text of the International Covenant on Civil and Political Rights (ICCPR). For example, the text does not mention what sort of evidence is required to justify detention. Review of the laws in Part II of this book will reveal that the use of secret evidence is predominant in detention cases. To counter this, the Working Group on Arbitrary Detention has recommended that "no person should be deprived of liberty or kept in detention on the sole basis of evidence to which the detainee does not have the ability to respond."[9]

Legal representation

The United Nations Body of Principles for the Protection of All Persons under Any Form of Detention or Imprisonment states that detained persons are entitled to legal representation "as prescribed by law."[10] The ICCPR does not mention the right to legal counsel in *habeas* proceedings, but until recently the HRC seemed to imply that such a right exists.[11] In *Berry v. Jamaica* the petitioner had been detained for two and a half months on a murder charge before he was brought before a judge to challenge detention. The state maintained that he could have made a *habeas* application in that time, but the HRC noted the petitioner's claim that throughout the period he had no access to legal representation. The HRC held that the right under Article 9(4) had been violated, "since he was not, in due time, afforded the opportunity to obtain, on his own initiative, a decision by a court on the lawfulness of his detention."[12] In *Obaidullah* in the HRC's discussion of numerous due process rights that had been violated, reference was made to the fact that the detainee had been denied legal counsel in all administrative and legal hearings.[13] In *A. v. Australia* the HRC "acknowledged the importance of access to counsel while accepting that some reasonable limits on that access did not violate Article 9(4)."[14] General Comment No. 35 has now addressed this issue in one sentence: "To facilitate effective review, detainees should be afforded prompt and regular access to counsel."[15]

European Convention

Knowing the reason for detention

Pursuant to Article 5(2), every person has the right to be told why he or she has been arrested and detained. In *Fox, Hartley and Campbell v. United*

Kingdom the applicants were all told merely that they had been arrested on suspicion of terrorism. The Court stated that:

> any person arrested must be told, in simple, non-technical language that he can understand, the essential legal and factual grounds for his arrest, so as to be able, if he sees fit, to apply to a court to challenge its lawfulness in accordance with paragraph (4).[16]

There is, however, no requirement that all the relevant information be given at the moment of arrest.[17] Although the bare statement that they had been arrested on suspicion of terrorism was deemed inadequate, the Court considered that the applicants would have found out the reasons during their interrogations.[18]

Challenging detention

Article 5(3) deals with the obligation to bring detained persons promptly before judicial authorities. In *Lawless* the Court confirmed that this requirement applies to persons detained on preventive grounds.[19] The meaning of "promptly" was analyzed in *Brogan v. United Kingdom.*[20] Four applicants were each arrested on reasonable suspicion of involvement in the commission, preparation, or instigation of acts of terrorism and detained for less than seven days without being brought before a judge. Under the relevant legislation, detention was permissible for an initial period of forty-eight hours, and then a further period of up to five days with the authorization of the secretary of state.

The Court noted that the assessment of "promptness" had to be made in the light of the object and purpose of Article 5,[21] and that in view of the differences in between the English word "promptly" and the French word "aussitôt" (meaning immediate) in Article 5(3), and the fact the French version was to be given precedence,[22] the scope for flexibility in interpreting and applying the notion of "promptness" was very limited.[23] The Court concluded that the "undoubted fact that the arrest and detention of the applicants were inspired by the legitimate aim of protecting the community as a whole from terrorism is not, on its own, sufficient to ensure compliance with the specific requirements of Article 5 para. 3." Similarly, in *Brannigan and McBride v. United Kingdom* both applicants were detained for less than seven days without charge and without judicial control. In the light of all the circumstances the Court did not consider this unacceptable.[24]

The right to challenge the legality of the detention pursuant to Article 5(4) gives the arrested or detained persons entitlement to a review "bearing upon the procedural and substantive conditions which are essential for the 'lawfulness', in the sense of the Convention, of their deprivation of liberty."[25] In essence, this is the right to *habeas corpus* proceedings.

Legal representation

Article 5(4) does not state that a person challenging detention has the right to be represented by legal counsel. Article 6 mandates legal representation for everyone charged with a criminal offense.[26] Thus anyone detained after being charged has the right to a lawyer, but the position is not so clear for those held without charge. The laws of some countries allow representation from the moment of arrest, or soon after, and others may not. It seems from *Salduz v Turkey* that a right to counsel could be implied because of the obligation to ensure that any subsequent trial is fair. So if there is a right to counsel during pre-charge interrogation, as recommended in *Salduz*[27] and/or from the moment a person is taken into custody, as held in *Dayanan v Turkey*,[28] unless there are compelling reasons not to permit this, then the detainee is more likely to be represented during *habeas* proceedings if detention continues without charge. The fact that this issue is unclear may have been one of the triggers for the Proposal for a Directive of the European Parliament and Council on the right of access to a lawyer in criminal proceedings and on the right to communicate upon arrest. The Proposal recommends access to a lawyer from the time any deprivation of liberty begins and the scope of the lawyer's duties would include representation at any *habeas* hearing.[29]

American Convention

The process relating to detention is clearly set out in Article 7, and broadly corresponds to the equivalent provisions in the ICCPR and European Convention. Frequent concerns center on the denial of access to *habeas corpus* proceedings,[30] and the conduct of those proceedings.[31]

Guidance

In *Ferrer-Mazorra*, a case under the American Declaration, the Commission clarified that the procedure in *habeas* proceedings should comply with the fundamental rules of procedural fairness, requiring an opportunity to present evidence, and know and meet the claims of the opposing party.[32]

In 2006, the Commission made a number of recommendations about how deprivation of liberty should be dealt with in the context of terrorism.[33] In 2009, the Commission's Report on Citizen Security and Human Rights laid out some principles about process,[34] and in *Valencia and Llanos* in 2011 the Court stated its position regarding process:

> Both the Inter-American Court and the European Court of Human Rights have attached special importance to prompt judicial control of detentions, to prevent arbitrary detentions. A person who has been deprived of his liberty without any type of judicial control should be released or immediately placed at the disposal of a judge, since the main

duty established in Article 7 of the Convention is protection of personal liberty against the interference of the State. The Court has emphasized that failure to recognize the detention of an individual is a complete denial of the guarantees that should be granted and an even more serious violation of the article in question.[35]

Challenging detention

One area of criticism concerns the duration of detention without access to a judicial authority. For example, in *Castillo Peruzzi* the Court held that the period of up to thirty days preventive detention for persons suspected of treason as permitted by Peruvian law contravened the American Convention.[36] The victim's period of thirty-six days detention was excessive.[37] Indeed, the Commission has stated that a "delay of more than two or three days in bringing a detainee before a judicial authority will generally not be considered reasonable."[38]

Another example concerns the case of Peruvian *Jose Cantoral* who was arrested in Bolivia in August 2011 on "terrorism charges" and held for twenty-two days without due process or access to lawyers.[39] He was also allegedly beaten whilst in custody. The Inter-American Commission granted precautionary measures on his behalf.[40]

A delay in ruling on a *habeas* petition can also contravene the American Convention, such as in *Acosta Calderon*, where the court considering the victim's *habeas* petition took forty-four days to rule.[41]

Legal representation

Detainees must have an opportunity to be represented by legal counsel or some other representative.[42]

African Charter

No specific rights relate to challenging detention. However, the general wording in Article 7, concerning the right to have one's cause heard, including the right to appeal against acts violating fundamental rights (such as the right to liberty) may cover this. Nothing in the Charter mandates a right to a prompt hearing to challenge detention. The general language gives a right to counsel for the purposes of criminal defense – this may or may not cover appeals to challenge detention.

Limited guidance

The African Commission on Human and Peoples' Rights has issued some general principles, some of which apply to arrest and detention. These include the right for a detained person to be kept in an officially recognized place of detention with a register of persons detained, the right of access to necessary facilities to communicate with lawyers, family and friends, and the right of *habeas corpus*.[43] The extent to which these principles have been adopted is as yet unknown.

Arab Charter

Detainees are entitled to be told at the time of arrest why they are being held, and must be brought before a judge promptly for a determination as to whether the detention is lawful.[44]

LOAC

The Geneva Conventions (GCs) contain very few provisions relating to detention, and the few that do exist are found within the context of international armed conflicts (IACs), and link to the duration of hostilities. GC IV, Article 43 sets out a procedure for prompt review after detentions of civilians, followed by a minimum of twice yearly further reviews.

Some procedural guidance for detention in the non-international armed conflict (NIAC) context is found in the non-binding Copenhagen Process.[45] In particular, it recommends that detainees must be informed promptly in a language they understand of the reasons for the detention.[46] Promptness is interpreted nebulously as "within a reasonable time."[47] Detainees are to have contact with the outside world, subject to security considerations, their families notified of their detention, and be held in a designated place and on a register of detainees.[48] Security detention must be initially reviewed promptly and subject to a further review and continuing periodic reviews, if possible every six months, to determine whether on-going detention is justified.[49] Although there is a reference to a right of a detainee to have a personal representative present at reviews, there is no right of access to a lawyer.[50] Detention must end when circumstances justifying detention have ceased.[51]

Conclusions to Part 1

The human rights treaties

Both commonality, and subtle yet important differences emerge from the analysis of the treaty detention jurisprudence. These are laid out in Appendix 3, Table 2. Two basic points of commonality are that detention can only be in accordance with, and on grounds that are prescribed by, law, and arbitrary detention is prohibited.

Arbitrary detention is expressly proscribed in international human rights law. This is found in the texts of all the treaties except the European Convention, but is frequently stated in European Court of Human Rights

(ECHR) jurisprudence.[52] However, the definition of arbitrary is not consistent in the guidance and jurisprudence of any of the HRC, ECHR, and Inter-American Court of Human Rights (IACHR). The broadest definition can be found in HRC cases.[53] Common core elements seem to be necessity[54] and proportionality.[55]

The most significant difference relating to detention is the scope of the detention power. In all the treaties other than the European Convention, the only restrictions on detention are that it must be in accordance with and on grounds prescribed by law, and not arbitrary. The European Convention's approach is different in that it permits detention only in six specified cases. The relevant provision for preventive detention is Article 5(1)(c). This is discussed extensively above, but in sum, jurisprudence relating to this Article narrows the scope of the detention power to preventing "a concrete and specific offense … as regards, in particular, the place and time of its commission and its victim(s)."[56] Thus, if authorities detain suspects without establishing that the potential offense is concrete and specific, a state could face ECHR censure for violating Article 5, unless the state had derogated from the European Convention at the relevant time during a state of emergency. In that situation, a state would not be obligated to provide any of the guarantees set out in Article 5.

Many procedural requirements are nebulous, inadequate, or absent. For example, although the ICCPR and the Arab Charter require that persons arrested shall be informed of the reasons for arrest at the time of arrest,[57] and the European Convention requires that the reason for arrest should be given "promptly,"[58] the American Convention does not specify a time limit for giving reasons, and the African Charter is silent on this issue. Detainees should be told why they are held as soon as possible after arrest. Comprehensive guidance on this issue is required.

With the exception of American Convention jurisprudence, which guarantees legal representation in *habeas* proceedings,[59] and one sentence in the HRC's General Comment 35, neither specific treaty wording nor jurisprudence gives a right to a detained person to have access to a lawyer. After a suspect has been *charged*, the right to have a lawyer is mandated by the ICCPR and the European Convention and the African Charter.[60] All detainees should be entitled to have the assistance of counsel during detention. This significant deficiency requires remedy.

The ICCPR and American Convention and their jurisprudence envisage court proceedings to challenge detention, even during a state of emergency.[61] In each case the court is required to *adjudicate* without delay, but the treaties and jurisprudence offer no guidance as to how promptly a detainee may make his challenge. The European Convention provides that detainees must be brought before a court promptly and be entitled to a *trial* without delay, but there is only a right to have the lawfulness of detention adjudicated speedily, with no mention of when this challenge may be made.[62] Furthermore, the European Convention does not mandate that the right to challenge detention during a state of emergency is non-derogable. The African Charter does not specify any rights of challenging detention. The Arab Charter contains similar general wording to that found in the ICCPR, European Convention, and American Convention, but the right to liberty is non-derogable.[63] None of the wording gives any real guidance on how to challenge detention, and these are all important matters that should be addressed in core principles.

No uniform right of redress exists for victims of violations.[64] Very little real redress is given to the victims of the continuing treaty violations in the field of detention matters, and in any event, the treaties bodies lack the power to compel state parties to comply with treaty obligations.

One of the biggest problems with current international human rights law standards is that no effective mechanism exists to ensure compliance. Although many of the provisions in treaties purport to offer protection, they are only effective if state parties choose to honor them.[65] Many countries have incorporated international human rights law directly into their domestic law,[66] or have implemented specific legislation.[67] However, the interpretation of human rights law is often stretched by the way governments deal with difficult security issues. Little heed is paid to the risk of an almost meaningless censure by an international body and international law does not have the mechanism of a "Super Court" to sanction treaty violations.

Could this problem be addressed by making each country more responsible for human rights violations through domestic sanctions? To whom would those sanctions be applied? Would the risk of sanctions deter law enforcement authorities from detaining an individual, in case their conduct fell short of the required standards, or if mistakes were made? No solution to this conundrum is immediately obvious.

Two versions of an international human rights law framework for detention principles could be extrapolated from the analysis in Part I. A narrower approach comprises the very small set of abstract common principles mentioned above, which can be extracted from the combination of the five human rights treaties. The narrow framework is not useful because of its limited scope, as insufficient material is yielded to create a meaningful set of detention guidelines.

A broader approach might be to select one of the treaties as a general framework. If so, which one? Does one treaty stand out as an obvious best example for the detention guidelines? The answer is no, and this approach also does not work either because there are inconsistencies between the treaties, particularly in respect of the detention power provisions in the European Convention that differs from all the others. Furthermore, as many states are party to more than one human rights instrument,[68] problems can be caused by conflicts between treaty provisions.

In the event of conflicts between the treaties, or treaty case law, there is "no supreme arbiter of international human rights law as a whole."[69] Little authority exists outside of consulting general rules on treaties about how to resolve the type of conflict where the provisions relating to detention are inconsistent. The ICCPR came into force after the European Convention. Theoretically, in accordance with the relevant rules of the Vienna Convention on Treaties, where states parties belong to both treaties, "the earlier treaty applies only to the extent that its provisions are compatible with those of the later treaty."[70] The detention provisions in the two treaties are different, so it might be concluded that the provisions of the ICCPR ought to prevail. Opinions differ on this. One approach is that the global instrument (i.e. the ICCPR) would contain the minimum normative standard and the regional document might go further by refining or adding rights.[71] Applying this reasoning, although the regional instrument came first, one might argue that the earlier regional treaty refines the general prohibition on arbitrary detention. The problem with this argument is that the drafters of the ICCPR specifically considered, and rejected the formula of listing specified grounds as in Article 5 (1) of the European Convention.[72]

Another approach to resolve treaty conflicts is to apply the *lex specialis* doctrine. This will focus on the scope of the treaties and give effect to the more narrowly gauged treaty.[73] Perhaps the application of *lex specialis* is what explains why the ICCPR has not trumped the European Convention.

The rights and guarantees of detainees, and powers to detain, differ depending on where the actors are, and which human rights treaty governs. From the perspective of a detained person, his rights seem better served if he is within the jurisdiction of the European Convention. From the perspective of law enforcement authorities, absent a state of emergency, the ability to preventively detain a terror suspect would appear more limited in countries within the jurisdiction of the European Convention than in countries that fall within the jurisdiction of the other treaties. There is no easy answer.

LOAC

Capture in an IAC is totally dissimilar to off-the-battlefield detention. Due process for detention is impracticable in IACs where the rules of engagement apply. IACs are a completely different scenario from random terror attacks carried out by non-state insurgents, who are neither lawful nor unlawful combatants in IACs. The question of whether the NIAC category applies to these sporadic terror attacks is also at best murky. Thus the LOAC is insufficiently developed to provide rules or afford adequate due process for detention relating to the special terrorist type of "combatant."

If guidance is sought from international human rights law, the current state of the jurisprudence relating to preventive detention as analyzed in Part I is insufficiently developed to address all the problems of preventive detention. The many flaws and deficiencies in the detention provisions in international human rights law demonstrate an urgent need for a clear and unambiguous set of core detention principles. In addition, the LOAC as currently formulated is not designed to deal with the current transnational terrorist threat.

Notes

1 International Covenant on Civil and Political Rights, G.A. res. 2200A (XXI), 21 U.N. GAOR Supp. (No. 16) at 52, U.N. Doc. A/6316 (1966), 999 U.N.T.S. 171 (entered into force March 23, 1976) [ICCPR]; European Convention for the Protection of Human Rights and Fundamental Freedoms, opened for signature Nov. 4, 1950, 213 UNTS 222 (entered into force September 3, 1953) [European Convention]; American Convention on Human Rights, O.A.S.Treaty Series No. 36, 1144 U.N.T.S. 123 (entered into force July 18, 1978) [American Convention]; African (Banjul) Charter of Human and Peoples' Rights, adopted June 27, 1981, OAU Doc. CAB/LEG/67/3 rev. 5, 21 I.L.M. 58 (1982) (entered into force October 21, 1986) [African Charter]; Arab Charter on Human Rights, adopted May 22, 2004, reprinted in 12 Int'l Hum. Rts. Rep. 893 (2005) (entered into force March 15, 2008) [Arab Charter].

2 Geneva Convention for the Amelioration of the Condition of the Wounded and Sick in Armed Forces in the Field, (August 12, 1949), 6 U.S.T. 3114, 75 U.N.T.S. 31 [GC I]; Geneva Convention for the Amelioration of the Condition of the Wounded, Sick and Shipwrecked Members of Armed Forces at Sea (August 12, 1949), 6 U.S.T. 3217, 75 U.N.T.S. 85 [GC II]; Geneva Convention Relative to the Treatment of Prisoners of War (August 12, 1949), 6 U.S.T. 3316, 75 U.N.T.S. 135 [GC III]; Geneva Convention Relative to the Protection of Civilian Persons in Time of War (August 12, 1949), 6 U.S.T. 3516, 75 U.N.T.S. 287 [GC IV]; Protocol Additional to the Geneva Conventions of August 12, 1949, and Relating to the Protection of Victims of International Armed Conflicts (June 8, 1977), 1125 U.N.T.S. 3 [AP I]; Protocol Additional to the Geneva Conventions of August, 12 1949, and Relating to the Protection of Victims of Non-International Armed Conflicts (June 8, 1977), 1125 U.N.T.S. 609 [AP II].

3 U.N. Human Rights Committee, General Comment No. 35, CCPR/C/G/35, ¶25 (December 16, 2014).

4 Berry v. Jamaica, Communication No. 330/1988, U.N. Doc. CCPR/C/50/D/330/1988 (1994) ¶11.1.

5 U.N.G.A. Human Rights Council, Report of the Working Group on Arbitrary Detention, A/HRC/22/44, 22, III D ¶66 (2012).

6 *Id.* (quoting Bousroual v. Algeria, Communication No. 992/2001 (March 30, 2006), ¶9.6; Bandajevsky v. Belarus, Communication No. 1100/2002 (March 28, 2006), ¶10.3; Borisenko v. Hungary, Communication No. 852/1999 (October 14, 2002), ¶7.4)).

7 Claire Macken, Counter-Terrorism And The Detention Of Suspected Terrorists, 58–61 (Routledge, 2011).

8 Australian Human Rights Commission, Response To Questionnaire From The Working Group On Arbitrary Detention, Judicial Review Of Lawfulness Of Detention, ¶23 (November 8, 2013), www.ohchr.org/Documents/Issues/Detention/DraftBasicPrinciples/AustralianNHRI.pdf (citing A. v. Australia, HRC Communication No. 560/1993, CCPR/C/59/D/560/1993 (1997), ¶9.5).

9 U.N.G.A. Human Rights Council, Report of the Working Group on Arbitrary Detention, 22, III D ¶72.

10 U.N. Body Of Principles For The Protection Of All Persons Under Any

Form Of Detention Or Imprisonment, A/RES/43/173 (December 9, 1988), Principle 11: "A person shall not be kept in detention without being given an effective opportunity to be heard promptly by a judicial or other authority. A detained person shall have the right to defend himself or to be assisted by counsel as prescribed by law."

11 Brian R. Farrell, *Access to Habeas Corpus: A Human Rights Analysis of U.S. Practices in the War on Terrorism*, 20 Transnat'l L. & Contemporary Problems 1, 11 (2011) (citing Berry v. Jamaica).

12 Berry v. Jamaica, ¶11.1.

13 HRC Communication No. 10/2013 (United States of America), ¶39.

14 Farrell, *Access to Habeas Corpus* (quoting A. v. Australia, ¶9.6).

15 U.N. Human Rights Committee, General Comment No. 35, CCPR/C/G/35, ¶46 (December 16, 2014).

16 Fox, Campbell and Hartley v. United Kingdom, Appl. No. 1244/86; 1245/86; 12383/86, ECHR (August 30, 1990), ¶40.

17 *Id.*

18 *Id.*, ¶41.

19 Lawless v. Ireland No. 3, ECHR Series A no. 3 (July 1, 1961), ¶14.

20 Brogan v. United Kingdom, App. No. 11209/84; 11234/84; 11266/84; 11386/85, ECHR (November 29, 1988).

21 *Id.*, ¶58.

22 *Id.*, ¶59.

23 *Id.*, ¶62.

24 Brannigan and McBride v. United Kingdom, Appl. No. 5/1992/350/423-424, ECHR (April 22 1993), ¶60.

25 *Id.*, ¶65.

26 European Convention, Art. 6: "1. In the determination of his civil rights and obligations or of any criminal charge against him, everyone is entitled to a fair and public hearing within a reasonable time by an independent and impartial tribunal established by law."

27 Salduz v. Turkey, Appl. No. 36391/02 ECHR (November 27, 2008) ¶51, 55.

28 Dayanan v. Turkey, App. No. 7377/03 ECHR (October 13, 2009), ¶¶31, 32.

29 European Commission Proposal for a Directive of the European Parliament and Council on the right of access to a lawyer in criminal proceedings and on the right to communicate upon arrest. COM(2011) 326/3, {SEC(2011) 686} {SEC(2011) 687}Arts. 3 and 4, *available at* http://ec.europa.eu/justice/policies/criminal/procedural/docs/com_2011_326_en.pdf, and latest draft of text, in Council of the European Union, Proposal for a Directive of the European Parliament and of the Council on the right of access to a lawyer in criminal proceedings and on the right to communicate upon arrest – Revised text, Interinstitutional File: 2011/0154 (COD), 7337/12, DROIPEN 25 COPEN 49 CODEC 574 (March 9, 2012), available at www.ecba.org/extdocserv/projects/ps/20120309_measureCrevtext.pdf.

30 Sergio Garcia Ramirez, *The Inter-American Court of Human Rights' Perspective on Terrorism*, 806, *in* Counter-Terrorism, International Law And Practice (Ana Maria Salinade Frias, Katja LH Samuel, Nigel D White, eds) (Oxford University Press, 2012). (citing Case of Neira Alegria, Inter-Am. C.H.R., Series C No. 21 (January 19, 1995) (Peru), ¶¶77–84); Brian Farrell, *The Right to Habeas Corpus in the Inter-American Human Rights System*, 33

SUFFOLK TRANSNAT'L L. REV. 197, 203 (2010) (quoting Coard v. United States, IACHR Case No. 10.951, Report No. 109/99 (Sep. 29, 1999), ¶55: "habeas corpus is not susceptible to abrogation").

31 Brian Farrell, *The Right to Habeas Corpus in the Inter-American Human Rights System*, 204 (citing Ferrer-Mazorra v. United States, Inter-Am. Comm'n H.R. Case 9903, Report No. 51/01, OEA/Ser.L./V/II.111, doc. 20 rev. P 213 (2001)).

32 *Id.*

33 INTER-AM. COMM'N H. R., RECOMMENDATIONS FOR THE PROTECTION OF HUMAN RIGHTS BY OAS MEMBER STATES IN THE FIGHT AGAINST TERRORISM, OEA/Ser.G, CP/doc.4117/06 (May 9, 2006) §B ¶1: "Where member states arrest, imprison or otherwise detain individuals as part of their anti-terrorism initiatives in situations outside of armed conflict, they must comply with minimum standards governing the right to personal liberty and security, from which derogation may never be justified. These include the following requirements:

(a) the grounds and procedures for the detention must be prescribed by law;
(b) the detainee must be informed of the reasons for the detention and afforded prompt access to legal counsel, family and, where necessary or applicable, medical and consular assistance;
(c) prescribed limits must be placed upon the length of detention;
(d) a central registry of detainees must be maintained;
(e) appropriate and effective civilian judicial review mechanisms must be in place to supervise detentions and to protect the non-derogable rights of detainees, promptly upon arrest or detention and at reasonable intervals when detention is extended."

34 INTER-AM. COMM'N H.R., REPORT ON CITIZEN SECURITY AND HUMAN RIGHTS, ¶¶146–7.

35 Case of Valencia and Llanos, IACHR, Report No. 79/11 Case No. 10.916 (July 21, 2011), (Colombia), ¶126.

36 Case of Castillo Petruzzi, IACHR, Series C No. 20, (May 30, 1999). (Peru), ¶110.

37 *Id.*, ¶111.

38 INTER-AM. COMM'N H. R., REPORT ON THE HUMAN RIGHTS OF PERSONS DEPRIVED OF LIBERTY IN THE AMERICAS, OEA/Ser.L/V/II. Doc. 64 (December 31, 2011), ¶122.

39 U.S. DEPT. OF STATE, 2011 COUNTRY REPORTS ON HUMAN RIGHTS PRACTICES, Bolivia (May 24, 2012), *available at* www.state.gov/j/rls/hrrpt/2011/wha/186494.htm.

40 INTER-AM. COMM'N H.R., ANNUAL REPORT 2011, 77, PM 291/11 – José Antonio Cantoral Benavides y otros, Bolivia.

41 Case of Acosta Calderon, IACHR Series C No. 129, Judgment of June 24, 2005 (Ecuador), ¶97.

42 *Id.*

43 Ibrahima Kane, *Reconciling the Protection of Human Rights and the Fight Against Terrorism in Africa*, 852–4 *in* COUNTER-TERRORISM, INTERNATIONAL LAW AND PRACTICE (Ana Maria Salina de Frias, Katja LH Samuel, Nigel D White, eds) (Oxford University Press, 2012) (citing African Commission on Human and Peoples' Rights, Principles and Guidelines on the Right to Fair

Trial and Legal Assistance in Africa (May 16, 2002) DOC/OS(XXX)247, §§M(6) 21, M(2)19 and M(2)20)).

44 Arab Charter, Arts. 14(3) (5) (6).

45 THE COPENHAGEN PROCESS ON THE HANDLING OF DETAINEES IN INTERNATIONAL MILITARY OPERATIONS [COPENHAGEN PROCESS] (October 19, 2012).

46 *Id.*, Principles, 7.

47 *Id.*, Guidelines, ¶7.1.

48 *Id.*, Principles, 8, 10, 11.

49 *Id.*, 12, Guidelines 12.1–3.

50 *Id.*, 12.4.

51 *Id*, Principles, 4.

52 *See e.g.* Lawless v. Ireland (No. 3) S (1961), ¶14.

53 The line of cases from Hugo van Alphen v. The Netherlands, HRC Communication No. 305/1988, CCPR/C/39/D/305/1988 (1990), ¶5.8; A. v. Australia, ¶9.2; C. v. Australia, HRC Communication No. 900/1999, CCPR/C/76/D/900/1999 (2002), ¶8.2, define arbitrary detention as reasonable, appropriate, predictable, necessary, proportionate, not unjust, not indefinite, not for a longer period than can be justified, not unjust, and not to be imposed if a less invasive method can be used to achieve the same ends.

54 Hugo van Alphen, ¶5.8; Saadi v. United Kingdom, App. No. 13229/03, ECHR (2008), ¶70; Case of Lopez-Alvarez, IACHR (Series C) No. 141 (2006), ¶¶67, 68.

55 *Id.*

56 M. v. Germany, App. No. 19359/04, ¶102 (December 17, 2009), ECHR.

57 ICCPR, Art. 9(2); Arab Charter, Art. 14(3).

58 European Convention, Art. 5(2).

59 Ferrer-Mazorra v. United States, Inter-Am. Ct. H.R., Case 9903, Report No. 51/01, OEA/Ser.L./V/II.111, doc. 20 rev. ¶213 (2001).

60 ICCPR, Art. 14(b); European Convention, Art. 6(3)(c); African Charter, Art. 7.

61 ICCPR, Art. 9(4); CCPR General Comment No. 29. States of Emergency (Article 4), U.N. Doc. CCPR/C/21/Rev.1/Add.11, ¶16 (2001); American Convention, Art. 7(6); Judicial Guarantees in States of Emergency (Arts. 27(2), 25 and 8 of the American Convention on Human Rights), Advisory Opinion OC-9/87, October 6, 1987, Inter-Am. Ct. H.R. (Ser. A) No. 9 (1987), ¶¶37–40.

62 European Convention, Art. 5(3).

63 Arab Charter, Art 14(5).

64 Art. 9(5) ICCPR and Art. 5(5) European Convention guarantee an "enforceable right" to compensation. Art. 14(7) Arab Charter guarantees "a right" to compensation, Art 10 American Convention ties the right of compensation to a sentence by a final judgment through a miscarriage of justice, and the African Charter offers no individual right of redress.

65 *E.g.*, HILARY CHARLESWORTH, HUMAN RIGHTS: AUSTRALIA VERSUS THE UN, Democratic Audit of Australia, Australian National University, 2, 3 (August 2006): "In response to almost every finding against Australia, the Commonwealth Government has reiterated that the Human Rights Committee is not a court and its views are not binding."

66 *E.g.* France and Spain.

67 *E.g.* Human Rights Act 1998 c.42 (U.K.).

68 All parties to the European Convention, other than Moldova, are also parties to the ICCPR. All parties to the American Convention, other than Jamaica, are also parties to the ICCPR. All parties to the African Charter, other than Comoros, Sahrawi Arab Democratic Republic, Sao Tome, Swaziland, and Tanzania are also parties to the ICCPR, and all parties to the Arab Charter, other than Palestine, Qatar, Saudi Arabia, and United Arab Emirates, are also parties to the ICCPR. Two countries, Algeria and Libya, are each party to the ICCPR and two regional instruments, the African Charter and the Arab Charter.

69 Lawrence R. Helfer, *Forum Shopping for Human Rights*, 148 U. PA. L. REV. 285, 301 (1999).

70 Vienna Convention on the Law of Treaties, U.N.T.S. vol. 1155, p. 331, dated May 23, 1969 (entered into force January 27, 1980), at arts. 30(3) (4)(a).

71 28th Report of the Commission to Study the Organization of Peace (1980) at 15, INTERNATIONAL HUMAN RIGHTS IN CONTEXT, 930 (Henry J. Steiner, Philip Alston and Ryan Goodman, eds) (3rd ed.) (Oxford University Press, 2007).

72 MARC J. BOSSUYT, GUIDE TO THE *"TRAVAUX PRÉPARATOIRES"* OF THE INTERNATIONAL COVENANT ON CIVIL AND POLITICAL RIGHTS (Martinus Nijhoff Publishers, 1987), 190–1, 193 (citing Commission on Human Rights, 5th Session (1949), 6th Session (1950), 8th Session (1952), A/2929, Chapt. VI, §28).

73 Christopher J. Borgen, *Treaty Conflicts and Normative Fragmentation*, 466, *in* THE OXFORD GUIDE TO TREATIES (Duncan B. Hollis ed.) (Oxford University Press, 2012) (quoting H. Grotius, De Jure Belli ac pacis Bk II, Ch XVI Sec XXIX; ILC Fragmentation Report pp. 36, 37: "Grotius explained that 'special provisions are ordinarily more effective than those that are general'").

Part II

The seven countries

5 United Kingdom

This Chapter analyzes detention without charge, the now abolished control orders, and their replacement Terrorism Prevention and Investigation Measures (TPIMs). These are measures that are specifically designed to detain or restrict liberty in order to prevent a terrorist act. However, United Kingdom law also permits forms of preventive detention both prior to deportation of aliens who have completed a sentence of imprisonment,[1] as well as in the case of immigration deportations, on grounds that continued presence in the United Kingdom would not be "conducive to the public good."[2]

Detention without charge

Persons reasonably suspected to be terrorists (i.e. persons who are or have been concerned in the commission, preparation or instigation of acts of terrorism)[3] may be arrested without a warrant.[4] As the definition of terrorism covers the use or *threat* of action, this means that people can be arrested without actually being in the act of committing or having committed an offense. As the Independent Reviewer of Terrorism Legislation[5] points out:

> [i]t is a notably wide power of arrest, in particular because the arresting officer need have no specific offence in mind. It is enough, under section 40(1)(b), for there to be a reasonable suspicion that a person is or has been concerned in the commission, preparation or instigation of acts of terrorism. The acts need not have been identified at the time of arrest.[6]

What does reasonable suspicion mean?

According to the European Court of Human Rights (ECHR):

> terrorist crime poses particular problems, as the police may be called upon, in the interests of public safety, to arrest a suspected terrorist on the basis of information which is reliable but which cannot be disclosed to the suspect or produced in court without jeopardizing the informant.

> However, though Contracting States cannot be required to establish the reasonableness of the suspicion grounding the arrest of a suspected terrorist by disclosing confidential sources of information, the Court has held that the exigencies of dealing with terrorist crime cannot justify stretching the notion of "reasonableness" to the point where the safeguard secured by Article 5 § 1 (c) is impaired … It may also be observed that the standard imposed by Article 5 § 1 (c) does not presuppose that the police have sufficient evidence to bring charges at the time of arrest. The object of questioning during detention under sub-paragraph (c) of Article 5 § 1 is to further the criminal investigation by way of confirming or dispelling the concrete suspicion grounding the arrest. Thus facts which raise a suspicion need not be of the same level as those necessary to justify a conviction, or even the bringing of a charge which comes at the next stage of the process of criminal investigation.[7]

Additionally, suspects can be arrested and prosecuted in the United Kingdom for committing certain terrorist offences outside the United Kingdom.[8] The law therefore permits detention both to prevent an attack and investigate and collect sufficient evidence to charge and prosecute. Some scholars regard the arrest without warrant as excessive and oppressive and damaging to community relations.[9]

Procedure

Suspects may be detained initially without charge for forty-eight hours, with their status subject to review every twelve hours by a police officer who has not been involved in the investigation.[10] The suspect has the right to make representations to the review officer about continued detention.[11] Continued detention is only permissible if the review officer is satisfied that it is necessary in certain specified conditions.[12] Whilst detained, a suspect has the right to have a person informed of the detention.[13] Access to counsel is permitted, but in certain circumstances access may be delayed for up to forty-eight hours as well as restricted in terms of having to take place within the sight and hearing of a police officer.[14] Once suspects have seen an attorney, those attorneys are entitled to be present at police interviews, unless specified exceptions apply.[15]

Police interviews are video taped, and suspects must be advised of their right to silence, although this right is not as extensive as in the United States. British juries are allowed to draw adverse inferences from a suspect's refusal to answer questions, both in pre-charge questioning and during trial.[16] The 2008 Counter-Terrorism Act introduced the concept of post-charge questioning, and extended the application of drawing adverse inferences from silence, to this stage of questioning.[17] However, if interviews take place when access to counsel has been delayed at the behest of the police, no inferences may be drawn from a suspect's silence.[18] The 2011 Review recommended that post-charge questioning should be introduced as an "additional investigative tool" and the impact of this measure on pre-charge detention should be "kept under review."[19]

After forty-eight hours, a senior police officer must apply to a judicial authority for a warrant to extend the detention for a period no longer than seven days from the date of arrest.[20] The grounds for extending the detention are either to obtain relevant evidence by questioning the suspect, or to obtain relevant evidence by other means, or to preserve relevant evidence.[21]

The suspect must be given a notice, specifying the grounds upon which further detention is sought.[22] The suspect or his attorney has the right to contest each application to extend the detention in court, but in certain circumstances a suspect and his lawyer may be excluded from the hearing.[23] The warrant will only be issued if the judicial authority is satisfied that there are reasonable grounds for believing that the further detention is necessary and that the investigation relating to the detention is being conducted diligently and expeditiously.[24] After seven days in custody, an application can be made to a court for an extension of detention for up to a further seven days.[25] It is unclear from the statute if the suspect is entitled to contest that application.

Duration of detention

From 2006 until the end of 2011, the length of detention increased to twenty-eight days.[26] Only six people were held for the maximum period of twenty-eight days,[27]and no one was held for longer than fourteen days after 2007.[28] Since January 2012, the maximum permissible period of detention has been fourteen days.[29] In 2014, forty-four out of sixty-five persons arrested under terror legislation were dealt with within seven days.[30]

Two Bills have been published which provide for the possibility of extending the maximum period to twenty-eight days temporarily in an emergency,[31] but debate continues as to whether the power to extend the detention period in exceptional circumstances should be enshrined in primary legislation, or be an "order-making power conferred on the Home Secretary, with safeguards."[32]

Legal challenges to detention without charge

The detention regime has been modified several times in response to a number of human rights challenges both in domestic courts and the ECHR, some of which are described below:

Equal treatment of British citizens and aliens

The United Kingdom's attempt to lock up "suspected international (i.e. alien) terrorists" indefinitely pending deportation was struck down in

December 2004 by the House of Lords who ruled that indefinite detention was incompatible with Article 5 of the European Convention.[33] A former home secretary, Charles Clarke, said that the governing legislation relating to detention without charge was being applied in a "disproportionate and discriminatory manner" against non-British citizens, whereas the government seemed to be "able to deal with the British-born without such draconian measures."[34] At the time these aliens were originally detained in 2001, British citizens could be held for up to seven days without charge.[35] Thus, all persons on British soil, suspected of terrorist involvement, irrespective of immigration status, are now treated in the same way.

Excluding suspects from all or part of detention challenge hearings

In *Ward v Police Services of Northern Ireland*[36] the suspect and his lawyer had been excluded[37] for about ten minutes from the court hearing dealing with extending the period of detention, whilst the prosecution explained to the judicial authority what topics they wanted to cover in further interviews with the suspect in a "closed evidence" process. The Appellate Committee noted that "[t]he interview must be conducted fairly. But advance notice of the topics to be covered is not a pre-requisite of fairness. The judicial authority may want to know what the topics are in order to be satisfied that the warrant or an extension of it should be granted."[38]As to the rationale of excluding the suspect from the hearing, the Court opined that closed hearings were in the "best interest" of the detainee, as they "enabled the judicial authority rigorously and conscientiously to explore the basis of the application for their detention."[39] The judiciary thus seems to be assuming a role of protecting the suspect.

Informing detainees of reason for detention

In *Sher v The Chief Constable of Greater Manchester Police*[40] the claimants were arrested without a warrant on suspicion on terrorism[41] and detained without charge for thirteen days. They challenged the legality of every aspect of their treatment, but the essential complaint was that they were "never told the basis on which they were being detained in sufficient detail in order to allow them properly to challenge their continued detention without charge, and that the legislation under which they were detained was incompatible with the European Convention."[42] Both British domestic law and European law require that an arrested man is to be told what is the act for which he has been arrested.[43] Here each claimant was told that they were being arrested because each was reasonably suspected of being a terrorist, and the court considered that nothing more was required at the time of arrest, noting that "a general statement of that sort will not usually amount to a breach of Article 5.2, *provided of course* that thereafter, further information as to how and why such suspicions are held is promptly given to the suspect."[44] As far as the compatibility claims were concerned, the claimant complained that in contrast to control order cases, where special advocates can make representations about closed evidence (see below), here decisions about further detention were made entirely on the basis of "closed evidence." The court rejected this claim, by following the precedent of *Ward v. Police Service of Northern Ireland* discussed above. Neither of the points raised in this case have been appealed.

Extraterritorial application of the European Convention to the United Kingdom in military detentions

Al-Jedda v. United Kingdom[45] concerned an Iraqi-born British national. He was arrested in Iraq by United States forces in October 2004, and then transferred into the custody of British forces, and was detained in a British detention facility for over three years on the basis that his internment was "necessary for imperative reasons of security in Iraq."[46] The detention was periodically reviewed, but no procedures were in place for disclosure of evidence, nor for an oral hearing. The detainee was permitted to submit written representations to the review committee. He challenged the lawfulness of his detention before the British courts. After his claims were rejected at each domestic court level, culminating in rejection by the House of Lords in December 2007,[47] he brought a claim to the ECHR, alleging a breach of Article 5(1) of the European Convention. The main issues in this case were jurisdiction, and whether the detention violated Article 5.

The Grand Chamber held that the applicant was within the authority and control of the United Kingdom throughout his detention, and therefore within the jurisdiction of the United Kingdom. Thus the European Convention was applicable to his case.[48] The Grand Chamber noted that "the list of grounds of permissible detention in Art. 5(1) does not include internment or preventive detention where there is no intention to bring criminal charges within a reasonable time."[49] In this case the United Kingdom government did not contend that the detention was justified under the list of grounds, nor did they purport to derogate under article 15.[50] The Grand Chamber concluded that there was no legal basis to displace Article 5, and therefore the applicant's detention constituted a violation of Article 5(1).[51]

In *Serdar Mohamed* (SM)[52] one of the issues related to the legality of 110 days detention of the Afghan appellant by British forces in Afghanistan in 2010. The British forces were part of the International Security Assistance Force (ISAF) in Afghanistan. ISAF detention policy permitted detention for only ninety-six hours before detainees were to be handed to the Afghan authorities.[53]

SM was arrested on April 7, 2010. His detention was reviewed every seventy-two hours between April 8 and May 10. The further detention was authorized in accordance with British detention policy for interrogation purposes,[54] and between May 6 and July 25, the British held him under "logistical detention" as the Afghan authorities had no space in in their facilities. Whilst in detention he had no access to a lawyer and did not receive family visits.[55]

The Court confirmed that the British forces were responsible for SM's detention in Afghanistan,[56] and that Article 5 European Convention applied to the detention.[57] The Court ruled that there was no authority to detain SM beyond the first ninety-six hours.[58] Thus the subsequent detention was unlawful and arbitrary.[59] Further, the Court ruled that SM had not been afforded certain "minimum procedural safeguards."[60]

Compatibility with Article 5 European Convention

In *Duffy*[61] a court in Northern Ireland rejected a challenge that Schedule 8 of the Terrorism Act 2000 (which dealt with extending detention after the first forty-eight hours has elapsed) was incompatible with Article 5 European Convention. The court confirmed that during the review process there was a continuing need to demonstrate reasonable suspicion: "Issues of proportionality and justification are … fundamental aspects of the review process."[62] The applicants complained that Article 5 required that a person be charged well before the expiration of the detention period, but the court found no authority to support that proposition.[63] An application to appeal this ruling was refused.[64]

Control orders

"Protecting the public"

Control orders were "neither punitive nor retributive."[65] The true purpose of the regime "was quite simply to protect members of the public from a risk of terrorism by preventing or restricting the controlled person's involvement in terrorism-related activity."[66] A control order was an order that could be made against an individual imposing obligations (such as curfews[67]) connected with preventing or restricting involvement by that individual in terrorism-related activity.[68] As one British judge described them:

> [a]t one extreme they are not far short of house arrest, which is plainly a form of detention or imprisonment. But they can be designed in such a way that their cumulative effect does not deprive the controlled person of his right to liberty within the meaning of article 5(1).[69]

The test for imposing a control order was derived from *Secretary of State for the Home Department v. MB:*

> Whether it is necessary to impose any particular obligation on an individual in order to protect the public from the risk of terrorism involves

> the customary test of proportionality. The object of the obligations is to control the activities of the individual so as to reduce the risk that he will take part in any terrorism-related activity.[70]

This measure was controversial from its inception because it could be used without a person being charged or convicted, orders were made based on "closed" or classified evidence that was not shown to the controlee (although controlees were entitled to be apprised of the essence of the case against them), and because some of the restrictions were extremely intrusive.[71]

The Prevention of Terrorism Act envisaged two distinct species of control order – derogating and non-derogating. The former contained obligations incompatible with the right to liberty under Article 5 of the European Convention on Human Rights.[72] The latter could impose conditions that fell short of actual deprivation of liberty under Article 5. No control orders derogating from Article 5 were ever made – only non-derogating control orders have been made.[73] Since March 2005 fifty-two people have been on control orders,[74] of which twenty-four were British subjects and twenty-eight were foreign nationals.[75] At the time control orders were abolished in December 2011, nine persons, all British citizens, were on control orders.[76] The longest period anyone was subject to a control order was in excess of fifty-five months,[77] and of the fifty-two control orders, only fifteen were in place for over two years.[78]

Non-derogating control orders could only be made against a person reasonably suspected of involvement in terrorist-related activity,[79] whether a British national or not, and whether the terrorist activity was domestic or international. The control order had to be considered necessary for purposes connected with protecting the public from a risk of terrorism.[80] In respect of a derogating control order a court had to be satisfied that there was evidence "capable of being relied on by the court as establishing that the individual is or has been involved in terrorism-related activity."[81] Thus a higher standard was required when liberty was to be deprived. Control orders could be made with court permission, or in certain urgent cases without prior permission, provided such order was promptly referred to a court to justify its validity.[82]

Procedure

When the matter came before a court, either for prior permission or review after the event, the special advocate system established by the Special Immigration Appeals Commission (SIAC) in 1997[83] was used, and still applies to the replacement regime. Special advocates are court appointed lawyers who have been security cleared. They are entitled to see material that for reasons of national security cannot be made public. Neither the detainee nor his lawyer are entitled to see this material, nor may the special advocate discuss the documents under consideration with, or show them to, the defendant's regular lawyers. "The special advocate acts in the 'best interests of an [appellant]. He does not act for the [appellant] and the [appellant] is not his client. He owes the [appellant] no duty of care in relation to the role he undertakes."[84]

Although the use of special advocates may at first sight seem a significant impediment to protecting civil liberties, in practice special advocates strive to gain an acceptable open summary of the closed materials. Once the closed materials have been revealed to them, special advocates dedicate a great amount of time in fighting for disclosure.[85] Nevertheless, the special advocate system has drawn much criticism, particularly in relation to the fact that special advocates are not permitted to communicate the contents of closed materials to their clients. This concern is one of several subjects discussed in a parliamentary Green Paper (a consultation paper produced by the government).[86]

The foreign secretary has justified the use of closed materials as being "surely fairer to ensure that sensitive material can be considered in court under these arrangements, than that it is excluded altogether."[87] In their response to the Green Paper, the special advocates expressed their concerns and described the shortcomings of the closed material procedures (CMPs).[88] They query why, in its survey of international approaches to the problem of sensitive information, the Green Paper did not discuss the way the United States gives security-cleared counsel access to certain materials and trusts them not to reveal sensitive information to their clients.[89] Judges too, have concerns about the procedures.[90]

Control orders were replaced by new measures on December 14, 2011 as described below. The closed materials procedures have been retained. The Independent Reviewer reports that none of the former controlees has been successfully prosecuted for a terrorism offense, because they are persons "in respect of whom the police will almost certainly already have confirmed that there is no evidence available that could realistically be used for the purposes of a prosecution."[91] Furthermore, "persons will normally choose not to commit terrorist offences while subject to restrictions which give the authorities a good opportunity to observe any such offences being committed."[92] However, the Independent Reviewer comments that the chief value of the replacement regime will "continue to lie in the 'prevention' rather than the 'investigation' of terrorism."[93]

Legal challenges to control orders

The main issues in litigation concerned the provision of fair hearings, and related to the problem that control orders were frequently made on the basis of evidence that could not be disclosed to the controlee because of national security concerns, a subject that is still currently relevant.

Deprivation of liberty

In *Secretary of State for the Home Department v. JJ* the House of Lords adjudicated on whether control orders violated article 5(1) by amounting to a deprivation of liberty.[94] The Court took notice of the ECHR principles set out in a number of cases, including *Guzzardi v. Italy*[95] where:

> the court has insisted that account should be taken of a whole range of factors such as the nature, duration, effects and manner of execution or implementation of the penalty or measure in question (… Guzzardi, ¶¶ 92, 94). There may be no deprivation of liberty if a single feature of an individual's situation is taken on its own but the combination of measures considered together may have that result (Guzzardi, ¶95).[96]

In this case the Court held that a curfew between the hours of 4 p.m. and 10 a.m. (eighteen hours) amounted to a deprivation of liberty.[97] Since this case, no periods of curfew exceeded sixteen hours.[98]

Informing detainees of the nature of the case against them

In 2007 in *Secretary of State for the Home Department v. MB (FC)* the House of Lords considered whether the making of a control order based on entirely undisclosed material, without any specific allegation of terrorism-related material in open material, violated Article 6 of the European Convention that guarantees a right to a fair trial.[99] The court held that control orders could be quashed if the court determines that the detainee has not had a fair trial. Baroness Hale advocated the creation of open material:

> Both judge and special advocates will have stringently to test the material which remains closed. All must be alive to the possibility that material could be redacted or gisted in such a way as to enable the special advocates to seek the client's instructions on it.[100]

The issue of how much information should be given to a controlee was considered by the ECHR in *A and Others v. United Kingdom* in February 2009.[101] In finding some violations of Article 6, the court ruled that it was essential that as much information about the allegations and evidence against each applicant was disclosed without compromising national security or the safety of others. If full disclosure was not possible, the difficulties caused by this should be counterbalanced to enable the applicant to challenge the allegations effectively. The Court endorsed the special advocate system, holding that SIAC was best placed to ensure that no material was unnecessarily withheld from the controlee, who must be given sufficient information to enable him to give effective instructions to the special advocate, although the amount would have to be decided on a case by case basis.[102]

In June 2009, in *AF (FC)* the House of Lords acknowledged the requirement to give a controlee sufficient information to enable him to give effective instructions to his lawyer in judicial review proceedings, or in any court hearings. Lord Phillips stated:

> Provided that this requirement is satisfied there can be a fair trial notwithstanding that the controlee is not provided with the detail or sources of the evidence forming the basis of the allegations. Where, however, the open material consists purely of general assertions and the case against the controlee is based solely or to a decisive degree on closed materials the requirements of a fair trial will not be satisfied, however cogent the case based on the closed materials may be.[103]

He continued, "The Grand Chamber [of the ECHR] has now made it clear that the non-disclosure cannot go so far as to deny a party knowledge of the essence of the case against him…"[104] but he also confirmed that it may be acceptable not to disclose the source of evidence.[105]

The effect of these decisions is that provided the above requirements were met, control orders were not invalid or in violation of the European Convention. Since the House of Lords' decision in June 2009,[106] three control orders were revoked because the courts decided that the controlees did not know the essence of the case against them.[107] In addition, the High Court ruled that bail applications for terror suspects "should be treated the same as control order cases, under which terror suspects must be given an 'irreducible minimum' of information about the case against them before being held under that regime."[108]

Terrorism prevention and investigation measures

In the wake of all the criticism described above, a revised form of control order regime was introduced by legislation in 2012.[109] The new regime is meant to be "more flexible and focused" with less stringent conditions than found in control orders,[110] but critics say it is "little more than 'control orders lite.'"[111]

TPIMs are designed to relate more closely to current civil law restrictions.[112] The aim of the measures is to have a "protective effect, whether through disruption or through facilitating investigation. The police will then be under a strengthened legal duty to ensure that the person's conduct is kept under continual review with a view to bringing a prosecution."[113]

Grounds

TPIMs are imposed by notice by the home secretary who must *inter alia* be satisfied on the balance of probabilities[114] that the individual is or has been involved in terrorism-related activity and be satisfied that it is necessary to apply any of a wide range of measures from the regime to protect the public from a risk of terrorism.[115] TPIMs may not exceed two years' duration,[116] but during the currency of a notice the home secretary must keep under review whether it is necessary to continue the measures.[117] The home secretary must consult with police about whether there is evidence available to prosecute the suspect,[118] and permission from the High Court must be sought before the measures may be imposed.[119]

Procedure

After permission is given, and the suspect is served with the notice detailing the measures, the High Court conducts a review hearing as soon as is reasonably practicable.[120] There is a right of appeal against any decision to vary or extend the notice, or any refusal to vary or discharge the notice.[121] In addition to judicial scrutiny, the home secretary must issue a quarterly report,[122] and the Independent Reviewer is required to report annually.[123] The TPIM powers are for a period of five years.[124]

If secret evidence is required, the special advocate system will be used,[125] but the Act is silent on when it is required to give the gist of allegations to the controlee. The Independent Reviewer has queried whether the obligation to give the suspect the gist of the case against him will apply to TPIMs.[126]

Reports

The first annual report by the Independent Reviewer on the operation of TPIMs in 2012 was published in March 2013.[127] Ten men were subject to TPIMs in 2012, of which nine were British citizens who had previously been subject to control orders and the tenth was a foreign national.[128] All were suspected of Islamist terrorism.[129] One absconded on December 26, 2012.[130] The Independent Reviewer commented that the allegations against some of the men were "at the highest end of seriousness, even by the standards of international terrorism,"[131] but none of the ten could be prosecuted because open court evidence sufficient to secure a conviction could not be introduced in an open criminal court.[132] Nine men were subject to TPIMs in 2013,[133] one of whom absconded in November 2013.[134] Partly because of the difficulties experienced by security services to prevent absconding, the power to relocate TPIM subjects was reintroduced in 2015.[135]

No TPIM notices have been in force since February 10, 2014.[136] The Independent Reviewer concluded that so far, TPIMs have been effective in preventing terrorist related activity, but not in enabling terrorist-related activity to be detected.[137]

Sixty-four applications were made to vary measures in TPIM notices, of which forty-five applications were refused.[138] One TPIM subject claimed that the imposition of certain restrictive measures affected his mental health to the extent that they constituted inhuman and degrading treatment and violated Article 3 European Convention. In June 2015 the High Court varied certain communication measures and quashed monitoring measures because their effect on the mental health of this particular subject amounted to a violation of Article 3.[139]

In assessing the fairness of TPIM notices, whilst the Independent Reviewer acknowledged that no closed material procedure can be wholly fair, he noted that the TPIM regime had been largely shaped by the experiences of legislators, officials, and judges in constructing a CMP for control orders that was "ECHR-compliant and aspire[d] to the highest standards of procedural fairness required in civil cases."[140]

The Independent Reviewer concluded that the power to impose TPIMs was appropriately used in the period under review, whilst emphasizing the importance of ensuring that the measures are proportionate.[141] A few potential TPIM cases were not put before the Home Office for permission to impose measures because it was believed that the necessary disclosure from sensitive human or technical intelligence sources would be harmful to national security.[142]

In sum, the Independent Reviewer concluded that TPIMs provided "a high degree of protection against untriable and undeportable persons who are judged on substantial grounds to be dangerous terrorists, while acknowledging that it is unacceptable to place persons who have not been charged with, or convicted of, a crime under indefinite constraint,"[143] but that it is necessary to give some constructive thought to exit strategies for use when TPIMs expire.[144]

In response to concerns that there might be exceptional circumstances requiring measures that are more stringent than TPIMs, the government published the Enhanced Terrorism Prevention and Investigation Measures Bill[145] in September 2011.[146] This Bill would apply a wider range of measures[147] and enhanced notices would only be issued in accordance with procedures in the Bill, if the home secretary reasonably considers it necessary to impose the stricter measures.[148] Thus this Bill imposes a more onerous threshold for the government to cross in order to issue enhanced measures.[149] In sum, this legislation would reintroduce the stricter restrictions characteristic of control orders, while granting the enhanced safeguards of TPIMs,[150] and is held ready for further parliamentary debate if the need arises.

Conclusions

The United Kingdom's detention framework has been described as being pre-trial,[151] investigative,[152] and pre-charge.[153] Although the model appears to be designed to detain suspects until sufficient evidence is obtained for the purpose of prosecution, the Home Office statistics on arrests can be interpreted another way. In 2014, 289 people were arrested on terrorist related charges; 38 percent of those arrested were charged, out of which 86 percent were terrorism related charges.[154] The pattern was similar in previous years.[155]

Thus, despite the label of pre-charge detention, which is an accurate description, the statistics can also be read to suggest that this type of detention may frequently be used preventively. This is corroborated by the 2011 Review of Counter-Terrorism, which states: "[t]o preempt a terrorist incident the police may need to arrest at an earlier point than would normally be the case"[156] and "[t]errorist suspects often need to be held in detention during the post-arrest phase of the investigation because of the public safety risk which they may represent."[157]

Thus the United Kingdom has a dual-purpose model. It permits detention for the purposes of investigation to facilitate decisions about whether or not to charge and prosecute. As a by-product, the model also permits preventive detention of terrorist suspects without charge for up to fourteen days.

The United Kingdom wields a delicate balance between security and liberty. In the face of significant actual threats and attacks, it understandably pushes the security side of the scale as far as it can. When prompted by the courts, the United Kingdom has pulled back and responded to findings of human rights violations by promptly changing its laws. For example, discriminating between British citizens and foreigners in terms of the length of detention periods[158] resulted in the repeal of the Anti-Terrorism, Crime and Security Act 2001 and the coming into force of the Prevention of Terrorism Act 2005. When the length of curfews under control orders reached eighteen hours and the ECHR considered that period amounted to a deprivation of liberty,[159] the government pulled back and reduced the curfew limit to sixteen hours. The government also listened to complaints about control orders and replaced them with TPIMs.

The ECHR has repeatedly "found internment and preventive detention without charge to be incompatible with the fundamental right to liberty under Article 5§1, in the absence of a valid derogation under Article 15."[160] Yet at the time of writing there are no cases pending in the United Kingdom domestic courts or the ECHR challenging the duration of detention in the pre-charge detention regime of up to twenty-eight days that existed between 2006 and January 2011, nor in respect of the current fourteen-day limit.

Almost every element of contemporary English detention law has been challenged on the grounds of violation of human rights in domestic courts as well as in the ECHR. The difficulties encountered in applying the detention laws and policies caused the government to do some serious and responsible rethinking and recrafting of the British counter-terrorism strategy. This experience provides important lessons for the drafters of global core detention principles.

Notes

1 *See*, *e.g.*, Lumba v Secretary of State for the Home Department (SSHD) [2011] UKSC 12 (March 23, 2011).

2 *See e.g.*, Mahajna v SSHD [2011] EWHC 2481 (Admin.) (September 30, 2011). Also, immigration detention in the UK is of indefinite duration. This has been adversely commented on and the subject of recommendations by a number of countries in the Working Group commenting on the UK's Periodic Report to the United Nations Human Rights Council, U.N.G.A. Draft report of the Working Group on the Universal Periodic Review, United Kingdom of Great Britain and Northern Ireland, Unedited Version, Human Rights Council Working Group on the Universal Periodic Review, ¶¶110.110–110.114, A/HRC/WG.6/13/L.7 (May 29, 2012).

3 Terrorism Act, 2000, c.11, §40, terrorism means the "use or threat of action" involving, *inter alia*, serious violence against a person, endangering a person's life, creating a serious risk to the health or safety of the public or a section of the public. Terrorist offenses include §§ 11 to 13 (offenses relating to proscribed organizations), §§15 to 19, 21A and 21D (offenses relating to terrorist property), §§38B and 39 (disclosure of and failure to disclose information about terrorism), § 54 (weapons training), §§56 to 58A (directing terrorism, possessing things, and collecting information for the purposes of terrorism) §§59 to 61 (inciting terrorism outside the United Kingdom), ¶14 of Sch. 5 (order for explanation of material: false or misleading statements), ¶1 of Sch. 6 (failure to provide customer information in connection with a terrorist investigation), ¶18 of Schedule 7 (offenses in connection with port and border controls). The definition of "terrorism acts" has been further extended in Anti-Terrorism, Crime and Security Act, 2001, c.24, §113 (1)(c); Terrorism Act, 2006, c.11, §34 and Counter-Terrorism Act, 2008, c.28, §27.

4 Terrorism Act 2000, § 41, and Sch. 8. Note also that Schedule 7 of this Act gives an examining officer (police, immigration, or customs) the right at the UK border to detain for up to nine hours a person for the purpose of determining whether he appears to be a person who is or has been concerned in the commission, preparation or instigation of acts of terrorism. There does not even have to be reasonable suspicion that the person has been so concerned. The detainee is required to give the examining officer any information and documents that he is requested to give. An example of this law in operation is the case of the detention at a London airport of David Miranda, partner of a Guardian newspaper journalist who covered the story of the US whistleblower Edward Snowden. *See e.g.* Nicholas Watt, *Theresa May rejects claim Miranda was detained with no legal basis*, THE GUARDIAN (August 21, 2013), www.theguardian.com/politics/2013/aug/21/theresa-may-david-miranda-legal-basis. In R. v. Gul [2013] UKSC 64, ¶64, the Court commented on the power to stop and detain at ports, and stated that this power "is not subject to any controls" and that this type of detention "represents the possibility of serious invasions of personal liberty."

5 Independent review of anti-terrorism legislation has existed in the UK since the 1970s. In the Prevention of Terrorism Act 2005, c.2, review by the Independent Reviewer was placed on a statutory basis.

6 DAVID ANDERSON Q.C., REPORT OF THE INDEPENDENT REVIEWER ON THE OPERATION OF THE TERRORISM ACT 2000 AND PART 1 OF THE TERRORISM ACT 2006, THE TERRORISM ACTS IN 2011, ¶7.2 (June 2012), https://terrorismlegislationreviewer.independent.gov.uk/wp-content/uploads/2013/04/report-terrorism-acts-2011.pdf.

7 O'Hara v. United Kingdom, Appl. No. 37555/97 Eur. Ct. H. R. (January 16, 2002), ¶¶35, 36.
8 Terrorism Act 2000, 17 (U.K.).
9 *See e.g.* CLIVE WALKER, TERRORISM AND THE LAW, 153, ¶4, 43–4 (Oxford University Press, 2011).
10 Terrorism Act 2000, Sch. 8, §24.
11 *Id.*, Sch. 8, §26.
12 *Id.*, Sch. 8, §23
13 *Id.*, Sch. 8, §6.
14 *Id.*, Sch. 8, §§§7, 8, 9; Police and Criminal Evidence Act 1984 Code H, Revised Code of Practice in connection with the detention, treatment, and questioning by police officers of persons in police detention under section 41 of, and Schedule 8 to, the Terrorism Act 2000, the treatment and questioning by police officers of detained persons in respect of whom an authorization to question after charge has been given under section 22 of the Counter-Terrorism Act 2008, §6.9 and Annex B (October 2013).
15 *Id.*
16 Criminal Justice and Public Order Act 1994, c.33, §§34, 35.
17 Counter-Terrorism Act 2008, §22.
18 Police and Criminal Evidence Act 1984 Code H, §§ 6.7, 10.9 and Annex C.
19 H.M. GOVERNMENT, REVIEW OF COUNTER-TERRORISM AND SECURITY POWERS, REVIEW FINDINGS AND RECOMMENDATIONS, CM 8004 January 2011 [PREVENT REVIEW] 5, ¶30(iii).
20 Terrorism Act 2000, Sch. 8 Pt. III, §29.
21 *Id.*, §32(1)(A).
22 *Id.*, §31.
23 *Id.*, §33.
24 *Id.*, §32.
25 *Id.*, §36.
26 Terrorism Act 2006, §§ 23(7), 25, amending Terrorism Act 2000, Sch. 8 §36(3). After the first seven days, an extension of the warrant from a judicial authority had to be sought for up to a further fourteen days, and thereafter extensions could be sought for further periods not exceeding an additional seven days. Note that non-terrorist suspects may be detained for up to an initial period of forty-eight hours, and this can be extended up to ninety-six hours – Police and Criminal Evidence Act 1984, §44, c.60 (U.K.).
27 HOME OFFICE, OPERATION OF POLICE POWERS UNDER THE TERRORISM ACT 2000 AND SUBSEQUENT LEGISLATION: ARRESTS, OUTCOMES AND STOPS AND SEARCHES, GREAT BRITAIN 2010/11, www.gov.uk/government/uploads/system/uploads/attachment_data/file/116740/hosb1511.pdf.
28 PREVENT REVIEW, 7.
29 Protection of Freedoms Act 2012, c.9, §57.
30 HOME OFFICE, OPERATION OF POLICE POWERS UNDER THE TERRORISM ACT 2000 AND SUBSEQUENT LEGISLATION: ARRESTS, OUTCOMES AND STOPS AND SEARCHES, GREAT BRITAIN, QUARTERLY UPDATE TO 31 DECEMBER 2014 (June 25, 2015) [HOME OFFICE, OPERATION OF POLICE POWERS 2014], ¶3.2.
31 Draft Detention of Terrorist Suspects (Temporary Extension) Bills, Cm 8018 (February 2011).

32 Parliamentary Business, Legislative Scrutiny: Protection of Freedoms Bill – Human Rights Joint Committee, 6. Pre-charge detention of terrorist suspects, ¶¶126–8 (October 7, 2011), www.publications.parliament.uk/pa/jt201012/jtselect/jtrights/195/19509.htm#n103.

33 A (F.C.) and Others (F.C.) v. SSHD [2004] UKHL 56.

34 Steve Hewitt, The British War On Terror, 45 (Continuum 2008), (quoting Charles Clarke, Parliamentary Introduction of the Prevention of Terrorism Bill 2005, Home Office, February 22, 2005, http://press.homeoffice.gov.uk/Speeches/0205-st-prevention-terrorism).

35 Terrorism Act, 2000, Sch. 8 ¶29.

36 Ward v. Police Service of Northern Ireland [2007] UKHL 50 (Northern Ireland).

37 Exclusion is permitted by Terrorism Act 2000, Sch. 8 ¶33. In Ward v. Police Service of Northern Ireland, ¶ 23, the Appellate Committee referred to the grounds for withholding information, as set out in Terrorism Act 2000 Sch. 8 ¶34, "which include such risks to the public interest as interfering with or harming evidence, making more difficult the apprehension, prosecution or conviction of a person suspected of terrorism and making prevention of the prevention of an act of terrorism more difficult as a result of a person being alerted."

38 Ward, ¶22.

39 *Id.*, ¶121.

40 Sher and Ors. v. The Chief Constable of Greater Manchester Police and Ors. [2010] EWHC 1859 (Admin.).

41 Terrorism Act, 2000, §41.

42 Sher, ¶2.

43 *Id.*, ¶¶86, 88 (citing Christie v. Leachinsky [1947] AC 573, 593 (U.K.)); Article 5.2 European Convention; Fox, Campbell and Hartley v. United Kingdom, ECHR [1991] 13 EHRR157.

44 Sher, ¶91.

45 Al-Jedda v. United Kingdom, Appl. No. 27021/08 (2011), ECHR (Jul. 7, 2011).

46 *Id.*, ¶10.

47 R. (on the application of Al-Jedda) v. Secretary of State for Defence (SSD) [2007] UKHL 58.

48 Al-Jedda, ¶¶85, 86.

49 *Id.*, ¶100.

50 *Id.*

51 *Id.*, ¶110. Also, on the same day, the Grand Chamber delivered judgment in Al-Skeini v. United Kingdom, Appl. No. 55721/07, ECHR (2011) 53 EHRR 18. That case related to the refusal of the British government to conduct an independent investigation into the death of five Iraqi citizens killed by British troops in Iraq. The judgment confirmed the extraterritoriality application of the ECHR to acts of British troops in Iraq. The exercise of authority and control by British troops of individuals killed in security operations established a jurisdictional link between the deceased and the UK for the purposes of Article 12, ECHR, *see* ¶149.

52 Serdar Mohamed and Ors. v. SSD [2015] EWCA Civ. 843.

53 *Id.*, ¶39–42.

54 *Id.*, ¶51.
55 *Id.*, ¶43.
56 *Id.*, ¶72.
57 *Id.*, ¶105.
58 *Id.*, ¶136.
59 *Id.*, ¶9(iv).
60 *Id.*, ¶¶297–8.
61 In the matter of an application for judicial review by Colin Duffy and others (No. 2) [2011] NIQB 16.
62 *Id.*, ¶30.
63 *Id.*, ¶36.
64 UKSC Permission to Appeal Results (November 2011), www.supremecourt.gov.uk/docs/PTA-1111.pdf.
65 SSHD (Respondent) v. MB (FC) (Appellant) [2007] UKHL 46, ¶24.
66 David Anderson Q.C., Final Report Of The Independent Reviewer Pursuant To Section 14(3) Of The Prevention Of Terrorism Act 2005, Control Orders In 2011, ¶2.2 (March 2012) [Anderson, Control Orders Final Report]. The report sets out all the shortcomings of the control order regime.
67 Lord Carlile Of Berriew Q.C., Sixth Report Of The Independent Reviewer Pursuant To Section 14(3) Of The Prevention Of Terrorism Act 2005, ¶19 February 3, 2011 ("There are currently up to 25 types of measures in use … In 2010 the average duration of a curfew was 11.9 hours per day.") [Carlile, Sixth Report].
68 Prevention of Terrorism Act, 2005, sets out the control order regime. *See* §1(4) for examples of obligations that could be imposed.
69 SSHD v. AF (FC), ¶77 (citing SSHD v. MB, ¶11).
70 SSHD v. MB [2006] EWCA Civ 1140, ¶63.
71 Prevent Review, ¶7.
72 This is because the obligations do not fall within the exceptions set out in the Article, and such a control order will only be lawful if the United Kingdom derogates from the European Convention.
73 Prevent Review, 41. *Also see* Carlile, Sixth Report, ¶13. This comment on derogation should not be confused with the Derogation Order made on November 11, 2001 when a public emergency was deemed to exist in the UK, apparently justifying the making of extended detention orders of foreign nationals under the 2001 anti-terrorism legislation. Although the determination of a state of emergency, justifying derogation, was upheld in A (F.C.) and Others (F.C.) v. SSHD, the court concluded that the detention regime of indefinite duration did not rationally address the threat to security and was a disproportionate response to that threat. Discussed in ¶20 and upheld in ¶190, A and Others v. The United Kingdom, Application no. 3455/05, ECHR (February 19, 2009).
74 Anderson, Control Orders Final Report, ¶3.13.
75 *Id.*, ¶3.14.
76 *Id.*
77 *Id.*, ¶3.47.
78 *Id.*, ¶3.48.
79 Prevention of Terrorism Act 2005, §2.

80 Carlile, Sixth Report, ¶9.
81 Prevention of Terrorism Act 2005, §4.
82 *Id.*, §3.
83 Special Immigration Appeals Commission Act 1997, c.68, §6.
84 Special Advocates: A Guide To The Role Of Special Advocates And The Special Advocates Support Office (Special Advocates Support Office, November 2006).
85 Daphne Barak-Erez and Matthew C. Waxman, *Secret Evidence – The Due Process of Terrorist Detentions*, 48 Colum. J. Transnat'l L. 3 (2009).
86 Justice And Security Green Paper, H.M. Government, CM 8194, 25–28 (October 2011), *available at* www.official-documents.gov.uk/document/cm81/8194/8194.pdf.
87 William Hague, Foreign Secretary, Speech at Foreign and Commonwealth Office, London: Securing our Future (November 16, 2011), *available at* www.fco.gov.uk/en/news/latest-news/?view=Speech&id=692973282.
88 Justice And Security Green Paper, H.M. Government, Response To Consultation From Special Advocates, ¶15 (December 16, 2011), http://consultation.cabinetoffice.gov.uk/justiceandsecurity/wp-content/uploads/2012/09_Special%20Advocates.pdf.
89 *Id.*, ¶29(i).
90 *See e.g.* Al Rawi v. The Security Service [2011] UKSC 34, Lord Kerr, ¶93, 94.
91 Anderson, Control Orders Final Report, ¶3.51.
92 *Id.*
93 *Id.*, ¶3.52.
94 SSHD v. JJ [2007] UKHL 45.
95 Guzzardi v. Italy, ECHR, 3 EHRR 333 (1980).
96 SSHD v. JJ, ¶16.
97 *Id.*, ¶¶21, 23, 24.
98 Anderson, Control Orders Final Report, ¶2.29.
99 Secretary of State for the Home Department v. MB (FC).
100 *Id*, ¶66.
101 A. v. The United Kingdom.
102 *Id.*, ¶¶218, 219, 220.
103 SSHD v. AF (FC), ¶59.
104 *Id.*, ¶65.
105 *Id.*, ¶66.
106 *Id.*
107 Carlile, Sixth Report, ¶15.
108 *See e.g.* R (Cart) v. Upper Tribunal, R (U) and (XC) v. Special Immigration Appeals Commission [2009] EWHC 3052 (Admin.); R. (on the application of BB) v. Special Immigration Appeals Committee and the SSHD [2011] EWHC 336 (Admin.) (U.K.).
109 Terrorism Prevention Measures and Investigation Act 2011, c.23.
110 *Id.*, Sch. 1.
111 *Teresa May: Control Orders to be replaced*, BBC News (January 26, 2011, 11:38 a.m.) www.bbc.co.uk/news/uk-12287074; Dominic Casciani, *U.K. counter-terror review explained*, BBC News (January 26, 10:09 a.m.) www.bbc.co.uk/news/uk-12289294.
112 Prevent Review, ¶23.

113 *Id.*, ¶ 26.
114 Terrorism Prevention and Investigation Measures Act, §3(1) as amended by §20(1) Counter-Terrorism and Security Act 2015, c.8. The evidential standard was increased from "reasonable grounds." Both of these are a lower standard than that required for control orders.
115 Terrorism Prevention and Investigation Measures Act, §§2, 3, Sch.1. The geographical condition was strengthened by §16 Counter-Terrorism and Security Act 2015, c.8.
116 *Id.*, §5.
117 *Id.*, §11.
118 *Id.*, §10.
119 *Id.*, §§6–9.
120 *Id.*
121 *Id.*, §16.
122 *Id.*, §19.
123 Prevention of Terrorism Act, 2005, §13.
124 Terrorism Prevention and Investigation Measures Act, §21.
125 *Id.* Sch.4.
126 Anderson, Control Orders Final Report, ¶5.36.
127 *Id.*
128 *Id.*, ¶4.7.
129 *Id.*, ¶4.8.
130 Rosa Silverman, *Terror suspect absconds while being monitored*, The Telegraph (Dec. 31. 2012), www.telegraph.co.uk/news/uknews/terrorism-in-the-uk/9773502/Terror-suspect-absconds-while-being-monitored.html.
131 David Anderson Q.C., First Report Of The Independent Reviewer On The Operation Of The Terrorism Prevention And Investigation Measures Act 2011, ¶5 (March 2013) [Anderson, TPIMS First Report].
132 *Id.*, 5, ¶¶7.8–23. Even if intercept evidence was admissible in UK courts, that would not have enabled a criminal prosecution to be brought in any of the cases. The main problem relates to concerns about compromising informants.
133 *Q & A: TPIMs explained*, BBC News (November 4, 2013), www.bbc.co.uk/news/uk-24803069.
134 Hayley Dixon and Tom Whitehead, *Counter-terrorism police hunt missing suspect disguised in a burka*, The Telegraph (November 4, 2013), www.telegraph.co.uk/news/uknews/terrorism-in-the-uk/10424152/Counter-terrorism-police-hunt-missing-suspect-disguised-in-burka.html; David Anderson Q.C., Second Report Of The Independent Reviewer On The Operation Of The Terrorism Prevention And Investigation Measures Act 2011, 1.15 (March 2014) [Anderson, TPIMS Second Report].
135 David Anderson Q.C., Third Report Of The Independent Reviewer On The Operation Of The Terrorism Prevention And Investigation Measures Act 2011, 3.8 (March 2015) [Anderson, TPIMS Third Report]; Counter-Terrorism and Security Act 2015, §16.
136 Anderson, TPIMS Second Report, ¶3.5; Anderson, TPIMS Third Report ¶1.10.
137 *Id.*, ¶11.5, 11.7, 11.10.
138 Anderson, TPIMS First Report, ¶4.4.

139 DD v. Secretary of State for the Home Department [2015] EWHC 1681 (Admin.), ¶¶78, 85.

140 *Id.*, ¶11.19–21. In the case of seven of the ten TPIM subjects, open judgments were handed down in 2012 confirming that the imposition of TPIMs was fair and reasonable. *See* SSHD v. BM [2012] EWHC 714 (Admin.); SSHD v. BF [2012] EWHC 1718 (Admin.); SSHD v. AM [2012] EWHC 1854 (Admin.); SSHD v. AY [2012] EWHC 2054 (Admin.); SSHD v. CC & CF [2012] EWHC 2837 (Admin.); SSHD v. CD [2012] EWHC 3026 (Admin.).

141 Anderson, TPIMS First Report, ¶11.28.

142 *Id.*, ¶11.27.

143 *Id.*, ¶11.56.

144 *Id.*, ¶11.34, 11.39–46.

145 Enhanced Terrorism Prevention and Investigation Measures Bill, CM 8166 (September 2011).

146 Anderson, Control Orders Final Report, ¶¶5.30-5.35. Enhanced T-Pims are only designed to be used "in the event of a very serious terrorist threat that cannot be managed by other means."

147 Enhanced Terrorism Prevention and Investigation Measures Bill, Sch. 1.

148 *Id.*, §2(4).

149 Anderson, Control Orders Final Report, ¶5.34.

150 Anderson, TPIMS First Report, ¶3.8.

151 *See e.g.* Stella Burch Elias, *Rethinking "Preventive Detention" From a Comparative Perspective: Three Frameworks For Detaining Terrorist Suspects;* 41 Colum. Hum. Rts. L. Rev. 99, 131 (2009).

152 *See e.g.* Dan. E. Stigall, Counterterrorism And The Comparative Law Of Investigative Detention, 116 (Cambria Press, 2009).

153 *See e.g.* Stephanie Cooper Blum, Preventive Detention In The War On Terror, 133 (Cambria Press, 2008); Claire Macken, Counter-Terrorism And The Detention Of Suspected Terrorists, 140 (Routledge, 2011).

154 Home Office, Operation Of Police Powers 2014, ¶3.3.

155 Of 222 people arrested on terrorist related charges in 2013, 51 percent were charged, of which only 48 percent were terrorist-related charges, *see* Home Office, Operation Of Police Powers Under The Terrorism Act 2000 And Subsequent Legislation: Arrests, Outcomes And Stops And Searches, Great Britain 2013, Quarterly Update To December 31, 2013 ¶1.1 (June 5, 2014). Of 246 people arrested in connection with terrorism in 2012, 41 percent were charged, of which 62 percen were terrorist related, *see* Home Office, Operation Of Police Powers, Operation Of Police Powers Under The Terrorism Act 2000 And Subsequent Legislation: Arrests, Outcomes And Stops And Searches, Great Britain 2012, Quarterly Update To December 31, 2012, ¶2.4, (June 13, 2013).

156 Prevent Review, ¶5.

157 *Id.*, ¶6.

158 A (F.C.) and Others (F.C.) v. SSHD.

159 SSHD v. JJ.

160 A. v. United Kingdom. For a discussion of derogation under Article 15, *see* Chapter 3 *infra; also see* Al-Jedda, ¶¶85, 86.

6 Three countries with strong foundations in British Law

This chapter examines the preventive detention laws of Australia, Canada, and India, all of which are modeled on various versions of British detention laws, and identifies several procedural problems.

Australia

Preventive detention

Preventive detention was introduced in 2005 in response to the London bombings.[1] Under federal law, an Australian Federal Police (AFP) officer may apply for a preventive detention order to be made to "prevent an imminent terrorist act occurring" or to preserve evidence from a recent terrorist act.[2] Although the stated aim of law enforcement is to act preventively in the early stages, this law can only be used when the planning is in its final stages.[3]

Grounds

In the case of preventing a terrorist act, the initial issuing authority (a senior AFP officer) must have reasonable grounds for suspicion and various criteria have to be met.[4] Some of the standards in those criteria, such as the "reasonable grounds" for suspicion and "reasonably necessary" requirement, are vague and difficult to contest.[5] Furthermore, the statute also permits the detention of someone in order to collect evidence of a recent terrorist attack,[6] yet there need not be any connection between the detainee and any terrorist activity.[7]

Procedure

An initial preventive detention order may not exceed twenty-four hours.[8] The period of detention under the initial order can be extended on the grounds of reasonable necessity[9] during that twenty-four period, but detention may not exceed twenty-four hours in total.[10] A continued detention order may be applied for. A magistrate or judge appointed by the appropriate minister may authorize detention for another twenty-four hours. Thus federal preventive detention may not exceed forty-eight hours from the time detention began pursuant to the initial detention order.[11]

At the end of that period, under federal law the detainee must either be charged or released, but the states have enacted "complementary legislation" that permits the period of detention to be extended to up to fourteen days.[12] An Australian crown prosecutor, Ben Power, has analyzed the state detention laws and concluded that although the legislation varies to some extent, every state authorizes detention without charge to prevent an "anticipated act of terrorism" for up to fourteen days.[13] Each state and territory has broadly similar legislation governing the issue of preventive detention orders, with provisions relating to details that must be given to detainees, access to a lawyer, but rights of challenge are more extensive than those in the federal legislation, as discussed immediately below.[14]

The police must explain the substance of the order to the detainee, and inform the detainee of his or her rights whilst detained.[15] The detainee must be given a summary of the grounds for detention,[16] but if information is deemed likely to prejudice national security, it need not be included.[17] The detainee must be given a copy of the order as soon as reasonably practicable.[18] This means that detainees may not see the application, or the underlying evidence and supporting materials.[19]

Rights to challenge the detention order are limited. Detainees must be told that they have a right to make representations to a senior AFP officer to have the detention order revoked[20] but the statute does not explain the mechanism for this. The law is unclear as to whether the detainee may be represented by a lawyer for this purpose. Additionally, limited rights to apply for *habeas corpus* exist under federal law, but only in the event of errors of law.[21] Appeals may be made to the Administrative Appeal Tribunal, but only after the detention order has expired.[22] Thus no meaningful right of challenge exists. Slightly more process is available to persons detained by the states.[23] For example, in both the Australian Capital Territory (ACT) and New South Wales (NSW), detainees can apply to a court to have a detention order revoked or set aside, and in Victoria, a detainee must seek leave of the court to apply for revocation.[24]

Access to lawyers

The detainee will have access to a lawyer, but only to discuss the rights of a person who is the subject of an order.[25] The police are entitled to monitor contact and communication between detainees and lawyers.[26] The detainee also has the right to notify specified persons that he or she is safe, but may not inform them that he or she is being detained.[27] Indeed, it is a criminal offense for either the detainee or his lawyer to disclose the existence of a preventive detention order, punishable with up to five years imprisonment.[28] In some circumstances the police may apply for a prohibited contact order.[29]

During the forty-eight hour period the detainee may not be questioned by the police except to verify identity and check on well-being.[30] However, after release from preventive detention, a suspect could be transferred to criminal custody and be questioned about alleged criminal offenses[31] or be placed in investigative detention by the Australian Security Intelligence Organization (ASIO), as described in the next section.

Preventive detention has never been imposed under federal law,[32] and only one state, Victoria, has used preventive detention, on one occasion in April 2015.[33] No special laws have been enacted to use detention in the immigration context as a means of preventing suspect terrorists from acting, because Australia's immigration laws are generally quite harsh, and until 2008 permitted mandatory indefinite detention of unlawful noncitizens.[34]

Investigative detention

Grounds and duration

Under the general criminal law a person suspected of a terrorist offense (which covers a wide range of activity, as mentioned above) may be arrested and detained for questioning without charge for up to four hours.[35] This period can be extended by warrant of a magistrate for up to a total of twenty-four hours.[36] However, the period of twenty-four hours does not include "dead time" such as sleeping, meal breaks, and contacting a lawyer.[37] The case of Mohamed Haneef, who was detained for twelve days without charge pursuant to the Crimes Act,[38] prompted a change in the law to prevent prolonged detention. Since December 2010, "dead time" may not exceed seven days.[39] In practice this means that pre-charge detention can last for up to eight days.

The Australian Security Intelligence Organization Act 1979 as amended (ASIO Act) permits the ASIO to seek a questioning and detention warrant from the issuing authority (a magistrate or judge) in relation to a terrorism offense.[40] However, between 2003 and the end of 2012, no questioning and detention warrants were issued.[41]

Procedure

The director general of the ASIO must first obtain approval from the relevant minister that all necessary criteria have been satisfied.[42] Application may then be made to an issuing authority, who must be satisfied that all the relevant criteria have been met.[43] The standard is that of "reasonable grounds." A key feature is that it is a measure of last resort to collect intelligence. A person may be detained and questioned for up to 168 hours[44] (seven days). The person being questioned must supply the information, and documents requested by the ASIO, and it is a criminal offense not to comply, punishable by imprisonment.[45] It is also an offense to make a statement that is materially misleading or false.[46]

Questioning and detention warrants have many of the same problems as prevention detention orders. The warrant must be explained to the detainee, but without any requirement to explain the grounds for detention.[47] No meaningful process of challenging the warrants exists, and the only recourse is to complain about the warrant and/or treatment, in appropriate circumstances.[48] Contact with family is forbidden except if authorized in the warrant,[49] and communications and contact with lawyers may be restricted and monitored.[50] The lawyer must be given a copy of the warrant.[51]

Control orders

Australian control orders are based on the British model, but there are a number of differences. In the United Kingdom, the now abolished control orders could only have been made against a person reasonably suspected of involvement in terrorist-related activity.[52]

Grounds

In Australia control orders may be issued if a court is satisfied on a balance of probabilities either that the order would substantially assist in preventing a terrorist act, or if the subject of the order has provided training to, or received training from, a listed terrorist organization, has engaged in hostile activity in a foreign country, or has provided support for or otherwise facilitated the engagement in a hostile activity in a foreign country.[53] In the case of the first limb, the Act is silent about whether a terrorist act must be imminent, and nor does the Act require mention of any specific terrorist activity.[54] As to a person who has received training, Kent Roach has criticized this status based approach, and queries whether is this a sufficiently reliable indicator that he or she is likely to commit a terrorist act so as to warrant the placing of restrictions on liberty.[55] The list of restrictions that might be imposed more or less mirror those found in British control orders, together with an additional condition that a person must receive specified counseling or education.[56]

Procedure

The attorney general's consent is needed before a senior AFP member can apply to a court for an interim control order.[57] Various details must be supplied in support of an application, but the summary of the grounds need not include any information prejudicial to national security.[58] Once a court has made an order for an interim control order, that order must be served on the subject within seventy-two hours, giving the person at least forty-eight hours notice to attend court for the confirmation of the control order.[59] Amongst other matters, the interim order must include a list of the restrictions as well as a summary of the grounds for making the order, but as before, those grounds need not include any information prejudicial to national security.[60] In its response to the United Nations Working Group on Arbitrary Detention, the Australian Human Rights Commission highlights the problem that no right exists for a suspect to appear before a court before the order is made.[61]

The Act does not deal with the type of evidence that might, or might not, be admissible in the confirmation hearing. The subject of the order may make representations to the court, either in person or through a representative.[62] Although there has been heavy criticism of the British requirements that the gist of the case must be given to the subject of the control order, and that special advocates will represent them, none of these civil liberty "safeguards" are present in the Australian model.

Confirmed control orders may last for no more than twelve months from the date of the interim order,[63] but the number of successive control orders that may be made in respect of the same person is not capped.[64] Unlike in the case of British control orders, the Australian authorities have no responsibility to review the viability of criminal prosecution; in Australia the AFP commissioner must apply to revoke a control order when the grounds upon which the order was issued cease to exist.[65]

Very few control orders have been made: two in 2007, in respect of Jack Thomas and David Hicks,[66] and two in December 2014.[67] The Independent National Security Legislation Monitor has recommended that preventive detention orders and control orders be abolished because they are "not effective, not appropriate and not necessary."[68]

Legal challenges

Domestic

Two control orders had been challenged as at 2011. The first case concerned an interim control order that was imposed on Jack Thomas after an appeal court reversed his conviction for receiving support from al-Qaeda.[69] The magistrate granted the control order on the basis of involuntary evidence that had been ruled inadmissible by the appeal court and should not have been used to support the applicant's conviction.[70] On appeal, the High Court held that the interim control order was constitutional. A majority held that the control order legislation was supported by the defense and external affairs powers in the Constitution.[71] A majority also held that courts are able to impose orders restraining liberty on the basis of a future risk.[72] Thomas also argued that the court did not have the constitutional power to issue a control order because it was an exercise of a non-judicial function. A majority of the court rejected this argument.[73] Thomas's control order had an extended duration of twelve months while he challenged its constitutional validity. It was not renewed after it expired.[74]

The second challenge was brought by David Hicks at the end of a short prison sentence served in Australia after his release from Guantánamo

Bay.[75] He was made the subject of a control order on the basis that the order would substantially assist in preventing a terrorist act, and because he had received training from al-Qaeda. His control order was confirmed in February 2008,[76] and expired in December 2008.[77] Kent Roach observes that the focus on status – the fact that a person has had terrorist training – means that control orders can still be imposed, even if intelligence authorities conclude those persons no longer present a security risk.[78] The Australian control order is thus quite different from its United Kingdom relation.

International

Australia has clashed on several occasions with the United Nations Human Rights Committee (HRC) about its immigration detention policy. Although the cases described below cases do not relate to preventive detention *per se*, the HRC's analysis of Article 9 in the Australian cases is relevant to the implementation of Australia's preventive detention in the counter-terrorism context.

A. v Australia concerned a Cambodian national who arrived in Australia by boat, seeking refugee status. He was held in detention for over four years, pursuant to Australia's mandatory immigration detention law.[79] The HRC interpreted 'arbitrary' in Article 9 to mean that detention should not be inappropriate or unjust, and that it must be necessary and proportionate.[80] Although the HRC did not consider that the mandatory detention law was arbitrary *per se*,[81] they stated that there was no justification for indefinite and prolonged detention, and that every detention should be periodically reviewed.[82] Furthermore, they found a violation of Article 9(4) because the detainee had no right to challenge his detention.[83]

The HRC has elaborated on the interpretation of arbitrary in three further Australian cases of immigration detention. In *C. v Australia* detention was required to be "reasonable, proportionate and necessary."[84] In *Danyal Shafiq v Australia* the test to ascertain arbitrary detention was to inquire whether the detention is "reasonable, proportionate and justifiable in all the circumstances."[85] In *D and E v Australia* the HRC emphasized the need for a state to "demonstrate that other, less intrusive measures could not have achieved the same end" as continued detention.[86]

Australia has come under HRC attack because of the lack of due process available to challenge detention.[87] Two states, ACT[88] and Victoria,[89] have enacted human rights legislation that contain language echoing Article 9(4) ICCPR, but the Australian Human Rights Commission considers the application of the rights to be of limited effect.[90] Although the states require their public authorities to act consistently with the human rights legislation, if there are inconsistencies between the states' human rights legislation and other state legislation, a declaration of inconsistent interpretation may be issued, but this will not affect the validity of the state law.[91]

In August 2013 the HRC adjudicated on two cases involving immigration detention[92] of fifty-two people who have been held "for nearly five years without trial, on secret evidence, with no prospect of release."[93]The majority of the detainees have been deemed security risks.[94]

Conclusions

Three reasons may explain the little use of the preventive detention and control order powers. First, Australia has not faced many terror threats comparatively speaking. Second, unlike the United Kingdom, Australia has had a number of very wide-ranging preparatory offenses under which terror suspects could be prosecuted since 2002. Third, again unlike in the United Kingdom, Australian law permits the use of intercept evidence in the prosecution of terror suspects.

Generally, Australia's attitude to its responsibilities under the International Covenant on Civil and Political Rights (ICCPR), including those related to detention, is problematic. The Democratic Audit of Australia, under the auspices of the Australian National University, noted in 2006 that the HRC had given forty-four decisions concerning Australia, and had found against it in twelve cases.[95]

This problem is not helped by the fact that Australia's Constitution does not contain a bill of rights. Detention is mentioned in the Constitution in a very limited way, in Chapter V, which deals with the states.[96] One scholar comments that without a federal bill of rights, the judiciary is virtually powerless to invalidate these laws that deprive suspects of any meaningful judicial review.[97] Another notes that generally there is no mechanism through which courts can analyze whether the violation of human rights is necessary or proportionate.[98] So the only "check" comes from political debate and the goodwill of political leaders.[99]

The detention legislation has produced a raft of significant problems, which include the following. Detainees are unable to have private conversations with lawyers as contact may be monitored. Preventive detention may be ordered without the subject knowing why, and without any meaningful method of judicial challenge. Questioning and detention warrants are coercive because failure to answer questions is a crime in itself. Little, or no, meaningful method exists to challenge judicially preventive detention, or investigative detention by the ASIO. Control orders may be imposed without the subject knowing why, and there is no mechanism comparable to the British special advocates, whereby a lawyer appointed to look after the detainee's interests may have access to evidence and make representations to the court, albeit without being able to communicate the gist of the evidence to the detainee.

Canada

Preventive detention

Grounds

Very limited circumstances exist under general criminal law to arrest without a warrant and detain a suspect for up to twenty-four hours. A peace officer may arrest a person if he or she has reasonable grounds to believe that the suspect has committed, or is about to commit an indictable offense.[100] The Supreme Court of Canada "graft[ed] on an objective test to this subjective belief by the peace officer."[101]

The Anti-terrorism Act 2001 introduced preventive detention without charge for up to seventy-two hours.[102] Detainees had the right under the Canadian Charter to be told the reason for their arrest and be given prompt access to a lawyer.[103] At the end of detention a judge could order the suspect to enter into a peace bond for up to a year. Refusal to enter into a peace bond carried a sentence of one-year imprisonment and breach of a peace bond was punished by two years imprisonment.[104] No preventive arrests were made since the provision was enacted, and the preventive detention provisions were allowed to expire in 2007,[105] but were revived in May 2013.[106] Since then two teenagers were detained without charge in April 2015 to avert the commission of a terrorist offense.[107]

Procedure

A peace officer may arrest a person without a warrant and detain him or her if that officer "suspects on reasonable grounds that the detention of the person in custody is necessary in order to prevent a terrorist activity."[108] The detainee must be brought before a judge within twenty-four hours, and the period of detention can be extended for an additional forty-eight hours.[109]

It is beyond the scope of this book to discuss the detention of persons detained by Canadian forces in Afghanistan, or Canadian citizens outside Canada, such as Maher Arar, Abdullah Almalki, Ahmad Abou-Elmaati, Muayyed Nureddin (all detained and tortured in Syria), and Omar Khadr detained in Guantánamo Bay, all of which has been extensively analyzed elsewhere.[110]

Immigration detention

Grounds

After 9/11, as in the U.K, United States, and Australia, Canada used and continues to use immigration law as a method of anti-terrorism preventive detention. It enacted the Immigration and Refugee Protection Act in 2001.[111] Immigration and public safety officials can declare in a security certificate that a permanent resident or a foreign national may not be admitted into Canada on security grounds,[112] which include engaging in terrorism,[113] being a danger to the security of Canada,[114] or being a member of an organization that there are reasonable grounds to believe engages, has engaged, or will engage in terrorism.[115]

The liability rules are broader than the terrorism offenses introduced into the Criminal Code by the Anti-terrorism Act, and membership in a terrorist organization can be proven on standards that are less onerous than the normal criminal law standard of beyond a reasonable doubt.[116]

Procedure

The immigration and public safety ministers can issue a warrant for the arrest and detention of a person named in a security certificate if they have reasonable grounds to believe that the person is a danger to national security or to the safety of any person, or is unlikely to appear at a proceeding or for removal.[117] Once a person is detained he must appear before a federal judge for a review of the detention after forty-eight hours, and then every six months until deportation.[118] As the Supreme Court prohibited the deportation of persons to countries where there is a "substantial risk of torture,"[119] detention may be extremely lengthy. In a later case, the Court, "by its silence," held that Section 12 of the Charter, which prohibits cruel and unusual punishment, was not violated by over five years' administrative detention without charge.[120]

Special advocates

Security certificates are subject to judicial review by specially designated judges to determine reasonableness in federal court. Special advocates will be appointed by the court to represent detainees in cases where evidence may not be disclosed to the detainee or his regular counsel, on the grounds of national security or possible danger to the safety of any person.[121] Similarities to, and differences from, the British use of special advocates in control order cases are apparent. Despite issues with regard to the use of secret evidence, which is discussed below, a higher level of disclosure to the detainee is required than in the United Kingdom.[122] Another significant difference is that the special advocate is entitled to see all of the government's evidence against the detainee. A judge must give directions as to the extent of any contact between the special advocate and detainee, because evidence may not be disclosed to the detainee after the special advocate has seen it.[123]

Peace bonds

Another cousin of the British control order is available to limit the freedom of potentially dangerous persons, including suspected terrorists. A provincial court judge can impose a recognizance with conditions, otherwise known as peace bonds, if he is satisfied that there are reasonable grounds to fear that a person may commit a terrorism offense.[124] The suspect will be present in court for the recognizance hearing,[125] but the Code is silent as to the type of evidence that is acceptable, and the extent to which the suspect can challenge it.

A judge may impose a number of conditions regulating conduct for twelve months,[126] but the period can be extended to two years if the suspect has been convicted previously of certain offenses.[127] A judge may order twelve months imprisonment if the suspect refuses to enter into the recognizance.[128] The punishment for breaching any of the conditions is up to two years imprisonment.[129] Appeal is limited to the right of the suspect to apply to a court to vary the conditions.[130]

Legal challenges

Domestic

The seminal case of *Charkaoui v Canada*[131] in 2007 was the trigger for several important changes to the law. The case concerned the detention pursuant to security certificates of Adil Charkaoui, a permanent resident, and two foreign nationals, Hassan Almrei and Mohamed Harkat, both of whose rights to remain in Canada had not been confirmed. All had been detained for some years but Charkaoui and Harkat had been released on conditions.

First, the Supreme Court ruled that the way secret evidence was used at the time violated the right to a fair hearing[132] pursuant to Article 7 of the Charter of Rights and Freedoms (Charter),[133] because Article 7 requires that in order to deprive a person of liberty, a fair process is essential.[134] That process has to involve a hearing, and the right to know, and answer the case against one.[135] However, that right is not absolute, particularly when there are national security concerns.[136] This ruling led to the introduction of special advocates, as described above.

Second, the Court considered whether the detention of foreign nationals without warrant violated the guarantee against arbitrary detention in Article 9 of the Charter. It decided that as a security certificate had been signed on national security grounds, the detention was not arbitrary.[137] At the time this case was litigated there was a difference in the way permanent residents and foreign nationals were treated as regards the review process. The former had to be brought before a judge within forty-eight hours of detention, but the latter could not seek a review for 120 days. The

Supreme Court held that the treatment of foreign nationals violated Article 9.[138] That ruling resulted in a change in the law ensuring that both permanent residents and foreign nationals are entitled to a review after forty-eight hours.[139]

The Court concluded that the principles in the Charter of fundamental justice and the guarantee of freedom from cruel and unusual treatment were not violated by long periods of immigration detention or onerous conditions of release, provided that meaningful opportunities are given to the detainee to challenge continued detention,[140] and onerous or restrictive release conditions.[141] Chief Justice McLachlin observed: "[t]he longer the period, the less likely that an individual will remain a threat to security."[142]

The Court declared that the immigration legislation did not authorize indefinite detention, and provided a meaningful review process.[143] In rejecting the applicant's claim that the legislation discriminated between citizens and non-citizens, the Court distinguished the United Kingdom case of *A. v Secretary of State*[144] on the basis that the United Kingdom legislation at the time did provide for indefinite detention.[145] The fact that the Court concluded that equality rights were not violated, precluded it from considering whether there were more proportionate means to address the terrorist threat – this was a central issue in *A*.[146]

Another case with human rights connotations is that of Abdullah Khadr, a Canadian citizen. The United States suspected that Khadr was supplying weapons to al-Qaeda forces in Pakistan and Afghanistan, and paid $500,000 to the Pakistani Intelligence Agency ISI to abduct him in Pakistan in 2004. He was held in secret detention for about fourteen months, interrogated by American and Pakistani authorities tortured, denied consular access for several months, and not permitted to challenge his detention in a court. When he was finally repatriated to Canada, the United States sought to have him extradited on terrorist charges.[147]

At the initial extradition committal hearing, although Justice Speyer did not accept that Khadr had been subjected to prolonged torture, he found that "the sum of the human rights violations suffered by Khadr is both shocking and unjustifiable."[148] He ordered Khadr released after he had spent a period of four and a half years in pre-extradition custody. In the Appeal Court, Justice Sharpe dismissed the appeal by the United States, saying "[t]here is no appeal against the extradition judge's finding that the human rights violations were shocking and unjustifiable. Because of the requesting state's misconduct, proceeding with the extradition committal hearing threatened the court's integrity."[149] The Court did not believe that denying the appeal would permit a suspected terrorist to walk free, because Khadr was liable to prosecution in Canada,[150] and commented that "[the rule of law must prevail even in the face of the dreadful threat of terrorism."[151]

In November 2011, the Supreme Court of Canada refused to hear an appeal by the United States.[152]

International

In *Ahani v Canada*[153] an Iranian citizen submitted a communication to the HRC in January 2002, alleging *inter alia* that article 9 of the ICCPR had been violated by his arbitrary detention in Canada for five years since 1993 without access to bail, detention review, and *habeas corpus*. He had been declared inadmissible to Canada on the grounds that there were reasonable grounds to believe that he would engage in terrorism, that he was a member of an organization that had engaged in terrorism, and that he had engaged in terrorism. He was deported to Iran in June 2002.

The Committee decided that the claim was admissible in respect of the first five years of detention, up to 1998, but thereafter the claim was inadmissible because of failure to exhaust domestic remedies in Canada.[154] The Committee observed that "an individual must have appropriate access, in terms of article 9, paragraph 4, to judicial review of the detention, that is to say, review of the substantive justification of detention, as well as sufficiently frequent review."[155] A majority of the Committee found a violation of article 9(4) because of the number of years between the commencement of detention and the date of the decision ruling whether the issue of the certificate was reasonable.[156]

Yet the majority also considered that the ineligibility of a foreign national to apply for release from detention for 120 days was not a violation of article 9, on the basis that such a period of detention in this case "was sufficiently proximate to a decision of the Federal Court."[157] This seems surprisingly deferential to the Canadian law of the time, but perhaps that ruling turned on specific facts. In any event, it was not until the decision of the Canadian Supreme Court in *Charkaoui*[158] that a change was triggered in Canadian law.

Conclusions

Security certificates have failed as a counter-terrorism policy.[159] After thirty-eight decisions in the federal court and two in the Supreme Court,[160] Charkaoui's security certificate was withdrawn in 2009.[161] After fourteen court judgments, Almrei's security certificate was quashed in 2009.[162] As at 2011, three security certificates remained, but each detainee had been released on a form of control order.[163]

The result of challenges to the security certificate regime has therefore been that it has "morphed into a *de facto* and controversial control order regime."[164] In any event, apart from problems about duration, and use of secret evidence, the usefulness of security certificates is limited. They do not address the Canada's problem of home-grown terror suspects[165] because security certificates may not be issued in relation to Canadian citizens.

As far as peace bonds are concerned, it is easy to break the onerous conditions. Moreover, "a peace bond with a hair trigger" could result in a state using prosecution and punishment for trivial violations of the peace bond in order to achieve tough preventive detention measures to counter terrorism.[166]

India

Preventive detention

Preventive detention without trial is another progeny of British colonial law and dates from 1784.[167] A line of colonial legislation followed[168] to combat the political terrorism in India that began at the start of the twentieth century.[169] The pre-independence detention legislation culminated in the Defence of India Act 1939,[170] which was modeled on British war-time emergency measures.[171] That act authorized detention if the government was satisfied that it was necessary to prevent persons acting in any manner that would prejudice the defense and safety of the country.[172]

Constitution

After independence, the new government was faced with an immediate dilemma – it wanted to "ensure the maximum liberty" for the individual, but at the same time it wanted to "nip in the bud every threat to national security from within."[173] The Constitution has a very short statement dealing with protection of life and liberty,[174] and after a series of stormy and acrimonious debates in the Constituent Assembly,[175] provisions relating to preventive detention were inserted into the Constitution.[176]

The Constitution gives with one hand and takes away with the other. Article 22(1) guarantees that a detainee is informed of the grounds for arrest and is given access to a lawyer. Article 22(2) requires that a detainee be brought before a court within twenty-four hours of arrest to have the detention confirmed. However, these guarantees do not apply to "enemy aliens" or persons "arrested under any law providing for preventive detention."[177] Detention can be for periods in excess of three months in certain circumstances as prescribed by Parliament.[178]

A series of detention laws

With the exception of two brief periods, Indian law has provided for preventive detention since independence.[179] The general criminal law, as set out in the Code of Criminal Procedure, allows an police officer "knowing of a design to commit a cognizable offense" to arrest without a warrant "if it appears that the offense cannot otherwise be prevented."[180] The suspect may only be detained for twenty-four hours, "unless his further detention is required or authorized under any other provisions of this Code or of any other law for the time being in force."[181] One state (Maharashtra) has amended the Code to permit detention under this section to continue for up to thirty days.[182] Once arrested, the accused must be told full particulars of the offense or the grounds for the arrest.[183] Normally the accused has to be brought before a magistrates' court within twenty-four hours.[184] If an investigation cannot be completed within twenty-four hours, a magistrate can remand a suspect in custody for an initial period of up to fifteen days, and thereafter for up to a period of ninety days in cases that might merit imprisonment for ten years or more.[185]

National security legislation has generally worked in tandem with the provisions of the Code of Criminal Procedure but extended the periods of detention under general criminal law. On the heels of the ratification of the Constitution, the Preventive Detention Act 1950[186] (PDA) was passed. This statute lapsed in 1969, and in 1971 the Maintenance of Internal Security Act[187] was passed, and it expired in 1978. This was followed by the National Security Act 1980 (NSA),[188] which generated a "rich, dizzyingly complex body of case law interpreting nearly every phrase of the act."[189] That Act permitted preventive detention for up to twelve months of an individual to prevent him from "acting in any manner 'prejudicial to' various state objective including national security and public order."[190] The courts permitted a very wide interpretation of "acts prejudicial to the maintenance of public order,"[191] bearing in mind that the scope of judicial review was hard to define precisely in preventive detention cases.[192] The law guarantees limited procedural rights that "arguably, fall well short of established international human rights standards."[193]

The NSA remains in force and has been supplemented by additional laws designed as counter-terrorism measures. More contemporary legislation includes the Terrorist and Disruptive Activities Prevention Act 1985 (TADA),[194] which was enacted specifically to counter the separatist movement in the Punjab and adjoining states.[195] It prescribed exceptions to the Indian Penal Code whereby prolonged detention was facilitated. Arrests were permitted without warrant and the periods of police and judicial custody in pre-trial remand were extended to a period of up to one year.[196] TADA's "sweeping powers" were mainly used as a "tool that enabled pervasive use of preventive detention and a variety of abuses by the police, including extortion and torture."[197] A government statistic in 1993 showed that a mere 0.81 percent of 52,268 persons detained under TADA were convicted.[198]

Equally, if not more controversial legislation followed: the Prevention of Terrorism Act 2002 (POTA).[199] Although neither TADA nor POTA were preventive detention laws *per se*, they appear to have existed in "a parallel legal system in aid of the Criminal Justice System."[200] POTA broadened the definition of terrorism to include membership, support and financial assistance, thus broadening the scope of the law generally.[201] The definition was broadened still further by the enactment of the Unlawful Activities (Prevention) Amendment Act of 2012, which added as a terrorist offense the causing of "damage to the monetary stability of India by way of production or smuggling or circulation of high quality counterfeit Indian paper currency, coin or of any other material."[202]

It also contained two very repressive measures relating to detention, which were inconsistent with the provisions of the ICCPR.[203] The period of pre-trial investigation without possibility of bail was reduced from one year to 180 days. However, this had the effect of extending the period of time permitted for the prosecutor to file a charge sheet to 180 days.[204] Also, although POTA required police to inform the accused persons of their right to counsel and meet counsel during the course of an investigation, legal counsel was not entitled to remain present throughout the period of interrogation.[205]

In addition, the substantive bail standard was nearly impossible for an accused person to meet. If the prosecutor opposed bail, the court could only release the accused if there were "reasonable grounds to believe that the accused is not guilty of the alleged offense and not likely to commit any offense while on bail."[206] The effect of this was to permit the prosecutor, rather than the court to determine whether bail would be granted. If the prosecutor opposed bail before filing the charge sheet, it would have been almost impossible for the accused to prove innocence, not only without a trial, but also without knowing the allegations or the grounds on which bail was opposed.[207] POTA was repealed in 2004. It had functioned more as a pure preventive detention law than as a general criminal law, and did not heed either the limited constitutional protections or the more exacting standards of international law.[208]

After POTA was repealed, an earlier statute, the Unlawful Activities (Prevention) Act 1967[209] was amended to become the Unlawful Activities (Prevention) Act 2004 (UAPA).[210] This legislation did not deal with preventive detention, which continued under NSA. After the Mumbai shootings in 2008, UAPA was amended again[211] and introduced a number of sections dealing with preventive detention. Any officer "knowing of a design" to commit an offense under the Act, or "having reason to believe" that a person has committed an offense under the Act, has the power to authorize the arrest of such a person.[212] Like POTA, bail can be denied for up to 180 days for investigation purposes.[213]

Legal challenges[214]

NSA

In *A.K. Roy v. India*[215] the constitutionality of the NSA was challenged. The Supreme Court held that preventive detention was not unconstitutional[216] but the power to detain preventively should be construed narrowly.[217]

TADA

In *Katar Singh v. State of Punjab*[218] the Supreme Court ruled that TADA was constitutional as regards the detention provision. It emphasized the necessity to strike a balance between liberty and security,[219] but acknowledged ways in which the law might be misused.[220]

POTA

In *People's Union for Civil Liberties v. Union of India*[221] the Supreme Court ruled that POTA was constitutional as regards the detention provisions.[222]

International

When India acceded to the ICCPR in 1979, it issued a declaration concerning the application of Article 9 ICCPR to the Constitution of India. In its view, Article 9 ICCPR had to be applied within the parameters of Article 22 of the Constitution of India.[223] Thus non-citizens of India and those arrested pursuant to Indian preventive detention laws are not entitled to the protections of Article 22 of the Constitution of India or Article 9 ICCPR.

India's most recent periodic report pursuant to Article 40 ICCPR was filed in 1996.[224] The report relating to Article 9 discussed TADA,[225] which had expired by the time the report was filed. The Indian government argued that the Supreme Court had ruled that the detention provisions in TADA were constitutional,[226] and declared that the period of pre-trial detention had been reduced from one year to 180 days.[227] In August 1997, the HRC published its concluding observations and invited India to review and withdraw certain of its reservations and declarations, including those relating to Article 9.[228] It also expressed concern at the continuing widespread use of preventive detention and pointed out that India's declaration in respect of the ICCPR did not exclude the requirement to inform an arrested person promptly of the reason for their arrest.[229]

Human Rights Watch has published a number of reports relating to India. Their 2008 report *inter alia* criticized the vague and overbroad definitions of terrorism,[230] the unlawful restrictions on freedom of association,[231] and condemned the provisions in UAPA[232] relating to arbitrary detention.[233] They echoed the words of the HRC in 1997 that pre-trial detention for up to 180 days was a violation of Article 9 ICCPR.

Human Rights Watch's 2011 special report on arbitrary detention and torture in India describes the numerous continuing violations of due process rights relating to detention, including failure to bring suspects before a court within twenty-four hours of arrest, delayed access to counsel, and excessive periods of detention.[234] The United States Department of State country report for India in 2011 also describes a number of human rights abuses, including those relating to detention.[235]

Conclusions

Indian detention laws are incompatible with Article 9 of the ICCPR. India's Constitution permits preventive detention and purports to afford safeguards, which are apparently meaningless as they do not apply to persons "arrested under any law providing for preventive detention."[236] Despite India's many protestations that its preventive detention provisions are constitutional, the periods of detention are excessive, with many violations of due process rights. Little prospect of any improvement in the near future is expected.

Notes

1 *7 July Bombings*, BBC NEWS, http://news.bbc.co.uk/2/shared/spl/hi/uk/05/london_blasts/what_happened/html/.

2 Criminal Code Act (Cth.) 1995, §105.1.

3 Katherine Nesbitt, *Preventative Detention of Terrorist Suspects in Australia and the United States: A Comparative Constitutional Analysis*, 17 PUB. INT. L. J. 39, 77 (2007).

4 Criminal Code Act (Cth.) 1995, §105.4, "(4) A person meets the requirements of this subsection if the person is satisfied that:

(a) there are reasonable grounds to suspect that the subject:
  (i) will engage in a terrorist act; or
  (ii) possesses a thing that is connected with the preparation for, or the engagement of a person in, a terrorist act; or
  (iii) has done an act in preparation for, or planning, a terrorist act; and
(b) making the order would substantially assist in preventing a terrorist act occurring; and (c) detaining the subject for the period for which the person is to be detained under the order is reasonably necessary for the purpose referred to in paragraph (b).
(5) A terrorist act referred to in subsection (4):
  (a) must be one that is imminent; and
  (b) must be one that is expected to occur, in any event, at some time in the next 14 days."

5 Nesbitt, *Preventative Detention*, 77.

6 Criminal Code Act (Cth.) 1995, §105.4.

7 Nesbitt, *Preventative Detention*, 77.

8 Criminal Code Act (Cth.) 1995, §105.8 (5).

9 *Id.*, §105.10 (3).

10 *Id.*, §105.10 (5).

11 *Id.*, §§105.12 (3) and (5).

12 KENT ROACH, THE 9/11 EFFECT: COMPARATIVE COUNTER-TERRORISM, 339 (Cambridge University Press, 2011); CRAIG FORCESE, INSTITUTE FOR RESEARCH ON PUBLIC POLICY, CATCH AND RELEASE: A ROLE FOR PREVENTIVE DETENTION IN CANADIAN ANTI-TERRORISM LAW, 10, Study No. 7 (Montreal, July 2010).

13 BEN POWER, PREVENTIVE DETENTION OF TERRORIST SUSPECTS. A REVIEW OF THE LAW IN AUSTRALIA, CANADA AND THE UNITED KINGDOM, (Paper prepared for the 21st International Conference of the International Society for the Reform of Criminal Law, Vancouver, Canada, June 22–26, 2007).

14 *See* for New South Wales, Part 2A, Terrorism (Police Powers) Act, No. 115 of 2002; for the Northern Territory, Part 2B Terrorism (Emergency Powers Act 2003, Act No. 22 of 2003; for Queensland, Terrorism (Preventative Detention) Act No. 73 of 2005; for South Australia, Terrorism (Preventative Detention) Act 2005; for Tasmania, Terrorism (Preventative Detention) Act No. 71 of 2005; for Western Australia, Terrorism (Preventative Detention) Act 2005; for Victoria, Terrorism (Community Protection) (Amendment) Act 2006; and for the Australian Capital Territory, Terrorism (Extraordinary Temporary Powers) Act 2006, A-2006-21.

15 Criminal Code Act (Cth.) 1995, §§105.28, 105.29, 105.30, 105.31 (Austrl.).

16 *Id.*, §105.8.

17 *Id.*, §105.8 (6A).

18 *Id.*, at §105.32.

19 Nesbitt, *Preventative Detention*, 78.

20 Criminal Code Act (Cth.) 1995 §§105.17(7), 105.28(2)(da) (Austrl.).

21 *Id.*, §105.51.

22 *Id.*

23 AUSTRALIAN HUMAN RIGHTS COMMISSION, RESPONSE TO QUESTIONNAIRE FROM THE WORKING GROUP ON ARBITRARY DETENTION, JUDICIAL REVIEW OF LAWFULNESS OF DETENTION (November 8, 2013), www.ohchr.org/Documents/Issues/Detention/DraftBasicPrinciples/AustralianNHRI.pdf.

24 *Id.*, ¶¶62, 63 (citing Terrorism (Police Powers) Act 2002 (NSW) §§26H, 26I and 26M; Terrorism (Extraordinary Temporary Powers) Act 2006 (ACT) §§18, 20 and 31, Terrorism (Community Protection) Act 2003 (Vic) §§13E and 13N).

25 Criminal Code Act (Cth.) 1995 §105.37.

26 *Id.*, 105.38.

27 *Id.*, §105.35.

28 *Id.*, §105.41.

29 *Id.*, §105.14A.

30 *Id.*, §105.42.

31 Crimes Act 1914 §§IAA, IC (Austrl.).

32 The Attorney General issues annual reports on the issue of preventive detention and control orders. *See e.g.* AUSTRALIAN GOVERNMENT ATTORNEY GENERAL'S OFFICE, CONTROL ORDERS AND PREVENTATIVE DETENTION ORDERS ANNUAL REPORT 2013-2014, *available at* www.ag.gov.au/NationalSecurity/Counterterrorismlaw/Documents/ControlOrdersandPreventativeDetentionOrders2013-14AnnualReport.pdf.

33 Alison Worrall, *Police use controversial anti-terror powers to detain teen terror suspect*, THE AGE (April 20, 2015), www.theage.com.au/victoria/melbourne-raids-police-use-antiterror-powers-to-detain-hampton-park-man-20150419-1mo78n.html.

34 ROACH, THE 9/11 EFFECT, 334 (citing Al-Kateb v Godwin, 218 CLR 562 (2004) (Austrl.)).

35 *Id.* §23CA(4).

36 *Id.*, §23DF(7).

37 *Id.*, §23DB(9).

38 Haneef v Minister for Immigration and Citizenship (2007) 161 FCA 40 (Austrl.).

39 Crimes Act 1914, §23DB(11).

40 Australia Security Intelligence Act 1979, No. 113 as amended, §34 (Austrl.).

41 Bret Walker, Independent National Security Legislation Monitor, Declassified Annual Report, 20 December 2012, 28 Commonwealth of Australia (2013), app. G.

42 *Id.*, §34F

(a) that there are reasonable grounds for believing that issuing the warrant to be requested will substantially assist the collection of intelligence that is important in relation to a terrorism offence; and

(b) that relying on other methods of collecting that intelligence would be ineffective; and

(c) that there is in force under section 34C a written statement of procedures to be followed in the exercise of authority under warrants issued under this Division; and

(d) that there are reasonable grounds for believing that, if the person is not immediately taken into custody and detained, the person:

(i) may alert a person involved in a terrorism offence that the offence is being investigated; or

(ii) may not appear before the prescribed authority; or

(iii) may destroy, damage or alter a record or thing the person may be requested in accordance with the warrant to produce.

43 *Id.*, §34G

(1) An issuing authority may issue a warrant under this section relating to a person, but only if:

(a) the Director General has requested it in accordance with subsection 34F(7); and

(b) the issuing authority is satisfied that there are reasonable grounds for believing that the warrant will substantially assist the collection of intelligence that is important in relation to a terrorism offence.

44 *Id.*, §34G(4).

45 *Id.*, §34L.

46 *Id.*

47 *Id.*, §34J.

48 *Id.*

49 *Id.*, §§34K10, 34K11.

50 *Id.*, §§34ZO, 34ZP, 34ZQ.

51 *Id.*, §34ZQ.

52 Prevention of Terrorism Act 2005, c.2, §2 (U.K.).

53 Criminal Code Act (Cth.) 1995, §104.4. Engaging in hostile activity, and supporting or facilitating engagement in hostile activity in a foreign country were added in December 2014.

54 Nesbitt, *Preventative Detention*, 86.

55 Roach, The 9/11 Effect, 340.

56 Criminal Code Act (Cth.) 1995, §104.5(3)(l).

57 *Id.*, §104.2.

58 *Id.*, §§104.2(3), 104.2(3A).

59 *Id.*, §§104.5, 104.12.

60 *Id.*, §104.5(2A).

61 Australian Human Rights Commission, Response To Questionnaire From The Working Group On Arbitrary Detention, Judicial Review Of Lawfulness Of Detention, ¶73.
62 Criminal Code Act (Cth.) 1995, §§104.14(1)(c),104.14(d).
63 *Id.*, §104.16(1)(d).
64 *Id.*, §104.16(2).
65 Andrew Lynch, *Control Orders in Australia: A Further Case Study in the Migration of British Counter-terrorism Law*, Oxford University Commonwealth Law Journal 159, 181 (2008); Criminal Code Act (Cth.) 1995 §104.19.
66 Walker, Declassified Annual Report, 18–25.
67 Dan Box and Michael McKenna, *Sydney men placed under tougher control orders after raids*, The Australian (December 20, 2014) www.theaustralian.com.au/in-depth/terror/sydney-men-placed-under-tougher-control-orders-after-raids/story-fnpdbcmu-1227162556776.
68 Walker, Declassified Annual Report, 40, 58.
69 Roach, The 9/11 Effect, 342–44 (citing Thomas v Mowbray, HCA 33 (2007) (Austrl.)).
70 *Id.*, 343.
71 Thomas v Mowbray (2007) 233 CLR 307, ¶6 (Austrl.).
72 *Id.*, ¶18, per Gleeson CJ, and ¶79, per Gummow and Crenna JJ.
73 Lynch, *Control Orders in Australia*, 171 (citing Thomas v Mowbray, ¶15).
74 *Id.*, 168.
75 Roach, The 9/11 Effect, 344–6 (citing Jabbour v Hicks, FMCA 2139 (2007) (Austrl.)).
76 Jabbour v Hicks, FMCA 178 (2008) (Austrl.).
77 Lynch, *Control Orders in Australia*, 169.
78 Roach, The 9/11 Effect, 346.
79 A. v Australia (560/1993) March 30, 1997, UN Doc CCPR/C/59/D/560/1993.
80 *Id.*, ¶9.2.
81 *Id.*, ¶9.3.
82 *Id.*, ¶9.4.
83 *Id.*, ¶9.5.
84 C. v Australia (900/1999) Nov. 13, 2002, UN Doc CCPR/C/76/D/900/1999. ¶14.
85 Danyal Shafiq v Australia (1324/2004) Nov. 5, 2004, UN Doc CCPR/C/88/D/1324/2004, ¶4.10.
86 Claire Macken, Counter-Terrorism And The Detention Of Suspected Terrorists, 50 (Routledge, 2011) (quoting D and E v Australia (1050/2002) July 25, 2006, UN Doc. CCPR/C/87/D/1050/2002, ¶7.2).
87 A. v. Australia, ¶9.5.
88 Human Rights Act 2004 (ACT) §18(6): "Anyone who is deprived of liberty by arrest or detention is entitled to apply to a court so that the court can decide, without delay, the lawfulness of the s release if the detention is not lawful."
89 Charter of Human Rights and Responsibilities Act 2006 (Vic.), §21(7): Any person deprived of liberty by arrest or detention is entitled to apply to a court for a declaration or order regarding the lawfulness of his or her detention, and

the court must (a) make a decision without delay; and (b) order the release of the person if it finds that the detention is unlawful."

90 Australian Human Rights Commission, Response To Questionnaire From The Working Group On Arbitrary Detention, Judicial Review Of Lawfulness Of Detention, ¶26.

91 *Id.*, ¶¶27–33.

92 M.M.M v. Australia, HRC Communication No. No. 2136/2012 (August 20, 2013); F.K.A.G. v. Australia, HRC Communication No. 2094/2011 (August 20, 2013). In both these cases the detention was deemed arbitrary and violated Article 9(1) and also violated 9(2) and 9(4) because of deficiencies in process.

93 Ben Saul, *Australia's Guantanamo Problem*, N.Y. Times (March 25, 2013), www.nytimes.com/2014/03/26/opinion/australias-guantanamo-problem.html?ref=opinion&_r=0.

94 *Id.*

95 Hilary Charlesworth, Human Rights: Australia Versus The UN, Democratic Audit of Australia, Australian National University, 2 (August 2006).

96 Australian Constitution § 120: "Custody of offenders against the laws of the Commonwealth. Every State shall make provision for the detention in its prisons of persons accused or convicted of offences against the laws of the Commonwealth, and for the punishment of persons convicted of such offences, and the Parliament of the Commonwealth may make laws to give effect to this provision."

97 Michael C. Tolley, *Australia's Commonwealth Model and Terrorism*, *in* Courts And Terrorism, 144, 145 (Mary L. Volcansek and John F. Styack Jr. eds) (Cambridge University Press, 2011).

98 George Williams, *Anti-terror legislation in Australia and New Zealand*, *in* Global Anti-Terrorism Law And Policy, 544–5 (Victor V. Ramraj, Michael Hor, Kent Roach and George Williams, eds) (Cambridge University Press, 2012).

99 *Id.*, 545.

100 Criminal Code R.S.C. 1985, c.A-1, §495.

101 Forcese, Catch And Release, 19–20 (quoting R. v Storrey [1990] 1 SCR 241; R.v Feeney [1997] 2 SCR 13, ¶24).

102 Anti-Terrorism Act, S.C. 2001, c.41 (Can.).

103 Canadian Charter of Rights and Freedoms, Article 10, Part I of the Constitution Act 1982, being Schedule B to the Canada Act, 1982, c.11 (U.K.).

104 Criminal Code, §83.3.

105 Roach, The 9/11 Effect, 390–1.

106 Combating Terrorism Act, S.C. 2013, c.9 amended the Criminal Code §§83.28–32.

107 *El Mahdi Jamali and Sabrine Djaermane arrested over terrorism fears*, CBC News (Apr. 15, 2015), www.cbc.ca/news/canada/montreal/el-mahdi-jamali-and-sabrine-djaermane-arrested-over-terrorism-fears-1.3034343.

108 Criminal Code §83.3(4)(b).

109 *Id.*, §§83.3(6) (7).

110 Roach, The 9/11 Effect, 410–16; *and see e.g.* International Civil Liberties Monitoring Group, Canada's Anti-Terrorism Laws in Violation of International Human Rights Standards, 4–5, Submission of Information by the International

Civil Liberties Monitoring Group to the Office of the High Commissioner for Human Rights (OHCHR) in relation to the Human Rights Council's Universal Periodic Review (UPR) of Canada to take place in February 2009 (2009), *available at* http://fileserver.cfsadmin.org/file/iclmg/1598bb0106ab8b8f1e2bcd5a89254cc32526a333.pdf.

111 Immigration and Refugee Protection Act, S.C. (2001) c.27 (Can.).
112 *Id.*, §34(1).
113 *Id.*, §34(1)(c).
114 *Id.*, §34(1) (d).
115 *Id.*, §34(1)(f).
116 Roach, The 9/11 Effect, 396.
117 Immigration and Refugee Protection Act, §81.
118 *Id.*, §82.1.
119 Roach, The 9/11 Effect, 402 (quoting Suresh v Canada, 1 S.C.R. 3, ¶¶47, 58 (2002) (Can.)).
120 Rayner Thwaites, The Liberty Of Non-Citizens: Indefinite Detention In Commonwealth Countries, 262 (Hart Publishing, 2014) (commenting on Charkaoui v Canada, 1 S.C.R. 350, ¶95 (2007) (Can.)).
121 Immigration and Refugee Protection Act, §§83, 85.1.
122 Roach, The 9/11 Effect, 400.
123 Bill C-3 and Special Advocates, Department of Justice, Canada, www.justice.gc.ca/eng/dept-min/sa-as/faq.html (last accessed Feb. 27, 2012). *Also see* Re Harkat, FC 1242, ¶¶139, 170 (2010) (Can.).
124 Criminal Code, §810.01.
125 *Id.*, §§810.01(2), 810.01(3).
126 *Id.*, §§ 810.01(3), 810.01(4.1), 810.01(5).
127 *Id.*, §810.01(3.1).
128 *Id.*, §810.01(4).
129 *Id.*, §811.
130 *Id.*, §810.1(6).
131 Charkaoui v Canada, 1 S.C.R. 350 (2007) (Can.).
132 *Id.*, ¶¶3, 23.
133 Constitution Act 1982, Art. 7 (Can.), *available at* http://laws.justice.gc.ca/eng/charter/CHART_E.PDF. (This guarantees the right to life, liberty and security of the person, and the right not to be deprived thereof except in accordance with the principles of fundamental justice.)
134 Charkaoui v Canada, ¶¶19, 20, 23, 28.
135 *Id.*, 29.
136 *Id.*, ¶¶57–62.
137 *Id.*, ¶89.
138 *Id.*, ¶¶91, 94.
139 Immigration and Refugee Protection Act, §82.1.
140 Charkaoui v Canada, ¶¶107–23.
141 *Id.*, ¶117.
142 *Id.*, ¶112.
143 *Id.*, ¶127.
144 A (F.C.) and Others (F.C.) v. Secretary of State for the Home Department [2004] UKHL 56 (U.K.).
145 Charkaoui v Canada, ¶¶127, 130.

146 ROACH, THE 9/11 EFFECT, 401.
147 United States of America v. Khadr, 2011 ONCA 358, ¶1(May 6, 2011).
148 *Id.*, ¶¶2, 8 (quoting United States of America v. Khadr (2010), 258 C.C.C. (3d) 231, at ¶124, 150).
149 United States of America v. Khadr, ¶4.
150 *Id.*
151 *Id.*, 76.
152 *Abdullah Khadr won't be extradited*, CBC NEWS (November 3, 2011), www.cbc.ca/news/canada/story/2011/11/03/scoc-abdullah-khadr.html.
153 Ahani v Canada (1051/2002), U.N. Doc. CCPR/C/80/D/1051/2002 (March 29, 2004).
154 *Id.*, ¶9.2.
155 *Id.*, ¶10.2.
156 *Id.*, ¶10.3.
157 *Id.*, ¶10.4.
158 Charkaoui v Canada.
159 ROACH, THE 9/11 EFFECT, 405.
160 *Id.*, 405, n.179.
161 *Id.*, 404 (citing Charkaoui v. Canada, FC 1030 (2009) (Can.)).
162 *Id.*, 404–5, n. 179 (citing Almrei v Canada, FC 1263 (2009)).
163 *Id.*, 405.
164 *Id.*, 405.
165 BUILDING RESILIENCE AGAINST TERRORISM: CANADA'S COUNTER-TERRORISM STRATEGY, GOVERNMENT OF CANADA, 7–9.
166 FORCESE, CATCH AND RELEASE, 21.
167 C.M. ABRAHAM, *India – An Overview*, 60 *in* PREVENTIVE DETENTION AND SECURITY LAW (Andrew Harding and John Hatchard, eds., Martinus Nijhoff Publishers, 1993).
168 *Id.* (citing regional legislation dealing with preventive detention in Bengal, Madras and Bombay in the early 19th century, the Defence of India Act 1915, and the Rowlatt Act 1919).
169 Peter Heehs, *Terrorism in India during the freedom struggle*, HISTORIAN, Vol. 55, Iss. 3 469 (Spring 1993).
170 Defence of India Act No. XXXV (1939).
171 Abraham, *India – An Overview*, 60.
172 *Id.*
173 *Id.*, 61 (quoting M.V. PYLEE, CONSTITUTIONAL GOVERNMENT IN INDIA 242–3 (Asia Publishing House, 1960)).
174 India Const., Art. 21, amended by The Constitution (Ninety-fourth Amendment) Act, 2006: "No person shall be deprived of his life or personal liberty except according to procedure established by law."
175 Abraham, *India – An Overview*, 60.
176 India Const., Art. 22(1).
177 *Id.*, Arts. 22(1) (2).
178 *Id.*, Arts. 22(4) (7).
179 Derek P. Jinks, *The Anatomy of an Institutionalized Emergency: Preventive Detentions and Personal Liberty in India*, 22 MICH. J. INT'L L. 311, 327 (Winter, 2001).
180 Code of Criminal Procedure 1973 (CrPc), §151(1).

181 *Id.*, §151(2).
182 *Id.*, §151(3), and Maharashtra Act 7 of 1981 (w.e.f. 27-5-1980).
183 *Id.*, §50.
184 *Id.*, §76. Human Rights Watch have reported that many people are detained for more than 24 hours before the first court appearance, Human Rights Watch, The "Anti-Nationals," Arbitrary Detention And Torture Of Terrorism Suspects In India, 44 (February 2011).
185 Code of Criminal Procedure 1973, §167.
186 Preventive Detention Act, No. 4 (1950).
187 Maintenance of Internal Security Act, No. 26 (1971).
188 National Security Act, No. 65 (1980).
189 Jinks, *The Anatomy of an Institutionalized Emergency*, 328–36.
190 *Id.*, 328 (quoting National Security Act §3(1)(a)).
191 *Id.*, 330.
192 *Id.*, 333.
193 *Id.*, 338; *see also* C. Raj Kumar, *Human Rights Implications of National Security Laws in India: Combating Terrorism while Preserving Civil Liberties*, 33 Denv. J. Int'l L. & Pol'y 195, 213 (2005): "the NSA has minimal procedural safeguards…"
194 Terrorist and Disruptive Activities (Prevention) Act, No. 28 (1987), It was first enacted in 1985 as a temporary measure for two years, but reintroduced through an Ordinance in 1987, with provision to extend it. It was extended periodically and permitted to lapse in May 1995.
195 Ujjwal Kumar Singh, *Mapping anti-terror regimes in India*, 421 *in* Global Anti-Terrorism Law And Policy (Victor V. Ramraj, Michael Hor, Kent Roach and George Williams, eds) (Cambridge University Press, 2012).
196 *Id.*, 423.
197 Anil Kalhan, Gerald P. Conroy, Mamta Kaushal, Sam Scott Miller and Jed S. Rakoff, *Colonial Continuities: Human Rights, Terrorism and Security Laws in India*, 20 Columbia Journal of Asian Law 93, 147 (Fall, 2006). They also note that there is evidence that thousands of people had been arbitrarily arrested under TADA for lengthy periods without being told the reason for arrest.
198 *Id.*, 148.
199 Prevention of Terrorism Act No. 15 (2002).
200 Ujjwal Kumar Singh, The State, Democracy And Anti-Terror Laws In India, 69 (Sage Publications, 2007).
201 Ujjwal Kumar Singh, *Mapping anti-terror regimes in India*, 421.
202 Unlawful Activities (Prevention) Act, 2012 No. 3 (2013), §4.
203 Kalhan and Ors, *Colonial Continuities*, 159–61.
204 *Id.*, 159 (citing Prevention of Terrorism Act §49(2)(a)–(b)).
205 *Id.* (citing Prevention of Terrorism Act §52(4)).
206 *Id.*, 160 (quoting Prevention of Terrorism Act §49(6)–(7)).
207 *Id.*, 160.
208 *Id.*, 174.
209 Unlawful Activities (Prevention) Act No. 37 (1967).
210 Unlawful Activities (Prevention) Act No. 29 (2004).
211 Unlawful Activities (Prevention) Amendment Act No. 35 (2008).
212 *Id.*, §43(A).

213 *Id.*, §43(D).
214 For a discussion of relevant cases, see SINGH, THE STATE, DEMOCRACY AND ANTI-TERROR LAWS IN INDIA, 102–42.
215 A.K. Roy v. Union of India (1982) SCR (2) 272.
216 *Id.*, 301, noting that preventive detention is dealt with in Article 22 of the Constitution.
217 *Id.*, 324.
218 Kartar Singh v. State of Punjab (1994) SCC (3) 569.
219 A.K. Roy v. Union of India, ¶351.
220 *Id.*, ¶352.
221 People's Union for Civil Liberties v. Union of India, AIR (2004) 456.
222 *Id.*, 479.
223 Declaration of India to Art. 9 ICCPR.
224 U.N. Human Rights Committee, Consideration of reports submitted by States parties under article 40 of the Covenant, Concluding observations of the Human Rights Committee, Third periodic reports of States parties due in 1992: India. CCPR/C/79/Add.81 (August 4, 1997).
225 *Id.*, ¶¶74–82.
226 Kartar Singh v. State of Punjab.
227 U.N. Human Rights Committee, Consideration of reports submitted by States parties under article 40 of the Covenant, Concluding observations of the Human Rights Committee, Third periodic reports of States parties due in 1992: India, ¶79(f).
228 U.N. Human Rights Committee, Consideration of reports submitted by States parties under article 40 of the Covenant, Concluding observations of the Human Rights Committee, India, CCPR/C/79/Add.81, ¶14 (August 4, 1997).
229 *Id.*, ¶¶24, 25.
230 HUMAN RIGHTS WATCH, BACK TO THE FUTURE, INDIA'S 2008 COUNTER-TERRORISM LAWS, 5–7 (July 2008).
231 *Id.*, 8–10.
232 Unlawful Activities (Prevention) Amendment Act.
233 HUMAN RIGHTS WATCH, BACK TO THE FUTURE, INDIA'S 2008 COUNTER-TERRORISM LAWS, 13–15.
234 HUMAN RIGHTS WATCH, THE "ANTI-NATIONALS," ARBITRARY DETENTION AND TORTURE OF TERRORISM SUSPECTS IN INDIA, 44–60.
235 US DEP'T. OF STATE, 2010 HUMAN RIGHTS REPORTS: INDIA (April 2011), www.state.gov/documents/organization/160058.pdf.
236 India Const., Arts. 22(1), 22(2).

7 Israel

This Chapter analyzes the mixture of detention models operated in Israel. Two types of detention are used in Israel, the first in accordance with domestic criminal law, and the second in accordance with administrative law.[1] Additionally, the detention laws applied in Israel differ from those administered in the Occupied Territories.

Terrorist activities are generally treated as crimes, and terrorists are prosecuted whenever reliable evidence is found.[2] However, in addition, the applicable normative system in many detention cases is the law relating to international armed conflicts (IACs).[3] Customary international law forms part of Israeli law.[4] Israel's use of law of armed conflict (LOAC) is "based upon a delicate balance"[5] of the rights of the individual, weighed against the military need to maintain and protect the security of the country and its citizens. Thus "human rights are protected by the law of armed conflict, but not to their full scope."[6]

Pre-trial detention in Israel

Criminal law

In cases where prosecution is envisaged, suspects may be arrested with or without a judicial warrant for interrogation and investigation, if there are reasonable grounds to suspect that an offense has been committed,[7] and if one ground out of a number of other criteria apply.[8] Arrests with a warrant are preferred.[9]

Procedure

In Israel, suspects who have not been charged must normally appear before a court after twenty-four hours in detention. In the case of security offenses, where suspension of an interrogation may impede an essential investigation that could save lives, the detention period can be extended for further interrogation for an initial period of up to forty-eight hours.[10] A judge can extend this period for fifteen days twice, up to thirty days, and thereafter with the approval of the attorney general in additional increments of fifteen days up to a maximum seventy-five days.[11] A new request has to be made to the court justifying why detention should be extended on each occasion that the detention is sought.[12]

Prior to 2012, in the Occupied Territories an initial period of ninety-six hours detention applied for security offenses, but an Israeli Defense Forces (IDF) officer could extend that period for up to eight days from the time of detention, if convinced that suspension of the interrogation would cause real harm to the interrogation, or that suspending the interrogation might damage an essential investigation intended to protect lives. Thereafter a judge could authorize successive periods of thirty days, up to ninety days. Appeal judges could authorize a further period of three months.[13]

Detention can also take place if bail is refused between indictment and trial. Cases are meant to conclude within nine months of the date of indictment but the Supreme Court has the power to prolong this period in tranches of three months for an unlimited number of times. Every time the prosecution seeks an extension of remand without bail, the defendants must come before the court.[14]

In 2012 the periods of extended detention in the Occupied Territories were reduced to six days in the case of concerns that interruption of interrogation would harm the investigation, and to two days instead of thirty for the first order by a judge. The judge can order successive periods of fifteen days, up to sixty days instead of ninety. Appeal judges can detain for additional thirty days, making a total of three months instead of six months.[15]

Access to lawyers

The security service Shabak can prevent the detainee having access to a lawyer for ten days. This denial of access can be extended by a court up to a total of twenty-one days, at a hearing in which the detainee will be produced in court.[16] The detainee will not have had access to a lawyer for that hearing but he can address the judge. In his absence, if his family has retained and given instructions to a lawyer, that lawyer can address the court before the ruling is made.[17] Human rights groups have complained about the lack of access to lawyers whilst people are detained for pre-charge interrogation purposes. For example, in the period between 2005 and 2007, the average period of incommunicado detention was 16.7 days.[18] It is not known if the 2012 law referred to above addresses this concern.

A new counter-terrorism bill, the Struggle Against Terrorism Law 2011, which is designed to draw together in one place a comprehensive and updated anti-terror law, was passed in June 2013.[19] It is designed to apply in times other than an emergency,[20] and deals with preventive arrests as well as introducing a form of control order along the lines of the United Kingdom model.[21] Details of this law are not yet available in English other than in a very limited overview,[22] so this cannot be analyzed in any meaningful way at this time.

Administrative detention in Israel

Grounds

In addition to the criminal law, and on a totally separate track, Israel operates a preventive detention regime called "administrative detention."[23] The goals of administrative detention are not arrest, trial, conviction, and punishment. It is purely and simply a tool to prevent terrorist attacks but was never intended to replace the enforcement of criminal law.[24] Essentially, it involves detention without charges or trial. However, administrative detention may only be imposed if it is the only means available to detain the person, i.e. if prosecution is not an option. The rationale of this regime is prevention of "danger to state or public security posed by a particular person whose release would likely threaten the security of the state and the ordinary course of life."[25]

Two separate administrative detention policies are in place, one for Israel and the other for the Occupied Palestinian territories. In Israel, administrative detention has its roots in British colonial law. In 1945, during the Mandate, the British government enacted as primary emergency legislation the Defence (Emergency) Regulations to deal with resistance.[26] That law permitted detention without trial by order of military commanders for renewable periods of six month, and provided a limited power to appeal to an advisory committee.

These regulations were incorporated into Israeli law after independence, virtually unchanged, until Israel enacted the Emergency Powers (Detention) Law of 1979 (EPDL).[27] Until August 2015 administrative detention orders had only been imposed on Palestinians, but three right-wing Jewish extremists were placed in administrative detention for six months following a deadly arson attack in the West Bank.[28]

The 1979 law only applies during a state of emergency.[29] It currently applies as Israel has been in a continuous state of emergency since the state was created.[30] The new counter-terrorism legislation, which has attracted criticism from human rights groups, will have implications for this detention law because this law (when it comes into force) will apply at all times, and not just in times of emergency.[31]

Procedure

"A particular person,"[32] presumably both citizens and non-citizens, can be detained if the defense minister has reasonable cause to believe that reasons of state security or public security require it (although these terms are not defined). Detainees have access to counsel. Within forty-eight hours of arrest detainees are brought before a district court for judicial review.[33] Hearings are held *in camera*,[34] but the detainee has a right to be present.[35] The judge will see all the evidence, without the detainee or his representative being present, and may decide to accept evidence without disclosing it to the detainee or his lawyer if he is "satisfied that disclosure of the evidence to either of them may impair state security or public security."[36] The language of this statute does not require the court to balance the individual's interests against those of the state at this stage.

Release will be ordered if the court does not find objective reasons of state security or public security to justify detention, or if the detention was made in bad faith or for irrelevant reasons.[37] Appeal may be made to the Supreme Court.[38] Judges have confirmed detention because of the likelihood of the suspect posing a danger to the community.[39] Detention orders made by the president of the District Court are limited to six months and subject to review every three months also by the president of the District Court, but they can be renewed unlimited times.[40] Every time an extension is ordered, a new request has to be made by the minister of defense, with an explanation of why it is necessary to prolong the detention.[41]

Access to lawyers

Access to counsel is permitted within seven days of detention[42] and judicial review takes place within fourteen days of arrest,[43] with a right of appeal to the Supreme Court within thirty days.[44] Detention may continue (with reviews every six months) until a minister of defense determines that the group with which the detainee is associated has ceased hostilities against Israel or a court has decided that the detainee's release would not threaten state security.[45]

Legal challenges

In 2000 more than twenty Lebanese citizens challenged their continuing detention. Some of them had been held in administrative detention since 1991, after serving sentences of imprisonment following convictions for membership of hostile organization and involvement in attacks against Israeli forces. They were being held as "bargaining chips" in negotiations under way to release prisoners and missing persons held by Israel's security forces.[46] Up to the point of this appeal, a number of hearings had taken place over the years, and the majority of the lower court, including Judge Barak (as he then was), had been satisfied that the return of prisoners was a purpose and interest included within the framework of national security, even where there was no danger from the detainees themselves.[47] Thus up to this point the courts had held that prisoners *could* be held as bargaining chips.

On appeal, President Barak changed his mind and noted that "[a] balance is required – a delicate and difficult balance – between the liberty and the dignity of the individual and national security and public safety."[48] In this case, a majority of the court (6:3) ruled that it was not lawful to administratively detain a person "from whom no danger is posed to national security and who merely constitutes a "bargaining chip." This type of detention does "a severe harm to human dignity, as the detainee is perceived as a means to achieving a goal and not as a goal in and of itself."[49] It is also prohibited by international law.[50] President Barak confirmed that the purpose of the EPDL "was to apply to the detention of a person from whom himself a danger is posed to security, and not beyond this."[51]

President Barak also noted that administrative detention "cannot go on endlessly. The more the period of detention that has passed lengthens, so too are weightier considerations needed to justify an additional extension of the detention. With the passage of time the means of administrative detention is no longer proportional."[52]

In 2002, the international atmosphere that prevailed after the events of 9/11 set the scene for Israel to enact another extreme law:[53] the Incarceration of Unlawful Combatants Law.[54] This law applies to "unlawful combatants" who are defined as persons who have "participated either directly or indirectly in hostile acts against the State of Israel" or are members of a "force perpetrating hostile acts against the State of Israel" where "the conditions prescribed in Article 4 of the Third Geneva Convention of 12th August 1949 with respect to prisoners of war and granting prisoner-of-war status in international humanitarian law, do not apply to him."[55] Detention may be ordered where the chief of general staff has "reasonable cause to believe that a person being held by the State authorities is an unlawful combatant and that his release will harm State security."[56] The status of unlawful combatant "rejects the dichotomy in the Geneva Conventions that divide persons into civilians or lawful combatants."[57]

A presumption exists that a person:

> who is a member of a force perpetrating hostile acts against the State of Israel or who has participated in hostile acts of such a force, either directly or indirectly, shall be deemed to be a person whose release would harm State security as long as the hostile acts of such force against the State of Israel have not yet ceased, unless proved otherwise.[58]

The first part of this presumption introduces the notion of association as a criterion for detention, rather than actual deeds, rather like in the United States detention authority under the law of armed conflict model, discussed *infra*.

Elements of LOAC

A v. State of Israel[59] concerned the legality of the detention under the Unlawful Combatants Law of two appellants from Gaza who allegedly belonged to Hezbollah. They petitioned the Supreme Court (sitting as the Court of

Criminal Appeals). Two questions were before the Court: (1) to what extent the Internment of Unlawful Combatants Law complied with international humanitarian law; and (2) whether the law passed constitutional muster against Israel's Basic Law: Human Dignity and Liberty. The Court emphasized that the purpose of the legislation was to "remove from the cycle of hostilities someone who belongs to a terrorist organization or who takes part in hostilities against the State of Israel … The law does not apply to innocent civilians."[60]

Consideration of the first question was dependent on the premise that Israel is engaged in an international armed conflict with the terrorist organizations operating outside Israel.[61] Although there is nothing in the text of the statute that states that the Incarceration of Unlawful Combatants Law applies to non-citizens of Israel, the Court interpreted the law to permit "the internment of *foreign* persons who belong to a terrorist organization or who participate in hostilities against the security of the state, and it was intended to prevent these persons returning to the cycle of hostilities against Israel."[62] In practice, the law has only been used for foreigners residing in the Gaza Strip, and not against Palestinians residing in Judea and Samaria.[63]

This Court and (earlier decisions[64]) treated unlawful combatants as a subcategory of civilians, "using the approach of customary international law, according to which the category of 'civilians' includes everyone that is not a 'combatant.'"[65] However in internment cases, all that need be shown is that "the conditions of the definition of 'unlawful combatant' in Section 2 are proved."[66] According to the Court, the relevance of this is that an unlawful combatant is subject to Geneva Convention (GC) IV and can be detained when he represents a threat to the security of the state.[67] An unlawful combatant would not, however, be entitled to the same degree of protection to which innocent civilians are entitled under GC IV.[68]

Nonetheless the Court satisfied itself that the legislation did not create a new reference group from the viewpoint of international law, but "merely determines special provisions for the detention of 'civilians' (according to the meaning of this term in international humanitarian law) who are 'unlawful combatants.'"[69] The then president of the Supreme Court dismissed suggestions that detention under this legislation was neither criminal arrest, nor administrative detention, but a third category of detention, unrecognized by both Israeli and international law.[70]

In its interpretation of the law in question the Court commented that the definition of unlawful combatant, which covers both a person taking part in hostilities as well as someone who is a member of a hostile force, should be interpreted with reference to the security purpose of the law, and require proof of an individual's threat as a ground for administrative detention.[71] In respect of the membership criterion:

> it is not necessary for that person to take a direct or indirect part in the hostilities themselves, and it is possible that his connection and

> contribution to the organization will be expressed in other ways that are sufficient to include him in the cycle of hostilities in its broad sense, in such a way that his detention will be justified under the law.[72]

This is a very broad and nebulous standard, but the same connection linking membership of a group to terrorist status or detention authority can be seen in the laws of other countries.[73]

The Court stated that the Incarceration of Unlawful Combatants Law should be interpreted in accordance with the holding in previous cases that "since administrative detention is an unusual and extreme measure, and in view of its violation of the constitutional right to personal liberty, clear and convincing evidence is required in order to prove a security threat that establishes a basis for administrative detention."[74] Clear and convincing evidence is required in order to prove that the detainee is an unlawful combatant (including being a person who merely "belonged to a terror organization and made a contribution to the cycle of hostilities in its broad sense") and also in the judicial review of the decision to continue detention.[75] "[A]dequate administrative evidence is required, and a single piece of evidence with regard to an isolated act carried out in the distant past is insufficient."[76]

The Court subjected the statute to a very thorough constitutional scrutiny. In the Court's opinion, *prima facie*, the law violated Section 5 of the Basic Law,[77] but that right to liberty "is not absolute, but a violation of the right is sometimes required to protect essential public interests" and the balancing formula is to be found in Section 8 of the Basic Law.[78] The Court held that the legislative purpose of this law, of removing terrorists from their cycle of hostilities against Israel, was a proper one.[79]

With echoes of the approach of the European Court of Human Rights (ECHR) to apply a "margin of appreciation,"[80] the Israeli Court applied a relatively broad "margin of constitutional appreciation" or a "margin of proportionality" to the three sub-tests of fundamental criteria it usually applied to assess proportionality.[81] The Court decided that the law satisfied the rational connection test.[82]

The Court then conducted a very lengthy examination of proportionality. It rejected the suggestions that detainees should be given a criminal trial or held pursuant to the EPDL, as alternative measures to administrative detention under this law.[83] It then considered whether the specific arrangements relating to hearings were proportionate. It found the arrangements relating to providing the detainee with a hearing no later than fourteen days from the issue of the order were within the margin of proportionality,[84] and that six monthly reviews were consistent with the provisions of GC IV in international humanitarian law and thus proportionate.[85]

As in the EDPL, the Court may make an order based on secret evidence.[86] Regarding the use of secret evidence, the Court noted that "[r]eliance on inadmissible administrative evidence and on privileged material for reasons of state security lies at the heart of administrative detention."[87] Thus "the judge is required to question the validity and credibility of the administrative evidence that is brought before him and to assess its weight."[88] Reliance on secret evidence was deemed to be "part and parcel of administrative detention" and proportionate.[89]

On the question of access to lawyers, the Court noted that the "right to legal counsel is also not absolute and it may be restricted if this is essential for protecting the security of the state."[90] A delay of seven days would not prevent the detainee seeing his lawyer within the fourteen-day deadline to appear before a court, and thus was proportionate.[91]

The Court went on to consider the issue of duration of detention. No maximum period of detention is specified, other than tying it to the end of hostilities against Israel by the force to which the detainee belongs. The Court found this to be proportionate, relying once more on the applicability of international humanitarian law, in particular to GC III, which allows prisoners of war to be interned until hostilities have ended.[92]

This is the same approach taken by the United States administration towards persons who are "part of" or "substantially supporting al-Qaeda, the Taliban and associated groups."[93] The Israeli Court did emphasize that "the question of proportionality of the duration of detention under the law should be examined in each case on its merits and according to its specific circumstances,"[94] and that a detention order under this law "cannot continue indefinitely."[95] It noted that the purpose of periodic judicial review every six months was to examine whether the threat presented by the detainee to the security of the state justified continued detention, and in making that assessment the court should take into account the length of time that has passed since the order was made.[96]

Finally the Court considered whether the combination of measures in this law satisfied the test of proportionality in the narrow sense – whether the violation of the right to personal liberty was reasonably commensurate with the public benefit that arises from this law, and concluded that the test was satisfied.[97]

Administrative detention in the Occupied Territories

Grounds

In the Occupied Territories administrative detention is enforced pursuant to military order.[98] If a military commander has "reasonable grounds to believe that a certain person must be held in detention for reasons to do with regional security or public security"[99] he may order that person to be detained for a period of up to six months. The period of detention can be renewed unlimited times, provided the military commander has reasonable grounds to presume that regional or public security require the continued detention.[100]

Procedure

The main difference from detention in Israel is that detainees have to be brought before a court for judicial review within eight days of arrest[101] instead of forty-eight hours. After forty-eight hours detainees can receive visits from the Red Cross and their families can be informed as to their whereabouts. Appeals may be made to a judge of the military court of appeals.[102] As with the other previously discussed administrative detention laws, a judge may rely on evidence that is not disclosed to the detainee or his legal representative,[103] and the hearing is *in camera*.[104]

In addition to administrative detention *per se*, a control order type of regime is also in place, called "restraining orders and supervision,"[105] which may only be used if the military commander deems it "necessary for imperative reasons of security."[106] Restraining orders cover restrictions on movement, contacts, employment, and possession of objects.[107] The order can be challenged in a hearing before an appeal committee of one member, and the adjudicator is permitted to rely on evidence not disclosed to the appellant or his representative.[108] Assigned residence and special supervision orders may also be issued,[109] and appeals are conducted in accordance with the same rules as restraining orders.[110] Hearings in respect of these orders are not open to the public.[111]

Legal challenges

Marab v. IDF Commander in the West Bank[112] challenged the legality of detention under Defense in Time of Warfare (Temporary Order) (Judea and Samaria) (Number 1500) – 2002, and Defense in Time of Warfare (Temporary Order) (Amendment) (Judea and Samaria) (Number 1502) – 2002. These Orders were promulgated because the then current order, Defense Regulations Order (Judea and Samaria) (Number 378) – 1970, appeared inadequate to detain large numbers of persons in connection with Operation Defensive Wall, which was aimed at destroying the infrastructure of terrorist groups that had carried out many attacks since September 2002.[113]

The petitioners in *Marab* questioned whether the law permitted detention for the purposes of investigation, and challenged the right to delay judicial review for twelve or eighteen days, and access to lawyers for thirty-two days. Despite the fact that Israel has maintained that Article 9 of the International Covenant on Civil and Political Rights (ICCPR) does not apply because it is in a state of emergency, President Barak began his consideration of the legal issues with a discussion of Article 9. He noted the prohibition against arbitrary detention and stated that it accorded with Israeli law:

> [a] person may be detained for investigative purposes – in order to prevent the disruption of an investigation or to prevent a danger to the public presented by the detainee – where the proper balance between the

> liberty of the individual and public interest justifies the denial of that right.[114]

The balance required in order to detain for investigatory purposes both in "regular" criminal detention and administrative detention "demands that the detaining authority possesses an evidentiary basis sufficient to establish suspicion against the individual detainee."[115] President Barak stated that internal Israeli law corresponded to international law on this matter and that the fundamental principles of Israeli administrative law applied to the military commander in the West Bank.[116] Crucially he emphasized: "[t]he fundamental principles which are most important to the matter at hand are those regarding the duty of each public authority to act reasonably and proportionately, while properly balancing between individual liberty and public necessity."[117]

Elements of LOAC

The Court went on to consider the question of detention during an occupation in times of war, pursuant to GC IV. Although noting that GC IV did not contain any specific article authorizing detention for investigative purposes, the Court decided that this authority could be "derived from the law in the area and is included in the general authority of the commander of the area to preserve peace and security."[118] The Court concluded that the detention authority in the military orders applicable to the area applies when there is a "cause for detention."[119] The cause here was that "the circumstances of the detention raise the suspicion that the detainee endangers or may be a danger to security."[120] However the detention authority is limited to "where there exists an individual cause for detention against a specific detainee," i.e. "the existence of circumstances which raise the suspicion that the individual detainee presents a danger to security."[121]

In answer to the complaint about the lack of judicial review, the Court emphasized that "judicial intervention with regard to detention orders is essential to the principle of rule of law,"[122] and "it is an inseparable part of the development of the detention itself."[123] The Court held that the detention periods of eighteen days and twelve days before judicial review were excessive,[124] and the proper approach was that adopted by international law, which requires that a judge be approached promptly.[125] The Court left the matter of fixing the length of a shorter period to the respondents.

On the issue of delaying access to lawyers, the Court commented that the right to meet with a lawyer was not an absolute right, but "rather a relative right, and it should be balanced against other rights and interests."[126] Meetings between lawyers and detainees could be delayed "if significant security considerations justify the prevention of the meeting."[127] Thus although the standard rule would permit prompt meeting with lawyers, significant security considerations, such as having meetings "during warfare or close to it," may prevent this.[128] The Court did not accept that lack of access to lawyers rendered the detainees incommunicado, because they would be moved to a detention facility within forty-eight hours of arrest, and would be permitted to have their families informed of their whereabouts and would be able to receive visits from the Red Cross.[129]

Secret evidence

In order to introduce some procedural fairness into the administrative detention hearings, the Israel Supreme Court has developed the "judicial management model,"[130] a practice that has "no basis in law."[131] The case will be decided *in camera* and the judge alone sees and reviews all the evidence. At no time will either the accused or his lawyer be given access to any classified information. This is because protecting the source of the intelligence information is "of the fundamental essence."[132] The Court has played a special role in trying to compensate for not giving the evidence to the detainee by applying a heightened scrutiny to the evidence.[133] The Court examines the evidence in a critical fashion, even from the viewpoint of the detainee.[134] The judge has to test the quality and credibility of the evidence and the government's case generally.[135] The Supreme Court has made it clear that the state must disclose the basic allegations to the accused, as an independent duty, as well as make full disclosure to the court.[136] This has similarities with the use of special advocates in United Kingdom, Canadian, and Australian law.[137] Doubts have been expressed as to whether the provision of core allegations is sufficient for a detainee to mount an effective defense.[138] Furthermore, defense lawyers and even some Israeli judges have agreed that the judicial management model "suffers from inherent weaknesses that prevent, at least to some extent, meaningful and independent judicial assessment of the secret evidence."[139]

Permanent state of emergency

Ever since it ratified the ICCPR, Israel has issued a declaration each year in accordance with Article 4,[140] stating that it is not subject to Article 9 because it is in a persistent state of emergency.[141] In order for this declaration to be valid Israel had to state that it had complied with Article 4.[142] Article 4 refers to an extreme situation, where there is a threat to the life of the nation as a whole, and debate has ensued as to whether Israel's state of emergency meets the requirements of the article and the continuous and persistent threats faced by Israel validate its declaration of a state of emergency.[143]

Israel's submission of its third periodic report in November 2008 to the Human Rights Committee (HRC) stated that it had been considering "refraining from extending the state of emergency any further."[144] However, before terminating the state of emergency, various laws would have to be revised.[145] Israel's report on compliance with Article 9 did not deal with administrative detention, which by dint of the declaration as to the state of emergency would not apply. It restricted its report to the application of Article 9 to its internal criminal law, in particular to issues relating to access to counsel, and detention pre-indictment and after sentence.[146] It also discussed the Application of Article 10 (treatment of persons deprived of their liberty) to the Incarceration of Unlawful Combatants Law of 2002,[147] and highlighted the case of *A v. State of Israel* (discussed above) in which the Supreme Court sitting as the Criminal Court of Appeals ruled that the 2002 law was constitutional.[148]

In the HRC's 2009 list of issues, Israel was asked to comment on the status of the state of emergency, and the frequent use of and details concerning administrative detention as well as an explanation of why access to counsel was delayed.[149] Israel gave certain details relating to administrative detention, describing the use of such measures as obligatory and essential to fight terrorism in the light of the current security situation.[150] In connection with the state of emergency, Israel further stated that new draft counter-terrorism legislation was under review.[151] In their concluding observations on this aspect of the report, the HRC merely urged Israel to complete their review of relevant legislation as soon as possible, refrain from using administrative detention, and ensure that detainees have prompt access to counsel.[152]

Three years later, the Israeli Supreme Court rejected a petition brought by the Association for Civil Rights in Israel (which had been pending for thirteen years) requesting an end to the state of emergency.[153] The Court held that the process of replacing, revoking, and enacting relevant pieces of legislation had to continue, together with the disentanglement of a large number of laws from the state of emergency declaration which gave validity to such laws. As long as this process has not been completed, and whilst the security conditions in the region require the existing laws to protect the Israeli population, the Court decided it should not intervene with the decision of the authorities to continue and renew the state of emergency.[154]

Conclusions

Of all the countries surveyed in this book, Israel is the one that faces the greatest number of threats,[155] and has the most liberty-repressive measures involving the right to detain indefinitely. This has given rise to many complaints from human rights organizations, despite Israel's efforts to put in place various measures to give some sort of process to detainees.

Israel is in a continual struggle to protect its citizens from the constant terror attacks it deals with on a daily basis. At the same time the Supreme Court is trying to dispense justice in accordance with human rights law as best it can against this backdrop of relentless terror attacks: "in devising any and all of its counter-terrorism strategy, the Israeli government takes into account the highly probable review of the lawfulness of the strategy by the Supreme Court."[156]

One of the most problematic aspects of this model is the use of secret evidence and the unusual, almost impossible, role played by judges who try to put themselves in the position of the defendant as well as issue rulings as to whether it is right and proper to detain. Another major problem involves the issue of the perpetual state of emergency. It remains to be seen what legislative reforms are in the new law, and what will be deemed appropriate to address the problem of securing the safety of citizens in the unique situation of daily incidents, and Israel's struggle to survive. However, the use of administrative detention at all times, and not just in times of emergency, will most likely violate Article 9 ICCPR.

The human rights group B'Tselem publishes monthly reports on the number held in administrative detention. In 2002–2003 this exceeded 1,000, and the numbers have slowly reduced, with some peaks and troughs, to 412 as at the end of March 2015, all of whom are held pursuant to military order.[157] As to duration of detention, the most recent report shows that of the 472 detained as at July 2014, four have been held for over two years, and 327 have been held for less than six months.[158]

The regime of administrative detention has attracted much criticism, particularly with regard to the use of secret evidence in the making of, and the legal challenges to, detention orders.[159] This criticism has been countered by Israel's claim that "the Supreme Court balances human rights and national security on a case by case basis," and is willing to hear almost any case without being concerned about standing or merits.[160]

Notes

1 *See* Dvorah Chen, *Prosecuting Terrorists: A Look at the American and Israeli Experiences*, Policy Watch #1162, The Washington Institute For Near East Policy, Nov. 14, 2006.

2 Daphne Barak-Erez, *Israel's Anti-Terrorist Law: Past, Present and Future*, 604, *in* Global Anti-Terrorism Law And Policy (Victor V. Ramraj, Michael Hor, Kent Roach and George Williams, eds) (Cambridge University Press, 2012); Interview with Advocate Dvorah Chen, Tel Aviv (August 15, 2013).

3 Public Committee Against Torture in Israel (PCAT) v. Government of Israel, HCJ 769/02, ¶18.

4 *Id.*, ¶19.

5 *Id.*, ¶22.

6 *Id.*

7 Criminal Procedure Law (Powers of Enforcement – Arrest) 1996, §§12–28. Terrorist acts are defined in the Prevention of Terrorism Ordinance No. 33 of 5708/1948, but the most detailed definition is found in the prohibition on Terrorist Financing Law 5765/2004: "(a) an act that constitutes an offence or a threat to commit an act that constitutes an offence that was committed or was planned to be committed in order to influence a matter of policy, ideology or religion" if all of a number of specified conditions are fulfilled.

8 *Id.*, §§12–28. Additional criteria apply if arrests are made by police without a

judicial warrant, and the additional criteria in both types of arrest include reasonable grounds to suspect that the suspect will endanger the safety of any person, public security or national defense.

9 *Id.*, §4.

10 Ido Rosenzweig and Yuval Shany, *IDF Publishes Amending Order Reducing Detention Periods in the West Bank [2.2.2012]*, THE ISRAEL DEMOCRACY INSTITUTE (March 2012), www.idi.org.il/sites/english/ResearchAndPrograms/NationalSecurityandDemocracy/Terrorism_and_Democracy/Newsletters/Pages/39/4/4.aspx.

11 *Id. Also see* Criminal Procedure Law (Detainee Suspected of Security Offense) (Emergency Order), 2006, §4, amending §17 Criminal Procedure Law (Powers of Enforcement – Arrest), 1996.

12 Interview with Advocate Chen.

13 *Id. Also see* Order regarding Security Provisions [Consolidated Version] (Judea and Samaria) (No. 1651), 5770-2009, Chap. C.

14 Interview with Advocate Chen.

15 Rosenzweig and Shany, *IDF Publishes Amending Order Reducing Detention Periods in the West Bank [2.2.2012]*.

16 Criminal Procedure Law (Powers of Enforcement – Arrest), 1996, §35D.

17 Interview with Advocate Chen.

18 WHEN THE EXCEPTION BECOMES THE RULE: INCOMMUNICADO DETENTION OF PALESTINIAN SECURITY DETAINEES, 7 THE PUBLIC COMMITTEE AGAINST TORTURE IN ISRAEL AND NADI AL ASIR PALESTINIAN PRISONER SOCIETY (November 2010), www.stoptorture.org.il/en/node/1659.

19 Jonathan Lis, *Israeli lawmakers blast Livni for rushing anti-terror bill through committee*, HAARETZ (Jun. 11, 2013), www.haaretz.com/news/national/.premium-1.529200.

20 Barak-Erez, *Israel's Anti-Terrorist Law*, 618.

21 *Id.;* KENT ROACH, THE 9/11 EFFECT: COMPARATIVE COUNTER-TERRORISM, 112 (Cambridge University Press, 2011).

22 Ido Rosenzweig and Yuval Shany, *New Comprehensive Counter-Terrorism Memorandum Bill [21.4.2010]*, THE ISRAEL DEMOCRACY INSTITUTE (May 2010), www.idi.org.il/sites/english/ResearchAndPrograms/NationalSecurityandDemocracy/Terrorism_and_Democracy/Newsletters/Pages/17th%20newsletter/1/1.aspx.

23 Chen, Prosecuting Terrorists; EMANUEL GROSS, THE STRUGGLE OF DEMOCRACY AGAINST TERRORISM, 122 (University of Virginia Press, 2006). Administrative detention is literally defined as "detention that is carried out by an administrative power and not by a judicial power or authority." *Also see e.g.*, STEPHANIE COOPER BLUM, THE NECESSARY EVIL OF PREVENTIVE DETENTION IN THE WAR ON TERROR, 117–33 (Cambria Press 2008); Stephanie Cooper Blum, *Preventive Detention in the War on Terror: A Comparison of How the United States, Britain and Israel Detain and Incapacitate Terrorist Suspects*, HOMELAND SECURITY AFFAIRS, VOL. IV, NO. 3 (October 2008); Amos Guiora, *An Israeli case for Administrative Detention*, OPINIO JURIS, June 15, 2009, http://opiniojuris.org/2009/06/15/an-israeli-case-for-administrative-detention/; Amos Guiora, *More on the Israeli Model*, OPINIO JURIS, June 16, 2009, http://opiniojuris.org/2009/06/16/more-on-the-israeli-model/; Amos Guiora, *Dilemmas in the Administrative Detention Paradigm*, OPINIO JURIS, June 17, 2009,

http://opiniojuris.org/2009/06/17/dilemmas-in-the-administrative-detention-paradigm/; Amos Guiora, *Judicial Review and Administrative Detention*, OPINIO JURIS, June 19, 2009, http://opiniojuris.org/2009/06/19/judicial-review-and-administrative-detention/; Daphne Barak-Erez and Matthew C. Waxman, *Secret Evidence – The Due Process of Terrorist Detentions*, 48 COLUM. J. TRANSNAT'L L. 3 (2009).

24 Barak-Erez, *Israel's Anti-Terrorist Law: Past, Present and Future*, 604.

25 COOPER BLUM, THE NECESSARY EVIL OF PREVENTIVE DETENTION IN THE WAR ON TERROR, 120 (quoting Emanuel Gross, *Human Rights, Terrorism and the Problem of Administrative Detention in Israel: Does Democracy Have the Right to Hold Terrorists as Bargaining Chips?* 18 ARIZ. J. INT'L. & COMP. L. 721, 757 (Fall, 2001)).

26 Barak-Erez, *Israel's Anti-Terrorist Law*, 598 (citing Defence (Emergency) Regulations 1945, Palestine Gazette no. 1442, Supp. No. 2, 1055 (Defence Regulations)).

27 Emergency Powers (Detention) Law, 5739-1979, S.H. 76, 33 L.S.I. 89-92 (Isr. 1979).

28 Revital Hovel, Chaim Levinson and Gili Cohen, *Israel Places Three Right-wing Extremists Under Administrative Detention*, HAARETZ (August 5, 2015), www.haaretz.com/news/diplomacy-defense/.premium-1.669624.

29 *Id.*, §1.

30 GROSS, THE STRUGGLE OF DEMOCRACY AGAINST TERRORISM, 124.

31 ASSOCIATION FOR CIVIL RIGHTS IN ISRAEL, THE COUNTER-TERRORISM BILL 2011, POSITION PAPER, EXECUTIVE SUMMARY (August 2011), www.acri.org.il/en/wp-content/uploads/2011/08/Counterterrorism-BillEng-3Aug2011.pdf.

32 Emergency Powers (Detention) Law, §2(a).

33 *Id.*, §4.

34 *Id.*, §9.

35 *Id.*, §8.

36 *Id.*, §6(c).

37 Emergency Powers (Detention) Law, §4(c).

38 *Id.*, §7.

39 Gross, *Human Rights, Terrorism and the problem of Administrative Detention in Israel*, 763 (quoting A.D.A. 1-2/88 Agbariya v. State of Israel, 42(1) P.D. 840, 844–45 (Heb.), "whether there is sufficient evidence to point to the fact that if the detainee were released, he would *almost certainly* pose a danger to public or State security").

40 Emergency Powers (Detention) Law, 57 §§1, 5.

41 Interview with Advocate Chen.

42 *Id.*, §6.

43 *Id.*, §5(a).

44 *Id.*, §5(d).

45 *Id.* §5(c).

46 John Does v. Ministry of Defense, CrimFH 7048/97, ¶1 (April 12, 2000).

47 *Id.*, ¶3.

48 *Id.*, ¶18.

49 *Id.*, ¶19.

50 *Id.*, ¶20.

51 *Id.*, ¶21.

52 *Id.*, ¶25.
53 Interview with Advocate Chen.
54 Incarceration of Unlawful Combatants Law, 5762-2002 (Isr. 2002).
55 *Id.*, §2.
56 *Id.*, §3(a).
57 ROACH, THE 9/11 EFFECT, 119.
58 Incarceration of Unlawful Combatants Law, §7.
59 A. v. State of Israel, CrimA 6659/06 (June 11, 2008).
60 *Id.*, ¶6.
61 *Id.*, ¶9 (citing PCAT v. Government of Israel, ¶¶18, 21).
62 *Id.*, ¶¶6, 11: "the express reference by the legislature to international humanitarian law, together with the requirement stipulated in the wording of the law that there is no prisoner of war status, show that the law was intended to apply only to *foreign* parties who belong to a terror organization that operates against the security of the state."
63 Interview with Advocate Chen.
64 *See e.g.* PCAT v. Government of Israel.
65 A. v. State of Israel, ¶12.
66 *Id.*
67 *Id.*, ¶13.
68 *Id.*
69 *Id.*, ¶14.
70 *Id.*, ¶15.
71 *Id*,. ¶¶19, 20, 21.
72 *Id.*
73 *See e.g.* the US case of Holder v. Humanitarian Law Project, 130 S. Ct. 2705 (2010), and US detention authority pursuant to National Defense Authorization Act of 2012, P.L. 112-88, §§1021, 1022.
74 A. v. State of Israel, ¶22 (citing *e.g.* Ajuri v. IDF Commander in West Bank [2002] IsrSC 56(6) 352, 372).
75 A. v. State of Israel, ¶22.
76 *Id.*
77 *Id.*, ¶27 (citing Basic Law (5752-1992), §5 Human Dignity & Liberty: "A person's liberty shall not be denied or restricted by imprisonment, arrest, extradition or in any other way").
78 *Id.*, ¶28 (citing Basic Law §8 Human Dignity & Liberty: "The rights under this Basic Law may only be violated by a law that befits the values of the State of Israel, is intended for a proper purpose, and to an extent that is not excessive, or in accordance with a law as aforesaid by virtue of an express authorization therein").
79 *Id.*, ¶30.
80 *See* Chapter 3, *infra*.
81 A. v. State of Israel, ¶31. The three subtests of fundamental criteria are i) "the rational connection test that requires the legislative measure that violates the constitutional right to correspond to the purpose that the law is intended to realize;" ii) "the least harmful measure test, which requires the legislation to violate the constitutional right to the smallest degree possible while achieving the purpose of the law;" and iii) "the test of proportionality in the narrow sense, according to which the violation of the constitutional right must be

commensurate with the social benefit arising from it."

82 *Id.* ¶32.
83 *Id.*, ¶¶33, 35.
84 *Id.*, ¶39.
85 *Id.*, ¶42.
86 Barak-Erez, *Israel's Anti-Terrorist Law*, 603 (citing Incarceration of Unlawful Combatants Law, §5(e)).
87 *Id.*, ¶43.
88 *Id.* (citing Justice A. Procaccia in Khadri v. IDF Commander in Judea and Samaria HCJ 11006/04 (unreported decision of December 13, 2004) ¶6, noting that the court has to act as "the mouth of the detainee").
89 *Id.*
90 *Id.*, ¶44 (citing Sufian v. IDF Commander in Gaza Strip, HCJ 3412/93 [1993] IsrSC 47(2) 843, 849).
91 *Id.*, ¶44.
92 A. v. State of Israel, ¶46 (citing Geneva Convention Relative to the Treatment of Prisoners of War (GC III) Art.118, August 12, 1949, 75 U.N.T.S. 135 (detention possible until the cessation of hostilities)).
93 National Defense Authorization Act of 2012, P.L. 112-88, §§1021, 1022, and Chapter 9, *infra*.
94 A. v. State of Israel, ¶46.
95 *Id.*
96 *Id.* (citing A v. Minister of Defence, CrimFH 7048/97 [2000] IsrSC 44(1) 721, 744).
97 *Id.*, ¶49.
98 B'TSELEM, THE BASIS FOR ADMINISTRATIVE DETENTION IN ISRAELI LAW (January 1, 2011), www.btselem.org/administrative_detention/israeli_law.
99 Order Regarding Security Provisions [consolidated version] (Judea and Samaria) (No. 1651) 5770-2009, Article B, Temporary Order §285(a).
100 *Id.*, §285(b).
101 *Id.*, §287.
102 *Id.*, §288.
103 *Id.*, §290.
104 *Id.*, §291.
105 *Id.*, Art. C.
106 *Id.*, §295.
107 *Id.*, §296(A).
108 *Id.*, §296(C).
109 *Id.*, §§297(A), 297(B).
110 *Id.*, §§§297(E), 297(H), 297(I).
111 *Id*, §298.
112 Marab v. IDF Commander in the West Bank, HCJ 3239/02 (February 3, 2003)
113 *Id.*, ¶¶1-4. Order 1500 permitted initial detention for eighteen days without a judicial order, and without judicial review during that period, and without access to a lawyer for a further fifteen days, although modifications were later made reducing the periods of detention without judicial review to twelve days, and without access to a lawyer to up to thirty-two days.
114 Marab v. IDF Commander in the West Bank, ¶20.
115 *Id.*

116 *Id.*
117 *Id.*
118 *Id.*, ¶21.
119 *Id.*, ¶23.
120 *Id.*
121 *Id.*
122 *Id.*, ¶26.
123 *Id.*, ¶32.
124 *Id.*, ¶34.
125 *Id.*, ¶35.
126 *Id.*, ¶43.
127 *Id.*
128 *Id.*, ¶44.
129 *Id.*, ¶46.
130 Barak-Erez and Waxman, *Secret Evidence*, 18.
131 *Id.*, 21 (quoting Itzhak Zamir, *Human Rights and National Security*, 23 Isr. L. Rev. 375, 399 (1989)).
132 Amos Guiora, *Dilemmas in the Administrative Detention Paradigm*, Opinio Juris, June 17, 2009.
133 Barak-Erez and Waxman, *Secret Evidence*, 21.
134 *Id.*
135 *Id.*, 22 (citing A v. State of Israel, ¶43).
136 *Id.*, 23 (citing Sofi v State of Israel, Administrative Petition Appeal 2595/09 (Isr. unpublished, Apr. 1, 2009)).
137 *Id.*, 35–47.
138 *Id.*, 24.
139 Shiri Krebs, *National Security, Secret Evidence and Preventive Detentions: the Israeli Supreme Court as a Case Study*, *in* Secrecy, National Security And The Vindication Of Constitutional Law, 147 (David Cole, Federico Fabbrini, and Arianna Vedaschi, eds) (Edward Elgar Publishing, 2013).
140 Barak-Erez and Waxman, *Secret Evidence*, 24 (referring to Art. 4 ICCPR).
141 U.N. Human Rights Committee, Consideration of Reports Submitted by States Parties under Article 40 of the Covenant, Third periodic report of States parties due in 2007: Israel, CCPR/C/ISR/3 ¶57 (November 21, 2008), *hereinafter* "HRC Israel's 3rd Report."
142 *See* U.N. Human Rights Committee, General Comment no. 29, States of Emergency (article 4), CCPR/C/21/Rev.1/Add.11 (August 31, 2001).
143 *See e.g.* Gross, *Human Rights, Terrorism and the Problem of Administrative Detention in Israel*, 767; *contra* John Quigley, *Israel's Forty Five Year Emergency: Are there Time Limits To Derogations From Human Rights Obligations?* 15 Mich. J. Int'l L. 491, 506–11 (Winter 1994).
144 HRC Israel's 3rd Report, ¶158.
145 *Id.*
146 *Id.*, ¶¶250–69.
147 Incarceration of Unlawful Combatants Law.
148 A v. The State of Israel.
149 U.N. Human Rights Committee, List of Issues to be Taken up in connection with the Consideration of the Third Periodic Report of Israel, ¶¶¶ 8, 16, 17 CCPR/C/ISR/Q/3 (November 17, 2009).

150 U.N. Human Rights Committee, Replies of the Government of Israel to the List of Issues (CCPR/C/ISR/Q/3/) to be taken up in connection with the consideration of the third periodic report of Israel (CCPR/C/ISR/3), 27–9 CCPR/C/ISR/Q/3/Add.1 (July 12, 2010).

151 *Id.*, 28.

152 U.N. Human Rights Committee, Consideration of reports submitted by States parties under article 40 of the Covenant, Concluding observations of the Human Rights Committee, 3 CCPR/C/ISR/CO/3 (Septembetr 3, 2010).

153 Ido Rosenzweig and Yuval Shani, *High Court of Justice Rejects Petition to End Israel's State of Emergency [HCJ 3091/99] [8.05.2012]*, The Israel Democracy Institute (May 8, 2012), www.idi.org.il/sites/english/ResearchAndPrograms/NationalSecurityandDemocracy/Terrorism_and_Democracy/Newsletters/Pages/41/1/1.aspx (quoting HCJ 3091/99 ACRI v. Knesset (Hebrew)).

154 *Id.*

155 *See* Appendix 2.

156 Gabriella Blum, *Judicial review of counterterrorism operations*, 47 Justice 17, 19.

157 B'tselem, Statistics On Palestinians In The Custody Of Israeli Security Forces, www.btselem.org/statistics/detainees_and_prisoners. Note that the numbers of detainees differ significantly according to who is preparing the report. E.g., the B'Tselem numbers are those supplied by the Israelis, who give the number of detainees in 2008 as 4,630, but the Palestinian Authority for Prisoner Affairs gives the number as 5,818. See The Public Committee Against Torture In Israel & Nadi Al Asir Palestinian Prisoner Society, When The Exception Becomes The Rule: Incommunicado Detention Of Palestinian Security Detainees (Nov. 2010) 12, fn.6, www.stoptorture.org.il/en/node/1659.

158 B'tselem, Statistics On Palestinians In The Custody Of Israeli Security Forces.

159 *See e.g.* Addameer Prisoner Support & Human Rights Organization, Administrative Detention In The Occupied Palestinian Territory, A Legal Analysis Report (July 2010), *www.addameer.org/files/Reports/administrative-detention-analysis-report-final.pdf;* Addameer Prisoner Support & Human Rights Organization, Administrative Detention In The Occupied Palestinian Territory (December 2010), www.addameer.org/files/Reports/en-addameer-administrative-detention-between-law-and-practice-december-2010.pdf; Association For Civil Rights In Israel, Five Questions On Administrative Detention And Administrative Control Orders In The Occupied Territories (April 17, 2012), www.acri.org.il/en/2012/04/17/five-questions-on-administrative-detention-and-administrative-control-orders-in-the-occupied-territories; Human Rights Watch, Israel: End Abusive Detention Practices (February 24, 2013), www.hrw.org/news/2013/02/23/israel-end-abusive-detention-practices.

160 Cooper Blum, The Necessary Evil Of Preventive Detention In The War On Terror, 128 (quoting Yigal Mersel, *Judicial Review of Counter-Terrorism Measures: The Israeli Model for the Role of the Judiciary during the Terror Era*, N.Y.U.J. Int'l. L & Pol, 38, 67–120 (November 2006)).

8 France

This chapter examines the preventive detention laws in a civil law country that has a long history of fighting terrorism with draconian laws. Two stages of detention are relevant in the terrorism context.

Garde à Vue[1]

Grounds

The French system of preventive detention in terrorism cases is an enhanced version of the regime of preventive detention used in general criminal cases.[2] A suspect is defined as a person who is suspected of having committed or is attempting to commit an offense.[3] The criteria for suspicion are "one or more plausible reasons to suspect a person of having committed or attempting to commit an offense."[4]

If evidence points to a person's involvement with a terrorist group, he or she can be arrested to prevent a terrorist act.[5] The suspect may be held preventively in Garde à Vue (GAV) for an extended period if a magistrate's preliminary investigation reveals a serious risk of an imminent act of terrorism. The initial length of GAV detention in terrorist cases is four days (as opposed to forty-eight hours in normal criminal cases), and this period can be extended twice by a judge for further tranches of twenty-four hours, totaling six days.[6] A French government comparative study of GAV in 2010 indicates that in 2009, of 617,849 persons held in GAV that year, 105,336 were held for more than twenty-four hours.[7]

The *procureur* or prosecutor has a dual role in GAV detention and interrogation: he is the person that is both involved in the police investigation of the potential crime and also authorizes detention for the first forty-eight hours.[8] In terrorism cases the investigating magistrate must approve the detention of the suspect for an initial period after arrest, during which time the suspect may be questioned.[9] In reality, in the vast number of cases, the magistrates get involved at a very early stage and give their approval in advance for the arrest of the suspect.[10]

In terrorism cases, extensions of detention may only be authorized by an independent judicial authority, called a *juge des libertes et de la detention*.[11] At the end of the detention period the suspect is either released or put under examination (*mis en examen*).[12] This occurs in about 4 percent of cases, when the inquiry is handed over to a *juge d'instruction*, who has wider powers of investigation in what is called the *instruction* inquiry, as well as having a judicial function.[13] In order to put a suspect under examination, the authorities need to find "serious and concordant indications that an offense has been committed."[14] At this point the magistrate can take into account "purely administrative intelligence material" supplied by intelligence agencies that has been collected by the agency in an administrative capacity, before they have begun working in a judicial framework to prepare a case for prosecution.[15] If the authorities want detention to continue, the suspect is held in *détention provisoire*, described below.

Concerns about the dual role of the judges were one of the reasons that prompted the establishment in 2008 of the Léger Commission to review criminal justice.[16] Although the Léger Commission believed that the *procureur's* role was key, the European Court of Human Rights (ECHR) had great misgivings about the judicial element of the *procureur's* role.[17] In April 2011 certain elements of the law relating to GAV were modified,[18] as discussed below. However, the new legislation did not alter the role of the *procureur* in supervising the conduct of the GAV.[19]

Procedure

The Code of Criminal Procedure gives detainees a limited number of rights: the right to be told the reason for arrest, to be given a medical examination, and to inform someone of their arrest, although that right can be denied if that contact is considered prejudicial to the investigation.[20] Although detainees had the right to silence, until the law was changed in April 2011, the police did not have to tell the detainees that they had that right.[21]

Access to lawyers

Until the recent change in the law, detainees' access to lawyers whilst in GAV was extremely limited. Access was allowed after seventy-two hours, but if the detention was extended, access to a lawyer was not permitted until the ninety-sixth hour, and even then only for thirty minutes.[22] Now detainees will be entitled to be notified of their right to have a lawyer present throughout the period of custody and during interrogations, but in terrorism cases, access to lawyers can still be delayed for seventy-two hours.[23] There does not appear to be a right of appeal against GAV detention.

Legal challenges

The law relating to GAV was amended in response to a number of both domestic and ECHR decisions, and certain aspects of the amended law were challenged during 2010 and 2011. In July and October 2010 there were a number of cases concerning access to lawyers both in the domestic courts and in the ECHR.[24] These cases triggered the passing of the amended law. In July, the French Constitutional Council in the case of *Daniel W.* declared it unconstitutional for a suspect not to have the benefit of counsel during questioning, and not to be informed of the right to silence.[25] On October 14, 2010, in *Brusco v. France* where the applicant had been denied access to a lawyer for twenty hours and not told of his right to silence, the ECHR ruled that these deprivations amounted to a violation of article 6 of the European Convention.[26] On October 19, 2010, in three judgments, the French Supreme Court declared that *Brusco* should be followed and that persons in GAV should be entitled to the assistance of lawyers at all times.[27] In addition, the right of a lawyer should be restricted only when there are compelling reasons based on the circumstances of the case.[28]

A group of French criminal lawyers challenged the GAV amendments on the grounds that they remained incompatible with Article 6 in a number of respects. For example, access to lawyers can still be delayed in terrorist cases, police can question a suspects before his lawyer arrives, lawyers still have a mere thirty minutes with their clients, they have limited access to the investigation files, lawyers may not attend searches, they can only ask questions at the end of interviews, and police have the right to bar questions they deem to interfere with the investigation.[29] The Constitutional Council ruled that the complaints had no merit.[30] That decision demonstrates that GAV occurs at a very early stage of an investigation, where evidence is provisional and untested, and that it is separate from any decision to prosecute.[31]

Détention provisoire

This is detention of a suspect under investigation for serious crimes including terrorism.[32] This tool can be used both *after* a crime has been committed pending trial, as well as *before* a crime has been committed, as suspects can be held with or without charge. For example, investigating magistrates can open an investigation into a possible crime of conspiracy to commit terrorism and use their expertise and judicial tools to prevent terrorist activity before these acts take place.[33] Despite the presumption of innocence in French law, in exceptional cases, for the necessity of the investigation or for reasons of security, a suspect may be placed in *détention provisoire*, provided a judge is satisfied that lesser measures would not suffice. Orders are made after an adversarial hearing with submissions made by the prosecutor, the accused, and his lawyer.

Since 2000, the initial maximum period for detention has been one year, but this can be extended after adversarial hearings, initially for six months, and thereafter for up to four years, as opposed to one year for non-terrorist offenses. (Prior to 2000, detention for serious crimes could be for an indefinite period.) The average length of *détention provisoire* in 2007 (the last year for which statistics are available) was 5.7 months.[34]

During the detention when investigation and interrogation may continue, suspects must be told about their right to silence and they are not held incommunicado. Once a person is subjected to *détention provisoire*, the detainee can request a review of detention at any time.[35]

Legal challenges

Many complaints have been made alleging violations of the European Convention, relating in particular to the length of time spent in detention and treatment of detainees. The ECHR has determined *détention provisoire* to be excessive and that it violates Article 5(3) on a number of occasions.[36] For example, in *Bernard v. France* the applicant was arrested on suspicion of being a member of the Breton Revolutionary Army and harboring members of ETA (Euskadi Ta Askatasuna) who had recently stolen explosives. He was placed under investigation for conspiring to commit terrorist acts and possessing explosives, and was held in *détention provisoire* for almost three years.[37]

In 1999, in *Tomasi v. France* the ECHR found numerous violations: of Article 3 for ill-treatment whilst in custody; of Article 5(3) because the applicant was detained for five years and seven months; and of Article 6 (1) because of the excessive time taken to investigate the complaints of ill-treatment.[38]

In 2011, in *Mourmand v. France* the applicants made various complaints relating to the treatment of their brother and son who had died whilst in police custody. They alleged that he had been excessively detained pending investigation for more than thirteen months in violation of Article 5(3), that his right to life had not been protected in violation of Article 2, he had not been given proper health care whilst in custody in violation of Article 3, and that the investigation into the cause of death had been far too slow in violation of Article 6(1). The case settled without an admission of liability on the part of France, with the applicants accepting 20,000 euros.[39]

Conclusions

Certain elements in each stage of the French detention model do not comply with the European Convention, as described above. Following the failure of the group of French lawyers to have some of the new GAV provisions declared unconstitutional by the Constitutional Council,[40] it remains to be seen if the challenge is taken to the ECHR.

The lengthy duration of *détention provisoire* has attracted much criticism. Between 1981 and 2002, France was condemned by the ECHR seventy times for different human rights violations, including for excessive length of detention both before trial and after completion of sentence, and treatment of detainees during detention.[41] Although France has reformed some aspects of the law relating to treatment of detainees, its only significant reaction to the condemnation in connection with the length of detention was to reduce the period in 2000 to the current levels.

So why, despite condemnation from human rights bodies and ECHR, as described above, does France retain such draconian laws? Above all, the French intend to stop terrorist attacks before they happen.[42] A tension in France exists between the right to freedom from arbitrary arrest and detention, enshrined in the French Bill of Rights of 1789, the International Covenant on Civil and Political Rights (ICCPR) and the European Convention, and the right of security as a condition of the exercise of freedoms. In 2003 legislation stated that the right to security was a fundamental right[43] and one of the conditions for the exercise of individual and collective freedom. To the French, it is the most important freedom[44] and supersedes other considerations.[45] Their experience dealing with Algerian resistance both in Algeria and in France may have reinforced the importance of the "security first" norm over adopting more proportionate responses to terrorism.[46] Furthermore, the lack of public debate, and little public opprobrium, suggests possible general public consensus about the security measures.[47]

French citizens appear more willing to give up greater degrees of fundamental liberties, in exchange for the services, safety, and stability that their government provides.[48] Collective safety is more important than individual rights.[49] The bottom line is that "freedom to walk the streets or take the subway without fear of bombs lies at the base of all civil liberties."[50]

Notes

1 *See* Jacqueline Hodgson, French Criminal Justice, (Hart Publishing 2005); Jacqueline Hodgson, *The French Prosecutor in Question*, 67 Wash. & Lee L. Rev. 1361 (2010).

2 *See* Dan E. Stigall, Counterterrorism And The Comparative Law Of Investigative Detention, 135–56 (Cambria Press, 2009).

3 Loi No. 2002-1138 (Fr.). (September 9, 2002).

4 Code de Procédure Pénale (CPP) Art. 77.

5 For example, on July 16, 2013, French authorities arrested and placed in GAV Norwegian neo-Nazi sympathizer, Kristian Vikernes, on suspicion of preparing to commit an act of terrorism on a large scale. Michael Sadkowski, *Varg Vikernes: meurtre, black metal et néopaganisme*, Le Monde (July 16, 2013), www.lemonde.fr/societe/article/2013/07/16/varg-vikernes-meurtre-black-metal-et-neopaganisme_3448253_3224.html?xtmc=vikernes&xtcr=1. Minister of the Interior Manuel Valls justified the arrest despite the fact that no target or plan had been identified, on the grounds that it was necessary when faced with terrorism to act before rather than after the event. ("M. Valls, tout en reconnaissant qu'il n'y a pour le moment *"ni cible, ni projet identifié"*, a justifié cette décision par la nécessité, face au terrorisme, *"d'agir avant, et non pas après"*.) *Valls justifie l'arrestation préventive du Norvégien Vikernes*, Le Monde (July 16,

2013), www.lemonde.fr/societe/article/2013/07/16/un-norvegien-neonazi-interpelle-en-correze_3448207_3224.html.

6 CPP, Art. 706-88.

7 Republique Française, Etude D'impact, Projet De Loi Relatif A La Garde A Vue, 15 (October 12, 2010), *available at* www.legifrance.gouv.fr/content/download/ei_garde_a_vue.pdf.

8 Jacqueline Hodgson, *The French Prosecutor in Question*, 1370.

9 Frank Foley, Countering Terrorism In Britain And France, 181 (Cambridge University Press, 2013).

10 *Id.*

11 Hodgson, *The French Prosecutor in Question*, 1369.

12 Foley, Countering Terrorism In Britain And France, 183.

13 Hodgson, *The French Prosecutor in Question*, 1369.

14 Foley, Countering Terrorism In Britain And France, 184.

15 *Id.*, 117, 185.

16 Hodgson, *The French Prosecutor in Question*, 1379–86 (discussing the Léger Report, Philippe Léger, Rapport Du Comite De Reflexion Sur La Justice Penale (2009)).

17 *Id.*, 1378–9; Medvedyev v. France, Appl. No. 3394/03, ECHR, (2010) 51 EHRR 39, ¶124 (March 29, 2010); Moulin v. France, Appl. 37104/06, ECHR (November 23, 2010), *available in French only at* http://cmiskp.echr.coe.int/tkp197/view.asp?action=html&documentId=877357&portal=hbkm&source=externalbydocnumber&table=F69A27FD8FB86142BF01C1166DEA398649.

18 Loi n° 2011-392 du 14 avril 2011 relative à la garde à vue (April 15, 2011).

19 Jacqueline Hodgson, *Extending the right to legal advice to suspects in police custody in France*, Jackie Hodgson's Blog (February 3, 2011), http://blogs.warwick.ac.uk/jackiehodgson.

20 Human Rights Watch, Preempting Justice. Counterterrorism Laws And Procedures In France, 57 (July 2008) (citing CPP, Art. 63).

21 Stigall, Counterterrorism And The Comparative Law Of Investigative Detention, 140.

22 CPP, Art. 63.

23 Loi n° 2011-392; Jacqueline Hodgson, *Extending the right to legal advice to suspects in police custody in France.*

24 Clifford Chance, Solicitors *From Courts to Parliament: an Imposed Reform of Police Custody* (client briefing, July 2011) (U.K.).

25 Decision n° 2010-14/22 QPC of July 30, 2010, ¶29 (July 31, 2010), *available in English at* www.conseil-constitutionnel.fr/conseil-constitutionnel/root/bank/download/201014_22QPCen201014qpc.pdf.

26 Jacqueline Hodgson, *Storming the Bastille…or at least the Police Station*, Jackie Hodgson's Blog, (May 2, 2011) (citing Brusco v. France, Requête no 1466/07, ECHR (October 14, 2010), *press release in English available at* http://cmiskp.echr.coe.int/tkp197/view.asp?action=open&documentId=875656&portal=hbkm&source=externalbydocnumber&table=F69A27FD8FB86142BF01C1166DEA398649).

27 Clifford Chance (citiing Cass. Crim., 3 arrets: n.10-82306. No. 10-82902, no. 10-85051 (October 19, 2010)); Jacqueline Hodgson, *Storming the Bastille…or at least the Police Station.*

28 Dean Spielman, *Jurisprudence of the European Court of Human Rights and the Constitutional Systems of Europe*, *in* THE OXFORD HANDBOOK OF COMPARATIVE LAW, 1239 (Michel Rosenfeld and Andros Sajo, eds) (Oxford University Press, 2012).

29 Clifford Chance; Jacqueline Hodgson, *French lawyers fail in their challenge to the new garde à vue regime.*

30 Jacqueline Hodgson, *French lawyers fail in their challenge to the new garde à vue regime* (citing Décision n° 2011-191/194/195/196/197 QPC).

31 *Id.*

32 CPP, Art. 144: Pre–trial detention can only be imposed if it is the sole means to:

 1 preserve material evidence or clues or to prevent either witnesses or victims being pressurized, or fraudulent conspiracy between persons under judicial examination and their accomplices;

 2 protect the person under judicial examination, to guarantee that he remains at the disposal of the law, to put an end to the offence or to prevent its renewal;

 3 put an end to an exceptional and persistent disruption of public order caused by the seriousness of the offence, the circumstances in which it was committed, or the gravity of the harm that it has caused.

 www.legifrance.gouv.fr/Traductions/en-English/Legifrance-translations.

33 Jeremy Shapiro and Benedicte Suzan, *The French Experience of Counter-Terrorism*, 45 SURVIVAL 67, 85 (Spring 2003).

34 *Id.*, 7.

35 CPP, Art. 148.

36 ANNA OEHMICHEN, TERRORISM AND ANTI-TERROR LEGISLATION: THE TERRORISED LEGISLATOR? 378 (Intersentia, 2009) (discussing Morgani v. France, Appl. No. 17831/91, ECHR (November 30, 1994) (detention for over three years) and Debboub v. France, Appl. No. 37786/97, ECHR (November 9, 1999) (detention for over four years)).

37 *Id;* Gerard Bernard v France, Appl. No. 27678/02, ECHR (September 26, 2006).

38 Tomasi v. France, Appl. No. 12850/87, ECHR (August 27, 1992) (1993) 15 EHRR 1.

39 Mourmand v. France, Appl. No. 4989/07, ECHR (November, 25, 2011).

40 Jacqueline Hodgson, *French lawyers fail in their challenge to the new garde à vue regime*, JACKIE HODGSON'S BLOG.

41 Jacqueline Hodgson, *Suspects, Defendants and Victims in the French Criminal Process*, 51 (4) I.C.L.Q. 781, 783 (2002).

42 *Detention of Terrorism Suspects in Britain and France, Hearing Before the Commission on Security and Co-operation in Europe*, July 15, 2008 (Statement of Jeremy Shapiro).

43 Loi No. 2003-239, art.1 (Fr. 18 March 2003).

44 HODGSON, FRENCH CRIMINAL JUSTICE, 39, 45.

45 FOLEY, COUNTERING TERRORISM IN BRITAIN AND FRANCE, 5.

46 *Id.*, 61.

47 *Id.*, 63.

48 Calliope Makedon Sudborough, *The War Against Fundamental Rights: French Counterterrorism Policy and the Need to Integrate International Security and*

Human Rights Agreements, 30 SUFFOLK TRANSNAT'L L. REV. 459 (Summer 2007).

49 CHATHAM HOUSE MEETING OF INTERNATIONAL LAW DISCUSSION GROUP, LEGISLATING AGAINST TERRORISM – THE FRENCH APPROACH (December 8, 2005).

50 Shapiro and Suzan, *The French Experience of Counter-Terrorism*, 67–98.

9 United States

This chapter analyzes preventive detention in the United States. Although preventive detention of terror suspects *per se* is not permitted in domestic law, a number of devices have been employed within the United States that have achieved that very goal. Beyond American shores, another device – the law of armed conflict (LOAC) – provides the framework to detain indefinitely persons categorized as some sort of combatant.

The LOAC section of the chapter[1] focuses on the detention of a discrete group of persons in detention at Guantánamo Bay, Cuba. Detention in Guantánamo is compared with that in Afghanistan[2] until the December 2014 closure of the last detention facility and release of all remaining detainees.[3]

Even before his election, President Obama pledged to close Guantánamo,[4] and he remains committed to this plan.[5] However, Congress has persisted in blocking the transfer of Guantánamo detainees into the United States, either for prosecution or long-term detention.[6]

Out of the 780 held since 9/11, 112 persons remain in LOAC detention in Guantánamo as at November 2015,[7] and 53 may be transferred out by the end of 2015.[8] None of the seven persons captured since January 2009 have been sent to Guantánamo. Six have been sent to the United States for criminal trial[9] and the seventh was transferred to the custody of the Kurds in Iraq, after being detained and interrogated by the United States for nearly three months.[10]

Preventive detention in U.S. domestic law

Under the general federal criminal law, suspects arrested without warrant[11] must be brought before a magistrate promptly to ensure that there was probable cause for the arrest.[12] In *County of Riverside v McLaughlin* the Supreme Court held that "prompt" generally means within forty-eight hours.[13] Even forty-eight hours may be deemed excessive if the suspect can prove unreasonable delay, which can include "delays for the purpose of gathering additional evidence to justify the arrest."[14]

Grounds

In order to obtain a warrant to seize or arrest terror suspects for any charge and to comply with the Fourth Amendment,[15] law enforcement officers are required to show probable cause that a crime has been, or is being, committed. There are some exceptions to the requirement to show probable cause, as discussed below.[16] Although the meaning of probable cause has been refined over time,[17] the Supreme Court has not used the words that a suspect was "about to" or "likely to" commit an offense, except in the short investigative stop context,[18] and nor has the Court ruled on the issue of probable cause for arrests to *prevent* offenses,[19] perhaps because by definition, probable cause relates to past or current activity.

The Obama administration has examined the question of whether the forty-eight hour period of detention before charge should be extended. The review was ordered in the wake of criticism about the handling of the arrest of Nigerian Farouk Abdulmutallab. He had attempted to blow up a Northwest Airlines flight en route to Detroit on December 25, 2009. Federal Bureau of Investigation (FBI) agents interrogated Abdulmutallab without *Mirandizing* him for nearly an hour.[20] Criticism erupted immediately, with cries that he "should have been designated an enemy combatant and shipped straight to Guantánamo,"[21] and complaints that he was *Mirandized* at all.[22]

Gaining intelligence is often hard to do once suspects have been arrested, because pursuant to *Miranda*, suspects have to be informed of their right to remain silent prior to custodial questioning.[23] If the warning is not given, any statements of the suspect may not be used in court. However, where there is a need to question a suspect in order to protect public safety, as in the case of *Quarles*,[24] there is no requirement to give the *Miranda* warning, and any un-*Mirandized* statements made by a suspect in such cases are likely to be admissible in court.[25]

If the fruits of the interview are to be used in a criminal trial, the law only affords a window of up to forty-eight hours to interrogate before a suspect must be charged and brought before a court. A broader use has been advocated of the *Quarles* public safety exception to enable a longer period of questioning in the counter-terrorism context.[26]

President Obama ordered a thorough review of the guidelines governing the arrest procedure, and his lawyers began to evaluate whether Congress could pass a law permitting detention longer than the current forty-eight hour period.[27] Whilst the deliberations were ongoing, another terrorist plot was disrupted on May 1, 2010. Faisal Shahzad, a United States citizen, attempted to detonate a car bomb in Times Square, New York. He was questioned under the public safety exception "until agents could determine that there was no imminent terrorist threat."[28] After he was read his rights, he waived them and continued talking for almost two weeks.[29]

Shortly after the Shahzad incident, the White House circulated to Congress a draft plan it had crafted. The plan included a proposal to codify the *Quarles* public safety exception into a "national security exception."[30] A second, more controversial, proposal extended the period of time in which a suspect could be detained without charge to seven days.[31]

Amidst all the predictable controversy,[32] the entire plan was "shelved."[33] Thus the forty-eight hour *status quo* remains.

Examples of preventive detention in U.S. law

Preventive detention has been in use in the United States for many years. It is "an established part of United States law ... an integral feature of the American legal landscape."[34] State and federal law permit the preventive detention of persons in diverse situations to prevent a variety of harms, including for example, refusal of bail to persons awaiting trial or deportation. In the context of pre-trial detention, a form of administrative detention exists as a measure to prevent terrorism by keeping suspects who are remanded in custody, prior to trial, in solitary confinement and incommunicado.[35] "Initial placement" of an inmate into administrative detention can be for up to one year.[36]

Other preventive detention measures include quarantine of persons with communicable diseases, detention of the mentally ill, as well as the continued detention of convicted sex offenders after the completion of prison sentences.[37] United States law possibly avoids preventive detention except when it is deemed necessary to prevent grave public harms.[38]

Turning specifically to preventive detention of terror suspects, Human Rights First has analyzed over a hundred cases relating to international terrorism that have been successfully prosecuted in the United States federal criminal system. Their survey highlights a wide range of relevant laws, including those dealing with immigration violations, money laundering, and fraud, that have been used successfully against suspected terrorists.[39] However, very few laws offer scope for making an arrest before an offense has actually been committed, unless the definition of the crime includes acts of conspiracy, planning, or preparation, attempts,[40] or even making threats.[41] In those situations any preventive detention would in fact be post-charge, pre-trial detention if the suspect is refused bail.

The United States has been able to use a number of offenses that by definition include inchoate elements to arrest and detain many suspects, by showing probable cause of early pre-crime activity.[42] In addition, several "devices" are used to detain certain groups of suspects preventatively.

Other ways to detain preventively in U.S. domestic law

Inchoate offenses

Conspiracy has been used frequently to charge suspect terrorists at an early stage.[43] Out of 415 charges connected with 155 al-Qaeda-related convictions between 1997 and 2012, 22 (5.30 percent) related to general conspiracy, and 121 (23.85 percent) related to conspiracy to commit specified offenses other than material support.[44] In cases other than conspiracy to give material support, an agreement to commit an offense is a fundamental requirement.[45] By definition this means that the growing phenomenon of the solo actor or "lone wolf"[46] cannot be charged with conspiracy. Prosecutors can arrest suspects at a fairly early stage in the commission of an offense, provided that the relevant statute is sufficiently specific and certain elements of the agreement between parties exist.[47]

Material support

The material support statutes[48] permit arrests to be made on a showing of probable cause that early pre-crime activity has occurred. Violation of material support statutes resulted in 100 out of 415 al-Qaeda-related convictions (24.09 percent) between 1997 and 2012,[49] and is now also being used to prosecute supporters of Da'esh.[50] These laws are so broadly drafted that people can be detained preventively, without proof of performance of any actual harmful acts.[51]

The scope of §2339A is vast.[52] It has no connection to foreign terrorist organizations, but instead is predicated on forty-seven offenses (which are not necessarily terrorism crimes).[53] These include bombing a place of public use, a government facility, or a transportation system,[54] or killing, injuring persons in the United States, or using a dangerous weapon in a way that involves conduct that transcends national boundaries.[55] It is irrelevant whether or not the predicate offense occurs: all that is required is that the suspect provided support with the intent or knowledge that the support would be used for, or in preparation for, the predicate offense, as well as conspiracy to commit the predicate offense.[56] This means that §2339A enables prosecutors to intervene in and disrupt nefarious activity at a very early stage. It covers both the activity of solo actors, who can provide themselves as personnel,[57] as well as conduct amounting to mere preparation,[58] provided that there is some connection with a predicate offense.

§2339A has been described as "perhaps the single most important charge" in terror prosecutions.[59] It has become useful charge from the point of view of prevention, but "by shifting the point of potential prosecutorial intervention further back along the continuum between thought and deed, the statute entails a variety of offsetting costs."[60] Those costs include the possibility of false positives where liability turns mainly on the intentions of the suspect and where opportunities to gather further intelligence and evidence are lost once a suspect is arrested and charged.[61]

§2339B criminalizes supporting the acts of others without establishing any sort of involvement by the suspect in a terrorist act, other than a suspect's provision of material support to a foreign terrorist organization. Thus §2339B will not apply to the activities of an unaffiliated suspect so from one point of view, it is narrower in scope than §2339A. However, certain activities covered by §2339B have been subject to challenge for over breadth as well as violation of the First Amendment.[62] Examples of the type of activities that constitute material support include speech advocating lawful and non-violent activity with a foreign terrorist organization,[63] and translating and disseminating pro-jihadist materials.[64]

Material witness statute[65]

This statute is used to preventively detain people who have not committed a crime and who are not even suspected of committing a crime. The power dates from 1789.[66] It has been described as "the most purely preventive detention authority within the criminal justice system."[67] Material witness warrants can be used to arrest and detain persons believed to be material witnesses to a crime if a judicial officer determines that such a person would flee if served with a subpoena to testify at grand jury proceedings or a trial. An order for detention is therefore made solely on the basis that the person might seek to avoid his civic duty of giving evidence. Although probable cause is required for a warrant, the authorities merely have to show probable cause that the person may have information relevant to a criminal investigation and will not respond to a subpoena. Commentators suggest that this is a lower standard than that required to arrest suspected criminals generally.[68] A person can be detained until he or she is required to give evidence, although no material witness may be detained if the testimony can be adequately acquired by deposition and if further detention is not necessary to prevent a failure of justice.[69]

Many commentators have criticized the misuse of this statute as a detention tool,[70] because, for example, the Bush administration failed to call its material witnesses to trial in many cases, and because of the handling of the cases of Jose Padilla, a United States citizen, and Ali Saleh Kahlah al-Marri, a citizen of Qatar but a United States resident, as discussed below. Human Rights Watch asserted that after 9/11 the government used the material witness law for reasons other than obtaining testimony of witnesses, such as detaining terror suspects in cases where probable cause to arrest had not been established.[71] Yet the Justice Department's Office of Professional Responsibility's inquiry into the use of the material witness law after 9/11 concluded that "the material witness statute was not misused in any of the cases it reviewed."[72]

Another controversial case is that of Abdullah al-Kidd,[73] who was detained in the United States at Dulles Airport as he was about to board a plane for Saudi Arabia and held for sixteen days in federal custody. He was then placed on supervised release for fourteen months until the trial of a terror suspect, but was never called as a witness. Al-Kidd issued a complaint seeking damages.[74]

Al-Kidd alleged that the then Attorney General John Ashcroft authorized federal prosecutors and law enforcement officials to use the material witness statute to detain individuals with suspected ties to terrorist organizations. It was alleged that federal officials had "no intention of calling most of these individuals as witnesses, and that they were detained, at Ashcroft's direction, because federal officials suspected them of supporting terrorism but lacked sufficient evidence to charge them with a crime."[75]

Ashcroft filed a motion to dismiss based on absolute and qualified immunity, which the District Court denied. A divided panel of the United States Court of Appeals for the Ninth Circuit affirmed, holding that the Fourth Amendment prohibits pre-textual arrests absent probable cause of criminal wrongdoing, and that Ashcroft could not claim qualified or absolute immunity.[76]

Ashcroft appealed to the Supreme Court. Justice Scalia, writing for the Court, reversed the Ninth Circuit decision and held that there was no violation of the Fourth Amendment:

> Because al-Kidd concedes that individualized suspicion supported the issuance of the material-witness arrest warrant; and does not assert that his arrest would have been unconstitutional absent the alleged pretextual use of the warrant; we find no Fourth Amendment violation. Efficient and evenhanded application of the law demands that we look to whether the arrest is objectively justified, rather than to the motive of the arresting officer.[77]

Justice Sotomayor commented: "Whether the Fourth Amendment permits the pretextual use of a material witness warrant for preventive detention of an individual whom the Government has no intention of using at trial is, in my view, a closer question than the majority's opinion suggests."[78] However, she did not consider that this case presented an occasion to address the proper scope of the material witness statute or its constitutionality.[79] Thus the Court neatly sidestepped the issue of deciding the constitutionality of pretextual arrests of suspected terrorists pursuant to the material witness statute. Al-Kidd's subsequent claim against the FBI relating to his sixteen-day detention was settled for compensation of $385,000.[80]

Immigration laws

Preventive detention pursuant to the immigration detention system affects more people than any other preventive detention regime in the United States.[81] For example, in 2010, almost 392,000 people were held in immigration detention.[82] Aliens can be detained without charge, without a showing of probable cause of any crime, merely to determine their immigration status, including in situations where there are visa violations.[83]

Dan Stigall and David Cole have separately highlighted the invidious position of immigration detainees as regards to, for example, not being informed of rights, the use of secret information, difficulty in gaining access to lawyers, and obtaining bail.[84] In 2009 Amnesty International argued that many of the conditions of immigration detention breached the right to liberty in Article 9 of the International Covenant on Civil and Political Rights (ICCPR).[85] In 2009 the United States Department of Homeland Security and Immigration and Customs Enforcement pledged to transform immigration detention by moving it away from its use of jails and jail-like facilities to places with conditions more appropriate to detain civil immigration law detainees. However, Human Rights First reported in 2011 that little improvement could be discerned.[86]

Aliens can be detained for a ninety-day removal period. This period can be extended if the alien has been ordered removed and the attorney general has certified the alien to be a risk to the community or unlikely to comply with the removal order. In the event of connections with terrorism, the period can be even longer.[87] However, the period of detention can range from 90 to 180 days,[88] and asylum seekers have been detained for an average of 102 days up to a year.[89]

However, the detention cannot be indefinite. In *Zadvydas v. Davis* the Supreme Court held that "once removal is no longer reasonably foreseeable, continued detention is no longer authorized by statute."[90] Further, the Court noted that Congress had "doubted the constitutionality of detention for more than six months," and it recognized that period as a limit on detention.[91] This did not mean that every alien had to be necessarily released after six months, rather, "an alien may be held in confinement until it has been determined that there is no significant likelihood of removal in the reasonably foreseeable future."[92]

The case of Ibrahim Turkmen is an example of the use of immigration law as a pretext to detain a terror suspect. He and seven non-United States citizens, of Middle Eastern, South Asian or North African origin, were arrested after 9/11 on alleged immigration violations and treated as "of interest" to the government's terrorist investigation. They were detained under a blanket "hold-until-cleared" policy, pursuant to which they were held without bond until cleared of terrorist ties by the FBI. Six of the detainees were Muslim and two were Hindu. They claimed *inter alia* that immigration violations were used "as a cover, as an excuse" to investigate whether they were tied to terrorism, and that their excessive detention violated their Fourth and Fifth Amendment rights. The District Court rejected these claims.[93]

The Second Circuit confirmed that ruling and held that the detention was supported by the Immigration Judge's findings of removability, which constituted "a good deal more than probable cause."[94] The government had shown an "objectively reasonable belief that the detentions were authorized."[95] Furthermore, no authority clearly established "an equal protection right to be free of selective enforcement of the immigration laws based on national origin, race, or religion at the time of plaintiffs' detentions."[96] The approach of the courts indicates deference to the executive branch of government, and an unwillingness to evaluate the underlying counter-terrorism policy in place at that time.

Section 412 USA PATRIOT Act[97]

This provision empowers the attorney general unilaterally to detain aliens for seven days without charge if he certifies that he has reasonable grounds (as opposed to probable cause) to believe that the person is a national security threat. This is another pure form of preventive detention of aliens only, but there is no equivalent law to deal with the homegrown United States citizen/national/resident terrorist threat. The detainee has a right of appeal to the United States Court of Appeals for the District of Columbia Circuit. After seven days, either charges must be filed or deportation proceedings begun. If removal is unlikely in the foreseeable future, the alien can still be detained if the attorney general re-certifies the national security risk every six months, thus raising the prospect of indefinite detention. Two of the most significant deficiencies of the section are that it allows indefinite detention on what may be called a technicality (the automatic re-certification as described above) and that it fails to provide adequate oversight from an authority outside the executive branch.[98] However, the section has never been used, and thus has not been judicially tested.[99]

Detention in a state of emergency

The laws of many countries permit the possibility of relaxing the obligation to guarantee *inter alia* the right to liberty when a state of emergency exists, subject to satisfying a number of criteria. International human rights jurisprudence sets the boundaries for preventive detention provisions found in domestic laws in times of actual and imminent terror attacks. The United States has a very limited version of this tool in the form of the Suspension Clause,[100] which "implies a *de facto* preventive detention authority in very limited circumstances."[101] The Suspension Clause permits Congress to suspend the writ of *habeas corpus* in times of "Rebellion or Invasion" where public safety requires it. If the writ of *habeas corpus* is suspended, this means that anyone detained during this time would not be able to challenge detention.[102] This power has been rarely invoked.[103]

Preventive detention under LOAC

Introduction

The shift after the events of 9/11 from the traditional criminal law approach in terrorism cases[104] to LOAC[105] may have occurred for several reasons, including the fact that United States domestic criminal law does not generally permit detention to incapacitate terrorists, disrupt terror plots, or gather information.[106]

Immediately after the attacks the Bush administration very quickly decided that America's old approach to treating terrorism as a crime was inadequate: "Almost without discussion, it was agreed that a new kind of enemy required new tactics."[107] The administration immediately went onto a war footing, but the legal framework to detain in accordance with LOAC principles evolved slowly.

On September 12, 2001, the United Nations Security Council passed a resolution recognizing the right of the United States to self-defense in response to the attacks, which it described as a "threat to international peace and security."[108] On September 18, 2001, Congress passed the Authorization for Use of Military Force (AUMF), which permitted the president to:

> use all necessary and appropriate force against those nations, organizations or persons he determines planned, authorized, committed or aided the terrorist attacks that occurred on September 11, 2001, or harbored such organizations or persons, in order to prevent any future acts of international terrorism against the United States by such nations, organizations or persons.[109]

Al-Qaeda, harbored by the Taliban, was quickly deemed the organization that had masterminded the terror. The Bush administration initially contended that the Geneva Conventions (GCs) did not apply to al-Qaeda or the Taliban.[110] This view prevailed until the 2006 Supreme Court ruling in *Hamdan*, which held that Common Article 3 applied to the conflict with al-Qaeda, i.e. treating the conflict as a non-international armed conflict (NIAC).[111] Despite denying the applicability of the GCs to the terrorists, the Administration wanted to treat the conflict as an international armed conflict (IAC) for the purposes of picking up and detaining terror suspects. The administration believed that it would then have the authority to hold the suspects until the cessation of hostilities – a power normally applicable to prisoners of war (POWs) – within the context of an IAC.[112]

In a 2011 White House fact sheet, under the heading of Support for a Strong International Framework,[113] the Obama administration urged the Senate to approve the adoption of Additional Protocol (AP) II (which has detailed humane treatment standards and fair trial guarantees in NIACs) and stated that the United States government chose "out of a sense of legal obligation" to treat the principles set forth in Article 75 of AP I as applicable to any person it detains in an international armed conflict, and it expected all other nations to adhere to these principles as well.[114] However, it appears that the White House subsequently decided that Article 75 would not apply to al-Qaeda or the Taliban.[115] In 2012, as a participant in the non-binding Copenhagen Process relating to NIACs,[116] and in the 2015 Department of Defense Law of War Manual,[117] the United States essentially endorsed most of the AP II provisions.

Detention authority

The power to detain derives solely from United States domestic law. In *al-Bihani v. Obama* the United States Court of Appeals for the DC Circuit stated "the international laws of war as a whole have not been implemented domestically by Congress and are therefore not a source of authority for the United States courts."[118] Thus the power to detain started with the AUMF, which does not mention detention. However, in 2004, in *Hamdi v. Rumsfeld*, which concerned a United States citizen who had been detained for two years on United States soil as an enemy combatant, a plurality of the Supreme Court held that the AUMF authorized the detention of United States citizens.[119]

The Obama administration adopted a new standard for the government's authority to detain in early March 2009. Instead of relying on the commander-in-chief authority, the administration claimed to "draw on the international laws of war."[120] That standard was set out in a filing with the District Court for the District of Columbia, and was still tied to the perpetrators of the 9/11 attacks, as well as persons "who were part of, or substantially supported, Taliban or al-Qaida forces or associated forces."[121]

Most detention provisions derive from National Defense Authorization Act (NDAA) of 2012,[122] as amended. Although this law was "intended to codify the present understanding of the detention authority conferred by the AUMF, as interpreted and applied by the Executive and D.C. Circuit,"[123] many issues were not addressed. These include the full scope of detention authority, particularly the circumstances in which United States citizens may be detained as enemy belligerents, and the extent of protections available to non-citizens held outside the United States.[124]

The NDAA of 2013 prohibited the indefinite detention of United States citizens and lawful permanent residents.[125] The position of United States citizens and permanent residents apprehended abroad was not clarified, nor the position of aliens without permanent resident status who are arrested in the United States, but these persons were permitted to seek *habeas corpus* review of their detention and were entitled to the Constitution's due process rights.[126]

Now that some terrorist groups have diminishing connections to al-Qaeda[127] and attention has been turned to combating Da'esh, many have questioned whether the AUMF is obsolete and should be replaced.[128] The administration's view in 2015 is that because the predecessor of Da'esh merged with al-Qaeda in 2004, it falls under the scope of the AUMF and no new statutory authority is required.[129]

Most of the detention authority provisions in the NDAA 2012 remain in place as at August 2015. Congress has affirmed that the authority of the president to use all necessary and appropriate force pursuant to the AUMF "includes the authority … to detain covered persons … pending disposition under the law of war."[130] The definition of "covered persons"[131] replicates the definition adopted by the administration in 2009.[132] For some time the federal courts had been upholding the detention of persons who are part of, or members of al-Qaeda.[133] The NDAA put "Congress's stamp on a dubious – and untested – interpretation of military detention authority" by leaving undefined what is meant by "substantial support" and "associated forces," and raised the question of whether detention of people in these two categories was permitted under LOAC.[134]

Four alternatives are listed as to "disposition under the law of war:"[135] trial by military commission; trial by an alternative court or tribunal having lawful jurisdiction (which could be a federal court); transfer to the detainee's country of origin or any other country; or detention without trial until the end of hostilities.[136] Yet linking the duration of detention to the end of hostilities (which is derived from GC III Article 118 and only applicable in IACs) is a difficult fit with the cessation of terrorist attacks. The non-binding Copenhagen Process relating to NIACs ties the duration of detention to when circumstances justifying detention have ceased to exist.[137] However, even that definition does not really assist in the context of ongoing and sporadic terrorist attacks worldwide, which are hard to classify as armed conflicts.

Section 1021(d) of the NDAA affirms that nothing in the section is intended to limit or expand the authority of the president or the scope of the AUMF.[138] Commentators are divided as to whether the legislation changes existing law.[139] Section 1021(e) states that nothing in the section shall affect existing law relating to the detention of United States citizens, lawful permanent resident, or anyone else captured or arrested in the United States.[140] Yet the law relating to detention is not settled. Although in *Hamdi* a plurality of the Supreme Court held that the AUMF authorized the detention of United States citizens,[141] Hamdi was a United States citizen captured outside the United States during an international armed conflict. The issues raised in the cases of United States citizen Padilla[142] and United States resident al-Marri,[143] both of whom were arrested inside the United States, are still unresolved.[144] It is still unclear whether the AUMF gives a future president the authority to place a citizen or permanent resident of the United States, who is arrested *inside* the United States, in long-term military detention.[145]

Section 1022 provides for military custody until "disposition under the laws of war" (as described in Section 1021) of covered persons. Section 1022 does not apply to United States citizens at all or to lawful permanent residents with respect to conduct inside the United States, except to the extent permitted by the United States Constitution.[146]

Military custody for this group of people is mandatory unless the president issues a waiver that must be certified to be in the national security interests of the United States.[147] However, military detention is limited to certain categories of persons. One such category includes foreign persons captured inside or outside the United States. Another category covers lawful permanent residents, captured inside or outside the United States in the course of AUMF-authorized hostilities, whose conduct took place outside the United States (that is, against United States interests abroad). This detention is subject to the proviso that such persons are either members of, or part of (but not providing support to), al-Qaeda, or an associated force working with or directed by al-Qaeda and that such persons participated in planning, or carrying out an attack, or attempted attack against the United States, or its coalition partners. However, the section does not cover persons who are part of the Taliban or its associated forces, nor, it seems, to arrests in the United States made by the FBI or other law enforcement agencies.[148] Indeed, it is made clear that nothing in the section will affect the authority of existing domestic law enforcement agencies, even if the person is held in military custody.[149]

Mandatory military detention cannot occur until the government has made a determination that a person is in the relevant category.[150] This can take a long time, particularly as the NDAA provides that it is not required to make a status determination until any ongoing interrogation – which does not appear to be subject to any time limit – has been concluded.[151]

"Member of," "part of," and "support of" al-Qaeda

What do these terms mean? Often these criteria are bound up together in factual situations and court opinions. Using membership as a criterion seems to be tricky. One view is that using membership or support is both "too broad and too narrow" an approach, which has proven "prone to overuse against individuals who, while perhaps individually dangerous, pose little or no threat of major terrorist attack." It may be more appropriate to ask if an individual operates "under the effective control" of an organization.[152]

Judges still do not agree on what conduct counts as membership, and nor do they agree whether detention may be used in the distinct situation in which a non-member provides support to "clandestine non-state actors with indistinct and unstable organizational structures."[153] In *Bensayah v. Obama* the government abandoned its claim that the petitioner's detention was lawful because of support rendered to al-Qaeda, and the claim rested on membership alone. The court decided that the government's authority to detain extends to individuals who are "functionally part of" al-Qaeda, but remanded the case to the District Court to determine the issue.[154] The issue of whether the authority extended to individuals who "substantially supported Taliban or al-Qaeda forces or associated forces"[155] was not dealt with.

The Court concluded that it was "impossible to provide an exhaustive list of the criteria for determining whether an individual is 'part of' al-Qaeda."[156] A case-by-case, functional, individualized approach was necessary to determine that question.[157]

On the question of membership, the Court in *Salahi* held that even though his "limited relationships" with certain al-Qaeda operatives "failed to prove that he was 'part of' al-Qaeda, those connections make it more likely that Salahi was a member of the organization when captured."[158] The Court opined that the District Court may have failed to consider that the "sporadic support" that Salahi "undoubtedly provided al-Qaeda demonstrates that he remained a member of the organization..."[159]

Does the word "member" mean an individual who provides "mere support"?[160] In *Gherebi v. Obama*[161] Judge Walton applied a combination of standards he deemed consistent with Common Article 3 and AP II to permit detention of anyone who is a "member of the armed forces" (defined in accordance with AP I) "of an organization that the President 'determines planned, authorized, committed or aided' the 9/11 attacks, as well as any member of the 'armed forces' of an organization harboring"[162] such members. Judge Walton did not reject outright the substantial support standard, except to determine membership of an organization.[163]

In *Hamlily v. Obama*[164] Judge Bates rejected the concept of substantial support as an independent basis for detention saying that it was "beyond what the law of war will support,"[165] but he did accept it as a criterion for membership. He cited with approval Judge Walton's statement in *Gherebi* that the key question was "whether the individual functions or participates within or under the command structure of the organization, i.e. whether he receives and executes orders or directions."[166]

There is no greater clarity about the meaning of support. Different district judges have adopted "as many as four distinct positions" in interpreting the meaning of support.[167] The difference between the approaches is critical in cases involving "independent actors who provide financial and other support services to al-Qaeda."[168]

In *al-Bihani v. Obama*[169] the petitioner had been a cook with a militia brigade associated with the Taliban. He claimed that although he carried a weapon, he never used it. The court noted that the Military Commissions Act (MCA) of 2006[170] lists persons who materially supported hostilities as being subject to trial by military commission. It held that al-Bihani was:

> lawfully detained whether the definition of a detainable person is, as the district court articulated it, "an individual who was part of or supporting Taliban or al-Qaeda forces, or associated forces that are engaged in hostilities against the United States or its coalition partners," or the modified definition offered by the government that requires that an individual "substantially support" enemy forces ... [F]or this case, it is enough to recognize that any person subject to a military commission trial is also subject to detention, and that category of persons includes those who are part of forces associated with al-Qaeda or the Taliban or those who purposefully and materially support such forces in hostilities against United States Coalition partners.[171]

The court seems to be using two different standards of support, referring both to "substantial" and "purposeful and material." As these are undefined qualitatively, it is hard to know what the difference is between them. In any event, as the Court had decided that al-Bihani could be detained for being a member, the finding as to support is merely a non-binding dictum.[172] Yet the Court was clear that the services provided by al-Bihani rendered him "detainable under the 'purposefully and material supported' language of both versions of the [Military Commissions Act]," but added that "[t]hat language constitutes a standard whose outer bounds are not readily available."[173]

Whatever support means, grounding the definition of an unprivileged enemy belligerent (essentially a civilian) in the international laws of war does not work so well in the context of providing support to terrorists because it does not square with the LOAC definition of direct participation in hostilities.[174]

Challenging LOAC detention

The detainees in the cases discussed above had claimed *habeas corpus* relief in District of Columbia courts. They were granted a right to claim *habeas corpus* relief through a series of Supreme Court cases that distinguished the precedent in *Johnson v. Eisentrager*[175] that enemy aliens held beyond the sovereign territory of the United States had no constitutional right to claim *habeas corpus* relief.

In *Rasul v. Bush*[176] statutory *habeas corpus* protection[177] was extended to detainees held at Guantánamo Bay. The Court distinguished *Eisentrager* on the grounds that the petitioners, who were two Australian and twelve Kuwaiti citizens, were:

> not nationals of countries at war with the United States, and they deny that they have engaged in or plotted acts of aggression against the United States; they have never been afforded access to any tribunal, much less charged with and convicted of wrongdoing; and for more than two years they have been imprisoned in territory over which the United States exercises exclusive jurisdiction and control.[178]

However, the Detainee Treatment Act of 2005[179] (DTA) appeared to proscribe jurisdiction to hear claims of Guantánamo detainees. *Hamdan*[180] held that the DTA did not preclude federal courts from hearing *habeas* petitions that were pending at the date the Act was passed. A further attempt to prevent federal courts from hearing *habeas* petitions was set out in the MCA of 2006.[181] Finally, in *Boumediene*[182] the Court held that the procedures in the MCA were not an adequate or effective substitute for *habeas corpus*, so Section 7 of the MCA "operate[d] as an unconstitutional suspension of the Writ."[183] Thus detainees in Guantánamo had the right to challenge their detention by claiming the constitutional privilege of *habeas corpus* in a federal court. The Court highlighted a number of factual differences to the situation in *Eisentrager*. For example, in *Boumediene* the petitioners had not been convicted by a military commission;[184] they were challenging their status as enemy combatants. In *Eisentrager* the United States did not have "absolute and indefinite" control over the German prison,[185] whereas Guantánamo is "within the constant jurisdiction of the United States."[186]

Standard of proof in habeas cases

After *Boumediene* Judge Hogan issued a Case Management Order designed to guide the Guantánamo *habeas* litigation.[187] For detention to be lawful, evidence had to be proved in accordance with the preponderance of evidence standard.[188] In *Hussein v. Obama* Judge Edwards explained the meaning of this evidential standard: "Under the preponderance of evidence standard 'the fact finder must evaluate the raw evidence, [and] find[ ] it to be sufficiently reliable and sufficiently probative to demonstrate the truth of the asserted proposition with the requisite degree of certainty.'"[189]

Duration of detention

In *Hamdi*, which concerned the capture of a United States citizen on the battlefield during the IAC with Afghanistan, the Supreme Court held that "indefinite detention for the purpose of interrogation is not authorized" in the AUMF,[190] and "[i]t is a clearly established principle of the law of war that detention may last no longer than active hostilities."[191] Furthermore, the Court's acknowledged that its understanding of the laws of war "may unravel" if "the practical circumstances of a given conflict are entirely unlike those of the conflicts that informed the development of the law of war."[192] Many circumstances indicate that this conflict is totally different from a traditional war, not least the debate as to whether the actors are combatants, who can claim POW privilege, or merely terrorists.[193]

Duration of detention authority is derived from *Awad v. Obama*. This affirms that "*Al-Bihani* makes plain that the United States' authority to detain an enemy combatant is not dependent on whether an individual would pose a threat to the United States or its allies if released but rather upon the continuation of hostilities,"[194] which is a nebulous standard in the context of countering violent extremism.

The formula relating to detention until the end of hostilities was repeated in *Ali v. Obama*.[195] Judge Kavanaugh acknowledged Ali's concern that even if his membership in a force associated with al-Qaeda justified detention as an enemy combatant for some period of time, it did not justify "a lifetime detention."[196] He commented:

> the 2001 AUMF does not have a time limit, and the Constitution allows detention of enemy combatants for the duration of hostilities ... absent

a statute that imposes a time limit or creates a sliding-scale standard that becomes more stringent over time, it is not the Judiciary's proper role to devise a novel detention standard that varies with the length of detention.[197]

Judge Edwards concurred with the holding in the case as he considered himself bound by precedent, but pointed to a "clear disjunction between the law of the circuit and the statutes that the case law purports to uphold. In other words, the 'personal associations' test is well beyond what the AUMF and the NDAA prescribe."[198] He was troubled as to "whether the law of the circuit has stretched the meaning of the AUMF and the NDAA so far beyond the terms of these statutory authorizations that habeas corpus proceedings like the one afforded Ali are functionally useless."[199]

The Copenhagen Process Principles relating to NIACs suggest that "when circumstances justifying detention have ceased to exist, a detainee will be released."[200] According to the Guidelines, this principle implies that the reasons for detention must be identified and assessed periodically from the moment of detention until release or transfer.[201] The 2015 *Law of War Manual* refers to the practice of periodic review, but states that there is no fixed requirement regarding frequency of reviews, and cites a number of factors that would determine the scheduling.[202]

Periodic review of detention

The NDAA of 2012 introduced status review procedures, which were to be issued with respect to all detainees who were ineligible to make *habeas* applications in a federal court (such as those in Afghanistan). Such detainees were entitled to be represented by military counsel in status determination proceedings before a military judge.[203]

On February 28, 2012, President Obama issued a set of procedures for the implementation of Section 1022 (PPD-14),[204] together with a fact sheet.[205] He issued seven waivers to the requirements of Section 1022(a)(1), including one with respect to lawful permanent residents of the United States arrested inside the United States on the basis of conduct taking place in the United States.[206] He also gave authority to the attorney general, in consultation with other national security officials, to issue further general and individual waivers in appropriate circumstances.[207] It is noteworthy that the list of laws with which PPD-14 is required to be consistent does not include the ICCPR.[208]

Section 1023 deals with procedures (to be issued within 180 days of the signing of the 2012 Act) for the periodic review of detainees held at Guantánamo.[209] One of the stated aims of the procedures is to "make discretionary determinations whether or not a detainee represents a continuing threat to the security of the United States."[210] What does continuing threat mean? How serious does this threat have to be? A previous test set out in an executive order signaled necessity to "protect against a significant threat to the security of the United States."[211] Civil libertarians may be less comfortable with "continuing threat" as opposed to "significant threat," as the former suggests a lower threshold for the government.

Classified evidence in habeas proceedings

The United States government has been able to rely on classified evidence in *habeas corpus* cases as "part (or all) of its legal justification for detention."[212] Security-cleared lawyers are entitled in principle to see the classified evidence, but may not disclose any of it to their clients, other than any classified information provided by the client.[213] Lawyers may use it to formulate questions that may be informed by having seen the secret evidence.[214] However, unless the detainee would otherwise have a right to examine the evidence – either because it is being used against him or her or because it is exculpatory – even the detainee's lawyer will not see it.[215] Even if the lawyer ought to have the right to see the evidence on behalf of his client, the government can still prevent him from seeing it if it successfully makes an *ex parte* and *in camera* application to a judge, arguing that the material is either highly sensitive, pertains to a highly sensitive source, or pertains to someone other than the detainee.[216] Furthermore, disclosure of classified evidence to the detainee's counsel can be avoided if the government can provide alternative, unclassified disclosures that are an effective substitute for the classified information.[217] Cleared counsel who act in different cases are entitled to share information amongst themselves in a secure facility.[218]

Access to lawyers

Detainees were not given access to lawyers until 2004, when the Supreme Court ruled that they had the right to assistance of counsel.[219] Communications between lawyers and detainees may not be monitored by the government.[220] In 2012, the DC District Court ruled the right of access to counsel continued after the detainees' *habeas* petitions have terminated.[221]

Giving detainees the reason for detention

The Copenhagen Process Principles provide that detainees are to be told the reason for their detention promptly in a language they understand.[222] The Guidelines suggest that "promptly" means within a reasonable time.[223] The 2015 *Law of War Manual*, which applies to both IACs and NIACs, replicates the wording of the Copenhagen Process but specifies that prompt notification should "generally occur within 10 days of detention."[224]

Contact with the outside world

The Copenhagen Principles advocate permitting detainees to have contact with family members, community, and religious representatives and other agencies, subject to security concerns.[225] The *Law of War Manual* provides for affording detainees contact with the outside world, subject to security measures, practical considerations, and other military necessities.[226] Detentions should be registered.[227] The International Committee of the Red Cross (ICRC) should be notified of detentions.[228]

International law

Do these procedures violate the United States Constitution and international law? They may not satisfy the all requirements of due process,[229] but the Supreme Court has not ruled whether detainees at Guantánamo have constitutional due process rights.[230] As to international human rights law, the United States is party to the ICCPR. Article 9(4) merely requires that a detained person be entitled to take proceedings before a court, so that the court may decide without delay, whether the detention is lawful. The treaty is silent as to the procedural details, and no jurisprudential guidance has been issued to shed any further light.

In June 2013 the HRC Working Group on Arbitrary Detention considered that Haneef Obaidullah's prolonged and indefinite detention by the United States in Guantánamo Bay since 2002 was arbitrary and constituted a violation of Article 9 ICCPR, that his rights to a fair trial and due process had been repeatedly violated, and that he had suffered discrimination because he had been subjected to prolonged detention due to his status as a foreign national.[231] The Working Group referred to a statement that it had made in May 2013 together with the Inter-American Commission of Human Rights and United Nations Rapporteurs on human rights and counter-terrorism, torture and health, in which it stressed:

> that even in extraordinary circumstances, when the indefinite detention of individuals, most of whom have not been charged, goes beyond a minimally reasonable period of time, this constitutes a flagrant violation of international human rights law and in itself constitutes a form of cruel, inhuman, and degrading treatment.[232]

Detention in Afghanistan

Detainees at Guantánamo fought a lengthy battle to achieve some procedural success, but detainees in Afghanistan were not so fortunate. Some were held "for as long as six years without access to counsel or a meaningful opportunity to challenge their imprisonment."[233] In 2010, the United States Court of Appeals for the District of Columbia ruled in *al Maqaleh v. Gates* that jurisdiction to hear *habeas* petitions of detainees did not extend to those held at Bagram.[234]

The *al Maqaleh* Court noted that the *Boumediene* Court "only told us that '*at least* three factors' are relevant"[235] to ascertain the reach of the Suspension of the Writ clause:

> (1) the citizenship and status of the detainee and the adequacy of the process through which that status determination was made; (2) the nature of the sites where apprehension and then detention took place; and (3) the practical obstacles inherent in resolving the prisoner's entitlement to the writ.[236]

The *al Maqaleh* Court reasoned that if the *Boumediene* Court had wanted to limit its understanding of the reach of the Suspension Clause to territories where the United States exercised *de facto* jurisdiction, it would not have needed to refer to the three factors mentioned above.[237] The Court specifically rejected the fact of United States control of Bagram under its lease of the military base, to trigger the extraterritorial application of the Suspension Clause. It did so on the grounds that this would "seem to create the potential for the extraterritorial extension of the Suspension Clause to noncitizens held in any United States military facility in the world, and perhaps to an undeterminable number of United States-leased facilities as well."[238]

The Court reached its conclusion by applying the three mentioned *Boumediene* factors to the facts of this case. Despite noting that the Unlawful Enemy Combatant Review Board process at Bagram afforded the petitioners even less protection than the Combatant Status Review Tribunal that the *Boumediene* petitioners complained about, the Court concluded that analysis of the second and third factors referred to above weighed more heavily in favor of the United States.[239] The Court ruled that "the writ does not extend to Bagram confinement in an active theater of war in a territory under neither the *de facto* nor *de jure* sovereignty of the United States and within the territory of another *de jure* sovereign."[240]

Conclusions

For years debate has raged about whether terrorists should be treated as criminals or combatants.[241] Yet irrespective of whether this group is labeled as combatant or terrorist, the rule of law requires that the governing law must adequately protect their fundamental human rights,[242] including the right to liberty. If law enforcement officers want to detain persons under domestic law to forestall terrorist acts, the scope to do so is extremely limited.[243] Other than in a very small category of cases involving special or exigent situations,[244] a suspect may not be arrested and detained, absent probable cause that a crime has been or is being committed.

The definition of probable cause has been discussed in many Supreme Court decisions[245] and the difficulty of giving it a precise meaning has been debated in many scholarly articles.[246] However, in addition to the difficulty of knowing exactly what probable cause means, it only applies when a crime has been or is being committed, or is being attempted. Unless the definition of the crime is sufficiently broad, such as in material support cases, arrest and prevention of a terrorist act may not be possible in cases where the only acts are those of preparation or planning, especially where a lone actor is involved.

The "devices" of inchoate offenses, material support, material witness, and immigration laws described above to detain people without charge for longer than the forty-eight hours permitted by law are problematic. They are all deficient from the human rights perspective, in that they do not afford adequate due process.

The current state of LOAC also does not provide an adequate blueprint to deal with either current or future detention challenges. For example, unresolved issues include questions relating to who may be detained. Although Da'esh appears to fall within the statutory detention authority, what if the threat diversifies to other terrorist groups with no connection at all to al-Qaeda, such as Hezbollah?[247] What if a suspected terrorist is inspired by jihad but acting alone?[248] In many of these cases there would not appear to be a legal framework for the United States to detain the perpetrators preventively without trial. The LOAC model also fails to cater for the United States citizen who travels overseas to a terrorist training camp and is captured overseas. Currently it is not clear what is to be done with such a detainee. Why should there be a difference in treatment relative to whether or not the detainee is a United States citizen?

Petitioners in *al Maqaleh* questioned whether the United States could "evade judicial review of Executive detention by transferring detainees into active conflict zones, thereby granting the Executive the power to switch the Constitution on or off at will."[249] Would the holding in *al Maqaleh* apply in places where the United States is in occupation, on a peace-keeping mission, or in other situations that are not deemed to be active theaters of war? Would it apply if the United States captured a suspected terrorist in Pakistan or Yemen and then held the suspect in a United States military base in Germany? Would this problem be addressed by Section 1024 of the NDAA of 2012?[250] These are not theoretical questions. The basis on which the United States detained Umm Sayyaf for three months in Iraq in 2015 is unclear.[251]

LOAC detention law has mainly been formulated by judges of the DC District Court and the DC Circuit Court of Appeals. Unresolved questions relate to boundaries of the president's detention power, burden of proof, the type of admissible evidence that can be used in *habeas* proceedings,[252] and the meaning of "part of" and "substantial support."

The denial of certiorari by the Supreme Court in a number of detainee cases, including *al-Adahi*,[253] *al-Odah*, *Ameziane*, *al-Bihani*, and *Awad*[254] suggested to some commentators that the Supreme Court has "no appetite for getting involved in the nitty gritty of the writing of the rules that will govern detention."[255] This view is perhaps reinforced by the fact that in June 2012 the Supreme Court denied certiorari in seven *habeas* cases,[256] and the practice has continued.[257]

Indefinite detention remains problematic. The war against al-Qaeda, its affiliates, and Da'esh is not a traditional conflict. How will the enemy manifest itself, and where or when will it strike again? How will the United States finally determine that hostilities have ended? As terror attacks are sporadic and in different locations, what period of time must elapse after an attack before the United States can declare that the war against al-Qaeda or Da'esh is over? Will the countdown start from the last terrorist event in the United States, or from the date of an event somewhere else in the world that caused United States casualties? What will happen if hostilities end but a group of individuals are still considered a threat? What is the solution for the group of detainees who cannot be prosecuted or released from Guantánamo?

Some suggest that military detention without trial for an indefinite period addresses the problems of trying suspected terrorists in either federal courts or military commissions.[258] However, military detention merely avoids the issue of having to decide an appropriate mode of trial. The fact remains that indefinite detention for terrorists does not sit comfortably in the LOAC paradigm.

Many problems relating to process have been identified. "The privilege of habeas corpus entitles the prisoner to a meaningful opportunity to demonstrate that he is being held pursuant to the erroneous application or interpretation of relevant law."[259] Yet LOAC does not provide an adequate framework for this to happen. The practice described above relating to the use of classified evidence often does not afford detainees the ability to know the case against them. Nor does LOAC provide meaningful time limits within which a *habeas* petition may be brought. From a human rights perspective LOAC detention, by its indefinite duration, by its failure to afford adequate procedures, and by the United States practice of applying it only to foreigners, is arbitrary.

The Obama administration continues to wrestle with the intractable problem of what to do with the Guantánamo detainees that cannot be prosecuted and are deemed too dangerous to release.[260] The United States maintains that LOAC prevails during an armed conflict to the exclusion of international human rights law. Yet LOAC is insufficiently developed to afford adequate due process for detention of this special terrorist type of "combatant."

Notes

1 An earlier version of the LOAC section appears in Diane Webber, *Preventive Detention in the Law of Armed Conflict: Throwing Away the Key?* 6 J. NAT'L SEC. L. & POL'Y, 167 (2012).

2 Reports vary, but between three and four thousand may have been detained between 2002 and 20014; *see* DETAINED BY U.S., NEW YORK LAW SCHOOL, www.detainedbyus.org/detainees/statistics/.

3 Frank Jack Daniel, *U.S. closes Bagram prison, says no more detainees held in Afghanistan*, REUTERS (December 11, 2014), www.reuters.com/article/2014/12/11/us-usa-cia-torture-bagram-idUSKBN0JO2B720141211. For an analysis of US detention in Iraq, see Robert M. Chesney, *Iraq and the Military Detention Debate: Firsthand Perspectives from the Other War, 2003–2010*, 51 VA. J. INT'L L. 549 (2011).

4 *Factbox: Has Obama delivered on his 2008 campaign promises?* REUTERS (October 28, 2011), www.reuters.com/article/2011/10/28/us-usa-campaign-obama-promises-idUSTRE79R3M920111028.

5 Jordan Fabian, *White House: Gitmo closing plan 'close'*, THE HILL (July 22, 2015), www.thehill.com/homenews/administration/248834-white-house-gitmo-closing-plan-close.

6 National Defense Authorization Act for Fiscal Year 2015, P.L. 113-291 (113th Cong.), §§1032, 1033; H.R. 1735 National Defense Authorization Act for Fiscal Year 2016, §§1036, 1037 [NDAA 2016].

7 GUANTANAMO BY THE NUMBERS, HUMAN RIGHTS FIRST, www.humanrights-first.org/sites/default/files/gtmo-by-the-numbers.pdf.

8 *Id.*

9 1) Ahmed Warsame in 2009, *see* Robert Chesney, *Ahmed Warsame and Law of War Detention*, LAWFARE (July 6 2011), www.lawfareblog.com/2011/07/ahmed-warsame-and-law-of-war-detention/; 2) Abu Anas al-Libi in 2013, *see* Benjamin Weiser and Eric Schmitt, *US Said to Hold Qaeda Suspect on Navy Ship*, N.Y. TIMES (October 6, 2013), www.nyAnas times.com/2013/10/07/world/africa/a-terrorism-suspect-long-known-to-prosecutors.html?hpw&_r=0; Benjamin Weiser, Charlie Savage & Eric Schmitt, *Qaeda Suspect is Brought to New York for a Hearing*, N.Y. TIMES (October 14, 2013), www.nytimes.com/2013/10/15/us/libyan-terror-suspect-brought-to-new-york-for-trial.html; 3) Irek Hamidullan in 2014, *see* Adam Goldman, *Russian accused of fighting with insurgents pleads not guilty to terrorism in U.S. court*, WASH. POST (November 7, 2014), www.washingtonpost.com/politics/russian-accused-of-fighting-with-insurgents-pleads-not-guilty-to-terrorism-in-us-court/2014/11/07/0f73dee8-66a5-11e4-836c-83bc4f26eb67_story.html; 4) and 5) Saddiq al Abbadi and Ali Alvi in January 2015, *see* Charles Hoskinson, *Captured al Qaeda fighters face civilian trial*, WASHINGTON EXAMINER (January 20, 2015), www.washingtonexaminer.com/captured-al-qaeda-fighters-face-civilian-trial/article/2558930?custom_click=rss; 6) Muhanad Mahmoud al Farekh, arraigned in April 2015, *see* Adam Goldman and Tim Craig, *American citizen linked to al Qaeda is captured, flown secretly to U.S.*, WASH. POST (April 2, 2015), www.washingtonpost.com/world/national-security/american-citizen-suspected-of-being-al-qaeda-member-captured-brought-to-us/2015/04/02/48e8cc4c-d89c-11e4-8103-fa84725dbf9d_story.html.

10 Umm Sayaf, widow of a Da'esh militant, captured in Iraq in May 2015; *see* Missy Ryan, *U.S. interrogation team sent to Iraq to question first Islamic State detainee*, WASH. POST (May 18, 2015), www.washingtonpost.com/world/national-security/us-interrogation-team-sent-to-iraq-to-question-first-islamic-state-detainee/2015/05/18/f5e4f04c-fd90-11e4-833c-a2de05b6b2a4_story.

html; Spencer Ackerman, *US transfers Umm Sayyaf, wife of suspected ISIS member to Iraqi Kurds*, THE GUARDIAN (August 7, 2015), www.theguardian.com/world/2015/aug/07/us-transfers-umm-sayyaf-wife-of-suspected-isis-member-to-iraqi-kurds.

11 Suspects can be arrested without a warrant where there is probable cause, and the arrest takes place in public, U.S. v. Watson, 423 U.S. 411, 423 (1976), or where there are exigent circumstances, Payton v. New York, 445 U.S. 573, 583 (1980); Kentucky v. King, 31 S. Ct. 1849, 1854 (2011).

12 Gerstein v. Pugh, 420 U.S. 103, 125, 126 (1975).

13 County of Riverside v. McLaughlin, 500 U.S. 44, 56 (1991).

14 *Id.*

15 US Const. Amend. IV: "The right of the people to be secure in their persons, houses, papers, and effects, against unreasonable searches and seizures, shall not be violated, and no Warrants shall issue, but upon probable cause, supported by Oath or affirmation, and particularly describing the place to be searched, and the person or things to be seized."

16 Gerstein v. Pugh, 111-2; *see also* Diane Webber, *Extreme Measures: Does the United States Need Preventive Detention to Combat Domestic Terrorism?* 14 TOURO INT'L L. REV. 128, 164–9 (2010).

17 *Id.*, 166–8.

18 United States v. Cortez, 449 U.S. 411, 417 (1981).

19 See discussion of Ashcroft v. al-Kidd, 131 S. Ct 2074 (2011) below, where the Court declined to discuss the constitutionality of using material witness arrest warrants as a means of preventively detaining terror suspects.

20 DANIEL KLAIDMAN, KILL OR CAPTURE, THE WAR ON TERROR AND THE SOUL OF THE OBAMA PRESIDENCY, 178 (Houghton, Mifflin Harcourt, 2012).

21 *Id.*, 178–9.

22 *Id.*, 179.

23 Miranda v. Arizona, 384 U.S. 436, 479 (1966).

24 New York v. Quarles, 467 U.S. 649 (1984).

25 David S. Kris, *Law Enforcement as a Counterterrorism Tool*, 5 J. NAT. SEC. L. & POL'Y 1, 20 (2011) (citing New York v. Quarles, 655–6), and 40 (citing United States v. Khalil, 214 F.3d 111, 121–122 (2d Cir. 2000), where an un-*Mirandized* suspect was asked questions about pipe bombs found in his apartment and his statements were admissible in court).

26 *Id.*, 77.

27 KLAIDMAN, KILL OR CAPTURE, 181.

28 *Id.*, 189.

29 *Id.*, 190. *See also* Stephanie Condon, *Faisal Shahzad Was Read Miranda Rights After Initial Questioning*, CBS NEWS (May 4, 2010), www.cbsnews.com/8301-503544_162-20004108-503544.html.

30 *Id.*, 191. *See also* Charlie Savage, *Holder Backs a Miranda Limit for Terror*, N.Y. TIMES, A1 (May 10, 2010), www.nytimes.com/2010/05/10/us/politics/10holder.html?pagewanted=all; Charlie Savage, *Obama Said to Be Open to New Miranda Look*, N.Y. TIMES at A11 (May 11, 2010), www.nytimes.com/2010/05/11/us/politics/11miranda.html; Charlie Savage, *Proposal Would Delay Hearings In Terror Cases*, N.Y. TIMES, A11 (May 15, 2010), www.nytimes.com/2010/05/15/us/politics/15miranda.html?_r=1&ref=politics.

31 KLAIDMAN, KILL OR CAPTURE, 191.

32 *See e.g. Pat Leahy Throws Cold Water On Obama's Hope For Miranda Fix*, HUFFINGTON POST (May 16, 2010, 11:27 A.M.), *available at* www.huffingtonpost.com/2010/05/16/pat-leahy-throws-cold-wat_n_577824.html. *Contra see* Benjamin Wittes, *President Obama needs more legal tactics against terrorists*, WASH. POST (May 14, 2010), *available at* www.washingtonpost.com/wp-dyn/content/article/2010/05/13/AR2010051303541.html.

33 KLAIDMAN, KILL OR CAPTURE, 191–2.

34 David Cole, *Out of the Shadows: Preventive Detention, Suspected Terrorists, and War*, 97 CALIF. L. REV. 693, 695 (2009).

35 28 C.F.R. §501.3(a): "… These special administrative measures ordinarily may include housing the inmate in administrative detention and/or limiting certain privileges, including, but not limited to, correspondence, visiting, interviews with representatives of the news media, and use of the telephone, as is reasonably necessary to protect persons against the risk of acts of violence or terrorism …" *See e.g.* United States v. Hashmi, 621 F. Supp. 2d 76 (S.D.N.Y. 2008), who was held in solitary confinement for two and a half years, cited in Laura Rover and Jeanne Theoharis, *Preferring Order to Justice*, 61 AM. U. L. REV. 1331, 1358–85 (2012).

36 28 C.F.R. §501.3(c).

37 Cole, *Out of the Shadows*, 700–03; Adam Klein and Benjamin Wittes, *Preventive Detention in American Theory and Practice*, HARV. NAT'L SEC. J. 85, 87 (2011).

38 Klein and Wittes, *Preventive Detention in American Theory and Practice*, 88.

39 RICHARD B. ZABEL AND JAMES J. BENJAMIN JR., IN PURSUIT OF JUSTICE: PROSECUTING TERRORISM CASES IN THE FEDERAL COURTS (HUMAN RIGHTS FIRST, MAY, 2008); RICHARD B. ZABEL AND JAMES J. BENJAMIN, JR., IN PURSUIT OF JUSTICE: PROSECUTING TERRORISM CASES IN THE FEDERAL COURTS, 2009 UPDATE AND RECENT DEVELOPMENTS (Human Rights First, 2009).

40 Arrests can be made for attempting to commit a terrorist act, provided there has been sufficient activity. Attempt generally involves the intent to do a bad act coupled with an act. The precise definition of what that act must be has been the subject of much debate, and includes "an act sufficiently proximate to the intended crime" or "an act which in the ordinary course of events would result in the commission of the target crime except for the intervention of some extraneous factor," or "an act of such a nature that it is itself evidence of the criminal intent with which it is done," or "an act or omission constituting a substantial step in a course of conduct planned to culminate in [the actor's] commission of the crime." *See* WAYNE R. LAFAVE, 2 SUBST. CRIM. L. §11.4 (West's Key Number Digest, 2d ed. 2011).

41 *See e.g.* N.Y. PENAL §420.20 (Consol. 2009): "1. A person is guilty of making a terroristic threat when with intent to intimidate or coerce a civilian population, influence the policy of a unit of government by intimidation or coercion, or affect the conduct of a unit of government by murder, assassination or kidnapping, he or she threatens to commit or cause to be committed a specified offense and thereby causes a reasonable expectation or fear of the imminent commission of such offense."

42 *See e.g.* the spate of ten preventive arrests prior to July 4, 2015: Greg Miller and Ellen Nakashima, *Recent Islamic State arrests include suspects in alleged July 4 plots*, WASH. POST (July 9, 2015), www.washingtonpost.com/world/

national-security/fbi-chief-describes-surge-in-arrests-related-to-islamic-state/2015/07/09/60d77998-2662-11e5-aae2-6c4f59b050aa_story.html.

43 *See e.g.* the conviction of Abu Ghaith for conspiracy to kill Americans and for providing material support to terrorists, *see* Benjamin Weiser, *Jurors Convict Abu Ghaith, Bin Laden Son-in-Law, in Terror Trial*, N.Y. TIMES, (March 26, 2014), www.nytimes.com/2014/03/27/nyregion/bin-ladens-son-in-law-is-convicted-in-terror-trial.html?_r=0; *Also see* Daphne Eviatar, *Bin Laden Relative Could Be Held Responsible for Deaths of Thousands*, HUFFINGTON POST (March 21, 2014), www.huffingtonpost.com/daphne-eviatar/bin-laden-relative-could_b_5008736.html (demonstrating the breadth of conspiracy law).

44 ROBIN SIMCOX AND EMILY DYER, AL-QAEDA IN THE UNITED STATES: A COMPLETE ANALYSIS OF TERRORISM OFFENSES, 675, Table 11C (Henry Jackson Society, 2013).

45 LAFAVE, 2 SUBST. CRIM. L., §12.

46 Reported numbers of lone wolves vary, *e.g.* In the United States there were 30 such cases between 1968 and 2007 (Ramon Spaaij, *The Enigma of Lone Wolf Terrorism: An Assessment*, 33 STUDIES IN CONFLICT AND TERRORISM 854, 859 (2010); Clark McCauley, Sophia Moskalenko and Benjamin Van Son, *Characteristics of Lone-Wolf Violent Offenders: a Comparison of Assassins and School Attackers*, 7 PERSPECTIVES ON TERRORISM, 4, 5 (2013) (citing CHARLES A. EBY, THE NATION THAT CRIED LONE WOLF: A DATA-DRIVEN ANALYSIS OF INDIVIDUAL TERRORISTS IN THE UNITED STATES SINCE 9/11. Monterey, CA: Naval Postgraduate School, www.hsdl.org/?view&did=710310, 53 lone-wolf terrorists between 2001 and 2011; and CHRIS JASPARRO, LONE WOLF: THE THREAT FROM INDEPENDENT JIHADISTS (Naval War College. 2010), 14 specifically jihadist lone-wolf U.S. terrorists). *Also see* Kendall Coffey, *The Lone Wolf – Solo Terrorism and the Challenge of Preventive Prosecution*, 7 FIU L. REV. 1 (2011) (discussing four jhadist lone wolf attacks or attempts since 2009, by Major Nidal Hassan, Abdul Muhammad, Faisal Shahzad, and Umar Abdulmutallab). In July 2015 Muhammad Youssef Abdulazeez killed five service personnel in Chatanooga, *see e.g. Chatanooga attack: Gunman Abdulazeez 'sent war text,'* BBC NEWS (July 19, 2015), http://www.bbc.com/news/world-us-canada-33581753.

47 Robert M. Chesney, *Beyond Conspiracy? Anticipatory Prosecution and the Challenge of Unaffiliated Terrorism*, 80 S. CALIF. L. REV. 425, 428 (2007).

48 18 U.S.C. §2339A, §2339B. 18 U.S.C. §2339A focuses on links between an individual and specified crimes, and §2339B centers on links between an individual and specified organizations.

49 SIMCOX AND DYER, AL-QAEDA IN THE UNITED STATES, 675, Table 11C. The data also shows that of 100 convictions for material support between 1997 and 2012, 24 were for providing material support to terrorists and 34 were for conspiring to provide material support to terrorists pursuant to §2339A, and 20 were for proving material support to a designated terrorist organization, and 22 were for conspiring to provide material support to a designated terrorist organization pursuant to §2339B.

50 Stephen Loiaconi, *Dozens of alleged ISIS supporters arrested in U.S. so far this year*, FOX11NEWS (Jul. 31, 2015) http://fox11online.com/news/nation-world/dozens-of-alleged-isis-supporters-arrested-in-us-so-far-this-year.

51 Chesney, *Beyond Conspiracy?* 479; Cole, *Out of the Shadows*, 723–4.

52 George D. Brown, *Notes on a Terrorism Trial – Preventive Prosecution, "Material Support" and the Role of the Judge after United States v. Mehanna*, 4 HARV. NAT'L SEC. J. 1, 4 (2012).
53 *Id.*, 475.
54 18 U.S.C. §2332(f).
55 18 U.S.C. §2332(b).
56 Chesney, *Beyond Conspiracy?* 479–80.
57 18 U.S.C. §2339A(b)(1).
58 Chesney, *Beyond Conspiracy?* 480. For examples of cases where the material support consisted of preparation, see United States v. Syed Haris Ahmed, U.S. District Court, N.D. Ga. (December 9, 2009), as described in SIMCOX AND DYER, AL-QAEDA IN THE UNITED STATES, 320-4, and U.S. v. Khaleel Ahmed, convicted 2009, described in SIMCOX AND DYER, AL-QAEDA IN THE UNITED STATES, 341–4.
59 Chesney, *Beyond Conspiracy*, 480.
60 *Id.*, 493.
61 *Id.*
62 *See e.g.* Holder v. Humanitarian Law Project, 130 S. Ct. 2705 (2010).
63 *Id.*
64 United States v. Mehanna, No. 9-cr-10017-GAO (D. Mass. 2011).
65 18 U.S.C. §3144 (2006), "if the testimony of a person is material in a criminal proceeding, and if it is shown that it may become impracticable to secure the presence of the person by subpoena, a judicial officer may order the arrest of the person and treat the person in accordance with the provisions of section 3142 of this title." §3142 authorizes detention.
66 Donald Q. Cochran, *Material Witness Detention in a Post 9/11 World: Mission Creep or Fresh Start?* 18 GEO. MASON L. REV. 1, 4 (2010) (citing Judiciary Act of 1789, ch. 20, 1 Stat. 73).
67 Klein and Wittes, *Preventive Detention in American Theory and Practice*, 133.
68 DAN E. STIGALL, COUNTERTERRORISM AND THE COMPARATIVE LAW OF INVESTIGATIVE DETENTION, 51 (Cambria Press 2009) (citing Ronald L. Carlson, *Distorting Due Process for Noble Purposes: The Emasculation of America's Material Witness Laws*, 42 GA. L. REV. 941, 973–74 (2008)).
69 *Id.*
70 *See e.g.*, Klein and Wittes, *Preventive Detention in American Theory and Practice*, 138–40; Cochran, *Material Witness Detention in a Post 9/11 World*, 4–7; Cole, *Out of the Shadows*, 704; STEPHANIE COOPER BLUM, THE NECESSARY EVIL OF PREVENTIVE DETENTION IN THE WAR ON TERROR, 3 (Cambria Press 2008).
71 Klein and Wittes, *Preventive Detention in American Theory and Practice*, 139–40 (citing HUMAN RIGHTS WATCH, WITNESS TO ABUSE: HUMAN RIGHTS ABUSES UNDER THE MATERIAL WITNESS LAW SINCE SEPTEMBER 11, 19 (2005)).
72 *Id.*, 140 (quoting OFFICE OF THE INSPECTOR GENERAL, DEPT. OF JUSTICE, REPORT TO CONGRESS ON IMPLEMENTATION OF SECTION 1001 OF THE USA PATRIOT ACT (2007), *available at* www.usdoj.gov/oig/special/s0703/).
73 Ashcroft v. al-Kidd, 131 S. Ct 2074 (2011).
74 Al-Kidd v. Gonzales, 2006 U.S. Dist. LEXIS 70283 (D. Idaho, September 27, 2006). He sought damages under Bivens v. Six Unknown Named Agents of the Federal Bureau of Narcotics, 403 U.S. 388 (1971), for violations of al-Kidd's

rights under the Fourth and Fifth Amendments to the Constitution (a "Bivens action"), and for a direct violation of §3144.

75 Ashcroft v. al-Kidd, 2079.

76 Al-Kidd v. Ashcroft, 580 F.3d 949 (2009).

77 Ashcroft v. al-Kidd, 2083.

78 *Id.*, 2090 (citations omitted).

79 *Id.*

80 *US Citizen Settles Lawsuit Over Post-9/11 Arrest With FBI*, N.Y. TIMES (January 16, 2015), www.nytimes.com/aponline/2015/01/16/us/ap-us-911-lawsuit.html?_r=0.

81 Klein and Wittes, *Preventive Detention in American Theory and Practice*, 140.

82 AMERICAN CIVIL LIBERTIES UNION, SECURELY INSECURE: THE REAL COSTS, CONSEQUENCES AND HUMAN FACE OF IMMIGRATION DETENTION (January 2011), *available at* www.detentionwatchnetwork.org/sites/detentionwatchnetwork.org/files/1.14.11_Fact%20Sheet%20FINAL_0.pdf.

83 8 U.S.C. §1226 (2008).

84 STIGALL, COUNTERTERRORISM AND THE COMPARATIVE LAW OF INVESTIGATIVE DETENTION, 55 (quoting Matthews v. Diaz, 426 U.S. 67, 79–80 (1976): " In the exercise of its broad power over naturalization and immigration, Congress regularly makes rules that would be unacceptable if applied to citizens"); Cole, *Out of the Shadows: Preventive Detention, Suspected Terrorists, and War*, 719–22.

85 AMNESTY INTERNATIONAL, JAILED WITHOUT JUSTICE, IMMIGRATION DETENTION IN THE U.S.A. (Mar. 25, 2009), *available at* www.amnestyusa.org/pdfs/JailedWithoutJustice.pdf.

86 HUMAN RIGHTS FIRST, JAILS AND JUMPSUITS, TRANSFORMING THE U.S. IMMIGRATION DETENTION SYSTEM – A TWO YEAR REVIEW, i-v (2011), *available at* www.humanrightsfirst.org/wp-content/uploads/pdf/HRF-Jails-and-Jumpsuits-report.pdf.

87 STIGALL, COUNTERTERRORISM AND THE COMPARATIVE LAW OF INVESTIGATIVE DETENTION, 55, 56, *citing* 8 U.S.C. §1231 (a)(2) and (6) (2009); §§ 1158(b)(2)(A)(v), 1182(a)(3)(B)(i)(I).

88 Klein and Wittes, *Preventive Detention in American Theory and Practice*, 151.

89 HUMAN RIGHTS FIRST, JAILS AND JUMPSUITS, 13.

90 Zadvydas v. Davis, 533 U.S. 678, 699 (2001).

91 *Id.*, 701.

92 *Id.*

93 Turkmen v. Ashcroft, No. 02 Civ. 2307, 2006 WL 1662663 (E.D.N.Y. June 14, 2006).

94 Turkmen v. Ashcroft, 589 F. 3d 542, 549 (2d Cir. 2009) (relying on and citing Whren v. United States, 507 U.S. 806, 813 (1996)).

95 *Id.*, 550.

96 *Id.*

97 USA PATRIOT Act, §412.

98 DANIEL B. PRIETO, "WAR ABOUT TERROR", CIVIL LIBERTIES AND NATIONAL SECURITY AFTER 9/11, 18, 34 (Council on Foreign Relations, Inc., February 2009).

99 Klein and Wittes, *Preventive Detention in American Theory and Practice*, 150.

100 US Const. art. 1 §9, cl. 2.

101 Cole, *Out of the Shadows*, 702.

102 *Id.*
103 *Id.*
104 Allison M. Danner, *Defining Unlawful Enemy Combatants: A Centripetal Story*, 43 TEX. INT'L L. J. 1, 8 (Fall 2007).
105 The relevant sources of LOAC in this section include customary international law; Geneva Convention for the Amelioration of the Condition of the Wounded and Sick in Armed Forces in the Field (August 12, 1949), 6 U.S.T. 3114, 75 U.N.T.S. 31 [GC I]; Geneva Convention for the Amelioration of the Condition of the Wounded, Sick and Shipwrecked Members of Armed Forces at Sea (August 12, 1949), 6 U.S.T. 3217, 75 U.N.T.S. 85 [GC II]; Geneva Convention Relative to the Treatment of Prisoners of War (August 12, 1949), 6 U.S.T. 3316, 75 U.N.T.S. 135 [GC III]; Geneva Convention Relative to the Protection of Civilian Persons in Time of War (August 12, 1949), 6 U.S.T. 3516, 75 U.N.T.S. 287 [GC IV]; Protocol Additional to the Geneva Conventions of August 12, 1949, and Relating to the Protection of Victims of International Armed Conflicts (June 8, 1977), 1125 U.N.T.S. 3 [AP I]; Protocol Additional to the Geneva Conventions of August 12, 1949, and Relating to the Protection of Victims of Non-International Armed Conflicts, (June 8, 1977), 1125 U.N.T.S. 609 [AP II]. The purpose of the GCs is to protect the sick and wounded, POWs and civilians; and UNITED STATES DEPARTMENT OF DEFENSE, LAW OF WAR MANUAL (June 2015). [LAW OF WAR MANUAL].
106 Matthew C. Waxman, *Administrative Detention of Terrorists: Why Detain, and Detain Whom?* 3 J. NAT'L. SECURITY L. & POL'Y 1, 14 (2009).
107 Jane Mayer, The Dark Side: The Inside Story of How The War on Terror Turned into a War on American Ideals 34 (Doubleday, 2008).
108 S.C. Res. 1368, ¶1, U.N. Doc. S/RES/1368 (September 12, 2001).
109 Authorization for Use of Military Force (AUMF), Pub. L. No. 107–40, 115 Stat. 224 (2001).
110 US Dept. of Justice, O.L.C., Memorandum from John C. Yoo and Robert Delahunty for Alberto R. Gonzales, Counsel to the President Re: Treaties and Laws Applicable to the Conflict in Afghanistan and to the Treatment of Persons Captured by U.S. Armed Forces in that Conflict (November 30, 2001), *available at* www.justice.gov/olc/docs/aclu-ii-113001.pdf.
111 Hamdan v. Rumsfeld, 548 U.S. 557, 629–630 (2006).
112 GC III, art. 118.
113 THE WHITE HOUSE, OFFICE OF THE PRESS SECRETARY, FACT SHEET: NEW ACTIONS ON GUANTÁNAMO AND DETAINEE POLICY (March 7, 2011).
114 This subject generated scholarly debate due to the fact that the White House statement purports only to refer to international armed conflicts, yet in *Hamdan* the Supreme Court determined that the US conflict with al-Qaeda is a non-international armed conflict. *See, e.g.*, John Bellinger, *Obama's Announcements on International Law*, LAWFARE (March 8, 2011), www.lawfareblog.com/2011/03/obamas-announcements-on-international-law/; Jack Goldsmith, *Why I Think the Obama Administration Did Not Extend Article 75 to Terrorists*, LAWFARE (March 11, 2011), www.lawfareblog.com/ 2011/03/why-i-think-the-obama-administration-did-not-extend-article-75-to-terrorists/; John Bellinger, *Further Thoughts on the White House Statement About Article 75* LAWFARE (March 13, 2011), www.lawfareblog.com/2011/03/further-thoughts-on-the-white-house-statement-about-article-75/.

115 John Bellinger, *When I'm 64: The Geneva Conventions and the Obama Administration*, LAWFARE, (August 11, 2013) www.lawfareblog.com/2013/08/when-im-64-the-geneva-conventions-and-the-obama-administration, *citing* Julian E. Barnes, *Geneva Protections for al Qaeda Suspects? Read the Fine Print*, WASHINGTON WIRE, WALL STREET JOURNAL BLOGS (March 14, 2011), http://blogs.wsj.com/washwire/2011/03/14/geneva-protections-for-al-qaeda-suspects-read-the-fine-print/?mod=google_news_blog.

116 THE COPENHAGEN PROCESS ON THE HANDLING OF DETAINEES IN INTERNATIONAL MILITARY OPERATIONS (October 19. 2012) [COPENHAGEN PROCESS].

117 US DEPT. OF DEFENSE, LAW OF WAR MANUAL (June 2015).

118 Al-Bihani v. Obama, 590 F.3d 866, 871 (2010) [al-Bihani]. In al-Bihani v Obama, 619 F.3d 1, 2 (2010), the Court declared the comments in the earlier case as dicta and denied an application to rehear *en banc* "to determine the role of international law-of-war principles in interpreting the AUMF because, as the various opinions issued in the case indicate, the panel's discussion of that question is not necessary to the disposition of the merits." This bare determination was accompanied by lengthy concurring judgments opining on the role of international law in US jurisprudence.

119 Hamdi v. Rumsfeld, 542 U.S 507, 517 (2004).

120 PRESS RELEASE, DEPARTMENT OF JUSTICE, OFFICE OF PUBLIC AFFAIRS, DEPARTMENT OF JUSTICE WITHDRAWS "ENEMY COMBATANT" DEFINITION FOR GUANTANAMO DETAINEES (March 13, 2009), *available at* www.justice.gov/opa/pr/2009/March/09-ag-232.html. The phrase "*draw* on the international laws of war" has changed subtly in various documents. For example, Executive Order 13,567 of March 10, 2011 defined detention authorized by the AUMF "as *informed* by the laws of war," and the National Defense Authorization Act of 2012 refers to detention "*under* the law of war." *See* Marty Lederman and Steve Vladeck, *The NDAA: The Good, the Bad, and the Laws of War – Part II*, LAWFARE (December 31, 2011), www.lawfareblog.com/2011/12/the-ndaa-the-good-the-bad-and-he-laws-of-war-part-ii/.

121 Respondents' Memorandum Regarding the Government's Detention Authority Relative to Detainees Held at Guantánamo Bay, *In re*: Guantánamo Bay Detainee Litigation, Misc. No. 08-442 (TFH) (D.D.C. March 13, 2009).

122 NDAA 2012.

123 JENNIFER K. ELSEA AND MICHAEL JOHN GARCIA, CONGRESSIONAL RESEARCH SERVICE, JUDICIAL ACTIVITY CONCERNING ENEMY COMBATANT DETAINEES: MAJOR COURT RULINGS, 1 Report R 41156, (December 11, 2012).

124 *Id.*

125 National Defense Authorization Act for Fiscal Year 2013, Pub.L.112-239 [NDAA 2013], §1033.

126 JENNIFER K. ELSEA, DETENTION OF U.S. PERSONS AS ENEMY BELLIGERENTS, 50 R42337 Congressional Research Service (December 4, 2012).

127 Greg Miller and Karen de Young, *Administration debates stretching 9/11 law to go after Al Qaeda offshoots*, WASH. POST, (March 7, 2013); ROBERT CHESNEY, JACK GOLDSMITH, MATTHEW C. WAXMAN AND BENJAMIN WITTES, A STATUTORY FRAMEWORK FOR NEXT-GENERATION TERRORIST THREATS, 3, Hoover Foundation, Stanford University (2013).

128 *See e.g.* CHESNEY AND ORS, A STATUTORY FRAMEWORK FOR NEXT-GENERATION TERRORIST THREATS, 10; Jennifer Daskal and Stephen I. Vladeck, *After the*

AUMF, LAWFARE (May, 9 2013), www.lawfareblog.com/wp-content/uploads/2013/05/After-the-AUMF-Final.pdf.

129 Stephen W. Preston, General Counsel for US Department of Defense, Address at Annual Meeting of the American Society of International Law, Washington D.C., "The Legal Framework for the United States' Use of Military Force Since 9/11," (April 10, 2015).

130 NDAA 2012, §1021. For a discussion about the meaning of "under the laws of war," see Lederman and Vladeck, *The NDAA: The Good, the Bad, and the Laws of War – Part I.* This section has been challenged as unconstitutional, see Hedges v. Obama, 12 Civ. 331 (S.D.N.Y., May 16, 2012).

131 NDAA 2012, §1021(b): a covered person is any person who is:
   (1) A person who planned, authorized, committed or aided the terrorist attacks that occurred on September 11, 2001, or harbored those responsible for those attacks.
   (2) A person who was a part of or substantially supported al-Qaeda, the Taliban, or associated forces that are engaged in hostilities against the United States or its coalition partners, including any person who has committed a belligerent act or has directly supported such hostilities in aid of such enemy forces.

132 Respondents' Memorandum Regarding the Government's Detention Authority Relative to Detainees Held at Guantánamo Bay.

133 *See* Lederman and Vladeck, *The NDAA: The Good, the Bad, and the Laws of War – Part I*; David Cole, *A Bill of Rights for Some*, NYRBLOG (December 16, 2011), www.nybooks.com/blogs/nyrblog/2011/dec/16/bill-rights-some/?printpage=true.

134 *Id.*

135 NDAA 2012, §1021(c).

136 Wittes and Chesney, *NDAA FAQ: A Guide for the Perplexed.*

137 COPENHAGEN PROCESS: PRINCIPLES, 4.

138 NDAA 2012, §1021(d).

139 *See e.g.* Wittes and Chesney, *NDAA FAQ: A Guide for the Perplexed*, commenting that that the detention authority is not expanded. Their view is that the DC Circuit courts have in fact articulated a broader standard than the NDAA's "substantial support" category on the basis that the court permits detention of those who "purposefully and materially support" the enemy. The wording in the NDAA may result in a narrower approach by the courts. *Contra* Benjamin Wittes, *Raha Wala Writes His Own FAQ*, reporting on Wala's fears that the authority has been expanded, although he is not sure that there is any practical difference between "material and purposeful" support and "substantial" support.

140 NDAA 2012, §1021(e). President Obama has issued a waiver in respect of US citizens and lawful permanent residents in MEMORANDUM, THE WHITE HOUSE, OFFICE OF THE PRESS SECRETARY, PRESIDENTIAL POLICY DIRECTIVE – REQUIREMENTS OF THE NATIONAL DEFENSE AUTHORIZATION ACT, PRESIDENTIAL POLICY DIRECTIVE/PPD-14, B (February 28, 2012) [PPD-14 MEMORANDUM].

141 Hamdi, 517.

142 Jose Padilla was initially detained in the United States in May 2002 as a material witness to grand jury proceedings investigating the attacks on 9/11. After being

detained as a material witness for a month with access to counsel, he was designated an enemy combatant and detained for three and a half years in military custody, initially with no access to counsel. He was then returned to civilian custody (just days before the government was due to respond to Padilla's petition for certiorari to the Supreme Court), and tried and convicted of conspiracy to murder, maim, and kidnap persons overseas, United States v. Padilla, 2007 U.S. Dist. LEXIS 26077 (S.D. Fla. April 9, 2007). See the line of cases claiming habeas corpus commencing with Padilla v. Bush, 233 F. Supp. 2d. 564 (S.D.N.Y. 2002), culminating in Padilla v. Hanft, 432 F.3d. 582 (4th Cir. 2005).

143 Ali Saleh Kahlah al-Marri was initially detained in the United States in December 2001as a material witness to grand jury proceedings investigating the attacks on 9/11. Two months later he was charged with fraud-related offenses. Further fraud charges were added a year later. These charges were dismissed in June 2003 and al-Marri was designated an enemy combatant and he was transferred to military custody, with no access to counsel for a year. He applied for *habeas corpus* and the denial was appealed all the way to the Supreme Court, but his case was dismissed as moot, because in February 2009, President Obama ordered him to be transferred to civilian custody to face criminal charges. See the line of *habeas* cases commencing with Al-Marri v. Rumsfeld, 360 F.3d. 707 (2004).

144 *See*, *e.g.*, Brian Michael Jenkins, *The NDAA Makes It Harder To Fight Terrorism*, FOREIGN AFF. (February 1, 2012), www.foreignaffairs.com/print/134333;. ELSEA, DETENTION OF U.S. PERSONS AS ENEMY BELLIGERENTS, 38–44.

145 Lederman and Vladeck, *The NDAA: The Good, the Bad, and the Laws of War – Part I.*

146 *Id.*, §1022(b).

147 *Id.*, §1022(a)(4).

148 Wittes and Chesney, *NDAA FAQ: A Guide for the Perplexed.*

149 NDAA 2012, §1022(2)(d).

150 Wittes and Chesney, *NDAA FAQ: A Guide for the Perplexed.*

151 NDAA 2012, §1022(c)(2)(C).

152 Waxman, *Administrative Detention of Terrorists*, 31.

153 Robert M. Chesney, *Who May Be Held? Military Detention Through the Habeas Lens*, 52 B.C. L. REV.769, 772 (2011).

154 Bensayah v. Obama, 610 F.3d 718, 720 (D.C. Cir. 2010).

155 *Id.*, 722.

156 *Id.*, 725.

157 *Id.* This approach has been emphasized in many cases, *e.g.* Al Adahi v Obama, 613 F.3d 1102 (D.C. Cir. 2010), *cert. denied*, 131 S.Ct. 1001 (2011), Salahi v. Obama, 625 F.3d 745, 752 (D.C. Cir. 2010), Uthman v. Obama, 637 F.3d 400, 407 (2011), Awad v. Obama, 608 F.3d 1, 7 (2010), Ali v. Obama, No. 11-5102, D.C. Ct. of App. (December 3, 2013).

158 Salahi v. Obama, 752.

159 *Id.*

160 David Mortlock, *Definite Detention: The Scope of the President's Authority To Detain Enemy Combatants.* 4 HARV. L. & POL'Y. REV. 375, 389–404 (2010).

161 Gherebi v. Obama, 609 F. Supp. 2d 43 (D.D.C. 2009).

162 Mortlock, *Definite Detention*, 390 (quoting Gherebi, 68–70).

163 *Id.*
164 Hamlily v. Obama, 616 F. Supp. 2d 63 (D.D.C. 2009).
165 Mortlock, *Definite Detention*, 391 (quoting Hamlily, 76).
166 *Id.*, 391 (quoting Hamlily, 75).
167 Benjamin Wittes, Robert Chesney and Rabea Benhalim, Emerging Law of Detention 17–21 (Brookings Institute, 2010) [Emerging Law of Detention]; Benjamin Wittes, Robert Chesney, and Larkin Reynolds, The Emerging Law of Detention 2.0: The Guantanamo Habeas Cases as Lawmaking 24 (Brookings Institute 2011) [Emerging Law of Detention 2.0].
168 *Id.*, 21–2.
169 Al-Bihani.
170 Military Commissions Act of 2006, Pub.L.109–366, §3, 120 Stat. 2600 (2006) (codified as amended in scattered sections of 10, 18, and 28 U.S.C.) amended by Military Commissions Act of 2009.
171 Al-Bihani, 872.
172 Mortlock, *Definite Detention*, 393.
173 Al-Bihani, 873.
174 These persons must comply with GC III, Art. 4(A) which requires: (a) being commanded by a person responsible for his subordinates; (b) having a fixed distinctive sign recognizable at a distance; (c) carrying arms openly; (d) conducting operations in accordance with the laws and customs of war.
175 Johnson v. Eisentrager, 339 U.S. 763, 778 (1950). The petitioners were German nationals taken into custody by the US military in China for continuing to take military action against the United States after Germany had surrendered. They were convicted of violations of the law of war by a US military commission in China, and were sent to serve their sentence in a prison in Germany under US control. The Court denied the applicability of *habeas corpus* because the petitioners were not at any relevant time "within any territory over which the United States is sovereign, and the scenes of their offense, their capture, their trial and their punishment were all beyond the territorial jurisdiction of any court of the United States."
176 Rasul v. Bush, 542 U.S. 466 (2004).
177 *Pursuant to* 28 U.S.C. §§2241–2243.
178 Rasul, 476.
179 Detainee Treatment Act of 2005, Pub. L. No. 109–148, 119 Stat. 2739 (2005).
180 Hamdan, 56.
181 Military Commissions Act of 2006.
182 Boumediene v. Bush, 553 U.S. 723 (2008).
183 *Id.*, 732.
184 *Id.*, 767.
185 *Id.*, 768.
186 *Id.*, 769.
187 In re Guantanamo Bay Detainee Litigation, No. 08-mc-0442, Doc 940 (D.D.C. November 6, 2008).
188 *Id.*, §IIA.
189 Hussain v. Obama, No. 11-5344, 4 D.C. Court of Appeal (June 18, 2013) 1 (of concurrence) (citing Concrete Pipe & Prods. of Cal., Inc. v. Constr. Laborers Pension Trust for S. Cal., 508 U.S. 602, 622 (1993)).
190 Hamdi, 521.

191 *Id.*, 520–1.

192 *Id.*

193 *See e.g.* YORAM DINSTEIN, THE CONDUCT OF HOSTILITIES UNDER THE LAW OF INTERNATIONAL ARMED CONFLICT 56 (Cambridge University Press, 2010) (arguing that al-Qaeda does not merit the status of POWs because they cannot meet the four requirements of GC III art. 4A).

194 Awad, 11.

195 Ali.

196 *Id.*, 19–20.

197 *Id.*, 20.

198 *Id.*, 22.

199 *Id.*, 23.

200 COPENHAGEN PROCESS: PRINCIPLES, 4.

201 *Id.*, GUIDELINES, ¶4.7.

202 LAW OF WAR MANUAL, §8.14.2.

203 THE WHITE HOUSE, FACT SHEET: PROCEDURES IMPLEMENTING SECTION 1022 OF THE NATIONAL DEFENSE AUTHORIZATION ACT FOR FISCAL YEAR (FY) 2012 (February 28, 2012) [DETAINEE POLICY FACT SHEET].

204 PPD-14 MEMORANDUM.

205 DETAINEE POLICY FACT SHEET.

206 *Id.*, §§IIC, IID.

207 *Id.*

208 International Covenant on Civil and Political Rights, December 19, 1966, 999 U.N.T.S. 171 [ICCPR].

209 NDAA 2012, §1023(a).

210 *Id.*, §1023(b)(1). Despite the 2012 Copenhagen Process Principles advocating in Principle 12 periodic review of security detainees in NIACs, it was not until October 2013 that the Department of Defense announced that the Periodic Review Board process was "now underway," see US Dept. of Defense, News Release No. 709-13 (October 9, 2013), www.defense.gov/releases/release.aspx?releaseid=16302.

211 Exec. Order No. 13,567, 76 Fed. Reg. 13,277, §2 (March 7, 2011).

212 David Cole and Stephen I. Vladeck, *Comparative Advantages: Secret Evidence and "Cleared Counsel" in the United States, United Kingdom and Canada*, *in* SECRECY, NATIONAL SECURITY AND THE VINDICATION OF CONSTITUTIONAL LAW, 176 (David Cole, Federico Fabbrini, and Arianna Vedaschi, eds) (Edward Elgar Publishing, 2013).

213 In re Guantanamo Bay Detainee Litigation, 577 F.Supp.2d 143, ¶29 (D.D.C. July 10, 2009).

214 Cole and Vladeck, *Comparative Advantages*, 177.

215 *Id.*, 177.

216 *Id.* (citing Bismullah v Gates, 501 F 3d 178, 187–88 (D.C. Cir. 2007), *and* In re Guantanamo Bay Detainee Litigation, 787 F Supp. 2d 5 (DDC 2011)).

217 *Id.* (citing Al Odah v United States, 559 F 3d 539, 547 (D.C. Cir. 2009)).

218 *Id.*, 186.

219 Hamdi, 539.

220 Al Odah v. United States, 346 F.Supp.2d 1, 15 (2004).

221 In re Guantanamo Bay Detainee Continued Access To Counsel, 892 F.Supp.2d 8 §VII (2012).

222 Copenhagen Process: Principles, 7.
223 *Id.*, Guidelines, ¶7.1.
224 Law Of War Manual, §8.14.1.
225 Copenhagen Process: Principles, 10, Guidelines, ¶10.1–3.
226 Law Of War Manual, §8.10.
227 Copenhagen Process: Principles, 8 where no time limit is suggested, and Law Of War Manual, §8.15.1, which states that registration should taken place promptly, defined as within a reasonable time.
228 Copenhagen Process: Principles, 11.
229 Matthews v. Eldridge, 424 U.S. 319, 335 (1976) In analyzing due process requirements three factors must be taken into account: "First, the private interest that will be affected by the official action; second, the risk of an erroneous deprivation of such interest through the procedures used, and the probable value, if any, of additional or substitute procedural safeguards; and finally, the Government's interest, including the function involved and the fiscal and administrative burdens that the additional or substitute procedural requirement would entail."
230 Cole and Vladeck, *Comparative Advantages*, 183.
231 HRC Communication No. 10/2013 (United States of America) concerning Obaidullah, ¶¶37–44.
232 United Nations Office of the High Commissioner for Human Rights, IACHR, UN Working Group on Arbitrary Detention, UN Rapporteur on Torture, UN Rapporteur on Human Rights and Counter-Terrorism, and UN Rapporteur on Health reiterate the need to end the indefinite detention of individuals at Guantánamo Naval Base in light of current human rights crisis, (May 1, 2013), www.ohchr.org/EN/NewsEvents/Pages/DisplayNews.aspx?NewsID=13278&LangID=E.
233 *Bagram FOIA*, American Civil Liberties Union (July 14, 2011), *available at* www.aclu.org/national-security/bagram-foia.
234 Al Maqaleh v. Gates, 605 F.3d 84, 99 (D.C. Cir. 2010).
235 *Id.*, 98.
236 Boumediene, 766.
237 Al Maqaleh, 95.
238 *Id.*
239 *Id.*, 97.
240 *Id.*, 98.
241 *See*, *e.g.*, Robert Chesney and Jack Goldsmith, *Terrorism and the Convergence of Criminal and Military Detention Models*, 60 Stan. L. Rev. 1079, 1080 (2008); Cole, *Out of the Shadows*, 697–8; Monica Hakimi, *International Standards for Detaining Terrorism Suspects*, 594–600; Oona Hathaway et al., *The Power to Detain: Detention of Terrorism Suspects After 9/11*, 38 Yale J. Int'l L. 123 (2013).
242 Tom Bingham, The Rule Of Law, 66, 84 (Penguin Books, 2011).
243 If a terror suspect is a United States citizen and is outside the United States, different options are open to the US government: targeted killing, capturing abroad, and criminal prosecution in US federal court; military detention; prosecution in the foreign country; and toleration. *See* Daniel Byman and Benjamin Wittes, Tools And Tradeoffs: Confronting U.S. Citizen Terrorist Suspects Abroad (Brookings Institution Press, June 17, 2013),

www.brookings.edu/research/reports/2013/07/23-us-citizen-terrorist-suspects-awlaki-jihad-byman-wittes.

244 *See e.g.* Payton v. New York, 445 U.S. 573, 583, 587 (1980); U.S. v. Watson, 423 U.S. 411, 277 (1976).

245 *See e.g.* Brinegar v. U.S., 338 U.S. 160 (1949); Illinois v. Gates, 62 U.S. 213 (1983); Maryland v. Pringle, 540 U.S. 366, 370-1 (2003).

246 *See e.g.* Craig S. Lerner, *The Reasonableness of Probable Cause*, 81 TEX. L. REV. 951 (March 2003); Bruce K. Antkowiak, *Saving Probable Cause*, 40 SUFFOLK U. L. REV. 569 (2007); Thomas Y. Davies, *The Supreme Court Giveth and the Supreme Court Taketh Away: The Century of Fourth Amendment" Search and Seizure" Doctrine*, 100 J. CRIM. L. & CRIMINOLOGY 933, 1009 (Summer 2010).

247 Daniel Benjamin, Coordinator, Bureau of Counterterrorism, Address at the Brookings Institution, Washington, D.C. (December 18, 2012) *available at* www.state.gov/j/ct/rls/rm/2012/202179.htm#.

248 *See, e.g.*, *Feds looking into Tenn. shooting as act of terror*, CBS NEWS (July 18, 2015), www.cbsnews.com/news/chattanooga-shooting-probe-terrorism-investigation/, relating to deadly attack on two military facilities in Chattanooga by Muhammad Youssef Abdulazeez.

249 Al Maqaleh, 98.

250 NDAA 2012, §1024(c) deals with status review of persons that are not entitled to *habeas* review in a federal court.

251 Jonathan Horowitz, *The U.S. Must Ensure Umm Sayyaf Is Not Subjected to Human Rights Abuses*, JUST SECURITY (July 9, 2015), http://justsecurity.org/24513/umm-sayyaf-nonrefoulement/.

252 EMERGING LAW OF DETENTION, 64–5.

253 Al-Adahi v. Obama, *cert. denied*, 131 S.Ct. 1001 (2011).

254 Larkin Reynolds, *Supreme Court Denied Cert. in Three More Gitmo Cases*, LAWFARE (April 4, 2011), www.lawfareblog.com/2011/04/supreme-court-denies-cert-in-three-more-gtmo-cases/.

255 Benjamin Wittes, *David Remes on Al Adahi Cert Denial*, LAWFARE (January 18, 2011), www.lawfareblog.com/2011/01/david-remes-on-al-adahi-cert-denial.

256 Wells Bennett, *SCOTUS Denies Cert in Seven GTMO Habeas Cases, and in Lebron Too*, LAWFARE (June 11, 2012), www.lawfareblog.com/2012/06/scotus-denies-cert-in-seven-gtmo-habeas-cases-and-lebron-too/. Certiorari was denied in Latif v. Obama, 11-1027; Al-Bihani v. Obama, 10-1383; Uthman v. Obama, 11-413; Almerfedi v. Obama, 11-683; Al-Kandari v. United States, 11-1054; Al-Madhwani v. Obama, 11-7020; and Al-Alwi v. Obama, 11-7700. *Also see* conversation between Steve Vladeck, Benjamin Wittes and Robert Chesney, commencing with Steve Vladeck, *D.C Circuit 1, Guantanamo Bar 0?* LAWFARE (June 11, 2012) www.lawfareblog.com/2012/06/d-c-circuit-1-guantanamo-bar-0/.

257 *See e.g.* Obaydullah v. Obama, 12-8932, cert. denied (June 24, 2013) www.supremecourt.gov/orders/courtorders/062413zor_n7ip.pdf.

258 *See, e.g.*, Benjamin Wittes and Jack Goldsmith, *Ghailani Verdict Makes Stronger Case for Military Detentions*, WASH. POST (November 19, 2010), A21.

259 Boumediene, 2267.

260 THE WHITE HOUSE OFFICE OF THE PRESS SECRETARY, REMARKS BY THE PRESIDENT AT THE NATIONAL DEFENSE UNIVERSITY (May 23, 2013): "one

issue will remain — just how to deal with those GTMO detainees who we know have participated in dangerous plots or attacks but who cannot be prosecuted, for example, because the evidence against them has been compromised or is inadmissible in a court of law. But once we commit to a process of closing GTMO, I am confident that this legacy problem can be resolved, consistent with our commitment to the rule of law."

Part III

Recommendations

10 Recommendations

The need for global core detention principles

Many countries have chosen to use preventive detention to pre-empt a terrorist act and/or ferret out vital information from suspected terrorists.[1] This book has conducted a detailed analysis of detention laws relating to suspected terrorists in a sample of those countries, LOAC,[2] and five general international human rights treaties,[3] together with related jurisprudence and guidance materials. The study has demonstrated that the procedures governing the use of preventive detention are deficient to a greater or lesser extent in each framework. These deficiencies often have an adverse and serious impact on the human rights of detainees, thereby delegitimizing the use of preventive detention.

The rule of law requires that the law afford adequate protection of fundamental human rights.[4] The right to liberty is one such fundamental right.[5] This book argues that neither domestic laws, nor LOAC, nor international human rights laws, as they currently apply to the deprivation of liberty in preventive detention, adequately protect this fundamental human right. The effect of this deficiency is that contemporary detention laws do not fully comply with the rule of law requirement.

In particular, and as explained more fully below, due process is lacking in many respects, and this adversely affects the human rights of detainees. If a person is detained anywhere in the world, he needs to know that he can find out why he has been arrested, that he can tell someone where he is and why, that he will be treated fairly, that he can challenge his detention without delay, and have the advice and assistance of a lawyer whilst detained. The laws as they currently stand do not properly provide these essential guarantees.

In order to prevent abuse, detention must be anchored and administered further within a coherent legal framework, based on international human rights and various good practices identified in domestic laws. This can serve as guidance for all countries wishing to use this counter-terrorism tool.

Drawing on the common elements found both in domestic law and international human rights law as a foundation and designed to address the current gaps and problems, this book proposes a set of recommendations.

These are crafted from international human rights law and guidance informed by both selected domestic laws as well as LOAC to provide a new, consistent, and principled approach to preventively detain terror suspects for the countries that choose to use this tool.

The recommendations

One possible approach for providing the appropriate legal framework might be the negotiation and conclusion of a formal and binding treaty on detention. However, the likelihood of this happening any time soon is extremely remote. In contrast, the adoption of guidance in the form of a non-binding Statement of Principles[6] is of greater likelihood, because the process is much more informal and faster. This approach is adopted here, with a suggested set of minimum essential core principles to give guidance on detaining suspected terrorists, before or without charge, to prevent the commission of a terrorist act.[7]

The aim of the recommendations is to reduce the potential for human rights violations, but some principles may have implications for security. In order to apply the rule of law consistently, "[t]he proper balance is a result of a clear position that recognizes both the need for security and the need for human rights."[8] Therefore each principle is subjected to a cost–benefit analysis in order to assess what, if any, tradeoffs might be required, from either the human rights or security perspective.

Each principle is subjected to three tests: (1) whether the principle is compatible with international human rights standards; (2) whether adopting the principle would affect the ability of law enforcement authorities to prevent terrorist acts; and (3) if the principle is adopted, how much change is needed in the domestic laws of the countries surveyed and LOAC.

The goal is to encourage states to comply with the principles at this basic level without having to make significant major adjustments to their own legal systems. States would then have the option to "gold plate"[9] the minimum detention standards, by imposing higher procedural standards for detention if they wish to do so. The recommendations are designed to improve the current lamentable level of process, without adversely affecting law enforcement tools to a significant extent.

Recommendation 1 – Clarify the requirement that preventive detention must be on grounds authorized by law

Four of the five human rights treaties prescribe that detention may only be used on grounds of and in accordance with procedures established by law.[10] In contrast, the European Convention erects a higher bar to detain, by listing six specific permissible reasons for detention.[11] The European Court of Human Rights (ECHR) has confirmed that no deprivation of liberty is regarded as lawful unless it falls within those six specified grounds.[12] In relation to preventive detention of terror suspects, Article 5(1)(c) requires a connection with a concrete and specific offense, and possibly a charge.[13] This means that an offense must be specific as to where and when it is to be committed, and as to who the intended victims are,[14] and also as to what actual crime is to be committed. For example, in *Shimovolos v. Russia* the applicant was detained for offenses "of an extremist nature." The ECHR considered this was too vague to satisfy the "concrete and specific" requirement of Article 5(i)(c).[15]

The Human Rights Committee (HRC)'s guidance on Article 9 of the International Covenant on Civil and Political Rights (ICCPR) in General Comment No. 35[16] considers that security detention "presents severe risks of arbitrary deprivation of liberty."[17] However, the need for states to clearly articulate grounds for national security detention is not adequately addressed.[18] General Comment No. 35 refers to the necessity of defining the substantive grounds for detention with sufficient precision to avoid overly broad or arbitrary detention.[19] This has particular relevance to preventive detention of terror suspects because many definitions of terrorist offenses are extremely broad.[20]

Should guidance recommend the adoption of the more restrictive approach of the European Convention? Adopting the Article 5(1)(c) formula would afford more protection to detainees, but would it be more difficult for states to detain suspected terrorists? The drafters of the ICCPR deliberately chose not to restrict detention to a specified list of grounds.[21] In General Comment No. 35, the HRC seems to acknowledge the problem, but is not advocating any change from the *status quo*.

One possible solution involves giving more precision to the general wording in Article 9 (and the American Convention, African Charter, and Arab Charter). This would address the concerns of the HRC relating to vague and very broad detention powers. The HRC appears to equate "overly broad" with arbitrary application of Article 9. Thus, over-broad application of the detention power would be unlawful. The following wording is suggested as a guide for more precision and specificity.

Principle 1 – Clarifying the requirement that preventive detention must be on grounds authorized by law

Subject to compliance with procedural guarantees set out in these Principles, detention of suspects is only permitted to prevent the commission of a terrorist offense that is concrete and specific as to (i) the type of conduct it is designed to proscribe, and (ii) where, and when, the offense is expected to be committed, and against whom, or what, the act is targeted.

Comments

Principle 1 does not affect the normal criminal power to arrest persons who have committed, or are in the course of committing, an offense. It is designed to address the detention of a suspect to *forestall* a terrorist attack. This is a minimum standard, so a state is free to use whatever evidential standard it chooses in order to arrest, and can impose additional restrictions if desired.

Would tweaking the broad treaty language as proposed in Principle 1, with echoes of European Convention jurisprudence, place law enforcers in a worse position? Many states will not be affected because they have quite precisely worded terrorism offenses, specifying acts that, for example, kill or injure persons, and damage property or infrastructures. Furthermore, preventive arrests are often made because of suspicions that persons have some connection to a particular imminent plot. This principle will adversely affect states that wish to detain to prevent offenses described only as "terrorist" or "extremist," without further explanation, or if it is not known in a general sense when or where the act is likely to take place, or its likely victims.

This does not mean that law enforcement authorities need to know that an attack will take place at 2 p.m. on Friday May 9, in Times Square, against particular people. It would be sufficient to know that an attack is likely to take place in New York City within, say, the next few weeks, and it may kill or injure anyone in its vicinity at the time. The wording of this Principle is suggested to give an idea of how to minimize vagueness and prevent indiscriminate dragnet arrests. As Principle 1 sets out a minimum standard, states that wish to apply more restrictive rights may continue to do so.

Principle 1 does not apply to the United States because its domestic law does not permit detention without charge to prevent a terrorist attack. The United Kingdom and France, as parties to the European Convention, are currently obliged to interpret their laws in such a way as to ensure that an arrest must be made for a specific and concrete offense. Both the United Kingdom and France, and the other countries in the European Union, have made many arrests to prevent terrorist attacks that comply with the European Convention standard. It is a standard that appears to work.

Australia, Canada, Israel, and India would need to adapt their interpretation of the law for them to continue with their current preventive detention practices. India is an example of a country where counter-terrorism laws have been interpreted so broadly that many human rights violations have resulted, prompting much criticism from the HRC and human rights non-governmental organizations (NGOs).[22] These countries should evaluate their laws and practices against the requirements of this standard. They should assess how great the cost to security would really be if they chose to adopt this principle, which has a proven successful track record in Europe.

Recommendation 2 – Provide guidance to understand the meaning of arbitrary detention

Although this essential and fundamental prohibition appears explicitly in the ICCPR,[23] the American Convention,[24] the African Charter,[25] and the Arab

Charter,[26] and in the jurisprudence of the European Convention,[27] it is not clear what arbitrary detention means. Dictionary definitions of arbitrary are unhelpful in terms of guidance.[28]

The definitional criteria of arbitrary detention are not consistent in the jurisprudence of all five sources.[29] Often the jurisprudence itemizes a long list of different criteria, such as that detention must only be on grounds, and in accordance with procedures established by law,[30] and it must be reasonable,[31] appropriate,[32] predictable,[33] necessary,[34] and proportionate,[35] it must be for an exceptional reason,[36] and it must afford due process.[37] Detention must not be unjust,[38] discriminatory,[39] or continue longer than can be justified,[40] it may not be indefinite,[41] and must not be imposed if a less invasive method can be used to achieve the same ends.[42] Detention should be a measure of "last resort."[43]

Only two definitional criteria are common to the jurisprudence of the ICCPR, the European Convention and the American Convention: that of necessity and proportionality.[44] With a more succinct and comprehensive definition, this Principle could form the basis of a test to be applied by arresting and judicial authorities. It would be more practical to have a short clear statement of essential criteria. All of the criteria set out below are equally important, and preventive detention should only be permitted if all of these tests are satisfied.

Principle 2 – Guidance to clarify the meaning of arbitrary detention

Detention may never be arbitrary. This means:

(i) Detention may only be imposed in accordance with procedures established by law;
(ii) Detention must not be unjust;
(iii) Detention must be proportionate;
(iv) Detention must be necessary;
(v) Detention may not continue for a longer period than can be justified in accordance with judicial assessment at regular specified intervals as to the continuing validity of the grounds that justified the initial detention, including the continuing threat posed by the terror suspect;
(vi) Detention must not be imposed if a less invasive method can be used to achieve the same ends.

Comments

This Principle expands on the criteria found separately in ICCPR, European Convention, and American Convention jurisprudence and guidance including that found in the HRC General Comment No. 35.[45]

The list of criteria in the preamble above Principle 2 has been examined and stripped down to essential elements by removing the synonyms found in the criteria mentioned above, which jurisprudential bodies have listed in various cases.

Principle 2 is a checklist for the authorities that detain, as well as the judicial authorities that evaluate and confirm detention orders. It is more practical to check the factual circumstances against six criteria, rather than the fifteen mentioned above. Principle 2(i) is derived from treaty language and it incorporates an obligation to afford due process. Principle 2(ii) incorporates the notions of reasonableness, non-discrimination, and predictability. Principle 2(iii) incorporates the notion of "appropriate." Principles 2(iv) and (vi) stand by themselves.

Principle 2(v) is derived from the jurisprudence that detention may not continue indefinitely,[46] or for a longer period that can be justified.[47] What does longer than can be justified mean – justified how, by whom, and according to what standards? Some cases touch on the meaning. For example, in *A. v. State of Israel* the Court required periodic judicial review every six months in order to examine whether the threat presented by the detainee justified continued detention. In making that assessment the Court is required to take into account the length of time that had passed since the detention began.[48] Principle 2(v) synthesizes national and international jurisprudence to make this criterion more meaningful. It adds useful criteria that are found in case law into the checklist. The procedural aspects are discussed below in connection with Principles 6 and 7.

The United Kingdom is the only country out of those surveyed in detail where preventive detention law currently complies with this principle. British law was amended in response to two cases where the essence of the rulings related to arbitrary detention, even though the word "arbitrary" barely appeared in the judgments. The first of these cases concerned the legality of control orders.[49] The law lords ruled that a curfew of eighteen hours amounted to a deprivation of liberty.[50] As a result of the ruling in this case, curfews were reduced to sixteen hours. In the second case,[51] the law lords ruled that it was discriminatory to detain foreign nationals (international terrorists) indefinitely, when the law did not permit this for British citizens.[52] The offending statute was repealed.

Every other country violates the prohibition on arbitrary detention in some way: Australia, India, France, because their laws do not afford adequate due process;[53] and Canada, because its use of immigration laws to detain suspected terrorists is discriminatory.[54]

Israel's jurisprudence has attempted to demonstrate that administrative detention is not arbitrary by highlighting a number of criteria that are found in Principle 2. For example, in *John Does v Minister of Defense* then Israeli Supreme Court President Barak emphasized that administrative detention "cannot go on endlessly. The more the period of detention that has passed lengthens, so too are weightier considerations needed to justify an additional extension of the detention. With the passage of time the means of administrative detention is no longer proportional."[55] The need for proportionality is referred to frequently in Israeli jurisprudence.[56] However, other deficiencies in process, as discussed below in connection with Recommendation 7, have the effect of making Israel's practice of administrative detention arbitrary.

In the United States, the essence of due process that is afforded by the Constitution[57] is the requirement that "a person in jeopardy of serious loss (be given) notice of the case against him and opportunity to meet it."[58] The criteria in Principle 2(i) comply with this, and the remaining criteria are within the spirit of due process. Detention under LOAC at Bagram in Afghanistan and in Guantánamo Bay has been ruled arbitrary by the HRC in the case of *Obaidullah*.[59] As long as the United States maintains its stance that its obligations under the ICCPR do not apply extraterritorially,[60] the likelihood of it adopting and applying this Principle to detentions outside the United States is remote.

Would this Principle inhibit the ability of countries to detain persons to prevent a terror attack? Much of the conduct that results in a determination of arbitrary detention relates to faulty, or no, process such as in Australia, India, France, and the United States' detentions in Afghanistan and Guantánamo.[61] Providing due process may legitimize many detentions. However, it may not address the needs of every country in every situation.

Some countries detain terror suspects preventively, but not arbitrarily, such as the United Kingdom, where such detentions have helped to prevent some terrorist attacks. However, operating in accordance with due process has meant that the British government has not always been able to detain all those it wanted. The United Kingdom decided that the tradeoff was acceptable. On the whole, the United Kingdom has been successful in thwarting terror plots since 2005. Their example should be borne in mind by countries that have concerns about the security/liberty tradeoff.

Recommendation 3 – Provide guidance for giving detainees the reason for detention

All detainees must be informed of the reason for their detention. Subtle differences are found in treaty terminology, as well as in the domestic laws of the countries surveyed in this monograph. For example, in the ICCPR, a detainee "shall be informed, at the time of arrest, of the reasons for his arrest and shall be promptly informed of any charges against him."[62] The reasons must include not only the general legal basis of the arrest, but enough factual specifics to indicate the substance of the complaint, such as the wrongful act and the identity of an alleged victim.[63] In the European Convention, a detainee "shall be informed promptly, in a language which he understands, of the reasons for his arrest and of any charge against him."[64] In the American Convention, a detainee "shall be informed of the reasons for his detention and shall be promptly notified of the charge or charges against him."[65] No right in the African Charter is specified relating to notification of the reason for detention, and in the Arab Charter, a detainee "shall be informed at the time of arrest, in a language which he understands, of the reasons for his arrest, and shall be promptly informed of any charges against him."[66]

Thus, other than in the case of the African Charter, the moment when information must be given varies from the time of arrest in the ICCPR and the Arab Charter, to the nebulous "promptly" in the European Convention, to no time mandated for the reasons of arrest in the American Convention. The United States 2015 Law of War Manual, which covers detention procedures, suggests that details should generally be given within ten days of capture.[67]

Principle 3 – Guidance for giving detainees the reason for detention

(i) All detainees must be told the reasons for arrest and detention at the time of arrest, or as soon as practicable thereafter, in a language the detainee understands.

(ii) The detainee is entitled to know the essential factual and legal grounds for the arrest. He must be sufficiently informed during the detention, in accordance with procedures set out in Principle 7, to be able to challenge his detention.

Comments

Principle 3(i) is derived from the treaty texts by selecting the words that afford the most protection to a detainee, without adversely impacting on law enforcement tools. Being told the reason for arrest "promptly" is not good enough, as different arresting officers may have conflicting ideas as to what "promptly" means. HRC guidance recommends that ordinarily this information must be provided immediately upon arrest. In exceptional circumstances, such immediate communication may not be possible. For example, a delay of several hours may be required before an interpreter can be present.[68]

Principle 3(ii) is inspired by the rulings in *Fox, Campbell and Hartley v. United Kingdom*[69] and *Drescher Caldas v. Uruguay.*[70] This Principle offers guidance not found in the bare treaty provisions. The explanatory wording does not adversely affect current counter-terrorism tools because it has not changed the law, but clarifies content and timing issues. This principle is designed to address the amount of minimum information that should be given to a detainee *on arrest* to enable him to know why he has been arrested. The giving of sufficient information to enable the detainee to challenge the detention can occur later. Giving more information may involve a number of security related issues that are discussed in connection with Recommendation 7.

India's detention laws and the domestic law of the United States comply with Principle 3, in that persons must be given full particulars of why they have been arrested.[71] LOAC detention at Guantánamo has not fully complied with this principle.[72] In Canada and Israel[73] the detention laws merely mandate that detainees must be given the "reasons for arrest" but do not specify what information must be given to a detainee on arrest. It is not known what is done in practice. In France, persons who have been arrested have the right to be told the "nature of the offense that is being investigated" within three hours of arrest, save in exceptional and unavoidable circumstances.[74]

United Kingdom law provides that a detainee may be told that he has been arrested on suspicion of terrorism offenses. The law does not specify that he be given all the relevant information at the moment of arrest.[75] *Sher v. Chief Constable of Manchester* held that this sort of very general statement at the time of arrest "will not usually amount to a breach of Article 5(2), *provided of course*, that thereafter further information as to why and how such suspicions are held is promptly given to the suspect."[76] United Kingdom practice would be improved by amending its practice to supply the information "as soon as practicable" rather than "promptly." In practice, if the suspect does not understand English, an interpreter will be provided at the police station to which a detained person is taken.

In Australia, the current process is deficient in many respects. The police must explain the substance of the order to the detainee and inform the detainee of his or her rights whilst detained.[77] The detainee must be given a summary of the grounds for detention,[78] but if information is deemed likely to prejudice national security, it need not be included.[79] The detainee must be given a copy of the order as soon as reasonably practicable.[80] This means that detainees may not see the application, or the underlying evidence and supporting materials.[81] If the detainee does not understand English, an interpreter must be provided to explain the substance of the order and the detainee's rights.[82] One reason why this process is particularly deficient is that the detainee is not given an opportunity to challenge his detention, so he may never know why he was detained.

Other than Australia, and the United States in respect of LOAC detentions, all of the countries largely comply with this principle, but may need to make small changes to their laws or produce guidance materials.

Recommendation 4 – Eliminate incommunicado detention

The domestic laws of some countries, such as Malaysia[83] and Algeria,[84] allow immediate notification of detention to designated persons, but elsewhere some domestic laws prevent or restrict detainees from making contact with lawyers or family.

Beyond restricted rights, there are cases of no rights, where people are detained in secret[85] and held totally incommunicado for lengthy periods in many countries, including Egypt,[86] Nepal,[87] Peru,[88] and Spain.[89] In Germany, incommunicado detention is still part of German counter-terrorism law, even though it has not been used for years.[90]

The Central Intelligence Agency (CIA) conducted an interrogation program between 2003 through 2009 in secret prisons known as "black sites" in a number of locations, including in Thailand, Poland, Romania,

Lithuania, Morocco, and Afghanistan.[91] In 2012 the United States participated in the Copenhagen Process concerning non-international armed conflicts (NIACs). The non-binding principles that resulted, address the eradication of incommunicado detention,[92] as does the United States Law of War Manual.[93]

Two terror suspects currently detained in Guantánamo petitioned the ECHR, claiming that the Polish government knew that they were being taken to a secret detention site for the purposes of interrogation, and that Polish government should have sought diplomatic assurances from the United States to avert the risk of the detainees being subjected to torture and incommunicado detention. The ECHR ruled in each case that by enabling the renditions to take place, Poland exposed the applicants to a serious risk of violations of Articles 3 (torture) and 5 (liberty) of the European Convention. Poland was adjudged to have breached Articles 3 and 5 in each case.[94]

The principle below is designed to offer guidance to ensure that these abuses are not repeated. Detainees must always have someone informed about the detention. Principle 4 builds upon provisions found in United Kingdom, Indian, and French law, the Enforced Disappearance Convention, the Arab Charter, and recommendations by the Inter-American Commission for Human Rights and the African Commission on Human and Peoples' Rights, as described below.

Of the human rights treaties analyzed in this book, only the Arab Charter mentions the right to ensure that third parties are informed of a person's detention.[95] Two treaty bodies have issued recommendations that touch on incommunicado detention. In 2002, the African Commission on Human and Peoples' Rights recommended that detained persons should be kept in an officially recognized place of detention with a register of persons detained, and that detainees should have the right of access to necessary facilities to communicate with lawyers, family, and friends, and the right of *habeas corpus*.[96] In 2006 the Inter-American Commission on Human Rights made some recommendations about how deprivation of liberty should be dealt with in the context of terrorism, some of which related to incommunicado detention, including that detainees be given "prompt access to legal counsel, family, and where necessary, medical and consular assistance."[97]

It is also relevant to look to the Enforced Disappearance Convention.[98] It offers limited guidance, to the extent that it recommends communication with lawyers, family, or other designated persons, but "subject only to the conditions established by law."[99] Theoretically, communication can still be denied or restricted if the law of the detaining country prevents contact.

In cases of incommunicado detention, how should the liberty/security balance be tilted? Some would argue that the law should weigh more in favor of liberty, because the deficiencies in process have resulted in egregious human rights violations. However, others might contend that these methods are essential from a security perspective. Undoubtedly, important reasons may justify preventing detainees from informing a family member about the detention, such as the fear of tipping off others involved in an imminent potential terror plot. Yet what purpose, other than a punitive one, is served by detaining them in this way for months or years, particularly if the danger posed by the suspects diminishes over time?

Principle 4 – Guidance for eliminating incommunicado detention

(i) Detainees must have the right to inform someone of their choice about their detention, either personally, or through the medium of police or some other acceptable third party.

(ii) This right must be exercised as soon as practicable after arrest and a record kept of the date when, and name of the person to whom, the information was given.

(iii) In exceptional circumstances this right may be delayed for up to forty-eight hours, provided that the detainee is told why this right is being delayed. To qualify as exceptional circumstances, investigating authorities must reasonably believe the consequences of exercising the right under 4(i) will carry a significant risk of:

  a) interfering with an on-going investigation;
  b) tampering with evidence;
  c) harming witnesses;
  d) the alerting of a person, thereby making it more difficult to prevent an act of terrorism;
  e) the alerting of a person and thereby making it more difficult to secure a person's apprehension, prosecution, or conviction in connection with the commission, preparation, or instigation of an act of terrorism;
  f) the alerting of persons who are suspected of having committed a serious offence but who have not been arrested for it.

(iv) Detainees must be kept in officially recognized facilities for detention.

(v) Each state must keep a central registry containing details of its detainees, including the detainee's full name and date of birth, date of commencement of detention, and place of detention.

Comments

Principle 4 is drawn from, and expands on, current guidance and some state practice. It addresses the tip-off problem, where an investigation might be prejudiced if persons connected with the matter under investigation are alerted, with the result that evidence is tampered with and witnesses are harmed.

In considering the permissible time period to delay making contact with authorized persons current practice, such as it is, was reviewed. For example in India, on arrival at a police station after arrest, police are obliged to inform the detainee of his right to have a nominated third party informed about the arrest. Police must record the details of the person to whom the information was given.[100]

In some situations, law enforcement persons might want to delay the right to inform a third party. One possibility is to delay communication with third parties until the first court appearance. In some countries, such as the United Kingdom and the United States, this occurs within forty-eight hours of being taken into custody. In some countries, the first appearance may take place after two weeks, or later, or not at all. Permitting contact with authorized persons at a time to coincide with a court appearance strikes an appropriate balance in addressing the tip-off issue, because once a public court hearing takes place, no reason remains to prevent contact. However, this might not deal with situations where hearings take place *in camera* without access to a lawyer. In Israel, although hearings are *in camera*,[101] the detainee will have had access to a lawyer and been able to contact family.[102]

The practice of the United Kingdom offers a reasonable solution and has been adopted in Principle 4(iii). In the United Kingdom a detainee has the right to have a relative or friend informed that he is in custody as soon as is reasonably practicable,[103] but the right to inform may be delayed for up to forty-eight hours[104] in certain specified circumstances that might involve for example, tipping off others, interfering with witnesses, evidence, or the carrying out of the investigation.[105] If this right is delayed, the detainee must be told the reason for the delay as soon as is reasonably practicable.[106]

Australia, Canada, France, and Israel all need to improve their procedures. In Australia, a detainee has the right to inform specified persons that he or she is safe, but may not inform them that he or she is being detained.[107] Indeed, it is a criminal offense for either the detainee or his lawyer to disclose the existence of a preventive detention order, punishable with up to five years imprisonment.[108] In some circumstances the police may apply for a prohibited contact order.[109]

Canada's laws do not specify any rights of a detainee to inform a family member or nominated third party of his arrest or detention. In France, detainees in *Garde à Vue* (GAV) have the right to inform someone of their arrest, but that right can be delayed for up to three hours if that contact is considered prejudicial to the investigation of the detainee.[110] Persons under *détention provisoire* may be prevented from contacting family members for up to twenty days.[111] In Israel's Occupied Territories, after forty-eight hours detainees can receive visits from the Red Cross and their families can be informed as to their whereabouts.[112]

The Principle does not appear to conflict with the United States Constitution. The Federal Rules of Criminal Procedure are silent about whether an arrested person has a right to notify anyone of his or her arrest. Under LOAC, a prisoner of war (POW) has the right to write to his family within one week of capture.[113] However, terror suspects do not usually have the rights of POWs, and detainees held in Guantánamo Bay and Afghanistan were not afforded this right. It remains to be seen if procedures in the United States Law of War Manual are applied to terror suspects captured overseas.

Recommendation 5 – Afford all detainees proper and consistent access to legal counsel

Little explicit reference to access to legal counsel during detention is found in the text of the five treaties, and practice in individual countries is extremely varied. ICCPR text refers to access to counsel in connection with the preparation of a defense after charge[114] and United Nations guidance mandates that detainees have the right to be assisted by counsel "as prescribed by law."[115] General Comment No. 35 states that in order to facilitate effective review of detention, detainees should be allowed "prompt and regular access to counsel."[116]

In the European Convention, no clear mandate is specified for legal representation of persons held without charge, but a right of access to a lawyer is prescribed once a charge has been preferred.[117] European Court judgments have considered the rights of accused persons to have legal representation as "soon as they are placed in custody or in pre-trial detention" in connection with Article 6 rights relating to fair trials,[118] but not Article 5 rights that refer to detentions without, or before, charge. Rights of access to lawyers vary in European Convention countries.

No mention of access to lawyers appears in the text of the American Convention, but a right of legal counsel in *habeas corpus*, or challenge of detention proceedings, is referred to in the jurisprudence.[119] The African Charter only mentions a right to counsel for criminal defense,[120] but African Commission guidelines recommend a right to access to lawyers for detained persons.[121] Rights vary from country to country: for example in Swaziland there is a right to counsel,[122] but not in Zambia, Nigeria, or Ethiopia. No right of access to lawyers is seen in the text of the Arab Charter.

The absence of treaty provisions and wide variations in practice demonstrate the need for guidance on this important matter. Detainees need help and advice to challenge detention. However, security considerations also weigh heavily. In some situations law enforcement will not want a detainee to consult with a lawyer, because the detainee may invoke a right to silence during interrogations. How should Principle 5 approach this dilemma?

As international law gives little guidance, some examples of domestic practice may indicate an approach that appears to work to the satisfaction of the countries concerned. In a number of countries, access to lawyers can be delayed for different periods: forty-eight hours in the United Kingdom;[123] seventy-two hours in France;[124] twenty-one days in Israel under the general criminal law,[125] and access to counsel is only permitted after seven days of detention under the Unlawful Combatants Law.[126] In contrast, in the United States and Canada, detainees have the right to counsel immediately after arrest. In countries where delays may be authorized, these apply in situations where the police are concerned about interference with witnesses, evidence, or the conduct of the investigation.[127]

The approach adopted in connection with Principle 4 (iii) has been followed, where contact with family members can sometimes be delayed for forty-eight hours. Here, access to legal counsel can be delayed for up to forty-eight hours in the specified circumstances, because this period is linked to the time of the first court appearance recommended in these principles. A detainee will need to have access to a lawyer, at the very least, before attending court.

Principle 5 – Affording access to legal counsel

(i) Every detainee must have immediate access to legal counsel for advice and representation after arrest, and in any legal proceedings.
(ii) Indigent detainees must be provided with legal counsel at the government's cost.
(iii) Lawyers must be given access to all facts of each case, and all evidence relevant to the detention, subject only to specified exceptions in cases of sensitive information and where there is a requirement for the authorities to protect sources, which is dealt with under Principle 7 below.
(iv) Confidentiality of communications between detainee and his lawyer must be respected, unless the investigating authorities have reasonable grounds to believe that the detainee's lawyer will, inadvertently or otherwise, pass on a message from the detainee or compromise the investigation in some other way. In these circumstances, either the communication will be monitored or the detainee must be permitted to choose another lawyer.
(v) Lawyers must be present during all interviews and examinations of detainees.
(vi) In exceptional circumstances this right may be delayed for up to forty-eight hours. To qualify as exceptional circumstances, investigating authorities must reasonably believe that the consequences of exercising the right under 5(i), (iii), and (vi) will carry a significant risk of:
   a) interference with an on-going investigation;
   b) tampering with evidence;
   c) harming witnesses;
   d) the alerting of a person, thereby making it more difficult to prevent an act of terrorism;
   e) the alerting of a person and thereby making it more difficult to secure a person's apprehension, prosecution, or conviction in connection with the commission, preparation, or instigation of an act of terrorism;
   f) the alerting of persons who are suspected of having committed a serious offence but who have not been arrested for it.

(vii) If the right of access to legal counsel is delayed, the detainee must be given an explanation.

Comments

Principle 5 has been designed to remedy the deficiencies in international human rights law, and is drawn from, and expands on current guidance, jurisprudence, and some domestic practice. The International Commission of Jurists has recommended that confidentiality of detainee-lawyer communications must be guaranteed from the outset of deprivation of liberty.[128] The Council of Europe has also recommended access to a lawyer from the time any deprivation of liberty begins. The scope of the lawyer's duties would include representation at any *habeas* hearing.[129]

In Canada, everyone has the right on arrest or detention to retain and instruct legal counsel without delay and to be informed of that right,[130] but it is not known if Canada complies with the remainder of Principle 5. In the United Kingdom, every person has the right to "consult a solicitor as soon as is reasonably practicable, privately and at any time,"[131] but a senior police officer may authorize a delay for such consultation for forty-eight hours in certain prescribed circumstances which might compromise the investigation.[132] However, United Kingdom practice permits a senior police officer to order that contact with a lawyer must take place within the sight and hearing of a police officer, if there are reasonable grounds to believe that the lawyer may pass information on to third party.[133]

There are many deficiencies in Australian process. Detainees have access to a lawyer, but only to discuss the legal rights of a person who is the subject of a detention order.[134] The police are entitled to monitor contact and communication between detainees and lawyers.[135] India's procedures are also sorely lacking. The Indian Constitution guarantees the right of any arrested person to consult and be represented by a lawyer,[136] but this right does not apply to anyone who is the subject of a preventive detention order.[137] Israel too must address deficiencies in its laws that currently would violate Principle 5. Detainees do not appear to have the right to have counsel present during interrogations.[138] The Supreme Court has held that the right to meet with a lawyer was not an absolute right, but "rather a relative right, and it should be balanced against other rights and interests."[139] French detainees are entitled to be notified of their right to have a lawyer present throughout the period of custody and during interrogations, but in terrorism cases, access to lawyers may be delayed by seventy-two hours.[140] Some amendment is required to make French law comply with Principle 5, by ensuring that detainees are given reasons for the delay.

The due process provisions of the United States Constitution comply with Principle 5. In domestic law, after arrest and before interrogation, detainees must be told of their right to remain silent and to have a lawyer.[141] Detainee–lawyer communications are confidential and privileged.[142] In 2008 the

Supreme Court ruled that the detainees at Guantánamo had a constitutional right to seek *habeas corpus* relief,[143] and in 2012, the DC District Court ruled that the right of access to counsel continues after the detainees' *habeas* petitions have terminated.[144] In Bagram, detainees were not permitted access to independent lawyers. Instead, they were assigned "personal representatives," who were non-legally trained members of the United States military supplied to represent the interests of the detainees.[145]

Neither law enforcement nor detainees can each avoid a tradeoff. The recommendations in Principle 5 will improve the current situation for detainees, but they must sacrifice immediate access to a lawyer and privacy of communication in exceptional circumstances in order to satisfy considerations of national security. The countries that postpone access to lawyers for lengthy periods should look to the experience of the United Kingdom in considering whether a shorter delay of forty-eight hours would significantly impede their counter-terrorism efforts.

Recommendation 6 – Work towards eliminating indefinite detention

Most, but not all, states specify the duration of pre-charge detention. Currently the period between arrest and charge ranges from twenty-four hours in Australia and Canada to indefinite pre-charge detention in Lebanon. Detention without charge is more problematic. In countries that use administrative detention, such as Israel and the United States under LOAC at Guantánamo or in Afghanistan, detention without charge is for an indefinite period. Out of the 112 persons currently held in Guantánamo, 53 may be released by the end of 2015, but 65 may still be held without prospect of a trial or release.[146] One suspected member of Da'esh, Umm Sayyaf, was detained in Iraq by United States forces for almost three months before being handed over to Iraqi Kurds on August 7, 2015.[147] Israel is holding 412 people who cannot be prosecuted in administrative detention.[148]

Indefinite detention of persons before or without charge is fundamentally unfair and arbitrary.[149] Ideally it should be eliminated, by giving it a time limit. It is, however, extremely difficult to recommend an acceptable maximum, because of the conflicting needs of law enforcement and detainees. In General Comment No. 35, the HRC has shied away from attempting this and merely repeated the formula seen in many Article 9 cases that detention should not last longer than necessary and should be subject to prompt and regular review.[150]

The suggested approach in Principle 6 is to expand upon the HRC pronouncements by introducing more procedural safeguards. In particular, regular reviews should take place to assess the threat posed by the detainee after passage of time. How frequently should periodic reviews take place? Some may think that three-month intervals would be appropriate, but this is likely to impose an unworkable and unacceptable administrative burden.

In Canada and Israel, detention is reviewed every six months. Under LOAC, periodic review is mandated to take place "at least twice yearly."[151] Principle 6 proposes that reviews should take place at least every six months after the first judicial confirmation that the detention is lawful, as discussed in Principle 7. This formula allows states the option of more frequent review.

This principle should not compromise counter-terrorism efforts, because if the detainee remains dangerous, a state will have grounds to order continued detention.

Principle 6 – Working towards eliminating indefinite detention

(i) After initial judicial confirmation, detention before, or without charge must be reviewed at least every six months.
(ii) Detainees, with the assistance of independent legal counsel, must have the right to challenge detention at each review before a judicial authority.
(iii) At each review hearing a number of specified criteria should be assessed, including the threat posed by the detainee at the time of the review, the continued necessity of detention, the length of time the suspect has been detained, and the availability of other appropriate methods to protect the community.
(iv) If the detainee is determined to pose a continuing threat, and detention is confirmed, he must be informed of the reasons for the decision.

Comments

Australia and India have no meaningful procedures to challenge detention generally, let alone in respect of periodic review. In France, the onus is on persons in *détention provisoire* to request a review at any time,[152] but no details are found in the code relating to the criteria that will be taken into account. In Canada,[153] the law provides for periodic review every six months for terror suspects held in immigration detention but it is not known what criteria are applied in the reviews. Israel's six-monthly procedures satisfy Principle 6,[154] with the exception of its use of secret evidence discussed below in Recommendation 7.

The United States' LOAC detentions in Guantánamo are tied to the continuation of hostilities[155] in something that is not a "war," as this term is traditionally understood. The United States started implementation of procedures for periodic review in 2013, whereby detainees are assessed as to the continuing threat they pose to security.[156]

Recommendation 7 – Improve the process of challenging detention

All detainees must have the opportunity to challenge their detention in a court of law. This includes persons detained during a state of emergency in cases where states have derogated from the obligation to guarantee the right to liberty.[157] Many variations in detention procedure are found in treaty texts. For example, the ICCPR does not state that a detainee should be brought promptly before a court, but the European Convention and the American Convention do. The jurisprudence of the adjudicating bodies interprets promptness differently. The process for challenging detention varies from treaty to treaty and from country to country.

Hearings must take place within a short time of the initial arrest and detention. The lack of clarity has produced a range of unacceptable times to hold review hearings in the case law. Current practice was reviewed for guidance in recommending how long should elapse between arrest and review of detention. In the United Kingdom, the United States, Israel, and for immigration detention in Canada, judicial review takes place not more than forty-eight hours after arrest.[158] In Israel's Occupied Territories, review hearings are held after eight days.[159] No review takes place for federal preventive detention in Australia,[160] preventive detention in India,[161] or GAV in France.[162] The period of forty-eight hours has been chosen as the prescribed period, as four of the countries above have found that this period is fair and workable. This period accords with the notion of "promptness" in international law (and in the Constitution, for the United States), and does not appear to have adverse security implications. Practice in countries such as the United Kingdom and Israel also underscores the importance of giving detainees a right of appeal to a higher court at every stage.

Many disputes have arisen concerning the type and extent of evidence to which a detainee should have access. The biggest problem relates to sensitive information and protecting sources. There are no easy solutions to resolving this problem. The dilemma is that on one side, law enforcement authorities want to protect sources and not divulge information considered harmful to national security; but on the other, procedures must be put in place to inform detainees why they are being detained, and allow them to challenge detention in an informed manner.

Israel, the United Kingdom, Canada, and the United States all approach this problem in different ways. Israel has procedures in place to challenge detention, with rights of appeal, but its most contentious practice is the frequent use of secret evidence to justify administrative detention. The Israeli Supreme Court has acknowledged that "[r]eliance on inadmissible administrative evidence and on privileged material for reasons of state security lies at the heart of administrative detention."[163] Israel's approach to this is unique. In the case of detention under the Emergency Powers (Detention) Law (EPDL), within forty-eight hours of arrest detainees are brought before a district court for judicial review.[164] The basic rule is that a detainee must be provided with the core allegations against him.[165] Hearings are held *in camera*,[166] but the detainee has a right to be present.[167] The judge will see all the confidential evidence, without the detainee or his representative being present, and may decide to accept evidence without disclosing it to the detainee or his lawyer if he is "satisfied that disclosure of the evidence to either of them may impair state security or public security."[168] A similar provision is found in the Incarceration of Unlawful Combatants Law.[169] In these cases, the judge is required to put himself in the position of the detainee and look at the evidence from his point of view.[170] In assessing the constitutionality of the Incarceration of Unlawful Combatants Law, the Israeli Supreme Court decided that the use of secret evidence was proportionate.[171]

The United Kingdom confronted the issue of sensitive evidence in applications for the now-abandoned control orders,[172] amongst other settings. The case law, following ECHR rulings, mandates that a detainee must be given sufficient information to instruct his lawyer in judicial review, or any court hearings.[173] The detainee must know the "essence of the case against him,"[174] which must comprise sufficient information to enable him to give effective instructions to the special advocate.[175]

Special advocates,[176] security cleared and appointed by the Court, represented detainees in the now-abandoned control order cases in addition to the detainee's regular lawyer. Special advocates are appointed in applications for Terrorist Prevention and Investigations Measures (TPIMs), which are imposed in place of control orders and impose lesser restrictions on liberty.[177] Special advocates are permitted to see sensitive evidence but may not discuss it with the defendant or his regular lawyer. They must act on his behalf by fighting to obtain an open summary of the evidence. Once the special advocate achieves a judicially confirmed open summary of evidence that expresses the essence of the case, he may give it to the regular lawyer, who then may discuss it with the defendant.

In Canada, special advocates represent detainees in respect of immigration detention (which has been used to detain terror suspects without charge) if sensitive evidence is involved.[178] They are entitled to see "all information and other evidence that is provided to the judge but that is not disclosed to the permanent resident or foreign national and their counsel."[179] They are permitted to speak to the defendant before seeing the sensitive evidence, but not thereafter, unless authorized by a judge.

In the United States, the Classified Information Procedures Act[180] (CIPA) offers another approach. Some evidence is so sensitive that it may only be disclosed to persons who have received the necessary security clearances. If a court finds that classified information is admissible and relevant at trial, CIPA establishes a framework by which the government may petition the court to permit certain alterations to evidence so that the relevant information may be introduced in an alternative form.[181]

Prior to introducing evidence, a court may permit the government to redact, summarize, or substitute classified information, but only so long as the substitution gives a defendant "substantially the same ability" to make his defense as would disclosing the specific classified information.[182] If the court rejects the substitute, the attorney general may file an affidavit objecting to the disclosure of the relevant evidence. In that situation the court may dismiss the application, find against the government on the issue in point, strike testimony, or take "any other action as may be appropriate in the interests of justice."[183] However, a court cannot require the disclosure of any evidence against the government's wishes.

In the case of *habeas* hearings of the Guantánamo detainees, the position is rather different. Security-cleared counsel are entitled in principle to see the classified evidence, but may not disclose any of it to their clients, other than any classified information provided by the client.[184] In many cases, however, the government can block even the detainee's cleared counsel from seeing the secret evidence,[185] and the government is entitled to provide alternative, unclassified disclosures that are "an effective substitute for the classified information."[186] Is this the same standard as the CIPA formula of providing the defendant with "substantially the same ability to make his defense as would disclosure of the specific classified information?" However, whatever the standard may be, the law does not require a detainee to be given access to any secret evidence.[187]

Would any of these examples serve as a blueprint to guide all the states that want to use this type of evidence? The Israeli approach where the judges try to place themselves in the position of the detainee is an impossible one. The practice whereby a judge assesses the evidence wearing three hats (prosecutor, defendant, and judge) is extremely problematic. Some of the judges have expressed their unease about this process[188] and would support the adoption of the special advocate model.[189] Perhaps justice is being done, but it also needs to be seen to be done. The Israeli approach does not answer this need.

The British approach is cumbersome, with two sets of lawyers, of whom only one is entitled to look at the classified evidence. The special advocate's position is not that much better than the Israeli judge's, because he can only attack the classified evidence on its face, without speaking to the detainee's regular lawyer after seeing the classified material. The special advocates themselves believe the procedures to be "inherently unfair; they do not work effectively, nor do they deliver real procedural fairness."[190] The Canadian approach is little better.

The simpler American approach seems the superior one. A security-cleared lawyer can speak to the defendant before and after seeing classified evidence that a defendant wishes to introduce. Because he is the only lawyer involved for the defense, he is in a better position to act in the defendant's interests generally, and when he argues for the summary of evidence.

Although the American approach with one lawyer acting for the detainee is preferable, what are the liberty/security implications of choosing to adopt the other elements of the American model? The British approach calls for telling the detainee the gist, or essence, of the case against him, which must comprise sufficient information to enable him to give effective instructions to the special advocate. The American model used in domestic criminal cases must provide the detainee with substantially the same ability to make his defense as would disclosure of the specific classified information. This is a higher level of disclosure than that of "gisting" required in the United Kingdom.

As the British detainee and his regular lawyer will never know the full facts, they are at an immediate disadvantage. Yet even the lower standard of providing the essence of the case has resulted in security costs to the British government. Control orders were revoked in cases where the government was unable to give this level of information to the controlee.[191]

The United States lawyer might know whether his client in a domestic criminal trial has substantially the same ability to make his defense because he will have seen the classified evidence. In the Guantánamo cases, the counsel and detainee may have been given material that is supposed to be an effective substitute for the classified evidence, or the counsel may have seen classified evidence but cannot share it with his client.

As to substance of the evidence, the British model permits the client to be given sufficient evidence to give instructions to his lawyer. The British detainee may in theory receive less information than his Guantánamo counterpart, but in reality, the American model does not require that this detainee be given any access to the classified evidence. The defendant in an American domestic criminal trial would be worse off than before, if the lower British standard were adopted. However, the principle below sets minimum criteria, so the United States would not be required to change its laws in respect of provision of classified evidence in domestic trials. This standard should apply for the benefit of the Guantánamo detainees.

A mixed approach is therefore chosen for Principle 7, with a single cleared counsel being provided with the essence of the case against his client, that he can discuss with the detainee. The detainee is best placed to challenge his detention if represented by cleared counsel who has seen the classified material.

Principle 7 – Improving the process of challenging detention

(i) All detainees must have the right to challenge detention before a judicial authority after forty-eight hours or as soon as is reasonably practicable.
(ii) All detainees have the right to attend a court for the purpose of challenging detention.
(iii) In the case of classified or otherwise sensitive information, the detainee is entitled to consult with, and be represented by a security-cleared lawyer who may see the confidential or classified evidence.
(iv) The detainee is entitled to know the essence of the case against him. The information must be sufficient to enable him to give effective instructions to his legal counsel.
(v) If detention is confirmed, every detainee must be given detailed reasons.
(vi) All detainees must have the right of appeal to a different or higher judicial authority within a specified timeframe.

Comments

Principle 7 expands on, harmonizes, and clarifies existing treaty texts and jurisprudence and draws on examples of national practice. Principle 7(i) replaces the notion of promptness in the European and American Conventions with a clear statement. Principle 7(ii) is drawn from Article 9(3) ICCPR. Principle 7(iii) is drawn from the United States CIPA.[192] Principle 7(iv) is drawn from ECHR jurisprudence.[193] Principle 7 (v) and (vi) are drawn from the practice of most states whereby appeals may be made to a different arbiter.

All of the national laws will require some amendment. The United Kingdom should adopt the single cleared counsel model in place of special advocates. Under French law, GAV detention carries no right of challenge. *Détention provisoire* may be challenged at any time by requesting a release from custody.[194] Applications for release may be made after each subsequent four-month period of detention,[195] but no criteria for assessing continued detention are found in the Code of Criminal Procedure.

No reference to procedures can be found in Indian legislative texts or jurisprudence. Australia does not have a proper mechanism to challenge detention until after it has ended. Slightly more rights exist to challenge detention orders made by the individual states.[196] The police must explain the substance of the order to the detainee,[197] and the detainee must be given a summary of the grounds for detention,[198] but if information is deemed likely to prejudice national security, it need not be included.[199] The detainee must be given a copy of the order as soon as reasonably practicable.[200] This means that detainees may not see the application, or the underlying evidence and supporting materials.[201]

United States domestic laws comply with, and provide more process than, the minimum standards in Principle 7. Detainees at Guantánamo are able to challenge their detention by bringing *habeas* petitions to the DC Circuit,[202] but detainees held in Afghanistan were unable to do so.[203] If the United States captures terror suspects outside the United States in the future, and wants to place them in LOAC detention, the recent experience with Umm Sayyaf demonstrates that it is still not known where, or under what law, they would be detained, or what detention principles would apply.

Recommendation 8 – Ensure fair treatment of detainees

In addition to protections provided by the Convention Against Torture,[204] this recommendation deals with the treatment of detainees in detention. It adds to the fundamental principle of prohibiting torture and cruel, inhuman, or degrading treatment by adding some other important criteria. It should not adversely affect lawful law enforcement methods.

Principle 8 – Ensuring fair treatment of detainees

(i) There must be a guarantee of no torture, or cruel, inhuman, or degrading treatment.
(ii) All detainees must have the right to medical examinations and treatment at any time.
(iii) Detainees may only be held in facilities officially acknowledged as places of detention.
(iv) All detainees must be confined in sanitary, properly heated, and ventilated conditions, with a right to regular periods of exercise.
(v) All interviews between detainees and authorities must be recorded, visually as well as audio, as a check on proper interrogation techniques.

Comments

Principle 8(i) is found in the text of all the treaties. Principle 8(ii) derives from United Nations guidance[205] and the Arab Charter.[206] Principle 8(iii) derives from HRC guidance.[207] Principle 8(iv) derives from United Nations guidance.[208] Principle 8(v) derives from state practice in most countries surveyed, such as in the United Kingdom[209] and the United States.[210]

The United Kingdom, Australia, Canada, and France currently comply with all of Principle 8. By contrast, India currently violates most of the criteria.[211] The Israeli Supreme Court, sitting as the High Court, outlawed the use of torture in interrogation in 1999.[212] However, Israel is not obliged to record police or army interrogations in security cases.[213] Israel has also been criticized for failing to meet the standards in some of the other criteria of Principle 8. For example, Palestinian prisoners have undergone hunger strikes to protest against prison conditions.[214] Israel thus needs to make changes to its laws and procedures to comply with Principle 8.

The United States' domestic law and practice currently complies with all of Principle 8. In the case of LOAC detention in Guantánamo, it is not known how much, if any, communication is permitted with family members. On the question of treatment, some inmates have gone on hunger strike to protest about conditions.[215] The United States Court of Appeals for the District of Columbia has ruled that detainees have the right to challenge the conditions of detention within the context of *habeas* proceedings, because "Habeas corpus tests not only the fact but also the form of detention."[216] United States Department of Defense policy has "explicitly incorporated the standards in [GC] Common Article 3 as minimum standards."[217]

Recommendation 9 – Provide all detainees with a right to seek compensation for violation of human rights

No uniform right exists in the human rights treaties to seek redress from a court if rights have been violated. A right to seek damages exists in some countries for wrongful imprisonment, but even when a judgment is obtained, this right is hard to enforce.

Principle 9 – Providing a right to seek compensation for violation of human rights

(i) Persons unlawfully detained shall be entitled to claim compensation or other redress from a court in the country where detention took place.
(ii) Persons who have been subjected to ill-treatment, or restriction of human rights during detention shall be entitled to claim compensation or other redress from a court in the country where detention took place.
(iii) States are required to enact legislation to enable persons to seek the redress referred to in Principles 9(i) and (ii).

Comments

This Principle is derived from the ICCPR, the European Convention and the Arab Charter, which guarantee the right of individuals to seek redress for treaty violations. The American Convention only guarantees the right to seek redress in connection with a miscarriage of justice arising out of a final judgment and the African Charter does not give any individual right of redress.

In brief, persons alleging treaty violations have the right to institute proceedings for compensation in the country in which they live, or in the place where the treaty violation took place, depending on different circumstances. If domestic remedies have been exhausted with no successful outcome, victims can petition the relevant treaty body. Although the HRC and the ECHR can recommend remedies, little or no effective mechanism exists to enforce judgments or rulings. Principle 9(iii) is designed to address this deficiency.

Some countries already have legislation that enables individuals to sue the government for compensation. For example, the British government has paid out millions of pounds in compensation to victims of torture in Guantánamo,[218] Kenya,[219] and Iraq.[220] In contrast, although United States law generally permits these types of claims,[221] the courts have ruled in a number of cases[222] that claims for compensation relating to ill-treatment in Guantánamo were barred by provisions in the Military Commissions Act (MCA) of 2006.[223]

Would this principle have an adverse effect on law enforcement methods? Would the obligation to pay a large sum of money to a victim inhibit a government from taking future counter-terrorism action? Perhaps it would, and this potential cost to security must be given full consideration and balanced against the right to take action that could provide a check on egregious conduct.[224]

Recommendation 10 – Provide a mechanism for independent oversight of detention

Many countries have recognized the importance of independent oversight of controversial measures, but current mechanisms vary in effectiveness, and guidelines are needed. This Principle provides an added safeguard on how detention operates, and should not adversely affect law enforcement methods.

Principle 10 – independent oversight of detention

(i) Each country must designate an independent person or body to monitor and report annually on the exercise and operation of preventive detention measures prevailing in the country in question, and make appropriate recommendations relating to the abolition or improvement of those measures.

(ii) The report should be presented to the governing body of the country, which is required to respond within a designated time period, and introduce changes to the detention laws if appropriate.

Comments

Current human rights guidance does not deal with this, but there is nothing in this Principle that would conflict with human rights standards. No independent oversight of the operation of terrorism legislation exists in India, Israel, or France. In Canada a bill was introduced in November 2013 to create a parliamentary committee to enhance the oversight of Canada's national security agencies.[225]

In the United Kingdom, annual review of the operation of the Terrorism Act 2000 and Part 1 of the Terrorism Act 2006 is required by section 36 of the 2006 Act. The reports of the Independent Reviewer of Terrorism Legislation are taken heed of and contributed to the government's decision to abolish control orders and create TPIMs in their place.[226] The United Kingdom's example could serve as a model for a person independent of government to check on proper and proportionate exercise of preventive detention powers. Australia has had an independent national security monitor since 2010. However, he does not appear to have effective powers. He has complained that the Australian government has taken no notice of the recommendations made in his three annual reports.[227]

The United States has a review for oversight of powers that enhance national security, with particular reference to the impact on civil liberties, in the form of the Privacy and Civil Liberties Board. This was originally established by Executive Order 13353 in August 2004, in response to a recommendation by the 9/11 Commission. The Board was criticized as not being sufficiently independent, and for appearing to be "a presidential appendage."[228] As a result, the Board was reconstituted in 2007.[229] The

American Civil Liberties Union (ACLU) has criticized the reconstituted body on the grounds that it has no powers to challenge the national security powers, nor has it any enforcement powers.[230]

A return to the scenario in the hypothetical example described in the Introduction illustrates how the adoption of these principles would affect the *status quo*.

The London arrest

This suspect was arrested on reasonable suspicion of "terror offenses." The application of Principles 1 and 3 would ensure that the suspect is told immediately, on arrest, the essential factual and legal grounds for that arrest. If Principle 7(iii) relating to representation by a security cleared lawyer were adopted, the suspect would still not be able to see, or be told, the contents of the sensitive evidence, but he would have the advantage of consulting with a lawyer with a full picture of the case against him.

The New York arrest

This suspect would be in no worse and no better position. As United States law provides a higher level of disclosure of classified evidence than that recommended in the minimum criteria, the United States would not need to amend its procedures applicable in domestic criminal trials.

The Mumbai arrest

The position of this suspect would be considerably improved by the adoption of these principles. He was arrested on suspicion of acting in a manner prejudicial to national security. Principle 1 requires that his arrest should be to prevent a concrete and specific offense. The vague nature of the reasons given to this suspect is likely to invalidate this arrest, at a possible security cost to Indian authorities. However, if the grounds of arrest are framed to substantiate a concrete and specific offense, both sides will gain.

Principle 5 will afford this suspect access to legal counsel from the beginning of detention. If, however, Indian authorities reasonably believe that the lawyer might pass a message to someone, thereby compromising the investigation, communications may be monitored. If the authorities reasonably believe that access to a lawyer might result in evidence being tampered with, or harming witnesses, that access can be delayed for forty-eight hours. Principle 7 will give this suspect the right to challenge his detention in a court within forty-eight hours of arrest. Principle 8 will ensure that he is detained in clean, well-ventilated conditions.

When the suspect is transferred to the United States and placed in LOAC detention on a navy brig, he will, pursuant to Principle 5, be entitled to consult with and be represented by a lawyer, subject to the same provisos as mentioned above. If that lawyer obtains the requisite security clearances, this suspect can be told the essence of the case against him, pursuant to Principle 7(iv), which will help him to challenge his detention in federal court. This principle does carry some cost to security, in terms of providing the detainee with the gist of the case. This must be balanced against the fairer procedures afforded to the suspect.

The Jerusalem arrest

This suspect will be in a better position than before. Principle 3 will permit him to be given the legal and factual grounds for his arrest. Principle 5 will give him immediate access to a lawyer, subject to the above provisos. Principle 8 will ensure he is not detained in overcrowded conditions. Principles 7 (iii) and (iv) assist him by facilitating access to a security-cleared lawyer who can see the classified evidence and contest the detention. Israeli authorities might believe that the adoption of this principle may result in some sacrifice in terms of security, but the judicial management model referred to above is already subject to much criticism.

The Melbourne arrest

This suspect, too, will be in a better position, but some security consequences may ensue because rights will now be afforded to the suspect where none existed before. Principle 3 gives the suspect the right to be told the legal and factual grounds of his arrest. Principle 4 will permit the suspect to tell his family where he is. If the Australian authorities reasonably believe that contact with his family, beyond telling them that he is safe, might result in the compromising of the investigation or tampering with evidence, this additional contact can be delayed for forty-eight hours. If detention extends beyond forty-eight hours, Principle 7 will give this suspect an automatic right to challenge it.

Concluding remarks

States should be free to adopt any lawful measures to prevent terrorist activity. At least forty countries use preventive detention as a counterterrorism tool. However, preventive detention has a bad reputation because its usage is often excessive, inappropriate, disproportionate, and abusive.

The above principles have been crafted to address to current deficiencies in preventive detention law and practice. All of them benefit both law enforcement and individuals because they provide clear parameters of when and how detention may be used. As can be seen from the application of the principles to the hypothetical example, preventive detention can be used in a way that both respects human rights and maintains security at what may be considered an acceptable cost.

For more than a decade, preventive detention has prompted heated debate, but no positive steps have been taken to resolve the issues. Since 9/11 a vast amount of laws have been introduced and refined with the aim of preventing terror attacks, and many of those laws have concerned preventive detention. The deficiencies in these laws as identified in this book indicate that the need for new principles remains constant and essential.

These principles should be adopted because they fill a void and are necessary. They will reduce the potential for human rights violations, but some tradeoffs, both from the human rights and security perspective, are unavoidable. The time has arrived for states and treaty bodies to cooperate and adopt these recommendations, as a first step to resolving the detention framework dilemma.

Notes

1 *See* Appendix 1 for list of countries where preventive detention is used.

2 This includes customary international law, Geneva Convention for the Amelioration of the Condition of the Wounded and Sick in Armed Forces in the Field (August 12, 1949), 6 U.S.T. 3114, 75 U.N.T.S. 31 [GC I]; Geneva Convention for the Amelioration of the Condition of the Wounded, Sick and Shipwrecked Members of Armed Forces at Sea (August 12, 1949), 6 U.S.T. 3217, 75 U.N.T.S. 85 [GC II], Geneva Convention Relative to the Treatment of Prisoners of War (August 12, 1949), 6 U.S.T. 3316, 75 U.N.T.S. 135 [GC III], and Geneva Convention Relative to the Protection of Civilian Persons in Time of War (August 12, 1949), 6 U.S.T. 3516, 75 U.N.T.S. 287 [GC IV].

3 International Covenant on Civil and Political Rights, G.A. res. 2200A (XXI), 21 U.N. GAOR Supp. (No. 16) 52, U.N. Doc. A/6316 (1966), 999 U.N.T.S. 171 (entered into force March 23, 1976) [ICCPR]; European Convention for the Protection of Human Rights and Fundamental Freedoms, opened for signature November 4, 1950, 213 UNTS 222 (entered into force September 3, 1953) [European Convention]; American Convention on Human Rights, O.A.S. Treaty Series No. 36, 1144 U.N.T.S. 123 (entered into force July 18, 1978) [American Convention]; African (Banjul) Charter of Human and Peoples' Rights, adopted June 27, 1981, OAU Doc. CAB/LEG/67/3 rev. 5, 21 I.L.M. 58 (1982), (entered into force October 21, 1986) [African Charter]; Arab Charter on Human Rights, adopted May 22, 2004, reprinted in 12 Int'l Hum. Rts. Rep. 893 (2005), (entered into force March 15, 2008).

4 TOM BINGHAM, THE RULE OF LAW, 66, 84 (Penguin Books, 2011).

5 *Id.*, 72 (quoting R. v. Secretary of State for the Home Department, ex parte Cheblak [1991] 1 WLR 890, 894 (U.K.): "We have all been brought up to believe, and do believe that the liberty of the citizen under the law is the most fundamental of all freedoms"); liberty is also the cornerstone of *e.g.* the United States Constitution and the French Declaration of the Rights of Man.

6 *See e.g.* U.N. Body of Principles for the Protection of All Person under Any Form of Detention or Imprisonment, A/RES/43/173 (December 9, 1988);

CONFERENCE ON SECURITY AND CO-OPERATION IN EUROPE, DOCUMENT OF THE MOSCOW MEETING OF THE CONFERENCE OF THE HUMAN DIMENSION, ¶23 (October 3, 1991).

7 The Core Principles do not include any recommendations relating to derogating the right to liberty in times of emergency, other than in respect of due process issues connected with challenging detention, because adequate guidance has been identified in the treaties, their jurisprudence and guidance materials.

8 ROBERT H. WAGSTAFF, TERROR DETENTIONS AND THE RULE OF LAW, 112 (Oxford University Press, 2014) (quoting AHARON BARAK, THE JUDGE IN A DEMOCRACY, 297 (Princeton University Press, 2006)).

9 R v. Gul [2013] UKSC 64, ¶53 (U.K.).

10 ICCPR, Art. 9(1); American Convention, Art. 7(2); African Charter, Art. 6; Arab Charter, Art. 14(2).

11 European Convention, Art. 5(1).

12 M. v. Germany, App. No. 19359/04, ¶86, ECHR (December 17, 2009).

13 *Id.*, ¶102.

14 *Id.*

15 Shimovolos v. Russia, Appl. No. 30194/09, ECHR ¶55 (November 28, 2011); *Also see* Schwabe and M.G. v. Germany, Appl. Nos. 8080/08 and 8577/08, ECHR, ¶¶70, 77 (March 1, 2012).

16 U.N. HRC, General Comment no. 35, CCPR/C/GC/35 (December 16, 2014).

17 ¶15.

18 Shaheed Fatima, *UN HRC'S General Comment 35 on the Right to Liberty and Security: A Missed Opportunity?* JUST SECURITY (Nov. 19, 2014), http://justsecurity.org/17587/uns-comment-liberty-security/.

19 U.N. HRC, General Comment no. 35, ¶22 (which cites examples where the HRC has expressed concerns about imprecise language).

20 *See* Introduction, *infra*.

21 MARC J. BOSSUYT, GUIDE TO THE *"TRAVAUX PRÉPARATOIRES"* OF THE INTERNATIONAL COVENANT ON CIVIL AND POLITICAL RIGHTS, XIX, 193, Commission on Human Rights, 5th Session (1949), 6th Session (1950), 8th Session (1952), A/2929, Chapt. VI, §28. (Martinus Nijhoff Publishers, 1987.

22 U.N. Human Rights Committee, Consideration of reports submitted by States parties under article 40 of the Covenant, Concluding observations of the Human Rights Committee, India, CCPR/C/79/Add.81, ¶14 (August 4, 1997); HUMAN RIGHTS WATCH, BACK TO THE FUTURE, INDIA'S 2008 COUNTERTERRORISM LAWS (July 2008); HUMAN RIGHTS WATCH, THE "ANTI-NATIONALS," ARBITRARY DETENTION AND TORTURE OF TERRORISM SUSPECTS IN INDIA, 44–60 (February 2011).

23 ICCPR, Art. 9(1).

24 American Convention, Art. 7(3).

25 African Charter, Art. 6.

26 Arab Charter, Art. 14(1).

27 *See e.g.* Lawless v. Ireland (No. 3) Series A no. 3. (July 14, 1961), ¶14.

28 *See e.g.* OXFORD DICTIONARIES, www.oxforddictionaries.com/us/definition/american_english/arbitrary?q=arbitrary ("based on random choice or personal whim, rather than any reason or system, unrestrained and autocratic in the use

of authority"); Webster's New World College Dictionary, 72 (4th ed. 2007): ("not fixed by rules, but left to one's judgment or choice, discretionary,"); Black's Law Dictionary, 42 (3d Pocket ed. 2006): ("depending on individual discretion; (of a judicial decision) founded on prejudice or preference rather than on reason or fact.").

29 *See* Table 2 in Appendix 3.

30 The most comprehensive definition in treaty texts of this principle is set out in ICCPR, Art. 9(1) and Arab Charter, Art. 14(2).

31 Hugo van Alphen v. The Netherlands, HRC Comm. No. 305/1988 (August 15, 1990) CCPR/C/39/D/305/1988, ¶5.8.

32 *Id.*

33 *Id.* There is similarity in the American Convention jurisprudence for a requirement of foreseeability, *see* Case of Gangaram Pandaray, IACHR (Ser. C) No. 16, Judgment of January 21, 1994, ¶47.

34 *Id;* Saadi v. United Kingdom, App. No. 13229/03 ECHR (January 29, 2008), ¶70; Case of Lopez-Alvarez, IACHR (Series C) No. 141, Judgment of February 1, 2006, ¶¶67, 68.

35 Hugo van Alphen v. The Netherlands, at ¶5.8; A v. Australia, HRC Communication No. 560/1993 (April 30, 1997), CCPR/C/59/D/560/1993, ¶9.2; Saadi v. United Kingdom, ¶70; Case of Lopez-Alvarez, IACHR, ¶¶67, 68.

36 Case of Lopez-Alvarez, IACHR, ¶¶67, 68.

37 HRC Communication No. 10/2013 (United States of America), A/HRC/WGAD/2013/10 (June 12, 2013), ¶42.

38 Hugo van Alphen v. The Netherlands, ¶5, 8.

39 HRC Communication No. 10/2013 (United States of America), ¶¶41, 42.

40 A v. Australia, ¶9.2.

41 HRC Communication No. 10/2013 (United States of America), ¶37.

42 C. v. Australia, HRC Communication No. 900/1999 (November 30, 2002), CCPR/C/76/D/900/1999, ¶8.2. The closest the American Convention jurisprudence gets to this standard is a requirement in Case of Lopez-Alvarez, IACHR, ¶¶67, 68, that the reason for the detention must be "exceptional."

43 Saadi v. United Kingdom, ¶70.

44 General Comment No. 29. States of Emergency (Article 4), U.N. Doc. CCPR/C/21/Rev.1/Add.11 (2001). ¶4; Brannigan and McBride v. United Kingdom, 5/1992/350/423-424 ECHR ¶43 (1993); Judicial Guarantees in States of Emergency (Arts. 27(2), 25 and 8 of the American Convention on Human Rights), Advisory Opinion OC-9/87, October 6, 1987, IACHR. (Ser. A) No. 9 (1987), ¶21.

45 HRC, General Comment no. 35, ¶12: "The notion of "arbitrariness" is not to be equated with "against the law", but must be interpreted more broadly to include elements of inappropriateness, injustice, lack of predictability, and due process of law, as well as elements of reasonableness, necessity and proportionality."

46 HRC Communication No. 10/2013 (United States of America), ¶37.

47 A v. Australia, ¶9.2.

48 A. v. State of Israel, CrimA 6659/06 (June 11, 2008), ¶46, (Isr.) (citing A v. Minister of Defence, CrimFH 7048/97 [2000] IsrSC 44(1) 721, 744) (Isr.). *See also* A. v. Australia, ¶9.4.

49 Secretary of State for the Home Department v. JJ [2007] UKHL 45, ¶16 (U.K.). Although the Court did not use the word arbitrary, the concept was implied. The Court tested control orders by assessing a number of restrictive measures considered together.
50 *Id.*, ¶¶21, 23, 24.
51 A (F.C.) and Others (F.C.) v. Secretary of State for the Home Department [2004] UKHL 56 (U.K.).
52 Anti-Terrorism, Crime and Security Act, 2001 §23(1) c.24 (U.K.).
53 *See post.*
54 Charkaoui v Canada, 1 S.C.R. 350, ¶89 (2007) (Can.).
55 John Does v. Ministry of Defense, CrimFH 7048/97, ¶25 (April 12, 2000) (Isr.).
56 A. v. State of Israel, ¶31 (June 11, 2008).
57 U.S. Const. amend. V, and XIV §1.
58 Matthews v. Eldridge, 424 U.S. 319, 348–9 (1976) (quoting Joint Anti-Fascist Comm. V. McGrath, 341 U.S. 123, 171–2 (1951)).
59 H.R.C. Communication No. 10/2013 (United States of America), ¶¶31, 37, 42.
60 Charlie Savage, *U.S., Rebuffing U.N., Maintains Stance That Rights Treaty Does Not Apply Abroad*, N.Y. TIMES (March 13, 2014), www.nytimes.com/2014/03/14/world/us-affirms-stance-that-rights-treaty-doesnt-apply-abroad.html?_r=1.
61 It remains to be seen if the revised procedural detention provisions in the UNITED STATES DEPARTMENT OF DEFENSE, LAW OF WAR MANUAL (June 2015) [LAW OF WAR MANUAL] as discussed in Chapter 9 *infra* have any effect on the procedural *status quo.*
62 ICCPR, Art. 9(2).
63 U.N. Human Rights Committee, General Comment no. 35, ¶25 (citing Ilombe and Shandwe v. Democratic Republic of the Congo, 1177/2003 (2006), ¶6.2).
64 European Convention, Art. 5(2).
65 American Convention, Art. 7(4).
66 Arab Charter, Art. 14(3).
67 LAW OF WAR MANUAL, §8.14.1.
68 U.N. Human Rights Committee, General Comment no. 35, ¶27 (citing Hill and Hill v. Spain, HRC Communication No. 526/1993, ¶12.2 (Apr. 2, 1997)); Borisenko v. Hungary, HRC Comm. No. 852/1999, ¶¶4.2, 7.3 (October 14, 2002).
69 Fox, Campbell and Hartley v. United Kingdom, Appl. No. 12244/86, 12245/86, 12383/86, ECHR (August 30, 1990).
70 Drescher Caldas v. Uruguay, HRC Comm. No. 43/1979, ¶13.2 (July 21, 1983).
71 Code of Criminal Procedure 1973 (CrPc), §50 (India); Matthews v. Eldridge, 348–9 (1976).
72 David Cole and Stephen I. Vladeck, *Comparative Advantages: Secret Evidence and 'Cleared Counsel' in the United States, United Kingdom and Canada*, *in* SECRECY, NATIONAL SECURITY AND THE VINDICATION OF CONSTITUTIONAL LAW, 174 (David Cole, Federico Fabbrini, and Arianna Vedaschi, eds) (Edward Elgar Publishing, 2013):"individuals can be deprived of their liberty on the

basis of secret evidence that is not disclosed to the affected individual." The LAW OF WAR MANUAL does not deal with the issue of specifically what information should be given to detainees.

73 The Canadian Charter of Rights and Freedoms, Art. 10, Part I of the Constitution Act 1982, *being* Schedule B to the Canada Act, 1982, c.11 (U.K.); Criminal Procedure Law (Powers of Enforcement – Arrest), 1996, §24(A) (Isr.).

74 Code de Procédure Pénale, Art. 63-1 (Fr.). The code does not specify what those "exceptional and unavoidable circumstances" might be.

75 Fox, Campbell and Hartley v. United Kingdom, ¶40.

76 Sher and Ors v. The Chief Constable of Manchester Police and Ors, [2010] EWHC 1859, ¶2 (Admin.) (U.K.).

77 Criminal Code Act (Cth.) 1995 §§§§105.28, 105.29, 105.30, 105.31 (Austrl.).

78 *Id.*, §105.8.

79 *Id.*, ¶105.8 (6A).

80 *Id.*, §105.32.

81 Katherine Nesbitt, *Preventative Detention of Terrorist Suspects in Australia and the United States: A Comparative Constitutional Analysis*, 17 PUB. INT. L. J. 39, 78 (2007).

82 Criminal Code Act (Cth.) 1995, §105.31(3) (Austrl.).

83 Security Offences (Special Measures) Act 2012, Act 747, §5(1)(a). (Malaysia).

84 Constitution of the Peoples' Democratic Republic of Algeria 1989 (amended by the constitutional revision of 1996), Art. 48.

85 U.N. HUMAN RIGHTS COUNCIL, JOINT STUDY ON GLOBAL PRACTICES IN RELATION TO SECRET DETENTION IN THE CONTEXT OF COUNTERING TERRORISM OF THE SPECIAL RAPPORTEUR ON THE PROMOTION AND PROTECTION OF HUMAN RIGHTS AND FUNDAMENTAL FREEDOMS WHILE COUNTERING TERRORISM, A/HRC/13/42 (February 19, 2010) [STUDY ON SECRET DETENTION], ¶¶216–21 (citing the reports by the Committee Against Torture, CAT/C/DZA/CO/3, ¶6, and two cases reported by the Working Group on Arbitrary Detention, of M'hamed Benyamina, Working Group on Arbitrary Detention, opinion No. 38/2006 (A/HRC/7/4/Add.1), and Mohamed Rahmouni, Working Group on Arbitrary Detention, opinion No. 33, 2008 (A/HRC/13/30/Add.1), both of whom were held in secret detention for six months).

86 Many people are held incommunicado, see e.g. Reporters sans Frontiéres, *Egypt: Journalist Held Incommunicado, Netizens Arrested, Censorship.* ALL AFRICA (August 2, 2013) http://allafrica.com/stories/201308050959.html

87 Maharjan v. Nepal, HRC Communication No.1863/2009, CCPR/C/105/D/1863/2009 (July 19, 2012).

88 *See e.g.* Case of Durand and Ugarte, Judgment of August 16, 2000, Inter-Am Ct. H.R. (Ser. C) No. 68 (2000).

89 Report to the Spanish Government on the visit to Spain carried out by the European Committee for the Prevention of Torture and Inhuman or Degrading Treatment or Punishment (CPT) from 31 May to 13 June 2011 (April 30, 2013), www.cpt.coe.int/documents/esp/2013-06-inf-eng.htm.

90 Anna Oemichen, *Incommunicado Detention in Germany: An Example of Reactive Anti-terror Legislation and Long-term Consequences*, 9 GERMAN L.J.

855 (2008), www.germanlawjournal.com/pdfs/Vol09No07/PDF_Vol_09_No_07_855-888_Articles_Oehmichen.pdf. In 1977, Germany enacted the *Kontaktsperregesetz* §§4, 31–8) to the *Introductory Act to the Judicature Act* (*Einführungsgesetz zum Gerichtsverfassungsgesetz*, in response to the terrorist threat from the Baader-Meinhof gang. Under this law a detainee could be held totally isolated from family, lawyers and prison inmates for up to 30 days, and in some situations this period could be extended indefinitely. Although the law has not been used since 1977, in 2006 § 38a extended its scope to organized crime. (855–7).

91 Adam Goldman, *The hidden history of the CIA's prison in Poland*, WASH. POST (January 23, 2014), www.washingtonpost.com/world/national-security/the-hidden-history-of-the-cias-prison-in-poland/2014/01/23/b77f6ea2-7c6f-11e3-95c6-0a7aa80874bc_story.html.

92 THE COPENHAGEN PROCESS ON THE HANDLING OF DETAINEES IN INTERNATIONAL MILITARY OPERATIONS, PRINCIPLES, 10, GUIDELINES, ¶10.1–3 (October 19. 2012) [COPENHAGEN PROCESS].

93 LAW OF WAR MANUAL, §8.10. However it is debatable whether the CIA is bound by these procedures.

94 Al Nashiri v. Poland, Appl. no. 28761/11, ECHR (February 16, 2015), ¶¶518–19, 531–2; Husayn (Abu Zubaydah) v. Poland, Appl. no. 7511/13, ECHR (February 16, 2015), ¶¶ 512–14, 525–6.

95 Arab Charter, Art. 14(3).

96 Ibrahima Kane, *Reconciling the Protection of Human Rights and the Fight Against Terrorism in Africa*, 852–4 *in* COUNTER-TERRORISM, INTERNATIONAL LAW AND PRACTICE (Ana Maria Salina de Frias, Katja LH Samuel, Nigel D White, eds) (Oxford University Press, 2012) (citing African Commission on Human and Peoples' Rights, Principles and Guidelines on the Right to Fair Trial and Legal Assistance in Africa (May 16, 2002) DOC/OS(XXX)247, §§M(6) 21, M(2)19 and M(2)20).

97 INTER-AM. COMM'N H. R., RECOMMENDATIONS FOR THE PROTECTION OF HUMAN RIGHTS BY OAS MEMBER STATES IN THE FIGHT AGAINST TERRORISM, OEA/Ser.G, CP/doc.4117/06 (May 9, 2006) §B ¶1.

98 International Convention for the protection of All Persons From Enforced Disappearance. U.N.T.S., Vol. 2715, Doc. A/61/448, https://treaties.un.org/pages/ViewDetails.aspx?src=TREATY&mtdsg_no=IV-16&chapter=4&lang=en (last accessed on February 16, 2014), hereinafter referred to as the Enforced Disappearance Convention. It came into force in 2010. As at February 16, 2014, 93 countries have signed it but only 42 have ratified. Of the countries discussed in this work, only France has ratified the treaty.

99 *Id.*, Art. 17(d).

100 Code of Criminal Procedure 1973 (CrPc), §50A (India).

101 Emergency Powers (Detention) Law 5737-1979, §9 (Isr.); Incarceration of Unlawful Combatants Law 5762-2002, §5(f) (Isr.).

102 Criminal Procedure Law (Powers of Enforcement – Arrest) 1996, §33A (Isr.).

103 Terrorism Act 2000 c.11 Sch. 8 §6(1) and (2) (U.K.).

104 Police and Criminal Evidence Act 1984, c.60, Code H. Revised Code of Practice in connection with the detention, treatment and questioning by police officers of persons in police detention under section 41 of, and Schedule 8 to, the Terrorism Act 2000, Annex B, ¶6 (October 2013) (U.K.).

105 Terrorism Act 2000, Sch. 8 §8(4) (a)–(g) (U.K.).
106 *Id.*, §7.
107 Criminal Code Act (Cth.) 1995, §105.35 (Austrl.).
108 *Id.*, §105.41.
109 *Id.*, §105.14A.
110 Code de Procédure Pénale, Art. 63–2 (Fr.).
111 *Id.*, Art. 145–4.
112 Order Regarding Security Provisions [consolidated version] (Judea and Samaria) (No. 1651) 5770-2009, Article B, Temporary Order §287 (Isr.).
113 G.C. III, Art. 69.
114 ICCPR, Art. 14(b).
115 U.N. Body of Principles for the Protection of All Person under Any Form of Detention or Imprisonment, A/RES/43/173 (December 9, 1988), Principle 11.
116 HRC General Comment No. 35, ¶46.
117 European Convention, Art. 6(3)(c).
118 Dayanan v. Turkey, App. No. 7377/03 ECHR (Oct 13, 2009), ¶¶31, 32.
119 *See e.g.* Ferrer-Mazorra v. United States, IACHR Case 9903, Report No. 51/01, OEA/Ser.L./V/II.111, doc. 20 rev. ¶213 (2001).
120 African Charter, Art. 7.
121 African Commission on Human and Peoples' Rights, Principles and Guidelines on the Right to Fair Trial and Legal Assistance in Africa (May 16, 2002) DOC/OS(XXX)247, §§M(6) 21, M(2)19 and M(2)20.
122 The Constitution of the Kingdom of Swaziland Act 2005 (Act No. 001 of 2005), Art. 16(2).
123 Terrorism Act 2000, Sch. 8, §8 and Police and Criminal Evidence Act 1984, Code H. Revised Code of Practice, Annex B, ¶6 (U.K.).
124 Loi no 2011-392 du 14 avril 2011 relative à la garde à vue (April 15, 2011). (Fr.).
125 Criminal Procedure Law (Powers of Enforcement – Arrest), 1996, §35D (Isr.).
126 Incarceration of Unlawful Combatants Law, 5762-2002, §6 (Isr.).
127 Terrorism Act 2000, Sch. 8 §8(4) (U.K.).
128 U.N. Human Rights Committee, International Commission Of Jurists, Initial Comments On Draft General Comment No. 35 On Article 9 Of The International Covenant On Civil And Political Rights, ¶13 (October 16, 2013).
129 Proposal for a Directive of the European Parliament and of the Council on the right of access to a lawyer in criminal proceedings and on the right to communicate upon arrest- Revised text, Interinstitutional File: 2011/0154 (COD), 7337/12, DROIPEN 25 COPEN 49 CODEC 574 (March 9, 2012), available at www.ecba.org/extdocserv/projects/ps/20120309_measureCrevtext.pdf.
130 Canadian Charter of Rights and Freedoms, Art. 10.
131 Terrorism Act 2000, Sch. 8, §7(1) (U.K.).
132 *Id.*, Sch. 8, §8 and Police and Criminal Evidence Act 1984, Code H. Revised Code of Practice, Annex B, ¶6 (U.K.).
133 Police and Criminal Evidence Act 1984, Code H. Revised Code of Practice, §6.5, and Annex B, ¶3 (U.K.).
134 Criminal Code Act (Cth.) 1995 §105.37 (Austrl.).
135 *Id.*, 105.38.

136 India Const., Art. 22(1), *amended by* The Constitution (Ninety-fourth Amendment) Act, 2006.
137 *Id.*, Art. 22(3)(b).
138 Rinat Kitai, *A Custodial Suspect's Right to the Assistance of Counsel – The Ambivalence of Israeli Law Against the Background of American Law*, 19 BYU J. PUB. L. 205, 219, fn.125 (2004).
139 Marab v. IDF Commander in the West Bank, HCJ 3239/02, ¶43 (February 3, 2003) (Isr.).
140 Loi no 2011-392 du 14 avril 2011 relative à la garde à vue (Fr. April 15, 2011)
141 Miranda v. Arizona, 384 U.S. 436 (1966).
142 Upjohn Co. v. U.S., 449 U.S. 383 (1981).
143 Boumediene v. Bush, 553 U.S. 723, 732 (2008).
144 In re Guantanamo Bay Detainee Continued Access To Counsel, 892 F.Supp.2d 8 §VII (2012).
145 JUSTICE PROJECT PAKISTAN, THE BAGRAM PRISONER CAMPAIGN, THE COMPLETE REPORT, 13 (September 5, 2013), www.jpp.org.pk/bagram/closing-bagram-the-other-guantanamo/.
146 GUANTANAMO BY THE NUMBERS, HUMAN RIGHTS FIRST (last visited July 8, 2015), www.humanrightsfirst.org/sites/default/files/gtmo-by-the-numbers.pdf (last visited Nov. 15, 2015).
147 Spencer Ackerman, *US transfers Umm Sayyaf, wife of suspected ISIS member to Iraqi Kurds*, THE GUARDIAN (August 7, 2015), www.theguardian.com/world/2015/aug/07/us-transfers-umm-sayyaf-wife-of-suspected-isis-member-to-iraqi-kurds.
148 B'TSELEM, STATISTICS ON PALESTINIANS IN THE CUSTODY OF ISRAELI SECURITY FORCES, www.btselem.org/administrative_detention/statistics (last visited June 8, 2015).
149 HRC Communication No. 10/2013 (United States of America), ¶37.
150 HRC General Comment No. 35, ¶15.
151 GC IV, Art. 43.
152 Code de Procédure Pénale, Art. 148 (Fr.).
153 Immigration and Refugee Protection Act, S.C. (2001), §82.1 c.27 (Can.)
154 The procedure used to review detention has been described in a number of cases, *e.g.* John Does v. Ministry of Defense, ¶25 (April 12, 2000) (Isr.); A. v. State of Israel, ¶¶39, 42 (June 11, 2008).
155 Awad v. Obama, 608 F.3d 1, 11 (D.C. Cir. 2010).
156 National Defense Authorization Act of 2012, Pub.L.112-181, at §1023 (b)(1).
157 ICCPR Art. 4 permits derogation of the right to liberty in Art. 9 in these circumstances. The HRC General Comment No. 29, ¶16 states that the right of detainees to challenge detention in emergency situations is not derogable. The European Convention, Art.15 permits derogation of the right to liberty in Art. 5 in an emergency. The American Convention Art. 7 permits derogation of the right to liberty in Art. 7, but the Habeas Corpus in Emergency Situations (Arts. 27(2) and 7(6) of the American Convention on Human Rights), Advisory Opinion OC-8/87, January 30, 1987, Inter-Am Ct. H. R. (Ser. A) No. 8 (1987) at ¶¶37–40 makes it clear that it is never lawful to suspend *habeas corpus* in a situation of emergency. The African Charter, does not permit any derogations in emergency situations. The Arab Charter, Art. 4 permits

derogation from the right to liberty in Art. 14, but not the right to challenge detention in Art. 14(6).

158 Terrorism Act 2000, Sch. 8 Pt. III, §29 (U.K.); County of Riverside v. McLaughlin, 500 U.S. 44, 56 (1991); Immigration and Refugee Protection Act, S.C. (2001), §82.1 c.27 (Can.); Emergency Powers (Detention) Law of 1979, §4 (Isr.).

159 Order Regarding Security Provisions [consolidated version] (Judea and Samaria) (No. 1651), §287 (Isr.).

160 Criminal Code Act (Cth.) 1995, §105.51 (Austrl.).

161 India Const. Art 22(3)(b).

162 No right of review is found in the Code de Procédure Pénale.

163 A. v. State of Israel, ¶43.

164 Emergency Powers (Detention) Law of 1979 §4 (Isr.).

165 Daphne Barak-Erez and Matthew C. Waxman, *Secret Evidence – The Due Process of Terrorist Detentions*, 48 COLUM. J. TRANSNAT'L L. 3, 24 and fn 83 (2009) (citing HCJ 2595/09 Sofi v. State of Israel ¶21 [2009] (unpublished), and HCJ 1510/09 Atamana v. State of Israel [2009] (unpublished)).

166 Emergency Powers (Detention) Law of 1979, §9.

167 *Id.*, §8.

168 *Id.*, §6(c).

169 Incarceration of Unlawful Combatants Law, §5(e) (Isr.).

170 Khadri v. IDF Commander in Judea and Samaria HCJ 11006/04 (unreported decision of December 13, 2004), ¶6 (Isr.).

171 A. v. State of Israel, ¶43.

172 Control orders were created and regulated in accordance with the Prevention of Terrorism Act 2005, c.2 (U.K.). They were abolished by the Terrorism Prevention and Investigation Measures Act 2011, c.23, §1 (U.K.).

173 Secretary of State for the Home Department v. AF (FC). (U.K.).

174 *Id.*, ¶66.

175 A. v. United Kingdom, Appl. No. 34455/05, ECHR (February 19, 2009) ¶¶21–220.

176 Special advocates were established by the Special Immigration Appeals Commission Act 1997, c.68, §6 (U.K.).

177 Terrorism Prevention and Investigation Measures Act 2011, §2 (U.K.).

178 Immigration and Refugee Protection Act, §§83, 85.1 (Can.).

179 *Id.*, §85(4)(1).

180 Classified Information Procedures Act, P.L. 96–456, codified at 18 U.S.C. app. 3 §1-16, §6 (1980).

181 EDWARD. C. LIU AND TODD GARVEY, PROTECTING CLASSIFIED INFORMATION AND THE RIGHTS OF CRIMINAL DEFENDANTS: THE CLASSIFIED INFORMATION PROCEDURES ACT, REPORT 41742, 6 (Congressional Research Service, April 2, 2012).

182 *Id.*, (quoting 18 U.S.C. app 3. §6(c)(1)).

183 *Id.*, 6–7 (citing 18 U.S.C. app 3.§6(e) (1) and (2)).

184 In re Guantanamo Bay Detainee Litigation, 577 F.Supp.2d 143, ¶29 (D.D.C. July 10, 2009).

185 Cole and Vladeck, *Comparative Advantages*, 176.

186 *Id.*, (quoting Al Odah v United States, 559 F 3d 539, 547 (D.C. Cir. 2009)).

187 *Id.*, 186.

188 Shiri Krebs, *National Security, Secret Evidence and Preventive Detentions: the Israeli Supreme Court as a Case Study*, *in* SECRECY, NATIONAL SECURITY AND THE VINDICATION OF CONSTITUTIONAL LAW, 145 (David Cole, Federico Fabbrini, and Arianna Vedaschi, eds) (Edward Elgar Publishing, 2013).

189 *Id.*, 147.

190 Cole and Vladeck, *Comparative Advantages*, 192 (quoting JUSTICE AND SECURITY GREEN PAPER, RESPONSE OF SPECIAL ADVOCATES, ¶15 (December 16, 2011)).

191 *See e.g.* Secretary of State for the Home Department v. AN [2009] EWHC 1966 (Admin.), ¶3 (U.K.).

192 Classified Information Procedures Act (U.S.).

193 A. v. United Kingdom.

194 Code de Procédure Pénale, Art. 148-1 (Fr.).

195 *Id.*, Art.148-5.

196 AUSTRALIAN HUMAN RIGHTS COMMISSION, RESPONSE TO QUESTIONNAIRE FROM THE WORKING GROUP ON ARBITRARY DETENTION, JUDICIAL REVIEW OF LAWFULNESS OF DETENTION, ¶¶62, 63 (November 8, 2013), www.ohchr.org/Documents/Issues/Detention/DraftBasicPrinciples/AustralianNHRI.pdf, *citing* Terrorism (Police Powers) Act 2002 (NSW) §§26H, 26I and 26M; Terrorism (Extraordinary Temporary Powers) Act 2006 (ACT) §§18, 20 and 31, Terrorism (Community Protection) Act 2003 (Vic) §§13E and 13N.

197 Criminal Code Act (Cth.) 1995, §§105.28, 105.29, 105.30, 105.31 (Austrl.).

198 *Id.*, §105.8.

199 *Id.*, §105.8 (6A).

200 *Id.* §105.32.

201 Nesbitt, *Preventative Detention of Terrorist Suspects in Australia and the United States* 78.

202 Boumediene v. Bush.

203 Al Maqaleh v. Gates, 605 F.3d 84 (D.C. Cir. 2010); Al Maqaleh v. Gates, 2011 WL 666883 (D.D.C. February 15, 2011); Al-Maqaleh v. Hagel, No. 12-5404, D.C. Cir. (December 24, 2013).

204 Convention Against Torture and Other Cruel, Inhuman or Degrading Treatment or Punishment, G.A. Res. 39/46, annex, 39 GAOR Supp. (No. 51) at 107, U.N. Doc. A/39/51 (1984) (entered into force June 26, 1987).

205 U.N.G.A. Res. 43/173, Body of Principles for the Protection of All Persons Under Any Form of Detention or Imprisonment, Principle 24 (December 9, 1988).

206 Arab Charter, Arts. 14(3), 14(4).

207 HRC Draft General Comment 35, ¶60.

208 Standard Minimum Rules for the Treatment of Prisoners, Adopted by the First United Nations Congress on the Prevention of Crime and the Treatment of Offenders, held at Geneva in 1955, and approved by the Economic and Social Council by its resolutions 663 C (XXIV) of July 31, 1957 and 2076 (LXII) of May 13, 1977, ¶10.

209 Police and Criminal Evidence Act 1984, c.60, Code F, Code of Practice on Visual Recording with Sound of Interviews with Suspects (2013) (U.K.).

210 THOMAS P. SULLIVAN, NORTHWESTERN UNIVERSITY SCHOOL OF LAW, CENTER ON WRONGFUL CONVICTIONS, POLICE EXPERIENCES WITH RECORDING CUSTODIAL INTERROGATIONS, 4 (2004).

211 Human Rights Watch, The "Anti-Nationals," Arbitrary Detention And Torture Of Terrorism Suspects In India, 40–60 (February 2011).
212 Public Committee Against Torture v. State of Israel, H.C. 5100/94 (1999).
213 Jonathan Lis, *Bill set to grant Israel Police immunity when quizzing suspects*, Haaretz (March 18, 2012) www.haaretz.com/print-edition/news/bill-set-to-grant-israel-police-immunity-when-quizzing-suspects-1.419237.
214 *Seven prisoners continue their hunger strikes despite increasing punitive measures*, Addameer Prisoner Support And Human Rights Association (February 18, 2014) www.addameer.org/etemplate.php?id=665.
215 *See e.g.* Charlie Savage, *Guantanamo Hunger Striker's Petition Divides Officials*, N.Y. Times (August 7, 2015), www.nytimes.com/2015/08/08/us/guantanamo-hunger-strikers-petition-divides-officials.html?emc=edit_tnt_20150807&nlid=67784019&tntemail0=y&_r=0.
216 Aamer v. Obama, No. 135223 (D.C. Cir. February 11, 2014) 15 (citing Hudson 424 F.2d 854, 855 (D.C. Cir. 1970)).
217 Law Of War Manual, §8.1.4.1.
218 John F. Burns and Alan Cowell, *Britain to Compensate Guantánamo Detainees*, N.Y. Times (November 16, 2010), www.nytimes.com/2010/11/17/world/europe/17britain.html?_r=0.
219 *U.K. to compensate Kenya's Mau Mau torture victims*, The Guardian (June 6, 2013), www.theguardian.com/world/2013/jun/06/uk-compensate-kenya-mau-mau-torture.
220 Ian Cobain, *MoD pays out millions to Iraqi torture victims*, The Guardian (December 20, 2012), www.theguardian.com/law/2012/dec/20/mod-iraqi-torture-victims.
221 *See e.g.* Alien Tort Statute, 28 U.S.C. 1350; Federal Tort Claims Act, 28 U.S.C 1346(b), 2761.
222 *See e.g.* Al Zahrani v. Rodriguez, 669 F.3d 315 (February 21, 2012); Ameur v. Gates, 950 F.Supp.2d 905 (Jun. 20, 2013); Janko v. Gates, 741 F.3d 136 (Jan. 17, 2014).
223 Military Commissions Act of 2006, Pub.L.109-366, §7.
224 *See e.g.* Parker Report (H.M. Stationery Office 1972) on the British interrogation methods in Northern Ireland, and ensuing litigation.
225 Liberals Introduce Legislation to Increase National Security Oversight for Canadians, Liberal (November 7, 2013), www.liberal.ca/newsroom/news-release/liberals-introduce-legislation-increase-national-security-oversight-canadians/.
226 See Chapter 5 *infra*.
227 Paul Osborne, *Govt ignored terrorist law improvements*, The Australian (December 16, 2013), www.theaustralian.com.au/news/latest-news/govt-ignored-terrorist-law-improvements/story-fn3dxiwe-1226784343490.
228 *See* Garrett Hatch, Privacy And Civil Liberties Board: New Independent Agency Status, 5, Congressional Research Service, CRS- 7-5700, RL 34385 (August 27, 2012), www.fas.org/sgp/crs/misc/RL34385.pdf.
229 *Id.*, The legislation implementing this is P.L. 110-53; 121 Stat. 226.
230 Jay Stanley, *What Powers Does the Civil Liberties Oversight Board Have?* ACLU (November 4, 2013), www.aclu.org/blog/national-security-technology-and-liberty/what-powers-does-civil-liberties-oversight-board-have.

Appendix 1

Table of countries using preventive detention of terror suspects before or without charge[1]

Country	*Population*[2]	*Period of detention before or without charge*	*Source*
Afghanistan	32,564,342	72 hours then up to 75 days for suspected felony	US Department of State[3]
Algeria	39,542,166	12 days	Code de Procédure Pénale, Art. No. 51 loi No. 01-08 (2001)
Australia	22,751,014	48 hours federal detention and then up to a total of 14 days by states, or by Australian investigation and security officers	SBE; Criminal Code Act (Cth.) 1995, §105.4. See Chapter 6 *infra*.
Bahrain	1,346,613	Initially 60 days, which can be increased in 45 days tranches, indefinitely	US Department of State[4]
Bangladesh	168,957,745	At least 30 days, but law can permit indefinite detention	SBE; US Department of State.[5] Article 33 Constitution of Bangladesh (Advisory Board has to confirm preventive detentions exceeding 6 months). Section 12 Special Powers Act 1974 envisages indefinite detention
Bulgaria	7,186,893	Initially 24 hours, but can be extended up to 18 months	US Department of State[6]
Burkina Faso	18,931,686	5 days after charge	US Department of State.[7]

Country	*Population*[2]	*Period of detention before or without charge*	*Source*
Burma	56,320,206	4 weeks	US Department of State.[8]
Canada	35,099,836	Indeterminate but not indefinite immigration detention pursuant to security certificates	SBE; Immigration and Refugee Protection Act, SC (2001), §81.See Chapter 6 *infra*.
China	1,367,485,388	37 days initially then up to additional 8.5 months	US Department of State[9]
Colombia	46,736,728	30 days	US Department of State[10]
Cote d'Ivoire	23,295,302	96 hours	US Department of State[11]
Egypt	88,487,396	45 days	US Department of State[12]
France	66,553,766	96 hours GAV, 4 years *détention provisoire* for investigation	SBE; Code de Procédure Pénale art. 706-88. See Chapter 8 *infra*.
India	1,251,695,584	90 days	SBE; Code of Criminal Procedure 1973, §167. See Chapter 6 *infra*.
Indonesia	255,993,674	4 months	US Department of State[13]
Iraq	37,056,169	Arrests can take place without warrant under the anti-terrorism law and detentions may last for the duration of the investigation	US Department of State[14]
Ireland	4,892,305	6 days	Offences Against the State Act, §30.
Israel	8,049,314[15]	Indefinite administrative detention	SBE; Emergency Powers (Detention) Law, 5739-1979, S.H. 76, 33 L.S.I. 89-92, §§1,5. See Chapter 7 *infra*.

Country	*Population*[2]	*Period of detention before or without charge*	*Source*
Italy	61,855,120	48 hours	US Department of State[16]
Japan	126,919,659	23 days	US Department of State[17]
Jordan	8,117,564	6 months	US Department of State[18]
Kenya	45,925,301	90 days	Security Laws (Amendment) Act 2014, §15(10)
Libya	6,411,776	8 days	US Department of State[19]
Malaysia	30,513,848	28 days on suspicion of security offenses, and indefinite detention of persons who have previously committed offenses, to prevent security offenses	Security Offenses (Special Measures) Act 2012, §4; Prevention of Crime (Amendment and Extension) Act 2013, §§7C, 19A
Mexico	121,736,809	40 days "precautionary measures" involving detention, known as *arraigo* has been used in terrorism cases for investigation purposes. Can be extended to 80 days by judicial warrant	US Department of State[20] Mexican Commission for the Defense and Promotion of Human Rights[21]
Morocco	33,322,699	12 days	US Department of State[22]
Mozambique	25,303,113	92 days plus another 84 days if judicially approved	US Department of State[23]
Pakistan	199,085,847	90 days	Protection of Pakistan Act 2014, §6
Peru	30,444,999	15 days	US Department of State[24]
Russia	142,423,773	48 hours, but can be detained for 2 months prior to arraignment, with possibility of further 12 month extension	US Department of State[25]

Country	*Population*[2]	*Period of detention before or without charge*	*Source*
Saudi Arabia	27,752,316	6 months	US Department of State[26]
Singapore	5,674,472	Indefinite, in tranches of 2 years	Internal Security Act 1960 (as amended), Chapter 143, §8
South Africa	53,675,563	48 hours	US Department of State[27]
Spain	48,146,134	5 days	Constitution of Spain, art. 17; §520bis 1 LECrim
Sri Lanka	22,053,488	18 months	Prevention of Terrorism (Temporary Provisions) Act No. 48 of 1979, §9
Sudan	36,108,853	4.5 months	National Security Act 2010, art. 50
Syria	17,064,854	60 days	US Department of State[28]
Tanzania	51,045,882	Indefinite	SBE; Preventative Detention Act 1962
Turkey	79,414,269	4 days	US Department of State[29]
United Kingdom	64,088,222	14 days	Terrorism Act 2000, §41 and Schedule 8. See Chapter 5 *infra*.
United States	321,368,864	48 hours under domestic criminal law; 7 days for aliens posing national security risk, renewable indefinitely Indefinite detention at Guantánamo Bay	USA PATRIOT Act, §412 P.L.107-56 (2001); National Defense Authorization Act of 2012, §1021, P.L. 112-181; Al-Bihani v. Obama, 590 F.3d 866 (2010) See Chapter 9 *infra*.
Zambia	15,066,266	Indefinite	Preservation of Public Security Regulations, §33
World (July 2014 estimate)	7,174,611,584		

Notes

1 This table reflects the domestic laws relating to detention before or without charge. It does not catalog the practices of countries that preventively detain outside their law. The source of much of this material is Stella Burch Elias, *Rethinking "Preventive Detention" From a Comparative Perspective: Three Frameworks for Detaining Terrorist Suspects*, 41 COLUM. HUM. RTS. L. REV. 99, 212 (2009). Materials derived from this source are marked "SBE" in the Source column, but she has combined pre-charge and pre-trial detention. The data has been rechecked and updated to reflect pre-charge or without charge detention and any changes in the law since publication of the source article.

2 CENTRAL INTELLIGENCE AGENCY, THE WORLD FACTBOOK: POPULATION (estimating world population at July 23, 2015), www.cia.gov/library/publications/the-world-factbook/fields/2119.html

3 U.S. DEPT. OF STATE, COUNTRY REPORTS ON HUMAN RIGHTS PRACTICES FOR 2014: AFGHANISTAN (June 25, 2015), www.state.gov/j/drl/rls/hrrpt/humanrightsreport/index.htm#wrapper.

4 *Id.*, BAHRAIN.

5 *Id.*, BANGLADESH.

6 *Id.*, BULGARIA

7 *Id.*, BURKINA FASO.

8 *Id.*, BURMA.

9 *Id.*, CHINA.

10 *Id.*, COLOMBIA.

11 *Id.*, COTE D'IVOIRE.

12 *Id.*, EGYPT.

13 *Id.*, INDONESIA.

14 *Id.*, IRAQ.

15 This figure includes populations of Golan Heights and East Jerusalem.

16 US DEPT. OF STATE, COUNTRY REPORTS ON HUMAN RIGHTS PRACTICES FOR 2013, ITALY.

17 *Id.*, JAPAN.

18 *Id.*, JORDAN.

19 *Id.*, LIBYA.

20 *Id.*, MEXICO.

21 MEXICAN COMMISSION FOR THE DEFENSE AND PROMOTION OF HUMAN RIGHTS, REPORT BEFORE THE COMMITTEE AGAINST TORTURE, ON THE OCCASION OF THE REVIEW OF THE 5TH AND 6TH PERIODIC REPORTS OF MEXICO, *ARRAIGO* MADE IN MEXICO: A VIOLATION TO HUMAN RIGHTS, 6 (October 2012).

22 US DEPT. OF STATE, COUNTRY REPORTS ON HUMAN RIGHTS PRACTICES FOR 2013, MOROCCO.

23 *Id.*, MOZAMBIQUE.

24 *Id.*, PERU.

25 *Id.*, RUSSIA.

26 *Id.*, SAUDI ARABIA.

27 *Id.*, SOUTH AFRICA.

28 *Id.*, SYRIA.

29 *Id.*, TURKEY.

Appendix 2

Table of Jihadi terror threats in surveyed countries since 9/11[1]

Country	*Thwarted atacks*	*Successful attacks*	*Victims killed and injured*	*Joined Da'esh to fight in Syria and Iraq*	*Official terror threat level*
Australia	7[2]	2[3]	2(k), 6(i)	100[4]	High – terrorist attack is likely[5]
Canada	5[6]	3[7]	2(k)	145[8]	Medium[9]
France	More than 8[10]	8[11]	152(k), 407(i)	Over 1,550[12]	Highest[13]
India	43 between 2008 and May 2012[14]	Over 204[15]	1,165(k), 3,168(i)	100[16]	High[17]
Israel	112 in 2012 190 in 2013[18]	39,918 9,233(i)	1,354(k),	40[19]	No formal national alert system
UK	More than 76[20]	2[21]	53 (k), 700 (i)	Over 1,000[22]	Severe – highly likely[23]
US	71[24]	7[25]	23 (k), 310(i)	Over 200[26]	No official alert issued[27]

Notes

1 It has not been possible to find exactly the same type of openly recorded data in respect of each country.

2 *Fact file: Five facts about terrorism in Australia*, ABC News (February 25, 2015), www.abc.net.au/news/2015-02-25/fact-file3b-five-facts-about-terrorism-in-australia/6226086; *Timeline: Australia's terror threat*, BBC News (April 20, 2015), www.bbc.com/news/world-australia-30474414.

3 *Id;* Australian Federal Police Media Release, *Police shooting in Endeavour Hills* (September 24, 2014), www.afp.gov.au/media-centre/news/afp/2014 september/media-release-police-shooting-in-endeavour-hills.

4 Daniel Hurst, *Dual-national jihadists face loss of Australian citizenship, but not sole nationals yet*, THE GUARDIAN (May 26, 2015), www.theguardian.com/australia-news/2015/may/26/dual-national-jihadists-face-loss-of-citizenship-but-not-sole-nationals-yet.

5 www.nationalsecurity.gov.au/Securityandyourcommunity/Pages/NationalTerrorismPublicAlertSystem.aspx.

6 *A recent history of alleged terror plots foiled in Canada*, CTV NEWS (April 23, 2013), www.ctvnews.ca/canada/a-recent-history-of-alleged-terror-plots-foiled-in-canada-1.1350923; Alastair Sharp, *Canada says foils plot to bomb Toronto financial district, U.S. consulate*, REUTERS (March11, 2015), www.reuters.com/article/2015/03/11/us-canada-security-deportation-idUSKBN0M71UT20150311; Allan Woods, *Two Montrealers held after alleged terror plot foiled*, THE STAR (April 16, 2015), www.thestar.com/news/canada/2015/04/16/two-montrealers-held-after-alleged-terror-plot-foiled.html.

7 Michele Mandel, *Homegrown terror strikes at the heart of Canada*, TORONTO SUN (October 23, 2014), www.torontosun.com/2014/10/22/canada-under-attack-by-homegrown-terrorists.

8 Colin Freeze and Ors, *Number of Canadians drawn to overseas jihad is rising, CSIS head say*, THE GLOBE AND MAIL (April 20, 2015), www.theglobeandmail.com/news/national/quebec-students-face-terrorism-and-explosive-charges-plead-not-guilty/article24029058/.

9 Vassy Kapelos, *EXCLUSIVE: Terrorist threat levels highest in Vancouver, Edmonton, Montreal, Toronto*, GLOBAL NEWS (June 23, 2015), http://globalnews.ca/news/2071369/exclusive-terrorist-threat-levels-highest-in-vancouver-edmonton-montreal-toronto/.

10 After the Charlie Hebdo attack in January 2015, seven attacks have been foiled. *France 'foils five terror attacks': PM Valls*, BBC NEWS (April 23, 2015), www.bbc.com/news/world-europe-32427129; Peter Allen and Sam Webb, *French Islamist terrorist suspect's alleged plot foiled after he shot himself in leg*, THE MIRROR (April 23, 2015), www.mirror.co.uk/news/world-news/french-islamic-terrorist-suspects-alleged-5566913; *France 'foils terrorist attacks on military sites,'* FRANCE24 (July 16, 2015), www.france24.com/en/20150715-france-foils-terrorist-attacks-military-sites; *France train shooting: Hollande thanks 'heroes' who foiled gunman*, BBC NEWS (August 22, 2015), www.bbc.com/news/world-europe-34023361.

11 Graham Lanktree, *France on alert after spate of Islamist terror attacks takes deadly toll in 2015*, INTERNATIONAL BUSINESS TIMES (Jun. 26, 2015,) www.ibtimes.co.uk/france-alert-after-spate-islamist-terror-attacks-takes-deadly-toll-1508105. Prior to the Paris attacks on November 13, 2015 (*see e.g.* Tim Shipman, Nicholas Hellen, Bojan Pancevski, *Massacre triggers hunt for ISIS killers among Syrian migrants,* SUNDAY TIMES, (Nov. 15, 2015) http//:www.thesundaytimes.co.uk/sto/news/uk_news/National/Terrorism?article1633542.ece) only 23 had been killed and 55 injured since 9/11.

12 *French jihadists carrying out suicide bombings in Syria and Iraq*, FRANCE24 (April 14, 2015), www.france24.com/en/20150414-france-jihadist-suicide-extremism-syria-iraq.

13 *Hollande raises French terror threat level*, ITV NEWS (June 26, 2015), www.itv.com/news/update/2015-06-26/hollande-raises-france-terror-threat-level/.

14 Rama Lakshmi, *India's counterterrorism measures remain in disarray*, WASH. POST (May 1, 2012), www.washingtonpost.com/world/asia_pacific/indias-counter-terror-measures-remain-in-disarray/2012/04/30/gIQAo5yktT_story.html.

15 Data relating to identified Islamist attacks in India, injuries and fatalities since 9/11 until the end of 2014 compiled from Global Terrorism Database, www.start.umd.edu/gtd/search/Results.aspx?expanded=no&casualties_type=b&casualties_max=&dtp2=all&success=yes&country=92&ob=GTDID&od=desc&page=54&count=100#results-table. Note that this database shows that the total number of terror attacks from all sources in India since 9/11 is 5,844.

16 Indrani Basu, *Indians In ISIS: Growing Link Sparks Concern*, HUFFINGTON POST (December 12, 2014), www.huffingtonpost.in/2014/12/12/indians-in-isis_n_6314384.html.

17 *High Alert Sounded Across Country After Punjab Terror Attack*, NDTV (July 27, 2015), www.ndtv.com/india-news/high-alert-sounded-across-country-after-punjab-terror-attack-1201115.

18 All data derived from www.shabak.gov.il/English/EnTerrorData/Reports/Pages/default.aspx

19 Hassan Shalaan, *Arab-Israeli family feared to have joined ISIS*, YNETNEWS (June 23, 2015), www.ynetnews.com/articles/0,7340,L-4671912,00.html.

20 Data compiled from number of successful criminal prosecutions between 2006, *see* Counter-Terrorism Division of the Crown Prosecution Service, Successful Prosecutions Since 2006, www.cps.gov.uk/publications/prosecution/ctd.html#a02; Kim Sengupta, *Charlie Hebdo attack: MI5 chief reveals Britain faced four major terror plots in past year*, THE INDEPENDENT (January 15, 2015), www.independent.co.uk/news/uk/home-news/charlie-hebdo-attack-britain-faced-four-major-terror-plots-in-past-year-reveals-head-of-mi5-9966385.html.

21 Ewen MacAskill and Ian Cobain, 7/7 seemed to herald a new era of terror on UK soil – one that did not materialize, THE GUARDIAN (July 7, 2015), www.theguardian.com/uk-news/2015/jul/07/london-bombings-new-era-terror-uk-did-not-materialise-mi5-mi6-gchq.

22 Sean O'Neill, *Son of Tottenham Ayatollah has gone to fight with jihadists*, THE TIMES (July 31, 2015), www.thetimes.co.uk/tto/news/uk/crime/article4513507.ece.

23 www.mi5.gov.uk/home/the-threats/terrorism/threat-levels.html.

24 Data compiled from Wm. Robert Johnston, *Terror attacks and related incidents in the United States* (last updated July 19, 2015) [Johnson's Archive], www.johnstonsarchive.net/terrorism/wrjp255a.html; Jessica Zuckerman, Steven P. Bucci and James Jay Carafano, *60 Terrorist Plots Since 9/11: Continued Lessons in Domestic Counterterrorism*, THE HERITAGE FOUNDATION, (July 22, 2013), www.heritage.org/research/reports/2013/07/60-terrorist-plots-since-911-continued-lessons-in-domestic-counterterrorism; David Inserra, *Terrorist Plot 72: Congress Needs to Address Rising Islamist Terrorism at Home*, THE HERITAGE FOUNDATION, (July 22, 2015), www.heritage.org/research/reports/2015/07/terrorist-plot-72-congress-needs-to-address-rising-islamist-terrorism-at-home. Note that twice as many fatalities are reported to have resulted from non-Islamist terror attacks in the U.S. since 9/11 than from Islamist plots, *see* Scott Shane, *Homegrown Extremists Tied to Deadlier Toll Than Jihadists in U.S. Since 9/11*, N.Y. TIMES (June 24, 2015),

www.nytimes.com/2015/06/25/us/tally-of-attacks-in-us-challenges-perceptions-of-top-terror-threat.html?_r=0.

25 Johnson's Archive.

26 *Counterterrorism, Counterintelligence, and the Challenges of Going Dark: Hearing Before S. Select Comm. On Intelligence*, 114th Cong. (July 8, 2015) (statement of James B. Comey, Director, F.B.I.).

27 *Despite Obama's Claim, Our Terror Threat Level Is High*, INVESTORS' BUSINESS DAILY (June 23, 2015), http://news.investors.com/ibd-editorials/062315-758709-diminishing-us-power-has-elevated-our-terror-threat-level.htm.

Appendix 3

Table 1 Detention provisions in human rights treaties

International Covenant on Civil and Political Rights[1]	*European Convention for the Protection of Human Rights*[2]	*American Convention on Human Rights*[3]	*African Charter on Human and Peoples' Rights*[4]	*Arab Charter on Human Rights*[5]
Article 2 – jurisdiction (1) Each State Party to the present Covenant undertakes to respect and to ensure to all individuals within its territory and subject to its jurisdiction the rights recognized in the present Covenant …	*Article 1 – jurisdiction* The High Contracting Parties shall secure to everyone within their jurisdiction the rights and freedoms defined in Section I of this Convention …	*Article 1 – jurisdiction* (1) The States Parties to this Convention undertake to respect the rights and freedoms recognized herein and to ensure to all persons subject to their jurisdiction the free and full exercise of those rights and freedoms …	*Article 2 – jurisdiction* Every individual shall be entitled to the enjoyment of the rights and freedoms recognized and guaranteed in the present Charter …	*Article 3 – jurisdiction* (1) Each State Party to the present Charter undertakes to ensure to all individuals within its territory and subject to its jurisdiction the right to enjoy all the rights and freedoms recognized herein …
Article 9 – liberty (1) Everyone has the right to liberty and security of person. No one shall be subjected to arbitrary arrest or detention. No one shall be deprived of his liberty except on such grounds and in accordance with such procedure as are established by law. (2) Anyone who is	*Article 5 – liberty* (1) Everyone has the right to liberty and security of person. No one shall be deprived of his liberty save in the following cases and in accordance with a procedure prescribed by law: (a) the lawful detention of a person after conviction by a competent court; (b) the lawful arrest or detention of a person for	*Article 7 - liberty* (1) Every person has the right to personal liberty and security.(2) No one shall be deprived of his physical liberty except for the reasons and under the conditions established beforehand by the constitution of the State Party concerned or by a law established pursuant thereto.	*Article 6 – liberty* Every individual shall have the right to liberty and to the security of his person. No one may be deprived of his freedom except for reasons and conditions previously laid down by law. In particular, no one may be arbitrarily arrested or detained. *Article 7* (1) Every individual shall	*Article 14 – liberty* (1) Every individual has the right to liberty and security of person and no one shall be arrested, searched or detained without a legal warrant. (2) No one shall be deprived of his liberty except on such grounds and in accordance with such procedures as are established by law.

International Covenant on Civil and Political Rights[1]	*European Convention for the Protection of Human Rights*[2]	*American Convention on Human Rights*[3]	*African Charter on Human and Peoples' Rights*[4]	*Arab Charter on Human Rights*[5]
arrested shall be informed, at the time of arrest, of the reasons for his arrest and shall be promptly informed of any charges against him. (3) Anyone arrested or detained on a criminal charge shall be brought promptly before a judge or other officer authorized by law to exercise judicial power and shall be entitled to trial within a reasonable time or to release. It shall not be the general rule that persons awaiting trial shall be detained in custody, but release may be subject to guarantees to appear for trial, at any other stage of the judicial proceedings, and, should	non- compliance with the lawful order of a court or in order to secure the fulfilment of any obligation prescribed by law; (c) the lawful arrest or detention of a person effected for the purpose of bringing him before the competent legal authority on reasonable suspicion of having committed an offence or when it is reasonably considered necessary to prevent his committing an offence or fleeing after having done so; (d) the detention of a minor by lawful order for the purpose of educational supervision or his lawful detention for the purpose of bringing him before the competent legal authority;	(3) No one shall be subject to arbitrary arrest or imprisonment. (4) Anyone who is detained shall be informed of the reasons for his detention and shall be promptly notified of the charge or charges against him. (5) Any person detained shall be brought promptly before a judge or other officer authorized by law to exercise judicial power and shall be entitled to trial within a reasonable time or to be released without prejudice to the continuation of the proceedings. His release may be subject to guarantees to assure his	have the right to have his cause heard. This comprises: (a) the right to an appeal to competent national organs against acts of violating his fundamental rights as recognized and guaranteed by conventions, laws, regulations and customs in force; (b) the right to be presumed innocent until proved guilty by a competent court or tribunal; (c) the right to defense, including the right to be defended by counsel of his choice; (d) the right to be tried within a reasonable time by an impartial court or tribunal.	(3) Anyone who is arrested shall be informed at the time of arrest, in a language which he understands, of the reasons for his arrest, and shall be promptly informed of any charges against him. Anyone who is arrested has a right to contact his relatives. (4) Anyone who has been deprived of his liberty by arrest or detention is entitled to be subjected to a medical examination, and shall be informed of such right. (5) Anyone arrested or detained on a criminal charge shall be brought promptly before a Judge or

International Covenant on Civil and Political Rights[1]	*European Convention for the Protection of Human Rights*[2]	*American Convention on Human Rights*[3]	*African Charter on Human and Peoples' Rights*[4]	*Arab Charter on Human Rights*[5]
occasion arise, for execution of the judgment. (4) Anyone who is deprived of his liberty by arrest or detention shall be entitled to take proceedings before a court, in order that that court may decide without delay on the lawfulness of his detention and order his release if the detention is not lawful. (5) Anyone who has been the victim of unlawful arrest or detention shall have an enforceable right to compensation	(e) the lawful detention of persons for the prevention of the spreading of infectious diseases, of persons of unsound mind, alcoholics or drug addicts or vagrants; (f) the lawful arrest or detention of a person to prevent his effecting an unauthorised entry into the country or of a person against whom action is being taken with a view to deportation or extradition. (2) Everyone who is arrested shall be informed promptly, in a language which he understands, of the reasons for his arrest and of any charge against him. (3) Everyone arrested or	appearance for trial. (6) Anyone who is deprived of his liberty shall be entitled to recourse to a competent court, in order that the court may decide without delay on the lawfulness of his arrest or detention and order his release if the arrest or detention is unlawful. In States Parties whose laws provide that anyone who believes himself to be threatened with deprivation of his liberty is entitled to recourse to a competent court in order that it may decide on the lawfulness of such threat, this remedy may not be restricted or abolished. The interested party or another person in his		other officer authorized by law to exercise judicial power, and shall be entitled to trial within a reasonable time, or to release. The release may be subject to guarantees to appear for trial. It shall not be a general rule that persons awaiting trial shall be held in custody. (6) Anyone who is deprived of his liberty by arrest or detention shall be entitled to proceedings before a court, in order that a court may decide without delay on the lawfulness of his arrest or detention, and order his release if the arrest or the detention is not lawful.

International Covenant on Civil and Political Rights[1]	*European Convention for the Protection of Human Rights*[2]	*American Convention on Human Rights*[3]	*African Charter on Human and Peoples' Rights*[4]	*Arab Charter on Human Rights*[5]
	detained in accordance with the provisions of paragraph 1.c of this article shall be brought promptly before a judge or other officer authorised by law to exercise judicial power and shall be entitled to trial within a reasonable time or to release pending trial. Release may be conditioned by guarantees to appear for trial. (4) Everyone who is deprived of his liberty by arrest or detention shall be entitled to take proceedings by which the lawfulness of his detention shall be decided speedily by a court and his release ordered if the detention is not lawful.	behalf is entitled to seek these remedies.		(7) Anyone who is the victim of unlawful arrest or detention shall be entitled to compensation.

International Covenant on Civil and Political Rights[1]	*European Convention for the Protection of Human Rights*[2]	*American Convention on Human Rights*[3]	*African Charter on Human and Peoples' Rights*[4]	*Arab Charter on Human Rights*[5]
	(5) Everyone who has been the victim of arrest or detention in contravention of the provisions of this article shall have an enforceable right to compensation.			
Article 4 – derogation (1) In time of public emergency which threatens the life of the nation and the existence of which is officially proclaimed, the States Parties to the present Covenant may take measures derogating from their obligations under the present Covenant to the extent strictly required by the exigencies of the situation, provided that such measures are not inconsistent with their other obligations under	*Article 15 – derogation* (1) In time of war or other public emergency threatening the life of the nation any High Contracting Party may take measures derogating from its obligations under this Convention to the extent strictly required by the exigencies of the situation, provided that such measures are not inconsistent with its other obligations under international law.	*Article 27 – derogation* (1) In time of war, public danger, or other emergency that threatens the independence or security of a State Party, it may take measures derogating from its obligations under the present Convention to the extent and for the period of time strictly required by the exigencies of the situation, provided that such measures are not inconsistent with its other obligations under		*Article 4 – derogation* (1) In time of public emergency which threatens the life of the nation and which shall be officially proclaimed as such, the State Parties may take measures derogating from their obligations under the pre- sent Charter to the extent strictly required by the exigencies of the situation, provided that such measures are not inconsistent with their other obligations under international law and do

International Covenant on Civil and Political Rights[1]	*European Convention for the Protection of Human Rights*[2]	*American Convention on Human Rights*[3]	*African Charter on Human and Peoples' Rights*[4]	*Arab Charter on Human Rights*[5]
international law and do not involve discrimination solely on the ground of race, colour, sex, language, religion or social origin.		international law and do not involve discrimination on the ground of race, color, sex, language, religion, or social origin.		not involve discrimination solely on the ground of race, colour, sex, language, religion or social origin. (2) No derogation from articles … 14 … shall be made under this provision.
Article 10 – treatment (1) All persons deprived of their liberty shall be treated with humanity and with respect for the inherent dignity of the human person.	*Article 3 – treatment* No one shall be subjected to torture or to inhuman or degrading treatment or punishment.	*Article 5 – treatment* (2) No one shall be subjected to torture or to cruel, inhuman, or degrading punishment or treatment. All persons deprived of their liberty shall be treated with respect for the inherent dignity of the human person.	*Article 5 – treatment* Every individual shall have the right to the respect of the dignity inherent in a human being and to the recognition of his legal status.	*Article 8 – treatment* (1) No one shall be subjected to physical or mental torture or to cruel, inhuman or degrading treatment or punishment.

Notes

1 International Covenant on Civil and Political Rights, G.A. res. 2200A (XXI), 21 U.N. GAOR Supp. (No. 16) at 52, U.N. Doc. A/6316 (1966), 999 U.N.T.S. 171, (entered into force March 23, 1976).

2 European Convention for the Protection of Human Rights and Fundamental Freedoms, opened for signature November 4, 1950, 213 UNTS 222 (entered into force September 3, 1953).

3 American Convention on Human Rights, O.A.S.Treaty Series No. 36, 1144 U.N.T.S. 123, (entered into force July 18, 1978).

4 African (Banjul) Charter of Human and Peoples' Rights, adopted 27 June 1981, OAU Doc. CAB/LEG/67/3 rev. 5, 21 I.L.M. 58 (1982), (entered into force October 21, 1986).

5 Arab Charter on Human Rights, adopted May 22, 2004, reprinted in 12 Int'l Hum. Rts. Rep. 893 (2005), (entered into force March 15, 2008).

Table 2 Detention principles in treaty texts, jurisprudence, and guidance

International Covenant on Civil and Political Rights	*European Convention for the Protection of Human Rights*	*American Convention on Human Rights*	*African Charter on Human and Peoples' Rights*	*Arab Charter on Human Rights*
Detention must be on such grounds and in accordance with such procedures as are established by law.[1]	Detention only allowed in six specified cases and in accordance with procedure prescribed by law[2] and may only be to prevent a specific and concrete offense.[3]	Detention only for reasons and under conditions established by law.[4]	Detention only for reasons and conditions laid down by law.[5]	Detention only on grounds and in accordance with procedures established by law.[6]
Detention may not be arbitrary.[7]	Detention may not be arbitrary.[8]	Detention may not be arbitrary.[9]	Detention may not be arbitrary.[10]	Detention may not be arbitrary.[11]
Not arbitrary means appropriate, not unjust, predictable, reasonable, necessary[12] proportionate, not continuing longer than justified,[13] not discriminatory[14] and may not be imposed if a less invasive method can achieve the same ends.[15]	Not arbitrary means compatible with the rule of law,[16] necessary, proportionate, a measure of last resort, in good faith, conforming with the purpose of restrictions in Art. 5(1), have some relationship between ground of detention and place and conditions of detention,[17] and there may have to be a relationship between detention and bringing future charges.[18]	Not arbitrary means reasonable, proportionate, foreseeable,[19] based on a legitimate purpose and necessary.[20]	(No guidance)	(No guidance)

International Covenant on Civil and Political Rights	*European Convention for the Protection of Human Rights*	*American Convention on Human Rights*	*African Charter on Human and Peoples' Rights*	*Arab Charter on Human Rights*
Detention guarantees can be suspended in a state of emergency which must be an exceptional situation of actual or imminent danger[21] that threatens the life of the nation, and is officially proclaimed.[22]	Detention guarantees can be suspended[23] in an actual or imminent[24] public emergency,[25] which affects the whole nation, threatens the organized life of the community, and in a situation of exceptional crisis when normal measures are plainly inadequate.[26]	Detention guarantees can be suspended in time of war, public danger, or other emergency that threatens the independence of security of a State party.[27]	There are no situations when detention guarantees may be suspended.	There are no situations where detention guarantees may be suspended.[28]
Detention in a state of emergency must be exceptional and temporary,[29] strictly necessary and proportionate, and consistent with other international law obligations.[30]	Detention only permitted to extent strictly required by the exigencies of the situation,[31] i.e. proportionate to strict necessity and a genuine response to the circumstances with safeguards against abuse,[32] and consistent with other obligations under international law.[33]	Detention limited to the extent and period of time strictly required by the exigencies of the situation,[34] and proportionate to the danger.[35]		

International Covenant on Civil and Political Rights	*European Convention for the Protection of Human Rights*	*American Convention on Human Rights*	*African Charter on Human and Peoples' Rights*	*Arab Charter on Human Rights*
Treatment in detention must be humane and respect the dignity of the person.[36]	No torture or inhuman, or degrading treatment or punishment.[37]	No cruel, inhuman, or degrading punishment or treatment. All persons deprived of liberty to be treated with dignity.[38]	Detainees must always be treated with due respect for human dignity.[39]	No physical or mental torture, or cruel, inhuman or degrading treatment.[40]
Detainees must be told reason for arrest and detention.[41]	Detainees must be told the reason for arrest promptly.[42]	Detainees must be told the reason for detention.[43]	(No guidance)	Detainees must be told the reason for arrest at the time of arrest.[44]
At all times detainee has right to challenge detention in a court that must adjudicate without delay.[45]	Anyone arrested or detained must be brought promptly before a court.[46] Detainees must be able to challenge detention in a court, which must adjudicate without delay.[47]	Detainees must be brought promptly before a judge and be entitled to a trial within a reasonable time.[48]	Every detainee may have his cause heard, including that relating to a violation of fundamental rights.[49]	Anyone detained on a criminal charge must be brought before a court without delay.[50] Detainee can challenge detention inn a court which must adjudicate without delay.[51]
Detainees should be afforded prompt and regular access to counsel.[52]	Implied right of access to legal representatives when challenging detention.[53]	Detainees have right of access to legal representatives when challenging detention.[54]	(No guidance)	(No guidance about counsel). Detainees have a right to contact relatives[55] and have a medical examination.[56]

Notes

1 ICCPR, Art. 9(1).
2 European Convention, Art. 5(1).
3 Guzzardi v. Italy, 7367/76, ECHR (1980); M. v. Germany, 19359/04 ECHR (2009).
4 American Convention, Art. 7(2).
5 African Charter, Art. 6.
6 Arab Charter, Art. 14(2).
7 ICCPR, Art. (1).
8 Lawless v. Ireland No. 3, ECHR Series A no. 3 (1961); Ammur v. France, 17/1995/523/609 ECHR (1996).
9 American Convention, Art. 7(3).
10 African Charter, Art. 6.
11 Arab Charter, Art. 14(1).
12 Hugo van Alphen v. The Netherlands, HRC Comm. No. 305/1988 (August 15, 1990) CCPR/C/39/D/305/1988.
13 A. v. Australia, HRC Comm. No. 560/1993 (1997) CCPR/C/59/D/560/1993.
14 HRC Comm. No. 10/2013 (United States of America) A/HRC/WGAD/2013/10 (2013).
15 C. v. Australia, HRC Comm. No. 900/1999 (2002) CCPR/C/76/D/900/1991.
16 Ammur v. France.
17 Saadi v. United Kingdom, 13229/03 ECHR (2008).
18 Al Jeddah v. United Kingdom, 27021/08, ECHR (2011).
19 Case of Gangaram Pandaray, IACHR (Ser. C) No. 16 (1994).
20 Case of Lopez-Alvarez, IACHR (2006).
21 U.N. ECONOMIC AND SOCIAL COUNCIL, COMMISSION ON HUMAN RIGHTS, THE SIRACUSA PRINCIPLES ON THE LIMITATION AND DEROGATION PROVISIONS IN THE INTERNATIONAL COVENANT ON CIVIL AND POLITICAL RIGHTS (September 28, 1984), E/CN.4/1985/4, [Siracusa Principles], ¶39; Richard B. Lillich, *The Paris Minimum Standards of Human Rights Norms in a State of Emergency*, 79 AM. J. INT'L L. 1072 (1985) [Paris Minimum Standards], ¶A(1)(b).
22 ICCPR, Art. 4(1); CCPR General Comment No. 29, ¶2, States of Emergency (Art. 4), CCPR/C/21/Rev.1/Add.11 (2001).
23 European Convention, Art. 15.
24 The Greek Case, European Commission's Report of Nov. 5, 1969, 12 Ybk, ¶153.
25 Lawless v. Ireland, Report of the European Commission, 332/57 (Commission), 1 ECHR (Ser. B) (adopted December 19, 1959), ¶90.
26 The Greek Case, ¶153.
27 American Convention, Art. 27(1).
28 Arab Charter, Art. 14(2).
29 CCPR General Comment No, 29, ¶2.
30 *Id.*, ¶4; ICCPR, Art. 4(1).
31 European Convention, Art. 15(1); Brannigan and McBride, v. United Kingdom, 5/1992/350/423-424, ECHR (1993), ¶43.

32 A. v. United Kingdom, 3455/05, ECHR (2009), ¶184.
33 European Convention, Art. 15(1).
34 American Convention, Art. 27(1); INTER-AM. COMM'N H.R. REPORT ON THE SITUATION OF HUMAN RIGHTS OF A SEGMENT OF MISKITO ORIGIN, at Pt. II, subdiv. E, ¶6–8, OEA/Ser.L/V.II.62 doc. 10, rev. 3 (November 29, 1983).
35 *Id.*
36 Habeas Corpus in Emergency Situations (Arts. 27(2) and 7(6) of the American Convention on Human Rights), Advisory Opinion OC-8/87, January 30, 1987, IACHR (Ser. A) No. 8 (1987), ¶21.
37 ICCPR, Art. 10.
38 European Convention, Art. 3.
39 American Convention, Art. 5.
40 African Charter, Art. 5.
41 Arab Charter, Art. 14(8).
42 ICCPR, Art. 9(2).
43 European Convention, Art. 5(2); Fox, Campbell and Hartley v. United Kingdom, 12244/86, 12245/86, 12383 ECHR (1990), ¶40.
44 American Convention, Art. 7(4).
45 Arab Charter, Art. 14(3).
46 ICCPR, Art. 9(4); General Comment No. 29, ¶4.
47 European Convention, Art. 5(3); Lawless v. Ireland, ¶14; Brogan v. United Kingdom, 11209/84, 11234/84, 11386/85, ECHR (1998) ¶¶58, 59, 62.
48 European Convention, Art. 5(4); Brannigan and McBride v. United Kingdom, ¶65.
49 American Convention, Art. 7(6).
50 African Charter, Art. 7(1).
51 Arab Charter, Art. 14(5).
52 *Id.*, Art. 14(6).
53 U.N. Human Rights Committee, General Comment No. 35, CCPR/C/G/35, ¶46 (December 16, 2014).
54 Salduz v. Turkey, 36391/02 ECHR (2008), ¶50; Dayanan v. Turkey, 7277/03 ECHR (2009), ¶¶31–2.
55 Ferrer-Mazorra v. United States, IACHR Case 9903, Report No. 51/01, OEA/Ser.L./V/II.111, doc. 20 rev. P 213 (2001).
56 Arab Charter, Art. 14(3).
57 *Id.*, Art. 14(4).

Select bibliography

Abraham, C.M., "India – An Overview", in Harding, A., and Hatchard, J. (eds), *Preventive Detention and Security Law*, Martinus Nijhoff Publishers, 1993.

Addameer Prisoner Support and Human Rights Organization, *Administrative Detention in the Occupied Palestinian Territory, A Legal Analysis Report*, July 2010, www.addameer.org/files/Reports/administrative-detention-analysis-report-final.pdf.

Addameer Prisoner Support and Human Rights Organization, *Administrative Detention in the Occupied Palestinian Territory, A Legal Analysis Report*, December 2010, www.addameer.org/files/Reports/en-addameer-administrative-detention-between-law-and-practice-december-2010.pdf.

American Civil Liberties Union, *Securely Insecure: The Real Costs, Consequences and Human Face of Immigration Detention*, January 2011, www.detentionwatchnetwork.org/sites/detentionwatchnetwork.org/files/1.14.11_Fact%20Sheet%20FINAL_0.pdf.

American Civil Liberties Union, *Bagram FOIA*, July 14, 2011.

Amnesty International, *Jailed Without Justice, Immigration Detention in the U.S.A.*, March 2009, www.amnestyusa.org/pdfs/JailedWithoutJustice.pdf.

Anderson, D., *Final Report of the Independent Reviewer Pursuant to Section 14(3) of the Prevention of Terrorism Act 2005, Control Orders in 2011*, Home Office, March 2012.

Anderson, D., *Report of the Independent Reviewer on the Operation of the Terrorism Act 2000 and Part 1 of the Terrorism Act 2006, The Terrorism Acts in 2011*, Home Office, June 2012.

Anderson, D., *First Report of the Independent Reviewer on the Operation of the Terrorism Prevention and Investigation Measures Act 2011*, The Stationery Office, March 2013.

Anderson, D., *Report of the Independent Reviewer on the Operation of the Terrorism Act 2000 and Part 1 of the Terrorism Act 2006, The Terrorism Acts in 2012*, Home Office, July 2013.

Anderson, D., *Second Report of the Independent Reviewer on the Operation of the Terrorism Prevention and Investigation Measures Act 2011*, The Stationery Office, March 2014.

Anderson, D., *Third Report of the Independent Reviewer on the Operation of the Terrorism Prevention and Investigation Measures Act 2011*, The Stationery Office, March 2015.

Antkowiak, B.K., "Saving Probable Cause," *40 Suffolk University Law Review 569*, 2007.

Arai-Takahashi, Y., *The Margin of Appreciation Doctrine and the Principle of Proportionality in the Jurisprudence of the ECHR*, Intersentia, 2002.

Association For Civil Rights in Israel, *The Counter-Terrorism Bill 2011, Position Paper, Executive Summary*, August 2011, www.acri.org.il/en/wp-content/uploads/2011/08/Counterterrorism-BillEng-3Aug2011.pdf.

Association For Civil Rights in Israel, Five Questions on Administrative Detention and Administrative CONTROL Orders in the Occupied Territories, April 17, 2012, www.acri.org.il/en/2012/04/17/five-questions-on-administrative-detention-and-administrative-control-orders-in-the-occupied-territories.

Australian Government, *Counter-Terrorism White Paper*, 2010.

Australian Government Attorney General's Office, *Control Orders and Preventative Detention Orders Annual Report 2013–2014*, www.ag.gov.au/NationalSecurity/Counterterrorismlaw/Documents/ControlOrdersandPreventativeDetention Orders2013-14AnnualReport.pdf.

Australian Human Rights Commission, *Response to Questionnaire from the Working Group on Arbitrary Detention, Judicial Review of Lawfulness of Detention*, November 8, 2013, www.ohchr.org/Documents/Issues/Detention/DraftBasic Principles/AustralianNHRI.pdf.

Barak-Erez, D., "Israel's Anti-Terrorist Law: Past, Present and Future", in Ramraj, V.V., Hor, M., Roach, K., and Williams, G. (eds), *Global Anti-Terrorism Law and Policy*, Cambridge University Press, 2012.

Barak-Erez D., and Waxman, M.C., "Secret Evidence – The Due Process of Terrorist Detentions", *48 Columbia Journal of Transnational Law 3*, 2009.

Bellinger, J.B. III and Padmanabhan, V.M., "Detention Operations in Contemporary Conflict: Four Challenges for the Geneva Conventions and Other Existing Law", *105 American Journal of International Law 201*, 2011.

Bingham, T., *The Rule of Law*, Penguin Books, 2011.

Blum, G., "Judicial review of counterterrorism operations", *47 Justice 17*, 2010.

Blum, G. and Heymann, P.B., *Laws, Outlaws and Terrorists*, Massachusetts Institute of Technology Press, 2010.

Blum, S.C., *The Necessary Evil of Preventive Detention in the War on Terror*, Cambria Press, 2008.

Blum, S.C., "Preventive Detention in the War on Terror: A Comparison of How the United States, Britain and Israel Detain and Incapacitate Terrorist Suspects", *Homeland Security Affairs, Vol. IV, No. 3*, October 2008.

Boghardt, L.P., *Saudi Arabia: Outlawing Terrorism and the Arab Spring*, Washington Institute For Near East Policy, Policy Watch 2187, December 27, 2013, www.washingtoninstitute.org/policy-analysis/view/25640.

Borgen, C.J., "Treaty Conflicts and Normative Fragmentation", in Hollis, D.B. (ed.), *The Oxford Guide To Treaties*, Oxford University Press, 2012.

Bossuyt, M.J., *Guide to the "Travaux Préparatoires" of the International Covenant on Civil and Political Rights*, Martinus Nijhoff Publishers, 1987.

Brauch, J., "The Dangerous Search for an Elusive Consensus: What the Supreme Court Should Learn from the European Court of Human Rights", *52 Howard Law Journal 277*, 2009.

Brown, G.D., "Notes on a Terrorism Trial – Preventive Prosecution, "Material Support" and the Role of the Judge after United States v. Mehanna", *4 Harvard National Security Journal 1*, 2012.

B'Tselem, *Statistics on Administrative Detention in Israel*, June 2015, www.btselem.org/statistics.

Byman, D.L. and Shapiro, J., *Be Afraid. Be a Little Afraid: The Threat of Terrorism From Western Foreign Fighters in Syria and Iraq*, Brookings, January 2015.

Byman, D., and Wittes, B., *Tools and Tradeoffs: Confronting U.S. Citizen Terrorist Suspects Abroad*, Brookings Institution Press, June 17, 2013.

Cahn, O., "The Fight Against Terrorism and Human Rights: The French Perspective", in Wade, M., and Maljevic, A. (eds), *A War on Terror? The European Stance on a New Threat, Changing Laws and Human Rights Implications*, Springer, 2010.

Carlile, Lord, *Independent Reviewer of Terrorism Legislation, The Definition of Terrorism*, Cm. 7052, Home Office, March 2007.

Carlile, Lord, *Sixth Report of the Independent Reviewer Pursuant to Section 14(3) of the Prevention of Terrorism Act 2005*, Home Office, February 3, 2011.

Cassel, D., "Security Detention: The International Legal Framework: International Human Rights Law and Security Detention", *40 Case Western Reserve Journal of International Law 383*, 2009.

Central Intelligence Agency, *The World Factbook: Population*, www.cia.gov/library/publications/the-world-factbook/fields/2119.html.

Cerna, C.M., "Extraterritorial Application of the Human Rights Instruments of the Inter-American System", in Coomans, F. and Kamminga, M.T. (eds), *Extraterritorial Application of Human Rights Treaties*, Intersentia, 2004.

Charlesworth, H., *Human Rights: Australia versus the UN*, Democratic Audit of Australia, Australian National University, August 2006.

Chatham House Meeting of International Law Discussion Group, *Legislating Against Terrorism – The French Approach*, December 8, 2005.

Chen, D., *Prosecuting Terrorists: A Look at the American and Israeli Experiences*, The Washington Institute For Near East Policy, Policy Watch 1162, November 14, 2006.

Chesney, R.C., "Beyond Conspiracy? Anticipatory Prosecution and the Challenge of Unaffiliated Terrorism", *80 South California Law Review 425*, 2007.

Chesney, R.C., "Who May Be Held? Military Detention Through the Habeas Lens", *52 Boston College Law Review* 769, 2011.

Chesney, R.C., "Iraq and the Military Detention Debate: Firsthand Perspectives from the Other War, 2003-2010", *51 Virginia Journal of International Law 549*, 2011.

Chesney, R., and Goldsmith, J., "Terrorism and the Convergence of Criminal and Military Detention Models", *60 Stanford Law Review 1079*, February 2008.

Chesney, R., Goldsmith J., Waxman, M.C., and Wittes, B., *A Statutory Framework For Next-Generation Terrorist Threats*, Hoover Institution, Stanford University, 2013.

Cochran, D.Q., "Material Witness Detention in a Post 9/11 World: Mission Creep or Fresh Start?" *18 George Mason Law Review 1*, 2010.

Coffey, K., "The Lone Wolf – Solo Terrorism and the Challenge of Preventive Prosecution", *7 Florida International University Law Review 1*, 2011.

Cohen, A. and Cohen, S.A, *Israel's National Security Law*, Routledge, 2012.

Cole, D., "Out of the Shadows: Preventive Detention, Suspected Terrorist, and War", *97 California Law Review 693*, 2009.

Cole, D., and Vladeck, S.I., "Comparative Advantages: Secret Evidence and 'Cleared Counsel' in the United States, United Kingdom and Canada", in Cole, D., Fabbrini, F., and Vedaschi, A. (eds), *Secrecy, National Security and the Vindication of Constitutional Law*, Edward Elgar Publishing, 2013.

Commission to Study the Organization of Peace, "28th Report of the Commission to Study the Organization of Peace (1980)", reprinted in Steiner, H.J., Alston, P., and Goodman, R. (eds), *International Human Rights in Context*, 3rd ed., Oxford University Press, 2007.

Committee of Experts, *Collected Edition of the "Travaux Préparatoires", Volumes I, III and IV*, Martinus Nijhoff, The Hague, 1976.

Conte, A., and Ganor, B., *Legal and Policy Issues in Establishing an International Framework For Human Rights Compliance When Countering Terrorism*, International Policy Institute For Counter-Terrorism (2005), www.ict.org.il/Portals/0/Articles/20471-Ganor_Conte_Human_Rights.pdf.

Coomans F. and Kamminga, M.T., "Comparative Introductory Comments", in Coomans, F. and Kamminga, M.T. (eds), *Extraterritorial Application of Human Rights Treaties*, Intersentia, 2004.

The Copenhagen Process on the Handling of Detainees in International Military Operations, October 2012, http://um.dk/en/~/media/UM/English-site/Documents/Politics-and-diplomacy/Copenhangen%20Process%20Principles%20and%20Guidelines.pdf.

Council of Europe, *European Court of Human Rights, Landmark Judgments*, http://human-rights-convention.org/the-main-judgments.

Crawford, E., *The Treatment of Combatants and Insurgents Under the Law of Armed Conflict*, Oxford University Press, 2010.

Crenshaw, M., *Explaining Terrorism: Causes, Processes and Consequences*, Routledge, 2010.

Danner, A.D., "Defining Unlawful Enemy Combatants: A Centripetal Story", *43 Texas International Law Journal 1*, Fall 2007.

Davies, T.Y., "The Supreme Court Giveth and the Supreme Court Taketh Away: The Century of Fourth Amendment 'Search and Seizure' Doctrine", *100 Journal of Criminal Law and Criminology 933*, Summer 2010.

Deeks, A.S., "Administrative Detention in Armed Conflict", *40 Case Western Reserve Journal of International Law 403*, 2009.

Dennis, M.J., "Application of Human Rights Treaties Extraterritorially in Times of Armed Conflict and Military Occupation". *99 American Journal of International Law 119*, January 2005.

Dennis, M.J., and Surena, A., "Application of the International Covenant on Political Rights in Times of Armed Conflict and Military Occupation: the Gap Between Legal Theory and State Practice", *6 European Human Rights Law Review 714*, 2008.

Desierto, D.A., *Necessity and National Emergency Clauses*, Martinus Nijhoff, 2012.

Dinstein, Y., *The Conduct of Hostilities Under the Law of International Armed Conflict*, Cambridge University Press, 2010.

Donkin, S., and Bronitt, S., "Critical Perspectives on the Evaluation of Counter-terrorism Strategies. Counting the Cost of the "War on Terror" in Australia", in Masferrer, A., and Walker C. (eds), *Counter-terrorism, Human Rights and the Rule of Law*, Edward Elgar Publishing Limited, 2013.

Donoho, D.L., "Autonomy, Self-Governance, and the Margin of Appreciation: Developing a Jurisprudence of Diversity within Universal Human Rights", *15 Emory International Law Review 391*, 2001.

Elias, S.B., "Rethinking "Preventive Detention" from a Comparative Perspective: Three Frameworks for Detaining Terrorist Suspects", *41 Columbia Human Rights Law Review 99*, 2009.

Eissen, M., "The Principle of Proportionality in the case Law of the European Court of Human Rights", in St. Macdonald, R., Matscher, F., Petzold, H. (eds), *The European System for the Protection of Human Rights*, Martiinus Nijhoff, 1993.

Elsea, J.K., *Detention on U.S. Persons as Enemy Belligerents*, R42337 Congressional Research Service, December 4, 2012.

Elsea, J.K., and Garcia, M.J., *Judicial Activity Concerning Enemy Combatant Detainees: Major Court Rulings*, R 41156, Congressional Research Service, December 11, 2012.

Farrell, B.R., "The Right to Habeas Corpus in the Inter-American Human Rights System", *33 Suffolk Transnational Law Review 197*, 2010.

Farrell, B.R., "Access to Habeas Corpus: A Human Rights Analysis of U.S. Practices in the War on Terrorism", *20 Transnational Law and Contemporary Problems 1*, 2011.

Foley, F., *Countering Terrorism in Britain and France*, Cambridge University Press, 2013.

Forcese, C., *Catch and Release: A Role for Preventive Detention in Canadian Anti-terrorism Law*, Institute for Research on Public Policy, Montreal, July 2010.

Frankowski, S. and Shelton, D. (eds), *Preventive Detention*, Kluwer Academic Publishers, 1992.

Glazier, D., "Playing by the Rules: Combating Al Qaeda Within the Law of War", *51 William and Mary Law Review 957*, 2009.

Gogarty, B., Bartl, B., and Keyzer, P., "The Rehabilitation of Preventive Detention", in Patrick Keyzer, P. (ed.), *Preventive Detention: Asking The Fundamental Questions*, Intersentia, 2013.

Gondek, M., *The Reach of Human Rights in a Globalising World: Extraterritorial Application of Human Rights Treaties*, Intersentia, 2009.

Goodman, R., "The Detention of Civilians in Armed Conflict", *103 American Journal of International Law 48*, 2009.

Government of Canada, *Building Resilience Against Terrorism: Canada's Counter-Terrorism Strategy*, 2011.

Gross, E., "Human Rights, Terrorism and the problem of Administrative Detention in Israel: Does a Democracy Have the Right to Hold Terrorists as Bargaining Chips?" *18 Arizona Journal of International and Comparative Law 721*, 2001.

Gross, E., *The Struggle of Democracy Against Terrorism*, University of Virginia Press, 2006.

Gross, E., "Fighting Terrorism with One Hand Tied Behind the Back: Delineating the Normative Framework for Conducting the Struggle Against Terrorism within a Democratic Paradigm", *29 Wisconsin International Law Journal 1*, 2011.

Gross, O., "'Once More Unto the Breach': The Systemic Failure of Applying the European Convention on Human Rights to Entrenched Emergencies", *23 Yale Journal of International Law 437*, 1998.

Gross, O., "'Chaos and Rules' Should Responses to Violent Crises Always be Constitutional?" *112 Yale Law Journal 1011*, 2003.

Hafner-Burton, E.M., Helfer, L.R., and Fariss, C.J., "Emergency and Escape: Explaining Derogations from Human Rights Treaties", *65 International Organization 673* (2011).

Hakimi, M., "International Standards for Detaining Terror Suspects: Moving Beyond the Armed Conflict-Criminal Divide", *40 Case Western Reserve Journal of International Law 593*, 2009.

Hakimi, M., "A Functional Approach to Targeting and Detention", *110 Michigan Law Review 1365*, 2012.

Harding, A. and Hatchard, J. (eds), *Preventive Detention and Security Law, A Comparative Survey*, Kluwer Academic Publishers, 1993.

Hatch, G., *Privacy and Civil Liberties Board: New Independent Agency Status*, Congressional Research Service, CRS- 7-5700, RL 34385, August 27, 2012.

Hathaway O., Adelsberg S., Amdur S., Levitz P., Pitts F., and Shebaya S., "The Power to Detain: Detention of Terrorism Suspects After 9/11", *38 Yale Journal of International Law 123*, 2013.

Peter Heehs, "Terrorism in India During the Freedom Struggle", *Historian*, *Volume 55*, *Issue. 3*, *469*, Spring 1993.

Helfer, L.R., "Forum Shopping for Human Rights", *148 University of Pennsylvania Law Review 285*, 1999.

H.M. Government, *Pursue*, *Prevent*, *Protect*, *Prepare: The United Kingdom's Strategy for Countering International Terrorism*, Home Office, CM 7547, March 2009.

H.M. Government, *Review of Counter-Terrorism and Security Powers*, *Review Findings and Recommendations*, CM 8004, January 2011.

H.M. Government, *Justice and Security Green Paper*, CM 8194, October 2011.

H.M. Government, *Justice and Security Green Paper*, *Response To Consultation From Special Advocates*, December 16, 2011.

H.M. Government, *CONTEST: The United Kingdom's Strategy for Countering Terrorism: Annual Report for 2014*, CM 9048, March 2015.

H.M. Government, *Operation of Police Powers under the Terrorism Act 2000 and Subsequent Legislation: Arrests*, *Outcomes and Stops and Searches*, *Great Britain*, *Quarterly Update to 31 December 2012*, Home Office, June 13, 2013.

H.M. Government, *Operation of Police Powers under the Terrorism Act 2000 and Subsequent Legislation: Arrests*, *Outcomes and Stops and Searches*, *Great Britain*, *Quarterly Update to 31 December 2013*, Home Office, June 5, 2014.

H.M. Government, *Operation of Police Powers under the Terrorism Act 2000 and Subsequent Legislation: Arrests*, *Outcomes and Stops and Searches*, *Quarterly Update to 31 December 2014*, *Great Britain*, Home Office, June 26, 2015.

Hewitt, S. *The British War on Terror*, Continuum, 2008.

Heymann, P.B., "Detention", *2 Harvard National Security Journal*, 2011, available at http://harvardnsj.com/wp-content/uploads/2011/03/Vol.-2.

Hmoud, M., "Negotiating the Draft Comprehensive Convention on International Terrorism", *Journal of International Criminal Justice*, *4 5 (1031)*, 2006.

Hodgson, J., Jacqueline Hodgson, "Suspects, Defendants and Victims in the French Criminal Process", *51 (4) International Comparative Law Quarterly 781*, 2002.

Hodgson, J., *French Criminal Justice*, Hart Publishing, 2005.

Hodgson, J., *The Investigation and Prosecution of Terrorist Suspects in France*, Report commissioned by Home Office, 2006.

Hodgson, J., "The French Prosecutor in Question", *67 Washington and Lee Law Review 1361*, 2010.

Hoffman, B., *Inside Terrorism*, Columbia University Press, 2006.

Hoffman, M.H., "State Practice, The Customary Law of War and Terrorism: Adapting Old Rules to Meet New Threats", in *34 Israel Yearbook on Human Rights 231*, Martinus Nijhoff Publisher, 2004.

Hughes, E., "Entrenched Emergencies and the 'War on Terror': Time to Reform the Derogation Procedure in International Law?" *20 New York International Law Review 1*, 2007.

Human Rights First, *Jails and Jumpsuits, Transforming the U.S. Immigration System – A Two Year Review*, 2011, http://humanrightsfirst.org/wp-content/uploads/pdf/HRF-Jails-and-Jumpsuits-report.pdf.

Human Rights First, *Guantanamo by the Numbers*, April 2015, www.humanrightsfirst.org/sites/default/files/gtmo-by-the-numbers.pdf.

Human Rights Watch, *Witness to Abuse: Human Rights Abuses under the Material Witness Law Since September 11* (2005).

Human Rights Watch, *Preempting Justice. Counterterrorism Laws and Procedures in France*, July 2008.

Human Rights Watch, *Back to the Future, India's 2008 Counterterrorism Laws*, July 2008.

Human Rights Watch, *The "Anti-Nationals," Arbitrary Detention and Torture of Terrorism Suspects in India*, February, 2011.

Human Rights Watch, *World Report 2011*, www.hrw.org/sites/default/files/reports/wr2011.pdf.

Human Rights Watch, *2012 World Report: India*, www.hrw.org/world-report-2012/world-report-2012-india.

Human Rights Watch, *In the Name of Security. Counterterrorism Laws Worldwide Since September 11*, 2012.

Human Rights Watch, *Israel: End Abusive Detention Practices*, February 24, 2013, www.hrw.org/news/2013/02/23/israel-end-abusive-detention-practices.

International Commission of Jurists, *Assessing Damage, Urging Action, Report of the Eminent Jurists Panel on Terrorism, Counter-Terrorism and Human Rights* (2009).

International Commission of Jurists, *Initial Comments on Draft General Comment No. 35 on Article 9 of the International Covenant on Civil and Political Rights*, October 16, 2013.

Jenkins, B.M., "The NDAA Makes It Harder To Fight Terrorism", *Foreign Affairs*, February 1, 2012.

Jinks, D.P., "The Anatomy of an Institutionalized Emergency: Preventive Detention and Personal Liberty in India", *22 Michigan Journal of International Law 311*, 2001.

Justice Project Pakistan, *The Bagram Prisoner Campaign, The Complete Report*, September 5, 2013), www.jpp.org.pk/bagram/closing-bagram-the-other-guantanamo/.

Kalhan, A., Conroy, G.P., Kaushal, M., Miller, S.S and Rakoff, J.S., "Colonial Continuities: Human Rights, Terrorism and Security Laws in India", *20 Columbia Journal of Asian Law 93*, Fall, 2006.

Kane, I., "Reconciling the Protection of Human Rights and the Fight Against Terrorism in Africa", in de Frias, A.M.S., Samuel, K.L.H., and White, N.D. (eds), *Counter-Terrorism, International Law and Practice*, Oxford University Press, 2012.

Karagiannis, S., "The Territorial Application of Treaties", in, Hollis, D.B. (ed.), *The Oxford Guide to Treaties*, Oxford University Press, 2012.

Kels, C.G., "The Perilous Position of the Laws of War", *Harvard National Security Journal*, December 6, 2012, http://harvardnsj.org/2012/12/the-perilous-position-of-the-laws-of-war/.

Kingsbury, B., "Foreword: Is the Proliferation of International Courts and Tribunals a Systemic Problem?" *31 N.Y.U. J. International Law and Policy 679*, 1999.

Kitai, R., "A Custodial Suspect's Right to the Assistance of Counsel – The Ambivalence of Israeli Law Against the Background of American Law", *19 Brigham Young University Journal of Public Law 205*, 2004.

Klaidman, D., *Kill or Capture, The War on Terror and the Soul of the Obama Presidency*, Houghton, Mifflin Harcourt, 2012.

Klein, A., and Wittes, B., "Preventive Detention in American Theory and Practice", *2 Harvard National Security Journal 85*, 2011.

Krebs, S., "National Security, Secret Evidence and Preventive Detentions: the Israeli Supreme Court as a Case Study", in Cole, D., Fabbrini, F., and Vedaschi, A. (eds), *Secrecy, National Security and the Vindication of Constitutional Law*, Edward Elgar Publishing, 2013.

Kris, D.S., "Law Enforcement as a Counterterrorism Tool", *5 Journal of National Security Law and Policy 1*, 2011.

Kumar, C.R., "Human Rights Implications of National Security Laws in India: Combating Terrorism while Preserving Civil Liberties", *33 Denver Journal of International Law and Policy 195*, 2005.

LaFave, W.R., *Substantive Criminal Law*, West's Key Number Digest, 2d ed. 2011.

Laqueur, W., *The Age of Terrorism*, Brown, Little, 1987.

Lawson, R., "Life After Bankovic: On the Extraterritorial Application of the European Convention on Human Rights", in Coomans, F. and Kamminga, M.T. (eds), *Extraterritorial Application of Human Rights Treaties*, Intersentia, 2004.

Léger, P., *Rapport du Comité de Réflexion sur la Justice Pénale*, 2009.

Legg, A., *The Margin of Appreciation in International Human Rights Law*, Oxford University Press, 2012.

Lerner, C.S., "The Reasonableness of Probable Cause", *81 Texas Law Review 951*, March 2003.

Lillich, R.B., "The Paris Minimum Standards of Human Rights Norms in a State of Emergency", *79 American Journal of International Law 1072*, 1985.

Liu, E.C. and Garvey, T., *Protecting Classified Information and the Rights of Criminal Defendants: The Classified Information Procedures Act*, Report 41742, Congressional Research Service, April 2, 2012.

Lynch, A, "Control Orders in Australia: A Further case Study in the Migration of British Counter-terrorism Law", *Oxford University Commonwealth Law Journal 159*, 2008.

Macken, C., *Counter-Terrorism and Detention of Suspected Terrorists*, Routledge, 2011.

Marcoux, L. Jr., "Protection from Arbitrary Arrest and Detention under International Law", *5 Boston College International and Comparative Law Review 345*, 1982.

Mayer, J., *The Dark Side: The Inside Story Of How The War On Terror Turned Into A War On American Ideals*, Doubleday, 2008.

McBride, J., "Proportionality and the European Convention on Human Rights", in Evelyn Ellis (ed.), *The Principle of Proportionality in the Laws of Europe*, Hart Publishing, 1999.

McCarthy, A., "We Need an Administrative Detention Law", *National Review Online*, September 21, 2009, www.nationalreview.com/articles/228277/we-need-administrative-detention-law/andrew-c-mccarthy.

McCaul, M., Chairman of the Committee on Homeland Security, Opening Statement at Hearing on Preventing Terror, Travel and Homegrown Terrorism,

February 11, 2015, http://homeland.house.gov/press-release/chairman-mccaul-opening-statement-hearing-preventing-terror-travel-and-homegrown.

McCauley, C., Moskalenko, S., and Van Son, B., "Characteristics of Lone-Wolf Violent Offenders: a Comparison of Assassins and School Attackers", *7 Perspectives on Terrorism, 4*, 2013.

McGarrity, N., "'Let the Punishment Fit the Offence": Determining Sentences for Australian terrorists", *2 International Journal of Criminal Justice 1*, 2013.

McGoldrick, D., "Extraterritorial Application of the International Covenant on Civil and Political Rights", in Coomans, F. and Kamminga, M.T. (eds), *Extraterritorial Application of Human Rights Treaties*, Intersentia, 2004.

Michaelson, C., "Permanent Legal Emergencies and the Derogation Clause in International Human Rights Treaties: A Contradiction?" in Masferrer, A. (ed.), *Post 9/11 and the State of Permanent Legal Emergency*, Springer, 2012.

Milanovic, M., *Extraterritorial Application of Human Rights Treaties*, Oxford University Press, 2011.

Mortlock, D., "Definite Detention: The Scope of the President's Authority To Detain Enemy Combatants", *4 Harvard Law and Policy Review 375*, 2010.

National Counterterrorism Center, *Country Reports on Terrorism 2013, Annex of Statistical Information*, May 2013, April 2014, www.state.gov/j/ct/rls/crt/2013/224831.htm.

Nesbitt, K., "Preventative Detention of Terrorist Suspects in Australia and the United States: A Comparative Constitutional Analysis", *17 Public Interest Law Journal 39*, 2007.

New York Law School, *Detained By U.S.*, 2015, www.detainedbyus.org/detainees/statistics/.

Oehmichen, A., "Incommunicado Detention in Germany: An Example of Reactive Anti-terror Legislation and Long-term Consequences", *9 German Law Journal 855*, 2008.

Oehmichen, A., *Terrorism and Anti-Terror Legislation: The Terrorised Legislator?* Intersentia, 2009.

Office of Legal Counsel, Memorandum from John C. Yoo and Robert Delahunty for Alberto R. Gonzales, Counsel to the President Re: Treaties and Laws Applicable to the Conflict in Afghanistan and to the Treatment of Persons Captured by U.S. Armed Forces in that Conflict, November 30, 2001.

Oraa, J., *Human Rights in States of Emergency in International Law*, Clarendon Press Oxford, 1992.

Pejic, J., "Procedural Principles and Safeguards for Internment /Administrative Detention in Armed Conflict and Other Situations of Violence", *858 International Review of the Red Cross 375*, 2005.

Pejic, J., "The European Court of Human Rights' Al Jedda judgment: the oversight of international humanitarian law", *883 International Review of the Red Cross 837*, 2011.

Pejic, J., "The protective scope of Common Article 3: more than meets the eye", *883 International Review of the Red Cross* 189, 2011.

Perry, N.J., "The Numerous Federal Legal Definitions of Terrorism: The Problem of Too Many Grails", *30 Journal of Legislation 249*, 2004.

Peters, A. and Schwenke, H., "Comparative Law Beyond Post-Modernism", *49 International and Comparative Law Quarterly 800*, 2000.

Power, B., *Preventive Detention of Terrorist Suspects. A Review of the Law in Australia*,

Canada and the United Kingdom, 21st International Conference of the International Society for the Reform of Criminal Law, Vancouver, Canada, June 22–26, 2007.

Preparatory Commission of the Council of Europe, Committee of Members, Consultative Assembly, 11 May–8 September 1949, *Collected Edition of the "Travaux Préparatoires," Volumes I, III and IV*, Martinus Nijhoff, 1975.

Prieto, D.B., *"War About Terror," Civil Liberties and National Security After 9/11*, Council for Foreign Relations, February 2009.

Public Committee Against Torture in Israel and Nadi al Asir Palestinian Prisoner Society, *When the Exception Becomes the Rule: Incommunicado Detention of Palestinian Security Detainees*, November 2010, www.stoptorture.org.il/en/node/1659.

Quigley, J., "Israel's Forty Five Year Emergency: Are there Time Limits To Derogations From Human Rights Obligations?" *15 Michigan Journal of International Law 491*, Winter 1994.

Ramirez, S.G., "The Inter-American Court of Human Rights' Perspective on Terrorism", in de Frias, S.M., Samuel, K.L.H., and White, N.D. (eds), *Counter-Terrorism, International Law and Practice*, Oxford University Press, 2012.

République Française, *Etude D'Impact*, *Projet De Loi Relatif à La Garde à Vue*, October 12, 2010, www.legifrance.gouv.fr/content/download/ei_garde_a_vue.pdf.

Rishmawi, M., "The Arab Charter on Human Rights and the League of Arab States: An Update", *10 Human Rights. Law Review 169*, 2010.

Roach, K., "The post-9/11 migration of Britain's Terrorism Act 2000", in Choudry, S. (ed.), *The Migration of Constitutional Ideas*, Cambridge University Press, 2006.

Roach, K., *The 9/11 Effect: Comparative Counter-Terrorism*, Cambridge University Press, 2011.

Rodley, N., "The extraterritorial reach and applicability in armed conflict of the International Covenant on Civil and Political Rights: a rejoinder to Dennis and Surena", *5 European Human Rights Law Review 628*, 2009.

Rosenzweig, I., and Shany, Y., *IDF Publishes Amending Order Reducing Detention Periods in the West Bank [2.2.2012]*, The Israel Democracy Institute, March 2012, www.idi.org.il/sites/english/ResearchAndPrograms/NationalSecurityandDemocracy/Terrorism_and_Democracy/Newsletters/Pages/39/4/4.aspx.

Rosenzweig, I., and Shany, Y., *New Comprehensive Counter-Terrorism Memorandum Bill, [21.4.2010]*, The Israel Democracy Institute, May 2010, www.idi.org.il/sites/english/ResearchAndPrograms/NationalSecurityandDemocracy/Terrorism_and_Democracy/Newsletters/Pages/17th%20newsletter/1/1.aspx.

Rosenzweig, I., and Shany, Y., *High Court of Justice Rejects Petition to End Israel's State of Emergency [HCJ 3091/99] [8.05.2012]*, The Israel Democracy Institute, May, 2012, www.idi.org.il/sites/english/ResearchAndPrograms/NationalSecurityandDemocracy/Terrorism_and_Democracy/Newsletters/Pages/41/1/1.aspx.

Rover, L., and Theoharis, J., "Preferring Order to Justice", *61 American University Law Review 1331*, 2012.

Saul, B., *Defining Terrorism in International Law*, Oxford University Press, 2006.

Saul, B., "Legislating from a Radical Hague: the United Nations Special Tribunal for Lebanon Invents an International Crime of Transnational Terrorism", *Leiden Journal of International Law 24(3) 677*, 2011.

Scheppele, K.L., Bermann, G.A., Glenn, P., Scheppele, K.L., Shalakany, A., Snyder, D.V., and Zoller, E., "Comparative Law: Problems and Prospects", *26 American University International Law Review 935*, 2011.

Schmid, A.P., *Political Terrorism: A Research Guide to Concepts, Theories, Data Bases and Literature*, Transaction Books, 1984.

Schmid, A.P., "'Terrorism on Trial': Terrorism – the Definitional Problem", *36 Case Western Reserve Journal of International Law* 375, 2004.

Setty, S., "What's in a Name? How Nations Define Terrorism Ten Years After 9/11", *33 University of Pennsylvania Journal of International Law 1*, 2011.

Shapiro, J., and Suzan, B., "The French Experience of Counter-Terrorism", *Survival, Vol. 45, No. 1*, Spring, 2003.

Simcox, R., and Dyer, E., *Al-Qaeda in the United States: A Complete Analysis of Terrorism Offenses*, Henry Jackson Society, 2013.

Singh, U.K., *The State, Democracy and Anti-Terror Laws in India*, Sage Publications, 2007.

Singh, U.K., "Mapping anti-terror regimes in India", in Ramraj, V.V., Hor, M., Kent Roach, K., and Williams, G. (eds), *Global Anti-Terrorism Law and Policy*, Cambridge University Press, 2012.

Slobogin, C., "Preventive Detention in Europe, the United States and Australia", in Patrick Keyzer, P. (ed.), *Preventive Detention: Asking The Fundamental Questions*, Intersentia, 2013.

Solis, G.D., *The Law of Armed Conflict*, Cambridge University Press, 2010.

Sottiaux, S., *Terrorism and the Limitation of Rights*, Hart Publishing, 2008.

Spaaij, R., "The Enigma of Lone Wolf Terrorism: An Assessment", *33 Studies in Conflict and Terrorism 854*, 2010.

Special Advocates Support Office, *Special Advocates: A Guide to the Role of Special Advocates and the Special Advocates Support Office*, November 2006.

Spielman, D., "Jurisprudence of the European Court of Human Rights and the Constitutional Systems of Europe", in Rosenfeld, M., and Sajo, A. (eds), *The Oxford Handbook of Comparative Law*, Oxford University Press, 2012.

Stigall, D.E., *Counterterrorism and the Comparative Law of Investigative Detention*, Cambria Press, 2009.

Sudborough, C.M., "The War Against Fundamental Rights: French Counter-terrorism Policy and the Need to Integrate International Security and Human Rights Agreements", *30 Suffolk Transnational Law Review 459*, Summer 2007.

Sullivan, T.P., *Police Experiences with Recording Custodial Interrogations*, Northwestern University School of Law, Center on Wrongful Convictions, 2004.

Thwaites, R., *The Liberty of Non-citizens: Indefinite Detention in Commonwealth Countries*, Hart Publishing, 2014.

Tolley, M.C., "Australia's Commonwealth Model and Terrorism", in Volcansek, M.L. and Styack J.F. Jr. (eds), *Courts and Terrorism*, Cambridge University Press, 2011.

United States Department of Defense, *Law of War Manual*, June 2015.

United States Department of Justice, Federal Bureau of Investigation, *Terrorism in the United States 1999: Thirty Years of Terrorism*, 1999, www.fbi.gov/stats-services/publications/terror_99.pdf.

United States Department of Justice, Federal Bureau of Investigation, Office of Legal Counsel, Memorandum from John C. Yoo and Robert Delahunty for Alberto R. Gonzales, Counsel to the President, Re: Treaties and Laws Applicable to the

Conflict in Afghanistan and to the Treatment of Persons Captured by U.S. Armed Forces in that Conflict, November 30, 2001.

United States Department of State, *2010 Human Rights Reports, France*, April 2011.

United States Department of State, *2010 Human Rights Reports: India*, April 2011.

United States Department of State, *2011 Country Reports on Human Rights Practices, Bolivia*, May 24, 2012.

United States Department of State, *Country Reports on Terrorism*, 2014.

Van Schaack, B., "The United States' Position on the Extraterritorial Application of Human Rights Obligations: Now is the Time for Change", *90 International Law Studies 20*, 2014.

Wagstaff, R.H., *Terror Detentions and the Rule of Law: U.S. and U.K. Perspectives*, Oxford University Press, 2014.

Walker, B., Independent National Security Legislation Monitor, *Declassified Annual Report 20 December 2012*, Commonwealth of Australia, 2013.

Walker, C., *Terrorism and the Law*, Oxford University Press, 2011.

Watt, G., "Comparison as Deep Appreciation", in Monateri, P.G. (ed.), *Methods of Comparative Law*, Research Handbooks in Comparative Law, 2012.

Waxman, M.C., "Administrative Detention of Terrorists: Why Detain, and Detain Whom?" *3 Journal of National Security Law and Policy 1*, 2009.

Waxman, M.C., "Administrative Detention", in Wittes, B. (ed.), *Legislating the War on Terror: An Agenda For Reform*, Brookings Institution Press, 2010.

Webber, D., "Extreme Measures: Does the U.S. Need Preventive Detention to Combat Domestic Terrorism? A Comparison of Preventive Detention Models in the United States, United Kingdom, France and Israel", *14 Touro International Law Review 128*, 2010.

Webber, D., "Preventive Detention in the Law of Armed Conflict: Throwing Away the Key?" *6 Journal of National Security Law & Policy 167*, 2012.

The White House, Office of the Press Secretary, *Fact Sheet: New Actions on Guantánamo and Detainee Policy*, March 7, 2011.

The White House, Office of the Press Secretary, *Memorandum, Presidential Policy Directive – Requirements of the National Defense Authorization Act, Presidential Policy Directive/PPD-14*, February 28, 2012.

The White House, Office of the Press Secretary, *Fact Sheet: Procedures Implementing Section1022 of the National Defense Authorization Act For Fiscal Year (FY) 2012*, February 28, 2012.

The White House, Office of the Press Secretary, *National Security Strategy*, February 2015.

Williams, G., "Anti-terror legislation in Australia and New Zealand", in Ramraj, V.V., Hor, M., Roach, K., and Williams, G. (eds), *Global Anti-Terrorism Law and Policy*, Cambridge University Press, 2012.

Wittes, B., *Detention and Denial: The Case for Candor After Guantanamo*, Brookings Institution Press, 2010.

Wittes, B., Chesney, R., and Benhalim, R., *Emerging Law of Detention*, Brookings Institution Press, 2010.

Wittes, B., Chesney, R., and Reynolds, L., *The Emerging Law of Detention 2.0: The Guantanamo Habeas Cases as Lawmaking*, Brookings Institution Press, 2011.

Yourow, H.C., "The Margin of Appreciation and the Dynamics of European Human Rights Jurisprudence", *3 Connecticut Journal of International Law 111*, 1987.

Zabel, R.B., and Benjamin J.J. Jr., *In Pursuit of Justice: Prosecuting Terrorism Cases in the Federal Courts*, Human Rights First, May, 2008.
Zabel, R.B., and Benjamin J.J. Jr., *In Pursuit of Justice: Prosecuting Terrorism Cases in the Federal Courts, 2009 Update and Recent Developments*, Human Rights First, 2009.

Index